The Monsters

Also by Dorothy and Thomas Hoobler

Nonfiction

Captain John Smith: Jamestown and the Birth of the American Dream
Vanity Rules: A History of American Fashion and Beauty
We Are Americans: Voices of the Immigrant Experience
Vietnam: Why We Fought
The Voyages of Captain Cook
The Trenches: Fighting on the Western Front in World War I
Photographing History
Photographing the Frontier
The Chinese American Family Album
The Italian American Family Album
The Irish American Family Album
The Jewish American Family Album
The African American Family Album
The Mexican American Family Album
The Japanese American Family Album
The Scandinavian American Family Album
The German American Family Album
The Cuban American Family Album

Novels

The Ghost in the Tokaido Inn
The Demon in the Teahouse
In Darkness, Death (Edgar Award winner)
The Sword That Cut the Burning Grass

The Monsters

MARY SHELLEY & THE CURSE OF FRANKENSTEIN

DOROTHY & THOMAS HOOBLER

LITTLE, BROWN AND COMPANY

NEW YORK BOSTON

Little, Brown and Company
Hachette Book Group USA
1271 Avenue of the Americas, New York, NY 10020

ISBN 978-0-7394-7509-6

Book design by Jo Anne Metsch

Printed in the United States of America

CONTENTS

The Monsters

CONCEPTION

It actually was a dark and stormy night. All through that chilly summer of 1816, ominous gray clouds had swept across the skies, bringing fierce thunderstorms to much of Europe and North America. Earlier in the year, astronomers had seen unusual sunspots through their telescopes. By June, the spots were plainly visible, and people began to fear that they were portents of doom. A pamphlet that was passed from hand to hand in Paris warned that the end of the world was near. In some parts of Europe and New England, snow fell in July. It would long be remembered as a year when summer never came.

So it was that a violent thunderstorm was raging on a frigid June night as five young people gathered inside the Villa Diodati, a luxurious summerhouse on the southern shore of Lake Geneva in Switzerland. One of the group would have been instantly recognizable to most people in Europe or America. His imposing profile aroused the envy of young men, who obsessively imitated his clothes and hairstyle, and the secret admiration of young women, who had heard it whispered (in the words of Lady Caroline Lamb, his onetime lover) that Lord Byron was "mad, bad, and dangerous to know." And in fact Byron had fled here to escape the scandal caused by the allegation that he had committed incest with his half-sister Augusta — a rumor that had caused Byron's young wife to leave him.

Though only twenty-eight, Byron was already the most famous English poet of the time — an era when writing verse was the equivalent of playing in a rock band today. Two years earlier, some ten thousand copies of Byron's book-length poem, *The Corsair,* had been sold the day it was published, and it went through seven printings in the following month, a record that has probably never been equaled for a book of verse.

At least two of the other members of the group assembled in his villa were also poets, though neither had anything like the reputation that Byron did. One was Byron's companion, the brilliant Dr. John Polidori, who had graduated from the medical school of the University of Edinburgh two years before at the tender age of nineteen. Polidori would have gladly given up his medical career for poetry, but Byron mocked Polidori's artistic efforts and made the earnest young man the butt of jokes. The third youthful poet in the room, however, had done what few men — and no women — had been able to do: earn Byron's respect as an intellectual equal. This was Percy Bysshe Shelley, age twenty-three, whose work was then known only to a small circle of literary friends. In contrast to the dark, brooding, cynical Byron, Shelley was angel-faced, blond, and ethereal. He felt he could change the world through the power of his words, despite the fact that the world had so far shown virtually complete indifference to his efforts.

The two women in the room were both in their teens. One was Mary Wollstonecraft Godwin, who had become Shelley's lover two years earlier despite the inconvenient fact that he had been (and still was) married to someone else. Mary's parents, Mary Wollstonecraft and William Godwin, two of the most famous radicals of their time, had condemned marriage as a form of prostitution. Nevertheless, Godwin regarded it as a betrayal when his sixteen-year-old daughter ran off with Shelley, a man who had declared himself Godwin's disciple. Mary hoped to placate Godwin by writing some great work that would prove her worthy of being not only his child, but also the child of the famous mother who had died giving birth to her. Thus far, Mary had not found a subject that would justify that sacrifice.

The last person in the circle was Mary's stepsister, the beautiful and seductive eighteen-year-old Claire Clairmont (as she currently called herself), the catalyst who had brought the group together. In the spring of 1816 she had boldly written Byron to request a meeting at his London townhouse. Though he received countless such appeals from young women, Byron was touched by Claire's declaration that her future was in his hands and "the Creator ought not to destroy his creature." That sparked a sexual tryst which resulted in less abstract creative activity: as the five listened to the thunderstorm raging outside, only Claire was aware that she was now carrying Byron's child.

To entertain his guests on that rainy summer evening, Byron opened a volume of German horror stories translated into French, and began to read aloud from it. Flickering candles and burning logs in the fireplace provided the only light, other than the flashes of lightning that abruptly illuminated the windows. Byron liked to frighten people, and as the others became increasingly agitated by the jarring crashes of thunder and the howling of the wind outside, his enjoyment increased. Upon finishing, Byron closed the book and proposed a contest: each of them would try to write a ghost story. He could hardly have imagined that his challenge would result in a novel that was destined to become more famous than his own work or that Mary Godwin, eventually to be known as Mary Shelley, would be the author.

Mary's novel *Frankenstein* first appeared in print two years later. It immediately attracted readers, soon appeared in a stage production, and has retained its hold on people's imaginations for almost two centuries. The novel has been translated not only into other languages but also other forms — stage, movies, television, comic books, breakfast cereals. The 1931 motion picture version of the tale made Dr. Frankenstein and his creation famous throughout the world, and for many, the movie's star Boris Karloff provided the truest image of the creature that sprang from Mary's imagination that summer.

A second modern myth was born that evening: the story of a creature (also resembling a human) whose fame rivals Mary's monster. As a result of Byron's challenge, Dr. Polidori wrote *The Vampyre,* the first and most influential novel about a human vampire; it was the model for all subsequent authors in the genre, from Bram Stoker to Anne Rice. Everyone at Byron's villa that night would have recognized the person Polidori portrayed. The aristocratic vampire who preys on the lifeblood of others was undoubtedly Byron himself.

A dark star hung over all the brilliant young people who listened to Byron read horror stories that night. Though their futures seemed limitless, early deaths or stunted lives awaited each of them. It almost might be said that the writing of *Frankenstein* placed a curse on the lives of those who were present at its birth. Only Mary and her stepsister survived for long, bearing the heavy memory of those with whom they had shared a unique moment that produced two masterpieces of the imagination.

Our book concerns the creation of monsters, literary and human, and the tragic consequences of those generative acts. We will delve into the wellsprings of inspiration that produced the works of literature that were begun at Villa Diodati in the summer of 1816 and try to discover the relationship between the creators and their creations. In the process, we hope to reveal the name of the nameless monster that has fascinated readers and audiences ever since.

CHAPTER ONE

LOVE BETWEEN EQUALS

Mary moves in soft beauty and conscious delight,
To augment with sweet smiles all the joys of the night,
Nor once blushes to own the rest of the fair
That sweet love and beauty are worthy our care.

. . . .

And thine is a face of sweet love in despair,
And thine is a face of mild sorrow and care,
And thine is a face of wild terror and fear
That shall never be quiet till laid on its bier.

— "Mary," William Blake, c. 1801–1803

THIS STORY BEGINS, as many tales do, with a love affair. It involved two brilliant yet very odd people who seemed utterly unsuited for each other. William Godwin was painfully shy, given to intellectualizing, and apparently a virgin at the age of forty, when he fell in love with Mary Wollstonecraft. She was passionate to the point of recklessness, heedless of the opinions of the world, and insistent that she never take second place to anyone, male or female. What brought them together was their common interest: revolution.

If the term "radical chic" had been current in the late eighteenth century, Mary and William would have been its personification, for they were the idols of a generation of young people who wanted to overturn the existing order. Both of them had been inspired by the French Revolution, which broke out in 1789 and promised a complete transformation of society. Wollstonecraft had stunned the British public in 1792 with the publication of *A Vindication of the Rights of Woman* (note the singular), which grew out of her defense of the French Revolution's Declaration of the Rights of Man. In those days, no one had previously thought it "sexist" to use the word *man* as a synonym for the human race; Wollstonecraft boldly spoke for half of all humanity, who desired their rights too.

A sample of the tart opinions expressed by the woman who is often called the first feminist:

> My own sex, I hope, will excuse me, if I treat them like rational creatures, instead of flattering their *fascinating* graces, and viewing them as if they were in a state of perpetual childhood, unable to stand alone. . . . I wish to persuade women to endeavour to acquire strength, both of mind and body, and to convince them that the soft phrases, susceptibility of heart, delicacy of sentiment, and refinement of taste, are almost synonymous with epithets of weakness, and that those beings who are only the objects of pity . . . will soon become objects of contempt.

Another: "A mistaken education, a narrow uncultivated mind, and many sexual prejudices, tend to make women more constant than men." Also: "An unhappy marriage is often very advantageous to a family, and . . . the neglected wife is, in general, the best mother." Finally: "It is vain to expect virtue from women till they are, in some degree, independent of men; nay, it is vain to expect that strength of natural affection, which would make them good wives and mothers. Whilst they are absolutely dependent on their husbands they will be cunning, mean, and selfish."

These were revolutionary ideas in an age when women were the legal property of their fathers and husbands. Horace Walpole, the Earl of Orford, otherwise famous for writing the first Gothic novel, expressed the verdict of England's upper classes when he called Wollstonecraft a "hyena in petticoats."

Wollstonecraft's future husband, though timid and withdrawn in person, threw off his reticence in his writing. In his most famous work, *Political Justice* (1793), Godwin set out to describe the social conditions under which the human race could achieve perfection. Though the excesses of the French Revolution had aroused deep fears among the English upper class, Godwin declared that "monarchy was a species of government unavoidably corrupt." But he went farther, much farther, claiming that *all* governments by their very nature stood in the way of the improvement of the human condition. Godwin believed that it would only be through the power of reason, not coercion or force, that society would be transformed. The publication of his book made him one of the most famous people in England, and for a time he was idolized by young people who were swept away by his vision of perfecting society. Freud wrote that every person has a "family romance," a narrative that explains the different relations of their life. Mary Shelley, the daughter of these two famous radicals, would be haunted by their love story and would use it (and her own life) as the narrative for much of her literary work.

For Mary Wollstonecraft, to borrow another phrase from the 1970s, the personal was the political, and all her writings used her own experiences to illuminate her ideas. Mary had tempestuous relationships, for she was a mercurial person who could be by turns passionate, domineering, needy, or depressed. Her life resembled a story from the literature of her time — the angst of Rousseau's *Julie: La Nouvelle Héloïse* or the melodrama of Goethe's international best-seller *The Sorrows of Young Werther*. She was a woman of contradictions who took actions that often seemed at odds with her own radical philosophy. Hard as a diamond, if tapped the wrong way she could shatter. As she wrote when she was thirty-eight, "There is certainly an original defect in my mind, for the cruelest experience will not eradicate the foolish tendency I have to cherish, and to expect to meet with, romantic tenderness." Few have carried that "defect" as far as Mary Wollstonecraft.

She was born in London on April 27, 1759, a year of military victories for the English that won them Canada and India, making England the most powerful nation on earth. At home, Englishmen were finding new wealth from the heightened economic activity called the Industrial Revolution. Wollstonecraft's grandfather had earned a fortune as a master weaver and supplier of cloth to the growing textile industry. His son,

Mary's father, heir to two-thirds of the fortune, was a big spender, heavy drinker, and a man of violent temper. According to Godwin, Mary recalled that her mother was "the first and most submissive of his subjects."

Mary had the kind of childhood that could either crush a spirit or rouse it to greatness. The second of six children, she resented the favoritism shown toward her brother Ned, two years older than herself. Ned's position as the family's golden child was quite literal, for in his grandfather's will, he had inherited the other one-third of the estate. Money was not what Mary craved, however. She envied the attention and warmth that her mother, Elizabeth Dickson, bestowed on Ned. A significant factor in Mary's sibling rivalry was the fact that her mother had breast-fed Ned, while a wet nurse was hired to nourish baby Mary. It isn't clear how she knew of her deprived condition, but once she did know she considered it a profound fact. As she later wrote, a mother's "parental affection . . . scarcely deserved the name, when it does not lead her to suckle her children."

Additional complaints show up in a novel she wrote in 1787, titled *Mary*. (The title character was, not by coincidence, "the daughter of Edward, who married Eliza," the same names as the real-life Mary's parents.) The book describes not only the way men repress women's individuality but also shows that women often accept this domination. It was clear that the author was recalling her own family when she wrote: "Her father always exclaimed against female acquirements, and was glad that his wife's indolence and ill health made her not trouble herself about them. . . . [He] was very tyrannical and passionate; indeed so very easily irritated when inebriated, that Mary was continually in dread lest he should frighten her mother to death." For those who knew that the real-life Mary often slept on the landing near her mother's bedroom to protect her when her father was in one of his drunken rages, the portrait was hardly veiled.

Mary had only a few years of formal schooling, but her parents' fecklessness also gave her the freedom to run and play outside rather than being confined indoors, the fate of most girls at the time. To compensate for the chill she encountered at home, she formed intense friendships. Her best friend when she was fourteen was a schoolgirl named Jane

Arden. The two girls exchanged letters in which they gossiped about "macaronis," the young fashionable men in the town. Then some incident led Mary to accuse Jane of favoring another girl. Mary wrote to her, "I am a little singular in my thoughts of love and friendship; I must have the first place or none." In another letter to Jane, she wrote, "I cannot bear a slight from those I love."

As Mary grew into adolescence, she was required to change from the loose shifts and comfortable petticoats of childhood to corsets with stiff stays of whalebone that constrained her body from chest to thigh. Compounding her sense of restriction, she lacked a room of her own where she could be alone. Displaying the signs of a growing rebellious streak, Mary announced that she would never marry for money, for she was seeking a nobler life for herself. She also became more socially concerned, especially about the living conditions of servants and the poor.

When Mary was fifteen, her family moved to Hoxton, outside London. Here she met Fanny Blood, with whom Mary immediately made "in her heart, the vows of an eternal friendship." Fanny too suffered from having a drunken father, and Mary soon confided to Jane that now she loved her new friend "better than all the world beside." Fanny, Mary wrote, "has a masculine understanding, and sound judgment, yet she has every feminine virtue." Their relationship would endure through additional relocations, and become one of the most important in Mary's life.

Marriage, whether for love or money, remained unattractive to Mary in view of the example given by her parents. As a result, she knew that she had to be self-supporting. ("I must be independent and earn my own subsistence or be very uncomfortable," she declared.) At the time, single women had limited options for work — teacher, governess, or companion. In 1778, Mary found employment as a companion to a wealthy widow. The job, despite its amiable name, could be quite unpleasant, for it required the hired person to cater to the whims of her employer: the author Fanny Burney called the occupation "toad-eating." But Mary made a success of it, staying for two years until she had to come home to nurse her mother through her final illness.

Mary faithfully attended her mother for the next two years. During that time, her brother Ned, now married, rarely came to visit. Though

Mary hoped for some sign of deathbed favoritism and affection, she was disappointed. Her mother's last words were, ". . . a little patience and all will be over." Mary, however, would improve on these — and gain the affection she yearned for — when she wrote her autobiographical novel *Mary*. There, the dying mother's last words to her daughter are: "My child, I have not always treated you with kindness. God forgive me! Do you?" One day, Mary's own daughter would follow her mother's example of using her pen to "improve" her real-life experiences.

Six months after her mother's death, Mary's younger sister Eliza married Meredith Bishop, a boat builder some ten years older than she. In less than a year Eliza gave birth to a daughter and suffered from what we now know as postpartum depression. A concerned Bishop asked Mary to come and stay with her sister. Instead, Mary "rescued" her: with Fanny Blood's help, she spirited Eliza away from home when Bishop was absent, leaving the infant behind. They went into hiding north of London, living under false names. Eliza might well have returned to her husband if left to her own devices, but Mary stiffened her resolve.

Now Mary set out to achieve her dream of self-sufficiency and establishing a life with Fanny Blood. In 1783, joined by another of Mary's sisters, Everina, the four young women opened a school at Newington Green, on the outskirts of London. There, Mary met Dr. Richard Price, who took her under his wing and became a bit of a father figure. Dr. Price was a devoted lover of liberty; he had fervently supported both the American Revolution and the cause of reform within England. He corresponded with intellectuals and scientists in the United States and France — Franklin, Jefferson, and Condorcet, to name just a few. Price helped Mary to understand the intellectual underpinnings of what she felt instinctively about liberty and human rights.

The all-female family life that Mary hoped for was, however, doomed. In August 1784, word came that Eliza's baby daughter, still with its father, had died. Eliza suffered another nervous breakdown, and later would come to view Mary as the person who had destroyed her marriage and caused the loss of her child. (The resentment had repercussions even years after Mary's death when her two sisters, Eliza and Everina, rejected Mary's own daughter, who wanted to find a refuge with them.) At this time, Fanny Blood was also suffering from ill health: tuberculosis. When her longtime beau Hugh Skeys, who had become a wine merchant in Lisbon, sent a proposal of marriage, Mary encouraged Fanny to accept, arguing that the climate of Portugal would be good for Fanny's health. But after her friend's departure, she wrote, "without someone to love this world is a desert."

When Fanny became pregnant, Mary made the sea voyage to Lisbon to be with her, arriving only a few hours before the delivery. But she was only to be a witness to tragedy. Fanny's illness affected the birth, and both mother and child died. Fanny's death haunted Mary for the rest of her life. She would write, "the grave has closed over my dear friend, the friend of my youth; still she is present with me, and I hear her soft voice warbling as I stray over the heath."

She closed the school in Newington Green when she returned to England and found work as a governess for an aristocratic family in Ireland. This lasted only a year, for the lady of the family thought that the children were more devoted to Mary than to herself. While in Ireland Mary read and became deeply influenced by the ideas of Jean-Jacques Rousseau. Rousseau was the most important thinker of the second half of the eighteenth century. Mary found his work particularly appealing because of its emphasis on the personal, particularly in his *Confessions.* Rousseau was also, like her, a person of internal contradictions. In a letter to her sister Everina on March 24, 1787, she wrote: "I am now reading Rousseau's *Émile,* and love his paradoxes. . . . He was a strange inconsistent unhappy clever creature — yet he possessed an uncommon portion of sensibility and penetration." She might have been describing herself.

While at Newington Green, Mary had written a book, *Thoughts on the Education of Daughters,* which a friendly clergyman, John Hewlett, had sent to the London publisher Joseph Johnson. Johnson had accepted it and paid Mary twenty guineas, a sum that she immediately turned over to two of Fanny Blood's needy brothers, ignoring her own debts and obligations. Now, in 1787, she wrote to Johnson about her newest plan for self-sufficiency: to become a full-time writer. "I am determined! Your sex generally laugh at female determinations; but let me tell you, I never yet resolved to do anything of consequence, that I did not adhere resolutely to do it, till I accomplished my purpose, improbable as it might have appeared to a more timid mind." She relocated to London, where Johnson helped her find lodgings. A liberal in politics, he had published the works of William Blake and Benjamin Franklin as well as Thomas Paine, scientist Erasmus Darwin (grandfather of Charles), poet William Cowper, and chemist Joseph Priestley.

Acclaimed as "the father of the book trade," for he was the first to commission books, rather than serve as a printer for those who wished to publish, Johnson became both a mentor and a friend. Mary bragged to Everina in a letter: "I am . . . going to be the first of a new genus," adding, "You know I am not born to tread in the beaten track — the peculiar bent of my nature pushes me on."

Publishers were aware that women made up a large part of the reading public, and women like Fanny Burney, Jane Austen, Ann Radcliffe, and Hannah More were well known for their novels that dealt with women's interests. The bestsellers of the day included two genres of particular appeal to women — the novel of sentiment and the Gothic novel. In some ways, these reflected opposite sides of female personality. Novels of sentiment celebrated delicacy of feelings, and even fostered the practice of weeping in public. Such works praised women for their purity of refinement and moral superiority, exalting the traditional roles of mother, wife, and loyal sister. Gothic novels, on the other hand, looked into darker corners. Often set in exotic locales, the Gothics dealt with fear and the irrationality that lies beneath the surface of so-called normal life. Women writing in the Gothic genre discovered they could explore emotions and daring actions outside the norms regarded as "proper" for women. (Men were often fans of the Gothic genre too; the young Lord Byron read Ann Radcliffe's novel *The Mysteries of Udolpho,* and modeled part of his own soon-to-be-famous persona after one of its characters.)

Johnson suggested that Mary try her hand at writing books in the new field of children's fiction. His neighbor John Newbery had made a good living at it. (Today a children's book award is named for him.) In 1788, Mary's *Original Stories* appeared, depicting women in many different roles — single, married, widowed, working, and at home. It showed Mary's concern for the condition of the poor by portraying the suffering of unmothered children, victims of bad housing and corrupt landlords. For the second edition of the book, Johnson hired William Blake to illustrate it. The eccentric Blake was then an unknown artist and Mary found in him a friend as well as a collaborator who shared her social concerns. Soon Blake would be illustrating his own poems rather than acting as a collaborator for others' work.

Mary found a new intellectual circle opening to her. She wrote to Fanny Blood's brother George, "Whenever I am tired of solitude I go to Mr. Johnson's and there I meet the kind of company I find most pleasure in." Johnson hosted afternoon dinners where he entertained many of the leading writers, philosophers, and artists of the day. With time, Mary became one of the regulars, whom she called "standing dishes"— the only woman so honored other than the writer Anna Barbauld. Besides Blake, the guests included the painters John Opie and Henry Fuseli; the political philosophers Thomas Paine and William Godwin; the American poet Joel Barlow; radical reformer Horne Tooke, who had actually raised money in Britain to support the American colonies' struggle for independence; and Thomas Holcroft, who went from peddler's son and stable boy to become one of England's leading dramatists, just to name a few. Many of those in Johnson's circle were free thinkers, English versions of the French *philosophes* who were then challenging people to use rationality rather than religious faith to guide their lives. Mary found herself in the midst of daring discussions that challenged and encouraged her.

All of these people appealed to Mary's mind, but the artist Henry Fuseli stoked the fire in her heart. Mary was approaching thirty, and she longed for a great passion. In Fuseli she thought that she had found the "soul mate" she had dreamed of. Born Johann Heinrich Füssli in Zurich in 1741, he had come to England in the 1760s, where he adopted his new name. He was the oldest son of a painter who insisted that he become a minister, so as a child he had painted only in secret. He became ordained when he was twenty, along with his best friend Johann Lavater, who would later become famous as the founder of physiognomy, a method of determining character through the examination of facial features. The two men had an intense relationship that may well have been sexual. Fuseli wrote in a letter to Lavater, "I grow too excited, I must stop here —

O you who sleep alone now — dream of me — that my soul might meet with yours." When Lavater married, Fuseli wrote that a disembodied spirit would be around the lips of him and his bride.

Fuseli was a brilliant scholar who knew eight languages and wrote essays about painting, sculpture, art history, and Rousseau. When he came to England, a meeting with the painter Joshua Reynolds set him on the road to his true calling and he spent some seven years in Italy studying art. In 1782, he completed his most famous painting, *The Nightmare,* which caused a sensation. Bizarre, erotic, and emotional, it was reproduced many times in prints, and became an icon of Romantic art. The work portrays a sleeping woman lying across a bed, arms open as if filled with erotic desire. Looking through the window at her is a ghostly horse — a symbol of sexuality — with bulging, pale eyes. Seated on the sleeping woman's chest, staring out at the viewer of the work, is a grinning incubus, a male demon who had sexual intercourse with women as they slept. For a while the painting hung in Joseph Johnson's home as a token of the two men's close friendship. As guests engaged in the intellectual conversation of Johnson's dinner parties, they could enjoy a little erotica at the same time. (A century later, Sigmund Freud also displayed a print of this painting on the wall of his office.) And the image of the woman in the painting would much later become an inspiration for Wollstonecraft's daughter, when she wrote her famous novel.

When Mary met Fuseli she was twenty-nine and relatively inexperienced; he was a worldly-wise forty-seven. The short, lecherous, vain bisexual was a walk on the wild side for Mary, but unfortunately he was not a person capable of the kind of attachment she wished for. She was fascinated by his paintings and drawings, and loved listening to him discourse authoritatively on many subjects. His descriptions of the seamier side of life engrossed her too. He spoke openly of frequenting prostitutes; some of the drawings that he showed her were pornographic. All this — novel, daring, on the edge — was stimulating to Mary, in a way that the high-toned conversation of the crowd at Johnson's was not. She plunged into a love affair, meeting Fuseli at her own flat as well as his studio. At his urging, she changed her appearance. Before meeting him, she had dressed in a plain, almost careless, manner in coarse clothes, black worsted stockings, and beaver hat with her hair hanging loose about her shoulders. The fastidious Fuseli showed her how to dress more fashionably, and she now pinned up her hair.

As Mary's ardor increased, however, Fuseli's interest in her cooled; his friendship for her, he claimed, had been strictly intellectual. As Mary tried more desperately to call attention to herself, writing feverishly and often, Fuseli withdrew from her. He would pointedly allow her letters to remain unopened for many days. For a sexual partner, Fuseli preferred another: he married Sophia Rawlins, one of the models he used for his paintings. Ironically, she would burn her husband's more explicit drawings after his death.

It took a revolution to distract Mary from her unrequited passion for Fuseli. The French Revolution, which began in 1789 when a mob stormed and captured the Paris prison known as the Bastille, was the central event of the time. Its rallying cry of "Liberty, Equality, Fraternity" and the Declaration of the Rights of Man and the Citizen, which proclaimed all citizens were equal under the law, not only electrified the French but inspired many Britons as well. Mary and her friends who gathered at Joseph Johnson's house cheered what was happening in France, for they felt it heralded a new day for all mankind. The young poet William Wordsworth summed up the feelings of many with the couplet: "Bliss was it in that dawn to be alive, / But to be young was very heaven!" In October, Joseph Priestley predicted that revolution would spread to other countries — something that did not thrill Britain's upper classes. Indeed, after Mary's old mentor, Reverend William Price, gave a public sermon praising the revolution, saying, "I see the ardour for liberty catching and spreading," a prominent member of Parliament, Edmund Burke, felt compelled to reply. Though Burke had earlier supported the American Revolution, his *Reflections on the Revolution in France* condemned the destruction of French aristocratic society and government. Burke used the language of a Gothic novel in his metaphor for the revolutionary forces: "Out of the tomb of the murdered monarchy in France has arisen a vast, tremendous, unformed spectre, in a far more terrific guise than any which ever yet have overpowered the imagination."

Mary Wollstonecraft wrote the first answer to Burke in her vigorous defense of the French Revolution, *Vindication of the Rights of Man,* which was published anonymously in December 1790; the first printing sold out in a month, and the next printing had her name attached to it. Overnight, Mary became a heroine to English supporters of the Revolution. William Roscoe, a friend of Fuseli's, wrote a ballad satirizing Burke in which this stanza appeared:

And lo! an Amazon stept out,
One WOLLSTONECRAFT her name,
Resolv'd to stop his mad career,
Whatever chance became.

The Revolution radicalized a number of women writers, who began to critique the role of women in society and the family. The revolutionary emphasis on the rights of *man* gave Mary the opening to write about the other half of the human race. She may have been inspired by a dinner at Johnson's house in September 1791, where Thomas Paine, the firebrand whose pamphlet *Common Sense* had helped spark the American Revolution, was a guest. Among those present was William Godwin, who had been looking forward to meeting Paine and was annoyed when, he felt, Mary monopolized the conversation.

Of course, Mary needed no other goad than her intelligence and social conscience, for the real-life circumstances of women were reason enough to protest. Women had very restricted opportunities. Indeed a married woman had *no* rights after her wedding; her very being and legal existence was incorporated into that of her husband. Britain's Matrimonial Act of 1770 called for the prosecution as witches "all women . . . that shall . . . impose upon, seduce, and betray into matrimony any of His Majesty's subjects by means of scent, paints . . . false hair . . . high shoes, or bolstered hips." Many people had little sympathy for the cause of women's rights, for they saw the humiliations inflicted on them as the will of God.

Socially, women were hemmed in by the customs and standards society set for the "Proper Lady," as a twentieth-century scholar, Mary Poovey, has called the ideal woman of that time. Etiquette books, intended for the young and for those who wished to "improve" themselves, described precisely how women should act. Women of the aristocracy were not limited by these values, but for the rest of women — particularly the middle class — they were essential to respectability. The ideal of the Proper Lady strongly handicapped ambitious women like Mary, for it ranked the virtues of modesty and moderation higher than any talent or ability. It even held in low esteem women who indulged in vigorous activities; sports of any kind were denied to them. The Proper Lady could only entertain herself by activities such as sewing, piano playing, singing, needlework, and painting. Modesty was carried to extremes, for no proper woman could admit to sexual urges. The double standard of sexual morality was everywhere the norm; for a woman to lose her virginity outside of marriage was equivalent to dishonor — but men were expected to seduce them if they could. In the words of an eighteenth-century text for the education of young women: "This [virginity] lost, every thing that is dear and valuable to a woman, is lost along with it; the peace of her own mind, the love of her friends, the esteem of the world, the enjoyment of present pleasure, and all hopes of future happiness."

Encouraged by Joseph Johnson, Mary used her newfound fame to take up the cudgels for her sex. Thoughts rushed from her brain as she wrote her magnum opus in just six weeks. Mary handed *A Vindication of the Rights of Woman* to the printer in January 1792. In it, she launched a frontal attack on the Proper Lady and defined as "negative virtues" such Proper Lady ideals as patience and docility. She urged women to demand their rights and declared that she wanted to "rouse my sex from the flowery bed, on which they supinely sleep life away." Wollstonecraft declared that women were human beings before they were women, and they were entitled to equal civil and political rights as well as opportunity for education and economic advancement. "I do not wish them to have power over men; but over themselves," she wrote. She boldly criticized no less an exalted personage than Rousseau for his notions of female inferiority.

Mary asserted that the differences between men and women were mainly the result of upbringing and education, not of biology. She insisted that women had the same capacity for learning that men did and she wanted girls to have equal opportunity for learning and education, preferably in coeducational schools outside the home. Recognizing the connection between equality and becoming financially independent, she insisted that girls be encouraged to aim for success in the professions.

Perhaps because of her own mixed feelings, Mary played down the importance of sexual relations, advocating friendship between men and women, rather than passion. (She was soon to change these views.) She constantly struggled with the conflict between her need for love and her desire to dominate —"to be first." Moreover, she wanted the respect and rewards that society gave to the Proper Lady, though she refused to abide by the standards that society demanded in return. In short, she wished to have it both ways.

With the publication of *Vindication of the Rights of Woman*, she reached the height of her fame. It became an immediate bestseller and made Wollstonecraft one of the most famous women in Europe. French, German, and Italian versions appeared. (The sister-in-law of Abigail Adams, wife of the man who would become the second president of the United States, demanded that Abigail buy her a copy when she accompanied her husband to London.) Not all the attention was favorable. Hannah More, a prolific writer of pious plays, stories, and poetry, wrote to Horace Walpole: "I have been much pestered to read the *Rights of Women* [*sic*] but am invincibly resolved not to do it . . . there is something fantastic and absurd in the very title. How many ways there are of being ridiculous! I am sure I have as much liberty as I can make a good use of, now I am an old maid, and when I was a young one, I had, I dare say, more than was good for me."

By 1792 Wollstonecraft had changed her appearance again, allowing her hair to assume its natural curl and cutting it in a fringe in the latest French style. Her new relaxed clothing reflected French revolutionary sensibility, as well as medical approval: Erasmus Darwin had written that less restrictive clothing styles were good for one's health, prompting many relieved Englishwomen to cast off their stays.

Mary's newfound fame had not lessened her obsession with Fuseli. In a desperate move, she went to his home and asked his wife to allow her to live there in a kind of ménage à trois. Despite Mary's willingness to take second place for once in her life, Sophia rejected her offer and warned her never to visit the house again.

Crushed, Mary wrote to Joseph Johnson, "I am a strange compound of weakness and resolution! . . . There is certainly a great defect in my mind — my wayward heart creates its own misery — Why I am made thus I cannot tell; and, till I can form some idea of the whole of my existence, I must be content to weep and dance like a child — long for a toy, and be tired of it as soon as I get it." Ironically, Mary's daughter would have to suffer the same "threesome" problem with her husband, Percy Shelley.

Mary escaped this humiliation by going to France in December 1792, arriving as the Revolution was entering a new, more radical phase: France was now at war with Prussia and Austria, and by a narrow margin the Revolutionary Convention had sentenced King Louis XVI to death, something that shocked even many of the original revolutionaries. Yet publicly, the situation seemed calm, even joyous. The common people felt they had triumphed. Dr. John Moore, an Englishman who lived in Paris at this time, reported,

> The public walks are crowded with men, women, and children, of all conditions, with the most gay, unconcerned countenances imaginable. A stranger just come to Paris . . . would naturally imagine from the frisky behaviour and cheerful faces of the company he meets that this day was a continuation of a series of days appointed for dissipation, mirth, and enjoyment. He could not possibly imagine that the ground he is walking over [had been] . . . covered with the bodies of slaughtered men; or that the gay lively people he saw were so lately overwhelmed with sorrow and dismay.

Mary's fame preceded her, and she soon made friends among the small English community in Paris, where she found many involved in love affairs. A freer attitude toward sex was part of the spirit of the revolution. Nuns and priests were encouraged to marry, for celibacy was regarded as unhealthy; unmarried mothers were helped rather than blamed;

women argued for their right to divorce their husbands. Mary also found kindred spirits among the Girondists, members of the more moderate revolutionary faction who often met at the Jacobin Club, particularly the wife of a Girondist government minister, Madame Roland, who was one of the social and intellectual leaders of revolutionary Paris.

But danger loomed. In January 1793, the king was guillotined, an act that led to a declaration of war from England and Spain, countries whose monarchs felt their own necks threatened. In France, foreigners now began to encounter hostile stares; the government told landlords and innkeepers to report any suspicious activity, especially by English and Spanish residents. Mary's friends whispered stories of people being taken from their homes by revolutionary guards in the middle of the night. She slept with a burning candle in her room, fearful of what might happen.

In these tense circumstances Mary met the American Gilbert Imlay, who would bring a personal revolution into her life. Mary was thirty-three and Imlay a bachelor of thirty-nine. Born in New Jersey, he had fought in the American Revolution and was now a businessman and writer. Tall, handsome, and skilled at seduction and flattery, he could claim literary kinship with Mary, for he was the author of a book, *A Topographical Description of the Western Territory of North America,* and at the time she met him, he was completing a novel, later published as *The Emigrants.* He told Mary openly that he had lived with other women and that he intended never to marry. Mary's fame as well as her attractiveness and lively spirit were attractions that led him to court her.

As Mary learned more about his business interests, Imlay took on a romantic image. He was involved in a shady project to organize a French expedition against the Spanish colony in Louisiana, and he may also have been engaged in smuggling goods through the blockade that Britain, now openly hostile to the French government, maintained off the coast of France. Mary began to idealize him as a model of Rousseauian simplicity, as Europeans liked to imagine Americans (a pattern set by Benjamin Franklin's wearing animal skins and posing as a frontiersman during his visits to France). Besides, she was growing older and the humiliation she suffered over Fuseli led her to overlook Imlay's faults. By April, the two were always together and they soon consummated their love. According to her, she experienced orgasm — what she called "suffusion" — for the first time.

The pace of events in France pushed the relationship along. After the king's head fell, no one was safe, and the Revolution began to turn on its own. In May and June, the Girondists were rounded up; Mary's close friend Madame Roland was among those arrested. To protect herself, Mary moved to the Parisian suburb of Neuilly. Here, in the summer months of 1793, she and Gilbert enjoyed the height of their affair. Now infatuated, Mary wanted to make the relationship permanent, but Imlay suddenly departed for the port of Le Havre to carry out one of his shady business deals. Not wishing to be alone, Mary moved back to Paris, where conditions were even more dangerous than before. Robespierre, the most radical French leader, had come to power and instituted the phase of the Revolution known as the Terror. Madame Roland was one of thousands of former supporters of the Revolution who now went to the guillotine. All British citizens fell under suspicion, and to protect Mary, Imlay had registered her as his wife and an American citizen. In October, the English who had remained in Paris — including many of Mary's friends — were placed under arrest, but Mary was protected by her new status.

Imlay was still spending much of his time in Le Havre, and Mary now realized she was pregnant: "I have felt some gentle twitches," she wrote Imlay, "which make me begin to think, that I am nourishing a creature who will soon be sensible of my care.— This thought has . . . produced an overflowing of tenderness toward you." Meanwhile Mary worked on a new book, *A Historical and Moral View of the French Revolution,* further endangering herself, for even her new citizenship status would not protect her if the work were to be discovered. She walked to the Place de la Revolution daily and witnessed the guillotine in action. When she expressed her horror at the gruesome sight, others in the crowd warned her to be silent.

Her days were taken up with writing: in her letters to Imlay she poured out her feelings: "I do not want to be loved like a goddess; but I wish to be necessary to you." She hinted that she wished an invitation to join him in Le Havre. Receiving none, she acted on her own, finding a carriage and driver to make the journey. There, on May 14, she gave birth to a daughter. Mary named the girl Fanny after her closest friend, Fanny Blood. Imlay signed the birth certificate, still claiming he and Mary were married.

They spent the next three months together, happy ones for Mary as she basked in the feeling of being wife and mother. She and Imlay talked of settling in America, but by this time he was growing tired of playing at marriage and his finances required attention. He told Mary he had to go to London on business. She returned to Paris, which was safer now that Robespierre had himself become a victim of the guillotine and the Terror was over.

Mary suffered through a very cold winter, waiting for Imlay to return but receiving nothing but excuses. Her own letters became more insistent, and she wrote to him much as she had earlier to Jane Arden. On January 9, 1795, she told him, "I do not chuse to be a secondary object." Little Fanny was a demanding child, although caring for her distracted Mary from allowing despair to overwhelm her. Finally she decided to return to England, writing Imlay from Paris, "My soul is weary,— I am sick at heart." When Mary reached London in April, she and Fanny and a French maid moved into a house Imlay rented for them, but he was cold to her; he had taken a new mistress, a pretty actress. After he told Mary frankly that he did not want to live with her and Fanny as a husband and father, Mary attempted suicide by taking laudanum. It was a cry for help, for she had sent suicide notes to both Imlay and her mentor Johnson. In Mary's novel *Maria,* when the heroine is deserted by her lover, she also takes laudanum, but a vision of the fictional Maria's baby girl makes her vomit the poison. In real life, Imlay, who had received Mary's suicide note in time, came to revive her.

As in her affair with Fuseli, Mary was blinded by her passion, still hoping to save her relationship with Imlay despite all indications that it was over. He was planning to go on a business trip to Scandinavia and she volunteered to take his place. Perhaps wishing to get rid of her, he agreed, giving her some assignments to carry out. She set off with Fanny and her nursemaid, visiting Sweden, Norway, and Denmark, and then continuing on to Germany. During this trip she kept writing to Imlay, hoping to revive his feelings for her. At the same time, she analyzed herself keenly:

> Love is a want [need] of my heart. Aiming at tranquility, I have almost destroyed all the energy of my soul. . . . Despair, since the birth of my child, has rendered me stupid . . . the desire of regaining peace (do you understand me?) has made me forget the respect due to my own emotions — sacred emotions, that are the sure harbingers of the delights I was formed to enjoy — and shall enjoy, for nothing can extinguish the heavenly spark.

When she returned, she found Imlay was now openly living with another woman. Mary's humiliation was now both complete and public. She again sought escape through suicide — this time with more determination. She wrote to Imlay, "I would encounter a thousand deaths, rather than a night like the last. I shall plunge into the Thames where there is the least chance of my being snatched from the death I seek." On a rainy afternoon in October 1795, Mary carried out her plan. She rented a boat and rowed herself up the Thames to the Putney Bridge, which she had learned was less crowded than Battersea Bridge, the closest span to her flat. Leaving the boat, she walked back and forth along the bridge in the pouring rain to make sure that her clothes were so wet that she would sink under the waters. As she threw herself into the dark cold river, she expected death to embrace her kindly, the way Goethe had described it in *The Sorrows of Young Werther:* "I do not shudder to take the cold and fatal cup." (*Werther* was a bestseller that had prompted many suicides throughout Europe and was later to be one of the books that the monster reads in *Frankenstein.*) But as water filled Mary's lungs, she began to choke and was in pain before losing consciousness. A man who had seen her leap off the bridge jumped in and saved her. He took her to a tavern, where a doctor revived her. Death, apparently, would not accept her sacrifice.

Imlay offered financial help but Mary was too proud to accept it. She saw Imlay for the last time in 1796 and wrote to him the next day, "I part with you in peace." She resumed her writing career to earn her keep and get on with her life. From the Scandinavian trip came a charming book,

Letters Written During a Short Residence in Sweden, Norway and Denmark. The act of writing it gave her some respite from the turmoil that raged within her, and she began to come to grips with Imlay's true character, realizing that the relationship could never have worked out the way she had wanted. Perhaps most importantly, *Letters* won the heart of William Godwin, whom Mary would meet a second time, with happier results than the first.

William Godwin described himself accurately as "bold and adventurous in opinions, not in life." Though not as well known today as he once was, Godwin was one of the most important radical thinkers of his time. His courage did not extend to his relations with women, and it was only after becoming involved with Mary that he explored the intricacies of love. Their short life together provided for each of them the emotional and intellectual companionship that they had lacked. For their daughter Mary Shelley, who never knew her mother, their mutual affection was an ideal that continually inspired her fiction and her own desires.

Godwin was born March 3, 1756, in Wisbech in the Cambridgeshire Fens — a bleak area where the North Sea constantly threatens to overwhelm the land. He was the son and grandson of clergymen — so-called Dissenters who were stricter in their beliefs than the members of the Church of England. This devout religious background created an emotional rigidity that made William more comfortable with books than with the love and affection of other people. It fostered his shyness and coldness and did long-term psychological damage that he would pass on to his daughter.

William was the seventh of thirteen children, many of whom did not survive to adulthood. His father, John Godwin, was the minister of the Wisbech Independent Chapel and took in paying pupils to supplement his meager income. Because of the large family, William got little attention even as a young child. He was sent to a wet nurse for the first two years of his life and later, like Mary Wollstonecraft, was to fault his parents for this neglect. His formative years were marked by poverty and a dreary existence. They put a chill into his soul that would never leave him.

John Godwin belonged to the Sandemanian tradition, a small and joyless sect of Dissenters who embraced "primitive" Christianity. He believed in predestination, original sin, and divine retribution. Indeed his Calvinist views were so rigid that he alienated his congregation and had to move to Debenham in Suffolk when William was two. Here again, William's father had difficulties and two years later he relocated once more — this time to Guestwick, north of Norwich, where he would remain till he died. Much of Godwin's childhood was spent here. The local meeting house's most treasured possession was a carved oak chair known as Cromwell's chair. The young William occasionally sat in it, taking the place of Oliver Cromwell, the hero of the Dissenters, who had ruled England for five years when the Puritans had controlled the country.

William remembered his father as a man who had little love of learning or books and that he usually scribbled his sermon for the Sunday service at tea on Saturday afternoon. By contrast William himself was a very early reader and soon went through the Bible, books of sermons, *The Pilgrim's Progress,* and other religious literature. As he recalled, "I remember, when I was a very little boy, saying to myself, 'What shall I do, when I have read through all the books that there are in the world?'" A favorite "improving" book for him was James Janeway's *A Token for Children, Being an Exact Account of the Conversion, Holy and Exemplary Lives and Joyful Deaths of Several Young Children* — a series of stories about children who were saved by obeying God's will and dying at a young age. Uncle Edward Godwin, another minister, had written a children's book called *The Death Bed, a poem concerning the Joyful Death of a Believer and the Awful Death of an Unbeliever,* which all the young Godwins had to read. The title tells it all.

Death in its reality was not unknown to the Godwins. One brother drowned at sea and another in a pond right outside the Godwin home. William himself was a sickly boy and was lucky to survive an attack of smallpox; his religion forbade him to be inoculated, and he said he was "perfectly willing" to die rather than disobey.

All this piety made the young William fear that he might be damned forever for any small infraction. Even as a child, he wished to become a preacher himself. At home, he would stand on his high chair in the legal wig that had belonged to his great-grandfather and deliver sermons to an imaginary congregation. Rather than enjoying his son's performances, however, John Godwin feared that William was acting like a showoff.

When he was eight, William began attending school at a town two and a half miles away. He practiced preaching as he walked through the woods. One day he made a friend collapse in tears when he described the damnation that awaited him for his sins. Later he secretly borrowed the key to the meeting house and preached and prayed over his friend like an ordained minister. (In a note that he wrote to himself, he said he allowed the boy to kiss him. The nature of the kiss was not noted.) The only errant act of his childhood that William remembered was attending the theater in Norwich, when he was nine. Though his father's female cousin accompanied him, theater-going was forbidden by his religion.

His father sent him back to Norwich when he was eleven to be educated as the only pupil of the Reverend Samuel Newton. His father chose Newton because he believed that William needed even stricter training to instill more humility in him. Newton's preferred method of instruction was beating for the smallest behavioral lapses. William was beaten only once, but even that was an astonishing experience to him. As he recalled, "It had never occurred to me as possible that my person . . . could suffer such ignominious violation." After his schooling, William returned to Guestwick, where he worked as an assistant schoolteacher until his father's death in 1772.

John Godwin's death was a liberation. William's mother, conscious of her son's intellectual gifts, took him to London to the Hoxton Academy. Hoxton was a rigorous college — far more rigorous than Oxford and Cambridge at the time. (As a Dissenter, Godwin was not able to attend those prestigious schools, which were for Anglicans only.) Lectures started at six or seven in the morning and included classics, theology, and Greek philosophy; students learned Latin, Greek, and Hebrew along with smatterings of French, Italian, and German. Most important, for the first time in his life, Godwin was exposed to honest, passionate debate.

Though he did well academically, he was not happy at Hoxton. He had an intense desire to be liked by others, yet had little ability in the art of making himself popular. He later noted ruefully that the schoolmaster and other pupils thought him "the most self-conceited, self-sufficient animal that ever lived." Though he began what would be a lifelong friendship with a boy named James Marshall, Godwin felt a strong sense of loneliness. It would stay with him throughout his life, be a recurrent theme in his novels, and would be passed on to his daughter Mary.

When, after five years, Godwin left Hoxton, he still wanted to be a preacher even though he had now developed many other interests and his religious views had broadened. Then only twenty-two, he obtained his first job as a temporary minister in the town of Ware, near his birthplace, but problems soon developed. Though Godwin had not yet been formally ordained, he felt entitled to perform the communion service, because he had the consent of his congregation. It sounds like a minor issue, but other ministers in the county took umbrage and refused to use the title of Reverend in addressing him. Four congregations rejected him in four years. Godwin tried to open a seminary, but failed to attract students. He would never become formally ordained.

As Godwin's failures as a minister increased, he found his faith starting to waver as well. During this time, Godwin had started to read the works of the *philosophes* — the same thinkers who influenced his future wife, Mary Wollstonecraft. Rousseau's effect on Godwin was to make him realize that religion and superstition could not stand the test of reason. It was a profound shock to the young man's worldview. At first he shifted from Calvinism to Deism, but would in time become an atheist.

Bereft of the only sure force that had guided his life, he settled in London in 1782 and began his career as a writer, joining a part of the English literary world known as "Grub Street," which published cheap novels, books of poetry, and nonfiction. Godwin had to produce copy quickly and in great quantity. "In the latter part of 1783," he recalled, "I wrote in ten days a novel entitled *Damon and Delia,* for which Hookham gave me five guineas, and a novel in three weeks called *Italian Letters,* purchased by Robinson for twenty guineas, and in the first four months of 1784 a novel called *Imogen, A Pastoral Romance,* for which Lane gave me ten pounds." *Imogen* was a spoof of *The Poems of Ossian,* a bestseller of the day that was supposed to be ancient Celtic lore, but was in reality a fake. Godwin's parody was spicy, including rape, a lecherous magician, and other highly un-Christian elements, although virtue did triumph in the end. He also wrote reviews for John Murray's *English Review,* a monthly that favored radical political positions. Publications called "reviews" were abundant in those days; they were often little more than collections of puff pieces used to push the newest books. (Murray was a book publisher as well; he would later publish Byron's works.) Godwin also took to critical writing — he attacked hack writers with relish, but was willing to praise writers who he thought were advancing knowledge. (Mary was equally honest; despite her feminism, she had no qualms about giving bad reviews to female writers, as when she called one book "one of the most stupid novels we have ever impatiently read. Pray, Miss, write no more!")

Though Godwin wrote for a radical publication, he was himself at first not politically active. In this he followed his father's example; the closest John Godwin had come to a political act was to take five-year-old William to a fireworks display in Norwich to celebrate the coronation of George III. Even so, at the time, the need for political reform was a hotly discussed topic, and William, with his background as a Dissenter, was particularly interested in it. The Act of Toleration of 1689 had given Dissenters only the freedom to practice their religion; English law still retained many restrictions against their conduct or liberties. For example, Dissenters were forbidden to hold civil or military offices, and were required to pay for the upkeep of local Church of England parishes.

The French Revolution inspired Godwin, as it had Mary Wollstonecraft. The issues being raised in France encouraged him to look for a way to bring about political justice through rational means in England. In 1791 he began planning a book that would "tell all that I apprehended to be truth," and secured an advance from a publisher to give himself the time to write it. The result, *An Enquiry Concerning Political Justice,* was published in February 1793; its appearance made Godwin famous overnight. His central premise was that humans were innately good; cruelty and injustice have made them what they are. Given that Godwin's original religious belief, as a boy and young man, was that humans are *inherently* mired in evil and need God's grace for salvation, it was clear that he was totally repudiating the faith in which he was raised.

Like his future wife, Godwin was not a philosopher who spoke in abstract terms alone. He intended to improve humankind by attacking the entrenched social and political institutions. Government, he wrote, was the central problem. In a time when the ruling class of England feared the French Revolution, Godwin was heedless of the consequences when he wrote such passages as, "With what delight must every well-informed friend of mankind look forward to the . . . dissolution of political government, of that brute engine which has been the only perennial cause of the vices of mankind." Considering that a man had recently been thrown into prison for three months for drunkenly shouting "Damn the king" in a public place, it is surprising that Godwin experienced no harassment for his views. Other critics of the government were put on trial for their lives — Horne Tooke, one of those whom Godwin and Wollstonecraft knew from Joseph Johnson's dinner parties, was among them. (He was acquitted.) Godwin later claimed the authorities thought the book was too expensive to reach a large audience. For whatever reason, he escaped prison and the noose.

This was all the more surprising since Godwin's *Political Justice* was if anything more extreme than Wollstonecraft's book. Godwin condemned *all* forms of coercion, including those used by the government to keep order, making him one of the founders of anarchism. Godwin envisioned a society in which people lived harmoniously without compulsion or force. At the top of the list of coercive social institutions that he attacked was marriage, which he called a slavery for women and "the most odious of all monopolies." The world of the future, in his view, would be egalitarian and people would use reason in all their relationships. Reasonable individuals would only act after considering the general good of the society, and limits on freedom would no longer be necessary. Godwin saw no obstacles to this ideal society, for progress was his true theme; he believed that it would inevitably appear. It was not stoppable.

Godwin's optimism and idealism seem excessive today, but at the time, revolutions — the American, the French, the scientific, and the industrial — seemed to promise that anything humans could envision was possible. Godwin instantly became one of the leading figures in the intellectual ferment of the time, and he became a hero to those who were most idealistic.

Political Justice was both expensive and difficult for the average person to read. Even so, groups of people raised the money to buy a copy, and then gathered to hear it read aloud. Godwin set out to reach a wider audience by writing a novel that would express his views in simpler form. He told his new story from the first-person point of view to get the reader more involved, a technique that his daughter would also employ. The year 1794 saw the publication of *Things as They Are; or The Adventures of Caleb Williams,* which combined psychological insight with a mystery — an unbeatable combination that produces bestsellers even today. Lower-class Caleb Williams, a servant, discovers that his otherwise upstanding employer, the upper-class Falkland, is a murderer. To prevent Caleb from revealing the secret, Falkland frames him for a crime. Caleb goes into hiding, and the two become locked in a pattern of pursuit, which ultimately destroys them both. Mary Shelley, who knew her father's novel well, would make use of the relentless pursuit between two self-destroying individuals when she wrote about Dr. Frankenstein and his monster.

Godwin continued to write novels for the next four decades. He was perennially in need of money, and novels were easier to write and sell than books of philosophy. Superficially — for he always used his novels as vehicles for his philosophy — his books employ Gothic elements, such as a struggle against a tyrannical authority figure, supernatural happenings, and a mysterious or exotic setting. (In *Caleb Williams* the narrator is warned never to open a trunk that stands in his master's room. Of course . . .) Despite Godwin's popular appeal, his novels posed important questions for society, and their resolutions were often tied to Godwin's radical proposals. He did not totally abandon nonfiction, writing the sensational *Lives of the Necromancers* (1834) two years before his death. It described such magicians as Cornelia Agrippa and Albertus Magnus of medieval times — questing figures who would interest both Percy Shelley and his fictional counterpart, Victor Frankenstein.

In 1796, William Godwin, at forty, was at the height of his fame. William Hazlitt, a contemporary essayist and critic, wrote that "he blazed as a sun in the firmament of reputation." But he had little experience with women, although recently he had shown some interest in two female writers, Elizabeth Inchbald and Amelia Alderson. Godwin feared that romantic involvement would take away energy from his intellectual activity.

In his mind, as expressed in his works, sexual relationships ranked well below friendship, and of course marriage was actually "evil." These ideas would be severely tested when he encountered Mary Wollstonecraft in January 1796. The two were reacquainted at a dinner at the house of Mary Hays, another writer and a great admirer of Wollstonecraft. Godwin expected, but did not find, the woman who had annoyed him in 1791, but Wollstonecraft was now a mother and had gone through considerable emotional trauma since then. She did not dominate the conversation.

Godwin's interest increased after he read Mary's *Letters Written During a Short Residence in Sweden, Norway and Denmark.* He later wrote, "If ever there was a book calculated to make a man fall in love with its author, this appears to me to be the book. She speaks of her sorrows, in a way that fills us with melancholy, and dissolves us in tenderness, at the same time that she displays a genius which commands all our admiration." Godwin went to call on Mary but she was away. When she returned, seeing his card, she paid a visit to him — a bold move, but one that was necessary to overcome Godwin's shyness. A romance blossomed that led to a love affair.

Godwin described his attachment to Mary in terms that were about as emotional as he ever got: "When we met again, we met with new pleasure, and I may add, with a more decisive preference for each other. It was however three weeks longer, before the sentiment which trembled upon the tongue, burst from the lips of either. There was . . . no period of throes. . . . It was friendship melting into love. Previous to our mutual declaration, each felt half-assured, yet each felt a certain trembling anxiety to have assurance complete." Nobody wanted to make the first move.

For Mary, this would be the first time she had been able to enter a relationship that satisfied both her intellect and her heart. She wrote to Godwin in September 1796, "When the heart and reason accord there is no flying from voluptuous sensations, I . . . do what a woman can — Can a philosopher do more?"

It was a particularly modern relationship. They wrote countless notes to each other, sometimes several times a day, developing a code to signal when it was a good time for sex. Godwin plotted Mary's menstrual cycle, which they used as a form of birth control. Mary assured William that he was free to see his other "Fairs"— there was to be no monopoly of affections. (Although in Mary's notes to him she referred to Elizabeth Inchbald as "Mrs. Perfection.") Indeed, it appears that Godwin proposed to Amelia Alderson in July 1796, but was turned down.

Wollstonecraft was more sexually experienced than Godwin but she was also emotionally fragile, and with the memory of Imlay still fresh, she feared her own vulnerability. Shortly after they began having sexual relations, she wrote Godwin about her doubts: "My imagination is for ever betraying me into fresh misery, and I perceive that I shall be a child to the end of the chapter. You talk of the roses which grow profusely in every path of life — I catch at them; but only encounter the thorns . . . Consider what has passed as a fever of your imagination; one of the slight mortal shakes to which you are liable — and I — will become again a *Solitary Walker*." (The italicized phrase, underlined in her letter, was from one of Rousseau's autobiographical writings.)

Godwin responded: "Do not cast me off. Do not become again a *solitary walker*. . . . Be happy. Resolve to be happy. You deserve to be so. Every thing that interferes with it, is weakness & wandering: & a woman, like you, can, must, shall, shake it off." It was the first time that Mary had a lover who was emotionally supportive. As the relationship deepened, Wollstonecraft felt secure enough to show Godwin her frank, honest, true self and to question intimately his interest. "Can you solve this problem?" she asked in one letter. "I was endeavouring to discover last night, in bed, what it is in me, of which you are afraid. I was hurt at perceiving that you were." In November, she wrote, "You tell me that 'I spoil little attentions, by anticipation.' Yet to have attention, I find, that it is necessary to demand it. My faults are very inveterate — for I *did* expect you last night — But, *never mind it*. You coming would not have been worth any thing, if it must be requested."

What Mary called Godwin's "chance medley system" of birth control did not work, and in December 1796 she realized that she was pregnant. Both she and Godwin were philosophically against marriage, but Mary worried about having a second illegitimate baby. Godwin agreed to marry her for the sake of their child. With Godwin's school friend James Marshall as witness, the couple wed at St. Pancras Church on March 29, 1797. For Fanny's sake, Mary had been calling herself Mary Imlay, but she signed the marriage certificate "Mary Wollstonecraft, spinster." It was to be a fresh start.

Godwin did not even mention the wedding in his journal. One of his chief objections to marriage was "co-habitation," the necessity for husband and wife to live together, denying "peace and privacy" to both. The newlyweds avoided that by continuing to occupy two residences. Though Mary and three-year-old Fanny, who called Godwin "Papa," moved into his home, Godwin maintained a separate office up the street where he could work privately during the day. Mary insisted that Godwin was still free to eat out with anyone he chose and that she was free to raise her children as she wished. They continued to communicate frequently by letter. Such was their answer to the problem of marriage "monopoly."

Meanwhile the two looked forward to the baby; they were sure it would be a boy and planned to name him William. Mary regained the enjoyment in motherhood and married life that she had experienced so briefly with Imlay. She wrote to Godwin in June 1797, "I begin to love this little creature, and to anticipate his birth as a fresh twist to a knot, which I do not wish to untie. Men are spoilt by frankness, I believe, yet I must tell you that I love you better than I supposed I did, when I promised to love you for ever."

The weather during that summer of 1797 was freakish; the strange phenomena would not be equaled until 1816. England experienced terrific storms that had been spawned by volcanic activity in the South American Andes. Unusually high tides struck the English coast, flooding the low-lying areas. The land was plagued by storms in which the lightning was so severe it seemed "to threaten the earth with universal conflagration." On the night of August 14, a comet appeared over London, bathing the city with its glow for the next eleven clear nights of calm weather. Mary and William called the comet their child's friendly star.

Since Mary's first pregnancy had gone well, she had no fears about this one. When she felt the onset of labor pains in the early morning of August 30th, she called Mrs. Blenkinsop, the midwife in charge of the famous Westminster Lying-In Hospital. She sent the first of several notes up the street to Godwin, informing him of her condition: "I have no doubt of seeing the animal [as she referred to the baby] today; but must wait for Mrs. Blenkinsop to guess at the hour. . . . I wish I had a novel, or some book of sheer amusement, to excite curiosity, and while away the time — Have you any thing of the kind?"

Mary's final note to Godwin reads, "Mrs. Blenkinsop tells me that I am in the most natural state, and can promise me a safe delivery — But that I must have a little patience"— it ends there, without a period at the end, or even her signature. Whether Mary was aware she was quoting her mother's last words, cannot be known. In any case, they were the last she herself would ever put on paper.

Wollstonecraft had a slow and painful labor, but a baby girl was born late that night. At three in the morning of the next day, William was told to find a doctor, for the placenta had not come out. When the doctor arrived, he had to take the placenta out by hand, for it had broken into pieces. With no painkillers the pain was excruciating; Mrs. Blenkinsop had to hold Mary's shoulders while the doctor worked for hours. Because he did not sterilize his hands or equipment, the doctor's treatment caused an infection that would kill Mary eleven days later.

For the first few days, a weakened Mary nursed her newborn, determined that her child should receive the maternal nurturing that she herself had not. By the end of a week Mary's strength had further declined and she suffered a fit of shivers that were so violent that the bed shook. When her condition worsened, the doctors believed that too much milk was the problem. The baby and Fanny were put in the care of Maria Reveley, a neighbor. Puppies were applied to Mary's breasts to draw off the milk; the doctors hoped that this might stimulate her womb to contract so the rest of the placenta could be expelled. By the time a surgeon came, hoping to remove the last parts of the placenta, Mary was too weak for surgery. Godwin stayed with her in the final days, giving her wine to ease her pain. "Oh, Godwin, I am in heaven," she murmured at one point. "You mean, my dear," he replied, "that your symptoms are a little easier." He was at her bedside when she died September 10. He entered in his diary only the words, "20 minutes before 8" followed by a long series of dashes. For once, words failed him.

Five days later, he was still too distraught to go to her funeral. She was buried in the churchyard at St. Pancras, where she had been married five months earlier. Godwin wrote to a close friend: "I firmly believe that there does not exist her equal in the world. I know from experience we were formed to make each other happy. I have not the least expectation that I can now ever know happiness again. Do not — if you can help it — exhort me or console me."

The political and literary journals of the time noted the obvious irony that Mary Wollstonecraft, the advocate of equality between the sexes, died as a result of giving birth. As the conservative *Anti-Jacobin Review* pointed out, her manner of death marked the differences between the sexes and pointed out the "destiny of woman." This kind of vicious reaction only underscored the effect Mary had wrought. She had challenged many of the prejudices of society in her short but productive life — doing so at great cost to herself. Her life and courage would be a source of inspiration and pride for her daughter, who would grow up with a name fraught with significance, reflecting both of her famous parents. The daughter, like her mother, would challenge propriety and pay a high price. Mary Wollstonecraft Godwin was aware from childhood that her birth was responsible for the death of her mother. This trauma and guilt would be one of the central factors in her life, and would find an outlet in *Frankenstein.*

CHAPTER TWO

"NOBODY'S LITTLE GIRL BUT PAPA'S"

Reaching the cascade . . . my soul was hurried by the falls into a new train of reflections. The impetuous dashing of the rebounding torrent from the dark cavities which mocked the exploring eye, produced an equal activity in my mind: my thoughts darted from earth to heaven, and I asked myself why I was chained to life and its misery . . . my soul rose, with renewed dignity, above its cares — grasping at immortality . . . I stretched out my hand to eternity, bounding over the dark speck of life to come."

— *Letters Written During a Short Residence in Sweden, Norway and Denmark,*
Mary Wollstonecraft, 1796

MARY GODWIN WAS the "dark speck of life to come." She started life with a loss and it left her with an unsatisfied need for love, for her father was incapable of that kind of nurturing. Instead, she learned in the most intimate manner that birth and creation can be fraught with dire consequences.

From childhood, Mary turned inward to find consolation, as a way of dealing with the emotional chaos she often felt. The unspoken fear that her birth had caused her mother's death would give great urgency to Mary's need to create a new, perfect human being to take her place. Like Mary, both Victor Frankenstein and his monster would be motherless.

Godwin's background and temperament had not prepared him for being a parent, especially a single one, and he realized it. His fears and doubts show in a letter to a friend, Anthony Carlisle: "One of my wife's books now lies near me but I avoid opening it. I took up a book on the education of children, but that impressed me too forcibly with my forlorn and disabled state with respect to the two poor animals left under my protection, and I threw it aside. . . . If you have any . . . consolation in store for me, be at pains to bestow it."

The first act Godwin was able to perform with his newborn daughter was a scientific one — at least, in terms of the science of the day. Before Mary was three weeks old, Godwin had her examined by a physiognomist named Nicholson, a practitioner of the Lavater method. Mr. Nicholson reported from assessing Mary's face that she "possessed considerable memory and intelligence" and her eyes, forehead, and eyebrows showed a "quick sensibility, irritable, scarcely irascible." Her mouth, which Mr. Nicholson found "too much employed" (she was crying), did indicate "the outlines of intelligence. She was displeased, and it denoted much more of resigned vexation than either scorn or rage."

Godwin finally dealt with his wife's death by deciding to recount her life story. This was the family way: write, write, write in the face of adversity. The day after Wollstonecraft's funeral, he began to sort through her papers. Before the end of the month, Godwin had begun to write what he believed would be a loving and candid re-creation of his late wife's life. He saw it as an act of dedication to her memory that would also serve as an expression of his deepest feelings. Godwin was inspired by the autobiography of a man both he and his wife had admired: Jean-Jacques Rousseau. But Rousseau's famous *Confessions* was the brutally frank account of a man writing about his *own* life. Godwin was relating the life story of *another* person, and he would go farther than most readers thought he decently should have.

Using collected letters and notes, Godwin described all of Mary's lovers, with a candor that ignored common delicacy. He sought letters from those other lovers; one was Henry Fuseli, who opened a drawer and showed him a bundle of Mary's correspondence but then slammed it shut, saying, "Damn you, that is all that you will see of them." Besides Mary's love life, Godwin discussed her suicide attempts and pregnancies, and praised her rejection of Christianity. (This was not actually true; she had retained her faith in the Church of England.) The intensity of Godwin's sorrow is reflected in the great detail he devotes in the *Memoirs* to his daughter's birth and his wife's death. Writing in a white heat, he finished the manuscript in less than three months; it was published in January 1798.

Godwin's painfully candid *Memoirs of the Author of "A Vindication of the Rights of Woman"* caused a sensation. His revelations about Mary Wollstonecraft's love affairs with other men caused a scandal in the increasingly conservative England. The Tory press had a field day, calling Mary a whore and Godwin a pimp. The *European Magazine* wrote that the *Memoirs* would be read "with disgust by every female who had pretensions to delicacy; with detestation by everyone attached to the interests of religion and morality; and with indignation by anyone who might feel any regard for the unhappy woman, whose frailties should have been buried in oblivion." Even more biting was the *Anti-Jacobin Review and Magazine,* which summed up its editors' feelings about the book with this ditty:

For Mary verily would wear the breeches
God help poor silly men from such usurping b——s.

Richard Polwhele, a poet and clergyman, in his antifeminist poem *The Unsex'd Females,* gave voice to sentiments that many people felt but refrained from saying: "I cannot but think that the Hand of Providence is visible in her life, her death, and in the Memoirs themselves. As she was given up to her 'heart's lusts,' and let 'to follow her own imaginations,' that the fallacy of her doctrines and the effects of an irreligious conduct might be manifested to the world." Others were appalled that Godwin could expose his dead wife to such scorn. Wollstonecraft's friend William Roscoe wrote:

Hard was thy fate in all the scenes of life,
As daughter, sister, parent, friend and wife
But harder still in death thy fate we own,
Mourn'd by thy Godwin — with a heart of stone.

Wollstonecraft's reputation would remain tarnished by Godwin's *Memoirs* until the middle of the twentieth century. Wollstonecraft's ideas of equality were so severely mocked by critics of Godwin's intended memorial that subsequently feminists would choose narrower goals, such as suffrage for women, rather than the broad demand for equal rights that Wollstonecraft had recommended. Though her daughter did not read the criticisms at the time they were published, she became aware of them, and even suffered personally. The *Memoirs* and her mother's reputation for immoral sexual behavior gave little Mary an unsavory notoriety even as a child. The world truly was aware of her before she was aware of the world.

Godwin was truly shocked by the response to his tribute, and it deepened his sorrow and depression over his wife's death. Having enjoyed his marriage, and wanting to find a mother for his two children, Godwin began to court a Mrs. Elwes, a widow, in the spring of 1799. His attentions cooled when he learned that his neighbor Maria Reveley's husband had died, and Godwin proposed to her. Though she had enjoyed caring for the children, she had no desire to marry Godwin. When he shifted his attentions back to Mrs. Elwes, she also turned him down. Next he tried to revive a friendship with the writer Elizabeth Inchbald by sending her an advance copy of his novel *St. Leon* with a note asking to visit her. She answered that she could only see him in company. "While I retain the memory of all your good qualities," she wrote, "I trust you will allow me not to forget your bad ones." This was hardly the response that Godwin had hoped for; worse yet, she enclosed an unfavorable critique of the book. Godwin was crushed — so depressed that he could barely go outside. He wrote in his journal, "This day I was desirous of calling on someone, to learn more exactly the character of the book, but had not the courage . . . to look an acquaintance in the face."

Godwin's declining fame and influence brought about a loss of self-confidence that led to the deterioration of his health. The first symptoms were seen at Johnson's dinner parties, where he would drop off to sleep or lose consciousness. It was the onset of narcolepsy, which would worsen over the years. During an attack, he would lose control of his muscles, his jaw would drop, his legs lose their strength, and then he would crumple into sleep. He had the first of these fits in February 1800, and they would recur sporadically for the rest of his life.

Some of his old friends now were shunning him for political reasons.

The French Revolution which he so admired had mutated into an aggressive nationalistic crusade. French troops were fighting successfully all over Europe, and in England as well as other countries, revolutionary supporters such as Godwin were reviled. Godwin was spat on in the street — to many English, he represented atheism, sexual immorality, and treason.

He was no less hard on himself than others were. In 1798, he made a personal assessment of his character:

> I am tormented about the opinion others may entertain of me; fearful of intruding myself, and cooperating in my own humiliation . . . and by my fear producing the thing I fear. . . . This, and perhaps only this, renders me often cold, uninviting and unconciliating in society. . . . My nervous character . . . often deprives me of self possession, when I should repel injury or correct what I disapprove. Experience of this renders me, in the first case a frightened fool, and in the last a passionate ass.

Godwin hired a female housekeeper to take care of the children while he was working. His friend James Marshall, who often served as Godwin's secretary and literary agent, took the place of a parent when Godwin was away on long trips. Godwin tried to keep in touch with his family through letters. On one occasion he wrote to Marshall:

> Their talking about me, as you say they do, makes me wish to be with them, and will probably have some effect in inducing me to shorten my visit. It is the first time I have been seriously separated from them since they lost their mother. . . . Tell Mary I will not give her away, and she shall be nobody's little girl but papa's. Papa is gone away, but papa will very soon come back again.

As Mary grew from infancy to childhood, she desperately wanted to please her father and resented his offering any attention to others. His method of disciplining her when he disapproved of her behavior was to retreat into a calm silence. Such treatment devastated Mary. Craving affection, she received coldness. Later, in her most personal novel, *Mathilda*, written at a time of loss and desolation in her private life, she would portray an incestuous father-daughter relationship. Mathilda's mother died a few days after her birth, intensifying the relationship between father and daughter, which appears to have been close to wish fulfillment.

When Mary was four, Godwin found a second wife — or rather, she found him. At the time, the Godwins lived at the Polygon, a recently built housing development on the outskirts of London. The community was a set of balconied houses on the edge of a field. One day in 1801, Godwin's new next-door neighbor, an attractive woman in her mid-thirties named Mary Jane Clairmont, called to him from her balcony: "Is it possible that I behold the immortal Godwin?" What man could resist?

Clairmont was a bit of a mystery woman. She called herself a widow, but the identity (and fate) of her two children's father or fathers is uncertain. Even her last name is in doubt — she registered herself under two different names when she and Godwin were married. Clairmont had a three-year-old daughter named Clara Mary Jane; this child would later call herself Claire. Mrs. Clairmont also had a son about Fanny's age named Charles. Charles was apparently the son of Karl Gaulis, a Swiss, but Clara Mary Jane may have had a different father. In later life Claire tried many times to find out the secrets of her birth, apparently without success.

Godwin was quite a catch for Mary Jane Clairmont, and she soon reeled him in. They were married in a church, apparently the bride's decision, in December of that year. James Marshall was the only witness present. The new Mrs. Godwin soon expelled him from the household.

Four-year-old Mary was devastated by her father's remarriage. She resented having to share his love with another and was jealous of her new mother. Moreover, there were obvious signs of the new bond between husband and wife: Jane was soon pregnant. Their first child was stillborn, but that was followed by a second child, born March 28, 1803. He was christened William — the namesake that William Godwin had expected from his first wife, the boy that little Mary had not been.

In Mary's eyes, Jane Clairmont would always compete with her mother's ghost. The two women were very different people — Wollstonecraft was emotional, almost manic-depressive, but Clairmont was shrewd and competent, ambitious, and a manager. She proved to have a head for business, but lacked warmth, at least toward her stepchildren. Many of Godwin's friends shared his daughter's dislike for her new mother. The children's book author Charles Lamb referred to her as the "widow with green spectacles," comparing her to Robespierre, who was also noted for wearing tinted eyeglasses. Usually generous in his opinions, Lamb called her "That damn'd infernal bitch Mrs. Godwin." Another visitor was more unkind, calling her "a pustule of vanity."

Mary grew up in a strange blended family of five children with no child having the same two parents. First there was Mary's older half-sister Fanny, who was quiet and withdrawn. Fanny's biological father had by now vanished, never to be heard from again, and Godwin brought her up as his own child, not revealing the truth until she was about eleven; she was called Fanny Godwin. In his novel *St. Leon*, Godwin describes a character who bears an eerie likeness to Fanny; the passage contains a key to her ultimate fate: "Uncommonly mild and affectionate. . . . She appeared little formed to struggle with the difficulties of life and frowns of the world; but, in periods of quietness and tranquillity nothing could exceed the sweetness of her character and the fascination of her manners."

Mary's new step-siblings, Charles and Clara Jane, visibly reflected the fact that each had different fathers: Charles was fair while the boisterous, temperamental Clara Jane had dark hair and eyes. Finally there was Mary's half brother William, the baby of the family, who was doted on by the second Mrs. Godwin. Mary had plenty of competition for her father's attention.

Aaron Burr, the former United States vice president, visited the Godwin family and found the household charming. He referred to the girls in mock-French as "les goddesses," and recalled that the children often gave little performances and lectures. He noted that eight-year-old William read "from a little pulpit . . . with great gravity and decorum" just as William Sr. had in his childhood. After little William's "sermon," the family had tea and "the girls sang and danced an hour." Fanny and Mary, he reported, were talented in drawing and Clara had a lovely singing voice.

The household's routine was organized around Godwin's work needs. In the mornings everyone was expected to be quiet while he wrote in his study. The poet Samuel Taylor Coleridge, after a visit to the Godwin home, described it as having a "cadaverous silence . . . quite catacombish." After lunch, Godwin would take the children for a walk, which he used for imparting lessons of natural history. Clara would recall that she and the others worked at "learning and studying . . . we all took the liveliest interest in the great questions of the day — common topics, gossiping, scandal, found no entrance in our circle."

In Godwin's philosophy, self-examination was the principal means of improvement. Once a person had concluded that his or her actions were correct, then he or she might disregard the criticism, indeed even the condemnation, of others. Mary would follow this philosophy to a fault. Clara Jane Clairmont, who was also raised according to Godwin's principles, recalled later in life: "Nothing could be more refined and amiable than the doctrines instilled into us — only they were utterly erroneous."

Though the two boys went to school, Godwin taught the girls personally, giving them the essentials of literacy and basic mathematics, the history of Greece, Rome, and England, as well as literature in both Latin and English. (Mary thus did not get the advantage of attending a coeducational school outside the home, which her mother had advocated in the *Vindication.*) The only outside teacher for the girls was a man who came to teach singing and reading music once a week. Even Clara was sent to a boarding school for a while, but Mary's teacher was the man she revered, her father. Years later, Mary admitted that Godwin "was too minute in his censures, too grave and severe." Yet she also wrote of him that "Until I knew Shelley, I may justly say that he was my God."

There were constant reminders of Mary Wollstonecraft in the Godwin home. Over the mantel hung a large portrait of her, which had been painted by Wollstonecraft's friend John Opie. Visitors to the house saw it when they entered, and it often stimulated stories and memories of her, while little Mary sat listening. Godwin himself continued to idolize her even though he had remarried.

One of Mary's earliest memories was of her father taking her to her mother's grave, teaching Mary to spell her own name by tracing the letters on the tombstone, which read:

MARY WOLLSTONECRAFT GODWIN
Author of "A Vindication of the Rights of Woman"
Born April 27th, 1759, Died September 10th, 1797

It is not known how old Mary was when she realized that she and her mother bore the same name, and that her mother had died giving birth to her, but later in life, Mary often wrote in her journal of her duty to fulfill the promise left unfulfilled by her mother's death.

Godwin realized quite early that Mary was extraordinarily intelligent, and he wished to create in her a wonderful specimen of learning. Once she learned to read, he gave her the use of his fine library, and she adopted the Godwin method of reading two or three volumes simultaneously. Books were her childhood companions, for she had few friends her own age. She could hear adults constantly discussing books in her home, which, despite Godwin's marginalization, remained a gathering place for intellectuals and writers. The two founders of English Romantic poetry, William Wordsworth and Samuel Taylor Coleridge, were frequent guests of the Godwins. In 1798 they had jointly published a collection of their poetry, *Lyrical Ballads,* which literary historians regard as the beginning of the Romantic movement in England. Wordsworth, in the preface to a later edition, called "all good" poetry the "spontaneous overflow of powerful feelings," a definition that inspired the next generation of poets. Among those who gathered in Godwin's drawing room were poets and writers such as political essayist William Hazlitt; Robert Southey, who would be poet laureate of Britain and a historian as well; the Irish patriotic poet Thomas Moore; dramatist Richard Brinsley Sheridan; Humphry Davy, then a young poet but in the future England's leading scientist; and Thomas Holcroft, dramatist and novelist, who was one of those who had been indicted for treason in 1794. All were eager to discuss poetry and ideas — political, philosophical, scientific, literary.

Mary always remembered one Sunday in 1806, when Coleridge and Charles and Mary Lamb came to tea and stayed for supper. It was a magical evening of poetry in the Godwin home. Though there was a strict bedtime, Mary and Clara sneaked behind the sofa to listen as Coleridge recited his poem *The Rime of the Ancient Mariner.* Throughout the rest of Mary's life, this was one of her most beloved works of literature, for she identified with the isolated mariner and his torment. She was particularly haunted by the words:

> *Alone, alone, all all alone,*
> *Alone on a wide wide sea!*
> *And Christ would take no pity on*
> *My soul in agony.*

Mary also began to learn about her mother through the books that bore her name; she was as attracted to Wollstonecraft's collection of letters from Scandinavia as her father had been. It was more than merely a travel narrative. Written at a time of great personal anguish, the book incorporated Wollstonecraft's passions and grief (often expressed in her letters to Imlay, which form part of the book) with vivid descriptions of places she visited. It would later prove particularly influential in the writing of *Frankenstein.*

Godwin was perennially in need of money, particularly now that he had a family of seven to support. Fortunately, his new wife had a good head for business. At her instigation they opened a bookshop in 1805 on Skinner Street, north of Blackfriars Bridge in the heart of London. (Thomas Wedgwood, philanthropic heir to a fortune from the pottery business, lent Godwin one hundred pounds to start the venture.) Two years later, the Godwin family moved in upstairs in the five-story building. It was not a pleasant neighborhood for ten-year-old Mary to grow up in. Only a hundred yards from the shop were the Fleet Prison and the Old Bailey, the scene of public executions that drew raucous and sometimes violent crowds. At a double hanging in 1807, twenty-eight spectators were crushed or trampled to death. Not much farther away was Smithfield Market, where cattle and pigs were slaughtered for sale; their bellowing sometimes wakened the children. Adding to the stench of animal dung was the Fleet Ditch sewer, a covered passage that carried human waste through the city. It is not hard to understand why Mary preferred to stay inside with her daydreams than to venture out into the gruesome reality outside.

Mary's personal problems were exacerbated by the fact that the family was always in financial trouble. Godwin, as a single man, had been able to support himself as a writer. Having a wife and five children made life a constant struggle. Godwin would be perpetually "borrowing" throughout his life. He traded on the admiration others felt for him by hitting them up for loans that were never repaid. In an uncompleted autobiography he wrote:

> As long as I remained alone, I neither asked nor would accept aid from any man — I lived entirely as I listed.
>
> Since I have been a married man, the case has been otherwise. I never repented the connections of that sort I have formed, but the maintenance of a family and an establishment has been a heavy expense, and I have never been able with all my industry, which has been very persevering, entirely to accomplish this object.

Godwin's bookstore sold standard titles along with supplies such as copybooks and pencils and pens, but the Godwins also began to publish children's books, then a growing field. Using a pen name because his own was too notorious for English parents, Godwin wrote titles for the list, among which were histories of Rome, Greece, and England. Godwin did not always hide his political opinions; he ended the history of Rome with the reign of Augustus, stating that the next four hundred years, during which "tyrants" (emperors) ruled, were unworthy of mention for when Rome "ceased to be a Republic it ceased to deserve the name of History." His wife contributed by doing translations from books in French, as well as writing books herself.

The Godwins were the original publishers of their friends Charles and Mary Lamb's classic *Tales from Shakespeare.* Few who have read the Lambs' loving versions of the stories from Shakespeare's plays, and their other tales for children — for they have remained in print to our own time — suspected that these siblings both were for some time confined to what were then known as "madhouses," and that Mary Lamb stabbed her mother to death with a kitchen knife. A jury's verdict of insanity saved her from the death penalty; afterward, she was in the care of her brother, who committed her to asylums whenever he thought it necessary.

Mary Godwin began to develop a double life in literature, learning to experience life vicariously through her reading. When she was growing up, works of fiction for children — like those of Helen Maria Williams, who had been a friend of Mary's mother in France — often portrayed the heroines as orphans all alone in the world, a situation Mary identified with. One of her favorite books was Charles Brockden Brown's *Edgar Huntly, or Memoirs of a Sleepwalker,* whose heroine was described: "Her mother died shortly after her birth. Her father was careless of her destiny. She was consigned to the care of a hireling." As her literary experiences grew wider than the narrow world she knew at home, Mary started to interpret and deal with real-life events from what she read. In her mind, fiction, fable, life, and experience became intertwined, a condition that would continue throughout her life.

Often, when Mary sought escape from her family problems, she retreated to St. Pancras churchyard, where her mother was buried. There Mary could commune with the only person who truly loved her as she wished to be loved. Just as that mother, Mary Wollstonecraft, had always insisted on coming first, so her daughter wished herself to be. Yet the daughter noted regretfully, "I did not make myself the heroine of my tales. . . . I could not figure to myself that romantic woes or wonderful events would ever be my lot." Otherwise, she hid from her anguish in books and imagination. Reading led Mary to daydreaming, or "waking dreams" as she called them: "My dreams were all my own; I accounted for them to nobody; they were my refuge when annoyed — my dearest pleasure when free." She soon started to write down the dreams that she imagined. From the examples of her youthful writing that survive, it is clear that she had learned no punctuation or spelling from her freethinking father. What she did receive from Godwin was the encouragement, even the expectation, that she would be a writer and artist. Having such famous parents put pressure on her to be worthy of their names. Mary herself said she had been from birth "nursed and fed with glory." Her stepsister, Clara Jane, described the same pressure from a more skeptical viewpoint. "In our family," she wrote, "if you cannot write an epic poem or novel, that by its originality knocks all other novels on the head, you are a despicable creature, not worth acknowledging."

As Mary grew from childhood into adolescence, her relationship with her stepmother, never very good, deteriorated further. A clash of wills between the two became virtually a part of daily life. Mary accused her stepmother of snooping in her mail, invading her privacy, and making her do housework (something Mary always loathed). Of course, these are normal manifestations of adolescence, but Jane Clairmont also had to deal with the fact that she was constantly compared to the dead, now idealized, Mary Wollstonecraft. Mary read and reread her mother's works, finding fuel for defying her stepmother's discipline, and now that Mary was a teenager, the sexual passages in Godwin's memoir of Wollstonecraft took on new meaning for her. Mary also clashed frequently with Clara Jane, who was not unnaturally favored by her mother. Clara was aware of Mary's superior intellect, a fact that Mary flaunted. The second Mrs. Godwin told a friend that Mary "always thought and called [Clara] . . . stupid."

Frustratingly for Mary, Godwin's favorite daughter at that time seems to have been Fanny. She was less trouble, and for that Godwin was grateful. To all appearances, Fanny had the sweetest temperament of the three girls in the household. Christy Baxter, a friend of Mary's, said she was "more reflective, less sanguine, more alive to the prosaic obligations of life. . . . Godwin, by nature as undemonstrative as possible, showed more affection to Fanny than to anyone else. He always turned to her for any little service he might require."

Seldom a source of emotional support to Mary, Godwin all but ignored his daughter's teenage angst. He wrote his wife to "tell Mary that in spite of unfavourable appearances, I have still faith that she will become a wise, & what is more a good & happy woman." Like her mother she suffered from extreme mood swings, and it was sometimes unclear if her physical maladies were actually psychosomatic. At thirteen, Mary had started to suffer from a wasting of her arm and hand, and developed a skin infection that would not heal. This certainly could also have sprung from the unhealthy climate — the sewer and livestock market — around the family home on Skinner Street, but there was some doubt as to its origin. Two years earlier Clara had spent three months at Margate on the southeast shore of England, for her health. Now Mrs. Godwin took Mary to the nearby Ramsgate health resort, which offered "water cures," then a popular health practice. Those who wished to immerse themselves would enter "bathing machines," which were carts dragged by horses into the sea. From a door in the rear, the bathers could descend into the water and lower a canvas awning to protect their privacy from prying eyes on the shore.

Unfortunately, the visit to Ramsgate did not improve Mary's health or temperament sufficiently. In May of 1812, Godwin asked William Baxter, an acquaintance from Dundee, Scotland, to take Mary for her health — and to restore domestic peace at Skinner Street. One can only imagine how Mary felt about being dumped with strangers. In a letter written the day after the fourteen-year-old Mary was on her way, Godwin wrote another letter to Baxter, which showed his doubtful feelings about his daughter. "I am quite confounded to think how much trouble I am bringing on you & your family." Godwin goes on to characterize Mary as a virtual problem child — indeed, even a "monster." He relates that she has talents but apologizes in advance for her: "I tremble for the trouble I may be bringing on you in this visit." Godwin certainly wasn't paving the way for a great first impression.

Prone to seasickness, Mary endured a long sea voyage up the east coast of England. (The chilly, forbidding scenes of that trip would find their way into descriptions in *Frankenstein.*) After arriving, however, Mary loved Scotland's stark landscape. She believed that it was here "beneath the trees of the grounds belonging to our house, or the bleak sides of the woodless mountains near, that my true compositions, the airy flights of my imagination were born and fostered."

The Baxters were a loving family group — the first that Mary had known outside of books. They accepted her. She became closest to the two daughters, Christina and Isabella; for the first time in her life, Mary had girlfriends. Staying with them improved Mary's physical and mental health, and her bad arm seems to have been cured. She remained with the Baxters for two years, making only one trip home between the summer of 1812 to early spring of 1814. Throughout her chaotic lifetime, she would continually seek to regain her ideal of the stable family that they represented.

On that single trip back to Skinner Street, accompanied by Christy Baxter, Mary found her family abuzz about a young man named Percy Shelley. He had discovered *Political Justice* and one day arrived to tell Godwin he wanted to dedicate his life to achieving the book's ideals. At the time Mary was just fifteen, and Shelley a married man of twenty. He seems to have made little impression on her. When she returned to London in March 1814, however, she was about to meet him again, and this time he would turn her life upside down.

CHAPTER THREE

IN LOVE WITH LOVING

While yet a boy I sought for ghosts, and sped
Through many a listening chamber, cave and ruin,
And starlight wood, with fearful steps pursuing
Hopes of high talk with the departed dead.
I called on poisonous names with which our youth is fed;
I was not heard — I saw them not —
When musing deeply on the lot
Of life, at that sweet time when winds are wooing
All vital things that wake to bring
News of birds and blossoming, —
Sudden, thy shadow fell on me;
I shrieked, and clasped my hands in ecstasy!

— "Hymn to Intellectual Beauty,"
Percy Shelley, 1816

SINCE HIS YOUTH, Percy Bysshe Shelley had been fascinated with the supernatural. As a boy, he collected "blue books," cheap editions of Gothic novels about haunted castles, murders, ghosts, pirates, magicians, and bandits. One of his favorites was *The Life and Adventures of Peter Wilkins, a Cornish Man,* about a race of flying people, the "glumms" and "glowries," and Wilkins, their Prometheus, who brought them the arts and civilization. Shelley fantasized about having a winged wife who would give birth to little flying cherubs.

He felt that there were mysteries hidden beneath the veneer of everyday reality and that, somehow, he could discover them. Secret societies such as the Freemasons and the Illuminati held great interest for him, and he recalled perusing "ancient books of Chemistry and Magic . . . with an enthusiasm and wonder, almost amounting to belief."

One of Shelley's scientific interests was astronomy, and he often speculated on the possibility that people would one day travel to the planets. His cousin Thomas Medwin wrote that Shelley hoped that, in the same way schoolboys were promoted from one grade to another, humans "should rise to a progressive state from planet to planet, till we become Gods."

Fantasizing about all these marvels and horrors often gave Percy vivid and terrifying dreams, and he was a lifelong sleepwalker. Like Mary Godwin, he had "waking dreams" as well, though his were virtually hallucinations. Medwin recalled that "a sort of lethargy and abstraction" would come over Percy, after which "his eyes flashed, his lips quivered, his voice was tremulous with emotion, a sort of ecstasy came over him, and he talked more like a spirit or an angel than a human being."

Shelley often saw himself as a solitary genius or a wandering poet, but though he would roam, he also liked to be the center — and leader — of a group. Indeed, his life and career were devoted to bringing others along with him toward his envisioned, more perfect, existence. His large blue eyes and high-pitched, hypnotic voice invited others to join in the visions he saw clearly. From his youth, when he had four younger, adoring sisters to enlist in the fantasies he concocted, he was able to persuade others to share his dreams. Eccentric and rebellious, Shelley was forever to be a visionary looking for a harem.

The Shelleys were part of a minor branch of an old aristocratic family in Sussex, south of London. Percy's great-grandfather had gone to America to seek his fortune, and his grandfather Bysshe had been born in Newark, New Jersey. Through the deaths of his father's elder brothers, Bysshe came to inherit the estate of his branch of the Shelley family, which included a property called Field Place. He came to England and increased the family fortunes by eloping with two wealthy heiresses. The first one was only sixteen, the same age of the two women his grandson would fall in love with. Bysshe's first wife bore him a son and heir, the poet's father, Timothy.

Bysshe was an eccentric and a dreamer who spent much of his time building a castle which he called his "Folly." It was never completed, nor did anyone ever want to live in it. Through political connections, Bysshe became a baronet but he took the title with a grain of salt. His son Timothy, on the other hand, proved to be a pompous snob, lived the life of a country squire at Field Place, and also served in Parliament. The elder Bysshe showed a talent for versifying when he joked of his son:

It's not my wish
To be Sir Bysshe,
But it's my son's whim
To be Sir Tim.

Timothy Shelley married Elizabeth Pilfold, a beautiful woman of high birth. On August 4, 1792, their first child was born and christened Percy Bysshe, though the family always called him Bysshe. His birth was followed by those of five little sisters — one died in infancy — and a brother who was born after Percy was a teenager. Timothy and Elizabeth did not seem close to any of their children, and Percy always displayed a virulent hatred for his father, who in turn forbade anyone to use his son's name in his presence for years after Percy's death. Timothy had hoped for a political career for his first-born son and disapproved of his literary efforts. He gave his younger son this advice: "Never read a book, Johnnie, and you will be a rich man." Percy later wrote, "The habits of thinking of my father and myself never coincided. Passive obedience was inculcated and enforced in my childhood. I was required to love, because it was my *duty* to love."

Percy's mother was a beautiful woman and she has been described as clever but lacking imagination — not a perfect fit for her son. Edward Dowden, an authorized biographer of the poet who talked to Shelley's siblings, wrote that Elizabeth's "temper was violent and domineering," and that she felt her elder son had inadequate enthusiasm for hunting and fishing. She had been brought up in a sporting household and wanted her son to conform. Sometimes she would force Percy to go out with the gamekeeper to hunt. As soon as they were out of sight, Percy would curl up under a tree with a book while the gamekeeper proceeded to shoot enough rabbits and squirrels to satisfy Elizabeth.

But in some ways, growing up at Field Place was Edenic for Percy. He could romp in the gardens with his adoring sisters. He invented fabulous stories about fantastic creatures who lived there, such as the Great Old Snake that lurked in the gardens. Sometimes he dressed as an alchemist, casting spells, while his sisters would don costumes to impersonate spirits that Percy would summon up. Percy had little contact with boys his own age, and he became accustomed to having a circle of young females around him to entertain and play games with. He enjoyed nature and often rode on his pony through the woods; his sister Hellen recalled that he loved to sneak out and look at the stars at night. The estate also had a pond where young Percy sailed toy boats. Throughout his life he would love being near water, though he never learned to swim.

Percy learned to read quite early and started to devour books with what would be a lifelong gusto. He learned Latin from the local clergyman; even at this time it was clear that the young boy had a wonderful memory and his sisters remembered him reciting Latin verses. He soon started to compose his own poetry. The earliest surviving effort, written when he was eight, is "Verses on a Cat." The second stanza shows that a strain of melancholy was already part of his personality:

You would not easily guess
All the modes of distress
Which torture the tenants of earth;
And the various evils
Which like so many devils,
Attend the poor souls from their birth.

Shelley received a shock in 1802, when he was sent to the Syon House Academy, a boys' school in Brentford. Here there were no adoring sisters to obey his instructions — instead, only boys who felt he was not "one of them." His classmates, used to rough play, thought Percy was girlish because he didn't want to take part in their sports or games. Shelley, recalled his cousin Thomas Medwin, who was also a student there, was mocked because he did not know how to play marbles, leapfrog, hopscotch, or cricket. Another schoolmate remembered him as "like a girl in boy's clothes, fighting with open hands and rolling on the floor when flogged, not from the pain, but from a sense of indignity." Yet another reported that because Shelley talked about "spirits, fairies, fighting, volcanoes, etc." he was considered "almost on the borders of insanity."

In such a situation a lesser person would try to change, to adapt, become more like others. That was not Shelley, who claimed that it was at Syon House that it became clear to him that he must change the world. Years later he wrote about this experience in the introduction to "The Revolt of Islam."

Thoughts of great deeds were mine, dear Friend, when first
The clouds which wrap this world from youth did pass
I do remember well the hour which burst
My spirit's sleep: a fresh May-dawn it was,
When I walked forth upon the glittering grass,
And wept, I knew not why; until there rose
From the near schoolroom, voices, that, alas!
Were but one echo from a world of woes —
The harsh and grating strife of tyrants and foes.

The one good thing Shelley acquired at Syon House was a love of science, acquired from attending the talks given by Dr. Adam Walker, a traveling lecturer who was a friend of the chemist Joseph Priestley. Walker introduced Percy to electricity, magnetism, and telescopes. Among the facts that fascinated the boy was that, as Benjamin Franklin and others had shown, electricity could be collected, stored in a device called a Leyden jar (an early type of storage battery), and used to perform experiments. On holidays and school vacations, Shelley returned to Field Place to introduce surreptitiously the world of scientific inquiry to his sisters, who were distressed as gunpowder, fire balloons, and "electrical kites" appeared in Shelley's repertoire of practical jokes. When he offered to cure one sister's chilblains by "electrifying" her, she turned traitor, informed their mother, and the scientific experiments were reined in.

After two years at Syon House, Shelley went to Eton, where he spent the next six years, the longest time he was ever to remain in one place during his entire life. Shelley, still stubbornly averse to games and "manly" activities, once more found school a hostile environment. The headmaster, a Dr. Keate, was generally known as "Flogger," and the school authorities tolerated the "fagging" system by which the younger boys had to get protection from bullies by performing menial tasks for the older students. Here, the harassing of Shelley became so commonplace that it received a name: the "Shelley bait." A classmate recalled hearing cries of "Shelley! Shelley! Shelley!" thundering through the hallways as groups chased him down, surrounded him, knocked his books from under his arm, pulled at him, and tore his clothes. "The result was . . . a paroxysm of anger which made his eyes flash like a tiger's, his cheeks grow pale as death, his limbs quiver, and his hair stand on end." Such demonstrations of rage only prompted the crowd to taunt him some more. He soon picked up the nickname "Mad Shelley."

During his later years at Eton, things improved. Many of the younger students liked him because he refused to abuse the fagging system. Shelley developed a crush on a boy during these years. "Every night when we parted to go to bed, I remember we kissed each other," Shelley wrote in some autobiographical notes he made years later. A strong bisexual component to his personality would always be with him.

A classmate recalled him as

> a thin, slight lad, with remarkably lustrous eyes, fine hair, and a very peculiar shrill voice and laugh. . . . At his tutor, Bethell's, where he lodged, he attempted many mechanical and scientific experiments. By the aid of a common tinker, he contrived to make something like a steam-engine, which, unfortunately, one day suddenly exploded, to the great consternation of the neighbourhood and to the imminent danger of a severe flogging from Dr. Goodall.

But his scientific pursuits did not overshadow his fascination with the supernatural. One time during the Eton years, he spent the night in a charnel house at Warnham Church, waiting nervously for the spirits of the dead to appear. Indeed, the invisible world, whether explained by science or spirits, was to him a tangible reality.

An elderly teacher at Eton, Dr. James Lind, took a keen interest in Shelley and encouraged his scientific pursuits. Lind had been one of King George III's doctors and was a member of the Lunar Society, whose members included such pioneers of science as Joseph Priestley, James Watt, and Erasmus Darwin. (The group took its name from the fact that its meetings were held on the night of the full moon so that the members could get home safely.) Lind had traveled to China and was interested in many phases of knowledge and new ideas. He introduced Shelley to the study of French and German, which were not stressed in Eton's curriculum of classical learning. Under Lind's guidance, Shelley began to read seriously the writings of such thinkers as Lucretius, Pliny, Franklin, and Condorcet. Most important, Lind put a copy of William Godwin's *Political Justice* in Shelley's hands. Godwin's opposition to government and all other large societal institutions, as well as his optimism that free inquiry would lead to a happy anarchy, appealed enormously to Shelley. The future envisioned by Godwin meshed with Shelley's emerging ideas about the importance of small self-sustaining groups with which he could pursue intellectual inquiry.

During his last year at Eton, Shelley wrote what was to be his first published work: *Zastrozzi*, a Gothic story of passion, betrayal, and vengeance. It was similar to the popular books that he had devoured since his years at Syon House. He took the name of the female protagonist, Matilda (along with many other "borrowed" elements), from the evil heroine in Matthew Lewis's notorious 1796 novel, *The Monk*. (Lewis's work was a favorite of both Percy and Mary, and Percy would meet Lewis at Lord Byron's chateau during the memorable summer of 1816.) Shelley's novel made its appearance in 1810; he modestly claimed authorship as "P.B.S." The title page, significantly, contained an epigraph taken from John Milton's *Paradise Lost*, a passage in which Beelzebub declares his intention to take revenge on God by attacking the creatures most dear to him. A few years later, Mary would employ a similar epigraph, and the same plot device, for *Frankenstein*.

In October 1810, Shelley traveled with his father to Oxford to enroll in the university. His father had studied there and wanted to give his son a good start by establishing him in comfortable surroundings. The Oxford that Shelley attended was not the great institution of today. The pace was leisurely and gentlemen often did little scholarly work at all. The Bodleian Library went almost unused.

Within the first few days, Shelley met Thomas Jefferson Hogg, a son of a Yorkshire barrister, and an intimate, lifelong friendship sprang up. We learn about Shelley at this time through Hogg's biography of his friend: a tall, thin, stooped young man with a high-pitched voice who walked briskly around Oxford always with a book in his hand, nearly covering his face. Though clumsy looking, he never seemed to trip over others' outstretched feet while reading and walking. "His features, his whole face, and particularly his head, were, in fact, unusually small; yet the last *appeared* of a remarkable bulk, for his hair was long and bushy and . . . he often rubbed it fiercely with his hands . . . so that it was singularly wild and rough." The nickname he had picked up at Eton was now flaunted; to Hogg and others, Shelley admitted that he and his behavior were odd, explaining merely, "I myself am often mad."

Hogg left a memorable description of Shelley in his room at New College:

> Books, boots, papers, shoes, philosophical instruments, clothes, pistols, linen, crockery, ammunition, and phials innumerable, with money, stockings, prints, crucibles, bags, and boxes, were scattered on the floor and in every place; as if the young chemist, in order to analyse the mystery of creation, had endeavored first to reconstruct the primeval chaos. The tables, and especially the carpet, were already stained with large spots of various hues, which frequently proclaimed the agency of fire. An electrical machine, an air-pump, the galvanic trough, a solar microscope, and large glass jars and receivers, were conspicuous amidst the mass of matter. Upon the table by his side were some books lying open, several letters, a bundle of new pens, and a bottle of japan ink, that served as an inkstand . . . and a handsome razor that had been used as a knife. There were bottles of soda water, sugar, pieces of lemon, and the traces of an effervescent

> beverage. Two piles of books supported the tongs, and those upheld a small glass retort above an argand lamp. I had not been seated many minutes before the liquor in the vessel boiled over, adding fresh stains to the table, and rising in fumes with a most disagreeable odour. Shelley snatched the glass quickly, and dashing it in pieces among the ashes under the grate, increased the unpleasant and penetrating effluvium.
>
> He then proceeded, with much eagerness and enthusiasm, to show me the various instruments, especially the electrical apparatus; turning the handle very rapidly, so that the fierce, crackling sparks flew forth; and presently standing upon the stool with glass feet, he begged me to work the machine until he was filled with the [electrical] fluid, so that his long, wild locks bristled and stood on end. Afterwards he charged a powerful battery of several jars; labouring with vast energy, and discoursing with increasing vehemence of the marvellous powers of electricity, of thunder and lightning; describing an electrical kite that he had made at home, and projecting another and an enormous one, or rather a combination of many kites, that would draw down from the sky an immense volume of electricity, the whole ammunition of a mighty thunderstorm; and this being directed to some point would there produce the most stupendous results.

It was, in so many ways, the image of the mad scientist that would be recreated on the Universal Studios backlot 122 years later.

Hogg noted Shelley's hypochondria and his charming effect on women. After traveling with a fat lady in a coach Shelley feared that he was catching elephantiasis and that others might be infected as well. So at a country dance, using the excuse of medical inspection, Shelley placed "his eyes close to [the women's] necks and bosoms" and "felt their breasts and their bare arms" until the hostess told him to stop.

Seldom did any woman tell him to stop. Hogg somewhat enviously noted, "The moment he entered a house, he inspired the most lively interest into every woman in the family; not only the mistress of the house, her daughters, and other lady relatives, but even the housekeeper and the humblest females in the establishment were animated alike by an active desire to promote and secure his well-being, in every way and to the utmost in their power."

Very likely Shelley enjoyed his first sexual experience with a woman around this time. He wrote a poem celebrating Margaret Nicholson, who had attempted to murder George II. It includes a fragment that seems to be a paean to oral sex:

Soft, my dearest angel, stay,
Oh! You suck my soul away:
Suck on, suck on, I glow, I glow!
Tides of maddening passion roll,
And streams of rapture drown my soul.
Now give me one more billing kiss,
Let your lips now repeat the bliss,
Endless kisses steal my breath,
No life can equal such a death.

Shelley and Hogg's own relationship was so intense that it was like a love affair, though there was no overt sexual component. Shelley wrote Hogg twenty-three letters over the thirty-one-day Christmas holiday, when they were separated for the first time. Shelley developed the idea that Hogg should fall in love with Shelley's sister Elizabeth and talked her up so much that his friend became attracted without even meeting her.

Shelley's study of Godwin hardened the young man's belief that any true reform required the destruction of religion. When he and Hogg returned to Oxford after Christmas, they set out to expose the "fraud" of Christianity by writing a pamphlet, *The Necessity of Atheism.* It got the two friends expelled from Oxford; Shelley borrowed enough money to take them to London. The expulsion caused a breach with his father that never healed. His father wrote a letter about his son to his solicitor, in which he blamed Percy's trouble on the pernicious influence of Godwin. "He is such a Pupil of Godwin," he wrote, "that I can scarcely hope he will be persuaded that he owes any sort of obedience or compliance to the wishes or directions of his Parents."

Refusing his father's demands to renounce his atheism and to abandon his friend Hogg, Shelley set out to make a living with his pen. One of his first purchases in London was a copy of a poem entitled *English Bards and Scotch Reviewers* in a shop on Oxford Street. Shelley had never heard of the author, Lord Byron, but was impressed by Byron's taking poetic revenge on the reviewers who had been harshly critical of his earlier poetry. Shelley read the poem aloud to Hogg and was inspired.

In the spring Shelley went home to try to make peace with his father and family. His uncle interceded for him, and Sir Timothy granted Percy an allowance of two hundred pounds a year. For someone else this might have been adequate, but for Shelley it was never enough; he would spend much of his life trying to avoid financial disaster and keeping ahead of debt collectors. While at Field Place, Shelley again tried to get his favorite sister Elizabeth interested in Hogg. She was not enthusiastic but Percy smuggled Hogg into Field Place, where he hid in Shelley's bedroom. Nevertheless, Elizabeth still refused to see him. Hogg only got a peep at the girl through the windows of the local church. Such matchmaking efforts were ultimately doomed. Three of Percy's sisters never married and the fourth, after giving birth to three children, deserted her husband for another man, causing a scandal that had to be settled in the House of Lords.

Hogg went home to York to pursue a legal career, leaving Shelley alone in London. He was plagued by bad dreams and, as he often did in times of stress, started to sleepwalk again. Two of his sisters, Hellen and Mary, went to a boarding school in the city and Shelley often visited them. On one occasion he met their fifteen-year-old friend Harriet Westbrook, who soon became another of Shelley's hero worshippers. She parroted his opinions on everything, including atheism. Soon Harriet claimed that she was picked on by her teachers and others at the school because of her new, enlightened views. Shelley had found a disciple.

Thomas Peacock, another young author who became Shelley's friend, said of Westbrook: "Her complexion was beautifully transparent; the tint of the blush rose shining through the lily. The tone of her voice was pleasant; her speech the essence of frankness and cordiality; her spirits always cheerful; the laugh spontaneous, hearty and joyous." Hellen Shelley thought she looked "quite like a poet's dream." Though Percy probably never passionately loved Harriet, the idea of rescuing her from a school where she was being persecuted, and from her overbearing father as well, increased his desire for her. "I was in love with loving," he later wrote, quoting what was originally a Latin epigram by St. Augustine, "I was looking for something to love, loving to love." At the same time that he was courting Harriet he wrote to Hogg, "*Your* noble and exalted friendship, the prosecution of your happiness, can alone engross my impassioned interest."

Percy had learned from reading Godwin that the institution of marriage was a form of slavery, but changed his mind after reading Amelia Opie's novel *Adeline Mowbray,* which Harriet sent to him. The novel, written by a former friend of Mary Wollstonecraft who was now the wife of John Opie (whose portrait of Mary hung in the Godwin home), showed that the problems for a woman who lived with a man and gave birth outside of marriage were far worse than for the man in the relationship. (Ironically, the novel appears to have been roughly based on Mary Wollstonecraft's own life; life and art constantly intersected for Shelley.) On August 25, Shelley and Harriet, aged nineteen and sixteen respectively, met in London and spent the day hiding in a coffeehouse. They took the night coach to Scotland, where after three days of travel they married.

Because Shelley was low on money, he wrote Hogg, asking him to meet them in Edinburgh. Hogg was enchanted with Shelley's wife, finding her "radiant with youth, health and beauty." Shelley departed to attempt to pry more money from his family, and in his absence Hogg made an attempt to seduce Harriet. She turned him down. After Shelley heard of the refusal, he was strangely disturbed because he cared as much about Hogg as Harriet and did not want to lose his friendship. After Hogg left, Shelley wrote to him, "Jealousy has no place in my bosom. I am indeed at times very much inclined to think that the Godwinian plan is best. . . . But Harriet does not think so. She is prejudiced: tho I hope she will not always be so — And on her opinions of right and wrong alone does the morality of the present case depend." Clearly Shelley would have shared Harriet with Hogg if she had agreed. His second wife would face similar problems.

Joined by Harriet's sister Eliza, the newlyweds traveled around, trying to find a place to settle. Eliza was twelve years older than Harriet, and

Shelley resented her influence on her sister; he referred to Eliza as a "loathsome worm." Their travels included a stop in the Lake District, where they visited the poet Robert Southey, a flaming radical in his youth, now turned conservative. Shelley had once loved the older man's poetry but came away unimpressed. They moved on.

Shelley had thought about establishing a community in which people would live according to Godwin's principles, with the goal of providing an example to guide the world to a higher form of civilization. In early 1812 Shelley and Harriet became part of a commune in Wales; a little later he tried to form his own commune in Lynmouth. Failing at these efforts, he and Harriet went to Dublin, where they distributed in the streets copies of a tract Shelley had written in support of home rule for Ireland. Sometimes Shelley threw the pamphlet into the windows of passing carriages; he knew that the wealthy passengers might not read it, but hoped their sons and daughters might. Next the earnest couple moved to the north coast of Devon, where Shelley tucked into bottles copies of a manifesto titled *Declaration of Rights,* based on the American and French revolutionary documents, and set them adrift in the sea. A local official found one of the bottles and reported that it appeared "intended to fall into the hands of the Sea-faring part of the People . . . and do incalculable mischief among them." Shelley seemed to take up almost any popular cause that presented itself: protesting the executions of Yorkshire workmen who had deliberately destroyed spinning machines that put hand laborers out of work; protesting the prison sentences meted out to writer Leigh Hunt and his brother for "libelling" the prince regent in their magazine. The causes and places went by in a blur. All this activity must have been a strain on Harriet, but she loyally stuck by her husband through every new enthusiasm.

Even those who sympathized with Shelley sometimes found his radical sentiments a little extreme. His friend Thomas Love Peacock satirized him in his novel *Nightmare Abbey* as a perpetual do-gooder:

> He now became troubled with the *passion for reforming the world.* He built many castles in the air, and peopled them with secret tribunals, and bands of illuminati. . . . As he intended to institute a perfect

> republic, he invested himself with absolute sovereignty over these mystical dispensers of liberty. He slept with Horrid Mysteries under his pillow, and dreamed of venerable elutherarchs and ghastly confederates holding midnight conversations in subterranean coves. He passed whole mornings in his study, immersed in gloomy reverie, stalking about the room in his nightcap, which he pulled over his eyes like a cowl, and folding his striped calico dressing gown about him like the mantle of a conspirator.

In January 1812 Shelley was taking laudanum for his nerves, and the medication may have set off a strange episode in which Shelley believed that he had been attacked at his cottage door. A neighbor heard his screams and came running only to find him unconscious and no one else around. Later Shelley played down the incident. The next year Shelley, Harriet, and Eliza were staying in a house in Wales when one night Shelley heard a noise and went downstairs with a pistol. Those upstairs heard a shot and rushed to help. Shelley claimed that a man leaving through a window had fired a pistol at him. Shelley urged his wife and sister-in-law to go back to bed while he and a servant waited up. Around four a.m., while the servant was in another room, more shots rang out. This time Shelley claimed that the same man had fired at him through the window and then fled. Shelley made a sketch of the so-called assassin; it resembled not a human, but a Satanic figure with horns.

Shelley had written some childish poetry, but in 1812 he set out to make his mark on the world through verse. He began working on his first long poem, *Queen Mab*, which was published the next year. Shelley was not writing to entertain; he saw himself as leading the way to a social revolution that would mirror the political changes of the American and French Revolutions. Shelley boldly declared, "Poets . . . are the unacknowledged legislators of the world," and in fact, long after Shelley's death, the Chartists, a radical movement of working-class Britons, used *Queen Mab* to educate and inspire their followers.

The poem combined two different traditions; it was both an elaborate allegorical fairy tale and a historical political argument. The poem describes the fairy Queen Mab with her girl pupil Ianthe traveling away from the earth through space in a magic chariot to envision a new organization of society. In more than two thousand lines, Shelley attacks war, the church, monarchy, and the consumption of meat — all in verse. He advocates freedom of speech, dietary reform, repeal of the Act of Union, and Catholic emancipation. Appended to the poem were Shelley's extensive notes explaining his philosophy more fully.

Queen Mab also attempted to discredit marriage. Though Shelley was a married man and dedicated the poem to Harriet, he shared Godwin's dim view of the institution. In the notes he wrote: "A husband and wife ought to continue united so long as they love each other: any law which should bind them to cohabitation for one moment after the decay of their affection, would be a most intolerable tyranny." He added, "Love is free; to promise for ever to love the same woman is not less absurd than to promise to believe the same creed." Fair warning to Harriet.

While at work on the poem, Shelley wrote a letter to William Godwin, expressing his admiration. "It is now . . . more than two years since first I saw your inestimable book on 'Political Justice,'" Shelley wrote. "It opened to my mind fresh & more extensive view; it materially influenced my character, and I rose from its perusal a wiser and a better man." These words, which would warm the heart of any writer, came with an appeal for Godwin to adopt Shelley as his pupil and devoted follower. Godwin, living in near obscurity, was flattered, even though Shelley tactlessly added that he had not written earlier because he thought Godwin was dead. The two men began a correspondence that would be life-changing for both.

In a rash moment, Shelley also offered to help Godwin financially. Godwin would henceforth hold Shelley to his promise even when Shelley himself was in need of funds. Shelley could obtain loans because it was expected that some day he would come into a considerable inheritance, and lenders would advance funds on the agreement that he would repay them afterward. But these financial instruments, known as obit loans, came at huge rates of interest, and Shelley had trouble servicing his debt. At the time, delinquent debtors were not only subject to losing their possessions, but they could also be thrown in jail. Shelley's kind offer would turn out to be a thorn in the relationship between the two men.

Later in the year Shelley and Harriet came to London and met the

Godwins at home for dinner. Harriet noted on the visit that Godwin looked like Socrates, Fanny Imlay was plain but sensible, and the portrait of Mary Wollstonecraft was lovely. Through Godwin, Shelley met John Newton, a vegetarian and health fanatic. Shelley was already a vegetarian, but henceforth he adopted a lifestyle based on Newton's philosophy that what was "natural" was good. Hogg had earlier complained about his friend's eating habits: he ignored mealtimes, eating only when he was hungry, and according to Hogg, the poet lived on bread, raisins, nuts, tea, and honey. Later in 1812, Shelley would publish another tract, titled *A Vindication of Natural Diet,* in which he confidently stated, "There is no disease, bodily or mental, which adoption of vegetable diet and pure water has not infallibly mitigated, wherever the experiment has been fairly tried."

Percy and Harriet seemed overjoyed by the birth of their first child, a daughter, in June 1813. They named her Ianthe, after the heroine of *Queen Mab.* Unfortunately, the deterioration in their marriage began with that event. Shelley was distraught when Harriet refused to breastfeed the child, a topic about which he was passionate. One of Shelley's fantasies was that he could change sex at will, and he went so far as to try to breastfeed the infant himself. When that failed, Peacock recalled, the couple hired "a wet-nurse whom he [Percy] did not like, and [the child] was much looked after by his wife's sister, whom he intensely disliked. I have often thought that if Harriet had nursed her own child, and if this sister had not lived with them, the link of their married love would not have been so readily broken."

At the end of July, Shelley, his wife, and their daughter moved into the home of John Newton's sister-in-law, Mrs. Jean Baptiste Chastel de Boinville, who lived about thirty miles outside London. Her French husband had died during Napoleon's Russian campaign. Also part of the household were Mrs. de Boinville's eighteen-year-old daughter Cornelia and her husband, a lawyer who was another devotee of Godwin's. Percy began taking Italian lessons from Cornelia, and a short-lived romance blossomed. Some months later, Shelley wrote Hogg about his experience:

> The contemplation of female excellence is the favorite food of my imagination. . . . I had been unaccustomed to the mildness

> the intelligence the delicacy of a cultivated female. The presence of Mrs. Boinville & her daughter afforded a strange contrast to my former friendless & deplorable condition. . . . I saw the full extent of the calamity which my rash & heartless union with Harriet . . . had produced.

Nonetheless, in March of 1814, Shelley agreed to go through a second marriage ceremony with Harriet. The event may have come at the insistence of Harriet's family, because they feared that her age at the time of the first wedding might make the union technically illegal and thus threaten the legitimacy of their child, along with her right to inherit the Shelley fortune. Harriet conceived another baby, but the relationship had lost its zest for Percy. He blamed many of their problems on Harriet's sister Eliza, who doted on Ianthe. But in his mind Harriet was to blame too. She had given up their former practice of reading books aloud to each other, and it seemed to Percy that her efforts to improve her intellectual talents were slackening. Nor was she as devoted a disciple of his social ideas as she had been. Shelley wrote that it was only "duty" that was keeping the marriage together, and in a letter to Hogg, he identified himself with the poet John Milton, whose words he echoed: "a dead & living body had been linked together in loathsome & horrible communion."

The couple separated in March 1814, with Harriet and Eliza taking Ianthe to the west country of England. By the time Harriet and Percy's son, Charles, was born in November of 1814, the separation was permanent. Shelley had met someone else: Mary Godwin.

The relationship with Harriet set a pattern for Percy's later loves. He combined sexual ambiguity with a sense of omnisexuality. For him there were no limits. "I go on till I am stopped," he later told a friend, "and I am never stopped." He was not faithful in his first marriage, and he would not be in his second either.

Mary had originally met Percy on November 11, 1812, when he, his wife, and Eliza were visiting Godwin; the encounter seemed to make little impression on any of those present. By the time they met again, on May 5, 1814, her father and Shelley had become good friends, and indeed

Godwin was by now financially dependent on the young poet. Since her return from Scotland, Mary had heard only good things about Shelley. On his part, now that his separation from Harriet had taken place, Shelley saw Mary with new eyes. He was immediately attracted to her because of her beauty, intellect, name, and personality. "The originality & loveliness of Mary's character was apparent to me from her very motions & tones of voice. . . . Her smile, how persuasive it was & how pathetic!" he wrote. Mary had a high, smooth brow, dazzling fair skin, light brown hair, and large hazel eyes. She was then sixteen, the same age as Harriet had been at the time she and Shelley had wed.

Shelley recognized in Mary the "woman-symbol of intellectual beauty" that he sought. Yet he was torn between his feelings and loyalties. Thomas Love Peacock saw him frequently at this time and noted the poet's agony. Peacock called his state of mind "suffering, like a little kingdom, the nature of an insurrection." He remembered Shelley as being in a mad state, his hair and clothes disordered and his eyes bloodshot as he clutched his bottle of laudanum for security. But Mary's allure won out over Shelley's doubts.

In a sense Shelley was preconditioned to love Mary, for he greatly admired both of her parents. He had ordered Mary Wollstonecraft's *A Vindication of the Rights of Woman* in 1812 and was strongly influenced by her ideas on women's rights, so much so that she became in his mind a figure of the ideal woman; he would use her as the model for Cythna, the New Woman in his later poem *The Revolt of Islam,* who "doth equal laws and justice teach / To woman, outraged and polluted long." Harriet was not merely expressing sour grapes when she later said that Shelley was in love with the *idea* of Mary Wollstonecraft's daughter: Mary, for Percy, was an intellectual trophy wife. He would write of her:

They say that thou wert lovely from thy birth,
Of glorious parents, thou aspiring Child
I wonder not — for One then left this earth
Whose life was like a setting planet mild,
Which clothed thee in the radiance undefiled

Of its departing glory; still her fame
Shines on thee, through the tempests dark and wild
Which shake these latter days; and thou canst claim
The shelter, from thy Sire, of an immortal name.

For Mary, the attraction was immediate as well. She had no experience with love. Her youth had been spent in a world of ideas, where it was taken for granted that ideas would change the world, and that ideas were more important than the conventions of society. Shelley, who had a lifelong love affair with ideas, was the embodiment of what she held dear. The fact that he was married and unconventional in other ways didn't matter to someone who had grown up in a family where all five children had a different set of parents, where adults with unconventional ideas constantly came to visit. Mary was innocent of actual experience, intellectually brilliant, but immature and insecure. Her passionate nature was given a chance to bloom, and it did.

It didn't hurt that Percy was epicenely handsome. His sandy, unkempt hair stuck out around his face like a halo. Mary, who had inherited her father's large nose, felt herself unattractive. Shelley, who charmed her with his brilliant conversation and his devotion to noble causes, loved her for the only thing she was sure of: her own intelligence, which in those times was commonly thought to be a quality women should best keep hidden. Shelley would become her mentor, picking up where her father had left off. And who better to take this role than a man who had absorbed Godwin's philosophy? To Mary, Shelley appeared as one of the select group of people charged with bringing about the Godwinian future.

Furthermore, Shelley brought adventure. He confessed to her that he was trapped in an unhappy marriage with a woman who wasn't capable of understanding him the way Mary could. Equally trapped in the Skinner Street household with a critical stepmother and a father who was emotionally distant, Mary saw Shelley as her way to escape.

Their emotions meshed with their literary bent. The whole Shelley / Godwin / Wollstonecraft circle were living out of novels — they wrote their lives in their books, and their lives were in turn influenced and formed by their reading and writing. Mary and Percy were the heroine and hero of the most romantic novel of all, and at the beginning of their relationship, life became enchantment.

Some of their feelings are captured in Thomas Jefferson Hogg's account of his first sight of Mary at Skinner Street.

> I followed him [Shelley, whom Hogg called Bysshe] through the shop, which was the only entrance, and upstairs. We entered the room on the first floor; it was shaped like a quadrant. In the arc were windows; in one radius a fireplace, and in the other a door, and shelves with many old books. William Godwin was not at home. Bysshe strode about the room, causing the crazy floor of the ill-built, unowned dwelling-house to shake and tremble under his impatient footsteps. He appeared to be displeased at not finding the fountain of Political Justice. "Where is Godwin?" he asked me several times, as if I knew. I did not know, and to say the truth, I did not care. He continued his uneasy promenade; and I stood reading the names of old English authors on the backs of the venerable volumes, when the door was partially and softly opened. A thrilling voice called "Shelley!" A thrilling voice answered "Mary!" And he darted out of the room, like an arrow from the bow of the far-shooting king. A very young female, fair and fair-haired, pale indeed, and with a piercing look, wearing a frock of tartan, an unusual dress in London at that time, had called him out of the room. He was absent a very short time — a minute or two; and then returned. "Godwin is out; there is no use in waiting." So we continued our walk along Holborn.
>
> "Who was that, pray?" I asked, "a daughter?"
>
> "Yes."
>
> "A daughter of William Godwin?"
>
> "The daughter of Godwin and Mary."

Shelley worked to establish a fund to support Godwin's work, and he was continually at the house. (Godwin also claimed later that he sheltered Percy from bill collectors who were looking for him.) By the end of June, Percy and Mary were seeing each other every day. Mary used her stepsister Clara Jane to conceal their relationship from Mrs. Godwin. The two girls would walk together in the forested grounds of a school, the Charterhouse, where they would meet Shelley. They also visited Mary Wollstonecraft's tomb. When that happened, Clara Jane recalled, "They always sent me to walk some distance from them — alleging that they wished to talk on philosophical subjects."

On June 26, 1814, the two of them first declared their feelings for each other while they were visiting the grave of Mary's mother under the willows in St. Pancras churchyard. Shelley was overcome. He afterward wrote: "The sublime and rapturous moment when she confessed herself mine . . . cannot be painted to mortal imaginations." Shelley told Mary of his long quest for love, and she responded that she was entirely his. It is difficult to pierce the flowery prose that he used to recall the occasion, but the two may well have consummated their devotion then and there.

A few days later, Percy wrote the following lines:

Upon my heart thy accents sweet
Of peace and pity fell like dew
On flowers half dead;— thy lips did meet
Mine tremblingly; thy dark eyes threw
Their soft persuasion on my brain,
Charming away its dream of pain.

On July 6, Shelley asked William Godwin's consent for a union with his daughter. That very morning he had loaned a large sum to Godwin. Shelley evidently believed that Godwin's principles would come before his parental concerns. Yet, even though Godwin had denounced marriage and declared that a person might flout the opinion of society if his or her actions were correct, he was outraged by the budding romance between a married man and his daughter, and forbade them to meet again.

Shelley brooded about the rejection for a few days and then, as Mrs. Godwin recalled, suddenly entered the shop when Godwin was absent and rushed upstairs to the living quarters. "He looked extremely wild" and carried a bottle of laudanum and a pistol. When Mrs. Godwin tried to stop him, he violently shoved her aside. Finding Mary sitting with

Clara Jane in one of the rooms, he said, "They wish to separate us, my beloved; but Death shall unite us," and held out the bottle of laudanum. "By this you can escape from tyranny," he said, "and this," he said, gesturing with the pistol, "shall reunite me to you." His talent for melodramatic scenes had not diminished.

Mary, in her stepmother's words, "turned as pale as a ghost," and Clara Jane "at the sight of the pistol filled the room with her shrieks." Tears streaming down Mary's cheeks, she pleaded with Shelley to calm himself and leave. "I won't take this laudanum," she said, "but if you will only be reasonable and calm, I will promise to be ever faithful to you." Shelley seemed mollified, and he departed, leaving the laudanum on a table.

After that, Godwin tried desperately to keep his daughter away from Shelley. He may have been haunted by the fear that Mary would follow her mother's pattern of chasing lovers who would bring her only pain and rejection. Both girls were kept inside the house, for Mrs. Godwin had her own memories of unhappy love affairs and didn't want Clara Jane to become an accessory to this one.

The efforts failed. Shelley bribed the porter in the bookshop to smuggle his letters into the house, and on July 28, Mary and Percy ran off together accompanied by Clara Jane Clairmont, whose motive seems to be that she too wanted to escape the Godwin household. (The other two agreed to let her go along because otherwise she might have revealed their plans, and also for the practical reason that she knew French better than they did.) Thus it was that two girls dressed in black left the Skinner Street house in the early morning hours. Shelley was waiting with a chaise and a little money. He wrote in his journal: "She was in my arms — we were safe; we were on our road to Dover."

CHAPTER FOUR

CRACKLING SPARKS AND FREE LOVE

We are as clouds that veil the midnight moon;
How restlessly they speed, and gleam, and quiver,
Streaking the darkness radiantly! — yet soon
Night closes round, and they are lost for ever:

Or like forgotten lyres, whose dissonant strings
Give various response to each varying blast,
To whose frail frame no second motion brings
One mood or modulation like the last.

We rest.—A dream has power to poison sleep;
We rise.— One wandering thought pollutes the day;
We feel, conceive or reason, laugh or weep;
Embrace fond woe, or cast our cares away:

It is the same!— For, be it joy or sorrow,
The path of its departure still is free:
Man's yesterday may ne'er be like his morrow;
Nought may endure but Mutability.

— "Mutability," Percy Shelley, 1815

MARY HAD DEVELOPED fantasies of what the experience of living with Shelley would be like, beginning with her vision of it as a replication of her illustrious parents' marriage, a partnership between equals that would result in the love and emotional warmth for which she yearned. But during their first year and a half together, Mary would learn that the dreams of her husband could bring nightmares to her. The elopement developed into an emotional roller coaster. Just as in Percy's poem "Mutability," one day would bring her joy, the next sorrow. She ended this period with the hard-won realization that she had not gained the stable home she had always dreamed of. It was a time of unrest and anxiety that would, in the following year, find expression in her great novel.

The day the lovers eloped was a warm one, and Mary became ill from the excitement. Seven months later she would give birth to a child said to be premature, so the early stages of pregnancy are also possible cause for her illness. At the post houses where the carriage stopped along the way, she had to get out for rest and fresh air. At some point, Shelley paid extra to hire a carriage with four horses instead of two because he felt they would be pursued.

They arrived at Dover at four in the afternoon and made arrangements to be taken across the Channel in an small open fishing boat. At first the water was calm, but then a storm blew up and the little craft was tossed back and forth in the water. Mary, still weak and sick, closed her eyes and laid her head on Shelley's knees as they sat on the bare wood of the boat's hull. He wrote later that he feared the little craft would be swamped: "I had time in that moment to reflect, and even to reason upon death; it was rather a thing of discomfort . . . than horror to me. We should never be separated, but in death we might not know and feel our union as now." The journey lasted all night, and as they came into Calais, dawn was breaking. "I said to Mary," Shelley recalled, "look, the sun rises over France." His spirits rose along with it, for he felt it was an augury of the bright future that lay before them.

Mary's stepsister looked back at the Channel, possibly because she had doubts about the wisdom of what she had done. "As I left Dover and England's white cliffs were retiring, I said to myself I shall never see these more," Clara Jane wrote. Little did she know that they would be back in six weeks — their lives forever changed.

Shelley could never be accused of being conventional, but taking his lover's stepsister along on their elopement was one of his oddest acts. The decision only increased the shock value of the affair as news of it spread. Gossips depicted Shelley as running off with a woman on each arm. Harriet, Shelley's abandoned wife, may have started the rumor that Godwin had sold his daughter and Clara Jane to Shelley for eight hundred and seven hundred pounds each (Mary bringing the higher price). In the beginning Mary may have regarded Clara Jane's presence merely as a comforting link to her old household. Not till later would she see her stepsister as a possible rival for Shelley's love.

From the pier at Calais, the three young adventurers walked along the sands to Dessein's hotel, where Laurence Sterne had begun writing his *A Sentimental Journey through France and Italy* in 1765. They arranged to get the very suite he had stayed in — an apartment that had both a sitting and sleeping room. Here the young couple started a journal together. "Mary was there," Shelley wrote at the beginning; Mary inscribed "Shelley was also with me." At the beginning most of the entries are in Shelley's handwriting, but Mary's contributions gradually increased. On August 2, the pen went to Mary and from then on the journal was mainly, but not exclusively, hers. She usually wrote very little about personal things, but since pages of it were later torn out it is impossible to know how frank she was at the time she wrote it. Many of the journal's pages describe the vigorous program of reading that she and Shelley did. The list was long and varied, including works in French and Latin. They brought along Abbé Barruel's four-volume *History of Jacobinism,* which Shelley found interesting for its information on secret societies, including the Illuminati, a mysterious group dedicated to revolution and centered in the Bavarian city of Ingolstadt. (Mary would have Victor Frankenstein study at the university there.) The two liked to read the same books together, often taking turns reading them aloud.

Calais, with its exotic sights and sounds, was exciting to the three young people. It had been just three months since Napoleon had abdicated power and was sent to exile in Elba. After two decades of war, English tourists were coming back to France. Mary later wrote: "We saw with extasy [*sic*] the strange costume of the French women, read with delight our own descriptions in the passport, looked with curiosity on every *plat,* fancying that the fried-leaves of artichokes were frogs; we saw shepherds in opera-hats, and post-boys in jack-boots . . . it was [like] acting a novel, being an incarnate romance."

Meanwhile, Mary's stepmother was in hot pursuit of the trio. The day they fled, Godwin had found "a letter on my dressing table, informing me what they had done. I had been of the opinion from the first that Mary could only be withheld from ruin by her mind; & in that, by a series of the most consummate dissimulation, she made me believe I had succeeded. . . . You will imagine our distress. If anything could have added to it, it was this circumstance of Jane's having gone with her sister." Inquiry at a nearby stables revealed that the young people had intended to go to Dover, and from there presumably to France. Mrs. Godwin set out on the mail coach and reached Calais on July 29. Godwin told a friend that he had allowed her to go only on condition "that she should avoid seeing Shelley, who had conceived a particular aversion to her as a dangerous foe to his views, & might be capable of any act of desperation." Why Godwin himself did not join the pursuit is unclear. Perhaps, as usual, though his words were forceful, he was content to let others perform the actions he recommended.

At Calais Mrs. Godwin soon found out where the three were staying, and sent a note to her daughter. Clara Jane responded, and even spent the night in her mother's room. According to Mrs. Godwin, Clara Jane promised to return to England with her, but in the morning she insisted on meeting one last time with Shelley and Mary. The smooth-talking Shelley persuaded her to remain in France. "Not the most earnest intreaties of a mother could turn her from her purpose," wrote Godwin, and Mrs. Godwin returned alone on July 31. Ironically, Mary felt she had triumphed over her stepmother, a victory she would later have cause to regret, for it put the burden of Clara Jane forever on her shoulders.

The one pang of regret Mary had was the necessity of making a break with her adored father. At the time Mary may have thought his disapproval would be temporary, but it was long-lasting and adamant. In a letter written in August of the year she left, he declared, "Jane has been guilty of indiscretion only, . . . Mary has been guilty of a crime." Godwin did not even speak to his daughter for three and a half years. He was never able to forgive what he saw as a betrayal by both his disciple and his daughter.

Clara Jane's courage in turning her back on her mother made her a firm part of what was now a threesome. They hired a carriage and headed for Paris. Shelley had left London so quickly that he did not bring adequate funds, but he had asked his publisher Thomas Hookham to forward money to him in Paris. Unfortunately Hookham sent only what Shelley called "a cold & stupid letter," because he disapproved of the elopement. Shelley pawned his watch and chain while scrambling from bank to bank in hopes of obtaining a loan. Despite the uncertainty, Mary had no fears. "Mary especially seems insensible to all future evil," Shelley wrote. "She feels as if our love would alone suffice to resist the invasions of calamity."

Further indication that the young people thought love could conquer all was the fact that Mary and Clara Jane had brought only the clothes they wore on their backs. But Mary's devotion to writing had led her to carry a box containing something more precious than clothes: her own early writings and letters from various people, including her father and Shelley. There was even a pre-elopement letter from Harriet, who had hoped Mary would help send Percy back to her. She advised Mary how to "calm" Percy and persuade him to subdue his passion for her. Obviously Mary hadn't followed the instructions.

After getting a loan of sixty pounds from a banker whom Shelley had earlier called an "idiot" and a "fool" in his journal, Shelley bought an ass to carry their baggage, for they intended to walk to Switzerland. In this plan too, can be seen Shelley's cracked recklessness. Though Mary's health was frail, Shelley thought nothing of asking her to take a 250-mile journey on foot. Moreover, people warned them that the countryside could be dangerous, for ex-soldiers of Napoleon's defeated army sometimes preyed on unwary travelers. The trio would also discover that lodgings outside the major cities were usually primitive and filthy.

As they proceeded southeast from Paris, they saw the terrible conditions that two decades of war had brought to France. They passed through ruined villages with houses reduced to charred rubble. They heard horror stories of families killed by invading Cossack soldiers, tales that they often recalled when night fell before they reached a town where they could find lodging. As a result, they slept in places, as Shelley wrote, where the "beds were infinitely detestable." At one inn, their room had "four-footed enemies," or rats. Clara Jane complained that she could not sleep because she felt their cold paws on her face. When a man sharing the room asked Clara Jane to sleep with him, she moved to Mary and Percy's bed. On another night, Clara Jane — who kept her own journal — recalled that the beds were "so dreadfully dirty we . . . slept all night on chairs round the kitchen fire."

On the first day of the journey, the ass had proved unreliable; they sold it at a loss and bought a mule. Mary and Clara Jane took turns riding on the mule's back, but then Shelley, clumsy as always, sprained his ankle, so at Troyes they sold the animal and hired an open carriage with a driver. All the while, their funds dwindled at an alarming pace. When a rainstorm drenched the travelers, they had to stop at an inn and go to bed almost at once, for the women's dresses had to be hung up to dry and they had no other clothes.

Soon Shelley hatched another idea: he wrote Harriet inviting her to join them — as a friend, not a wife. (He may have expected her to bring money.) As bizarre as this offer seems, it was consistent with Godwin's *Political Justice* theories. Shelley's lack of sensitivity to Harriet's feelings was astonishing, but so was that of Mary, who in the flush of romantic love had little sympathy for her rival. Harriet, demoted to platonic friendship, not surprisingly turned down the offer.

At times, the journals reveal a few blissful moments. On August 14, Shelley wrote, "We rest at Vendeuvre two hours. We walk in a wood belonging to a neighboring chateau, & sleep under its shade. The moss was so soft, the murmur of the wind in the leaves was sweeter than Aeolian music . . . we forgot that we were in France or in the world for a time." As they stopped to rest at a mountain stream, Percy took off his clothes and jumped into the water, asking Mary to strip down and bathe with him. Though an overcropping of the river bank offered them some privacy, Mary shyly refused, protesting that it would be indecent and that she had no towel. Shelley, in the spirit of nature, offered to bring her leaves that she could use to dry herself, but she would not be persuaded. Clara Jane, recalling the incident in her journal, said that the carriage driver, a witness to the scene, gave Shelley a look that implied "he thought he was rather crazy."

On August 19, the travelers' spirits rose as they entered Switzerland. The majesty of the Alps impressed Mary; she would describe this magnificent scenery in *Frankenstein.* Clara Jane was particularly happy because she believed she was coming to the land of her ancestors, still suspecting that her father had been a Swiss. She noted that "the moment we passed from France to Switzerland — the Cottages & people (as if by magic) became almost instantaneously clean & hospitable." Their new Swiss carriage driver told her the difference was "because we have no king to fear!"

Swiss independence was in fact the reason that the travelers had come here. They were heading for Lake Lucerne where, in the town of Uri, William Tell had led the Swiss fight for self-determination. It was, not by coincidence, also the setting for Godwin's 1805 novel *Fleetwood.* That book's hero looked to establish a community to escape the materialism of the world, and Shelley and Mary likewise dreamed of settling there and attracting like-thinking friends and relatives to join them. One of these later arrivals, Mary hoped, would be Godwin himself.

But grandiose plans require money, and the next day Shelley was off to find a friendly banker. When he returned with a large canvas bag filled with silver coins, Mary and Clara Jane were encouraged, but Shelley knew it was not as much as it seemed. He wrote that the money was "like the white & flying cloud of noon that is gone before one can say Jack Robinson."

They next headed for Brunnen, where Shelley took a six-month lease on a two-room house. Mary and Shelley read the Roman author Tacitus to each other, and Shelley began writing a planned novel, *The Assassins,* that was never finished. Clara Jane, after reading *King Lear,* Shakespeare's play in which an old king's daughters betray him, may have seen a parallel with her own situation. She had a nightmare that apparently woke the others; this was the beginning of what Mary, with asperity, called "Jane's horrors."

Only two days after moving in, Shelley calculated that they had just enough money to return to England, and suddenly declared they must set off at once. Clara Jane, understandably, found this bizarre, but faithful Mary didn't question Shelley when he'd made up his mind.

Thus on Mary's seventeenth birthday, August 30, she found herself nearly penniless and traveling with a married man and her stepsister in a boat down the Rhine. Shelley had determined that this would be the fastest and cheapest way home; now, at least, they didn't have to walk. As they headed downstream, Shelley read aloud to Mary passages from her mother's book, *Letters Written During a Short Residence in Sweden, Norway and Denmark,* which Mary would use as a model for her own travelogue of this journey. She found the scenery along the river gorgeous, but not so the German peasants who were their fellow passengers. She wrote of them in her journal, "our only wish was to absolutely anihilate such uncleansable animals. . . . Twere easier for god to make entirely new men than attempt to purify such monsters as these."

Making new men may thus have been on Mary's mind when they reached the town of Gernsheim in the afternoon of September 2. For some reason, the operator of the boat insisted on staying there until the moon rose. That gave Mary and Percy three hours to explore the area. They saw nothing they thought worthy of mention in their journal, which they still kept jointly. However, they must certainly have seen one of the most notable sights in the vicinity: the ruins of Castle Frankenstein, whose twin towers dominated the landscape. Shelley was somewhat fluent in German, and they may have heard the local legends of a man named Konrad Dippel. Son of a Lutheran minister, Dippel was born at the castle in 1673 when it served as a hospital in wartime. He became a physician, dabbled in alchemy, and was accused of robbing graveyards to obtain cadavers for his experiments. According to local legends, Dippel believed that he could bring dead bodies back to life by injecting them with a special formula he had invented. Darker versions of the tale said he had made a pact with the devil to attain immortality. Reportedly he predicted he would live to the age of 135, but died under mysterious circumstances — poison was suspected — in 1734.

Neither the castle nor the local legend inspired Mary to write anything at that point, but as the boat continued on its way, a seed had been planted in her mind. The travelers continued to read widely: Lord Byron had passed this way during his trip abroad and described the Rhine banks in the second canto of *Childe Harold.* Mary noted that "We read these verses with delight, as they conjured before us these lovely scenes with the truth and vividness of painting, and with the exquisite addition of glowing language and a warm imagination." It tells much about the couple that they enjoyed reading about the scenes around them as much as seeing them firsthand.

On September 8, they reached Rotterdam, where they faced an emergency: all their money had been spent. Shelley, however, still had silver in his tongue: he persuaded a ship's captain to take them to England on the strength of Shelley's promise to borrow enough on the other side to pay for the trip. The crossing was a rough one, and they passed the time by writing. Shelley's unfinished *The Assassins* has survived, but the two stories begun by the women have not: Mary's story was called, tantalizingly, "Hate," and Clara Jane's, "The Ideot."

They landed at Gravesend on September 13, having been away from England for exactly forty-two days. During that time they had slept in forty-one different places — the rented house in Switzerland was the only place they occupied for two consecutive nights. Mary had discovered that life with Shelley would require her to be ready to follow wherever his whims took him. Now, in England, she would learn more about the differences between the real world and Shelley's.

Their first problem was their debt to the captain who had brought them from Holland. Shelley found a boatman who agreed to take him and the two women up the Thames to London. ("Delightful row up the River," Clara Jane recorded blissfully.) There, he hired a carriage and went from place to place trying desperately to borrow money. Only Shelley would have had the nerve to do what came next: he stopped at the home of Harriet's father, where his estranged wife, pregnant with Shelley's child, was staying. Mary, also pregnant with Shelley's child, waited in front of the house in the carriage with Clara Jane for two hours. It is a tribute to Shelley's power of persuasiveness that he emerged with a loan. The boatman, who had been with them all this time, took his cut and promised to pay the ship captain, clearly a trusting man.

Funds partially replenished, the threesome took rooms at a hotel and began trying to re-establish their old relationships. Shelley wrote a series of letters to Harriet, who apparently at the urging of her father, asked

Shelley to make a financial settlement with her. Shelley's letters to her show that he still hoped to persuade her to join him and Mary, writing at one point, "Consider how far you would desire your future life to be placed within the influence of my superintending mind," and challenged her: "Are you above the world & to what extent?" She was no longer as far above the world as he. Her letters of reply are lost, but there is no doubt that she turned him down.

The Godwins also remained stonily unreconciled, though Mary and Clara Jane wrote them letters of entreaty. One night Charles, Clara Jane's half-brother, came to tell them that his parents had told the other children to have nothing to do with any of the runaways, and that they had discussed plans to send Jane to a convent. Another time, Shelley ran after Mrs. Godwin and Fanny in the street, but they refused to speak to him. After a similar incident, Godwin wrote in his journal that he had seen Percy in the street, but cut him dead, adding regretfully, "But he is so beautiful."

Though Godwin would not speak to Shelley, he did send him letters, in which the philosopher showed devotion to one of his principles, as expressed in *Political Justice,* which Mary was rereading: all wealth is held in common, and it is the rich man's duty to help his poor brethren. In particular, the rich Percy Shelley should be held to his promise to financially assist poor Godwin. Shelley had given him more than 1,100 pounds just before eloping with Mary in July, but it was clear nothing would ever be enough.

Shelley was willing to do his part; the trouble with Godwin's equation was that Shelley was only potentially rich. In actuality, his father had again cut off his allowance, and Shelley had been immediately hounded by creditors when he returned to London. He and the two young women continually moved from place to place to keep one step ahead of bill collectors and bailiffs armed with arrest warrants. By law, such warrants could not be served on the Sabbath, so Mary and Percy often looked forward to Sundays, the one day a week when they could walk together outside. It was a hectic life, and Mary wrote in her journal, "Here are we three persons always going about, & never getting anything. Good God, how wretched!!!!!"

Mary was also feeling lonely. She wrote to her closest friend, Isabella Baxter, now married in Scotland, and received in return only a cold letter from Isabella's husband (twenty-nine years older than she was), who had forbidden his wife to communicate with now-disgraced Mary. Mary was discovering that donning her mother's mantle carried a high price. The world was not filled with people like the admirers of Wollstonecraft who had once visited the Godwin home. Mary became as notorious and derided as her mother had been. Having a discreet affair was acceptable; running off with a man who was deserting his pregnant wife and a daughter was quite another.

Some of Shelley's friends did come to visit, among them his publisher Thomas Hookham and the faithful Thomas Peacock. Peacock often accompanied the trio to ponds in London parks, where they would make paper boats, set them on fire, and send them out into the water. At home Shelley read aloud to the two women *The Rime of the Ancient Mariner* and resumed his scientific experiments. There always seemed to be enough money to buy books, and the journals are filled with titles that they read at this time. Shelley started to teach Greek to Mary, part of the advanced education he planned for her.

On October 4, Shelley wrote Hogg, whom he had not seen in three years, bringing him up to date with a long account of his meeting and eloping with Mary. A note of triumph is evident in the letter: "Let it suffice to you, who are my friend to know & to rejoice that she is mine: that at length I possess the inalienable treasure, that I sought & that I have found." Shelley saw their relationship in terms of what it did for him. "How wonderfully I am changed!" he wrote Hogg. "Not a disembodied spirit can have undergone a stranger revolution! I never knew until now that contentment was any thing but a word denoting an unmeaning abstraction. I never before felt the integrity of my nature, its various dependencies, & learned to consider myself as an whole accurately united rather than an assemblage of inconsistent & discordant portions."

The letter to Hogg may have been prompted by a revival of Shelley's plans for a commune. On September 30, he had discussed "liberating" two of his sisters, who were in boarding school in Hackney, a borough of London. On the night of October 7, when Mary had gone to bed early, Shelley and Clara Jane sat up late discussing what Clara Jane called "an Association of philosophical people," including his sisters Elizabeth and Hellen. Awakening memories of childhood may have induced Shelley to try to frighten Clara Jane, as he had often done to his sisters. According to her, "the conversation turned upon those unaccountable & mysterious feelings about supernatural things that we are sometimes subject to." Shelley gave her a strange look with his large, penetrating blue eyes. He got the desired effect. "How horribly you look . . . take your eyes off!" Clara Jane cried.

She ran upstairs to bed, but the frightening impression persisted, and worked on her nerves. She placed her candle on a set of drawers and noticed that her pillow lay in the middle of her bed. For a moment, she glanced out the window, and when she turned back to the bed, the pillow was no longer there. It now lay on a chair. "I stood thinking for two moments," Clara Jane wrote. "Was it possible that I had deluded myself so far as to place it there myself & then forget the action? This was not likely." She ran downstairs. Shelley wrote that "Her countenance was distorted most unnaturally by horrible dismay . . . Her eyes were wide & starting: drawn almost from their sockets . . . as if they had been newly inserted in ghastly sport in the sockets of a lifeless head."

Clara Jane told him the story of the pillow and the two of them sat by the fire "engaging in awful conversation relative to the nature of these mysteries." Shelley read aloud from a novel Hogg had written, and then one of his own poems, and Clara Jane seemed to calm down. Toward dawn, however, she told Shelley he was giving her the same frightening look that he had earlier. He hid his face with his hands, he writes, but Clara Jane went into convulsions, shrieking and writhing on the floor. Shelley took her upstairs to Mary, who soothed her until Clara Jane finally slept. In the morning they looked in her room and found the pillow on the chair.

Mary, who by now had discovered she was pregnant, was somewhat annoyed that all this fuss had resulted over the placement of a pillow. Shelley didn't improve her mood two nights later when he began to read Clara Jane passages from Abbé Barruel's book about the mysterious Illuminati, causing her another sleepless night. Clara Jane, as even her mother said, had a somewhat hysterical nature and Shelley could not stop himself from taking advantage of it. Mary, on the other hand, suspected that Clara Jane actually enjoyed the attention her fits of hysteria brought her, and on October 14, the two stepsisters had an argument. Clara Jane wrote in her diary, "How hateful it is to quarrel — to say a thousand unkind things — meaning none — things produced by the bitterness of disappointment!" But that night she walked in her sleep again, and after listening to her groaning in the hallway for two hours, Shelley brought her once more to a less-than-thrilled Mary to calm her down.

Shelley tried to patch things up between the sisters. He wrote in the mutual journal, knowing Mary would read it: "Converse with Jane; her mind unsettled; her character unformed; occasion of hope from some instances of softness and feelings; she is not exactly insensible to concessions." A few nights later, Mary made her own contribution to the journal: "Shelley and Jane sit up and for a wonder do not frighten themselves."

There were threats beyond the imaginary. Godwin sent his friend James Marshall to persuade Clara Jane to return home, but Shelley advised her not to. Shelley received a letter from Hogg that he felt was cold and unfriendly. On top of everything else, the bill collectors were getting too close for comfort, and at times Shelley was forced to hide in Peacock's rooms, leaving the two women by themselves. Mary sometimes met him secretly at coffeehouses, and of course they sent letters to each other. Wrote Mary: "in the morning I look for you and when I awake I turn to look on you — dearest Shelley you are solitary and uncomfortable. Why cannot I be with you to cheer you and to press you to my heart . . . when shall we be free from fear of treachery?"

Percy replied in passionate prose: "My beloved Mary, I know not whether these transient meetings produce not as much pain as pleasure . . . I will not forget the sweet moments when I saw your eyes — the divine rapture of the few and fleeting kisses . . . Mary, love, we must be united. I will not part from you again after Saturday night." Yet on the very same day, he appealed to Harriet, "I cannot raise money soon enough — unless you can effect something I must go to Prison & all our hopes of independence be finished."

Mary had continued to believe that Godwin would become reconciled toward her elopement. She recalled the description her father wrote of her mother in the *Memoirs* — that she remained stoic in the face of criticism over her relationship with Imlay. But Godwin's shunning continued. Mary spent hours at her mother's grave, now her favorite place for reading and writing. She sometimes blamed her stepmother for her father's hostility. "She plagues my father out of his life," Mary wrote to Percy on October 28 (while he was hiding at Peacock's), ". . . do you not hate her my love?" Her father's rejection only made Mary more dependent on Shelley. "Press me to you and hug your own Mary to your heart," she pleaded, "perhaps she will one day have a father till then be every thing to me love — & indeed I will be a good girl and never vex you any more."

Mary's health suffered as her pregnancy proceeded. ("Mary is unwell" appears in her journal more than once.) Nonetheless, Mary and Percy established a rigorous schedule of reading and writing, which they would stick to whenever possible for the rest of their lives. In the morning they did their reading and writing separately. After the midday meal came the shopping, sightseeing, and housework. They read together in the evenings, unless, as was sometimes the case when Shelley was not hiding, they went to a play, an opera, or a lecture.

By the turn of the nineteenth century, awareness of scientific discoveries had filtered down from a small educated elite to the general population. Public reading and lectures about exciting new developments by such famous scientists of the day as Humphry Davy drew large crowds. Electricity and magnetism were among the much-discussed topics of the day. Speculation — sometimes informed, sometimes imaginative — about the possibilities of science fueled both hopes of progress as well as fears that science might be a danger.

Mary noted in her journal for December 28, 1814, that she and Percy went to Garnerin's theater to hear a lecture on electricity. Preceding the lecture was a display of "phantasmagoria," a kind of magic lantern show that Mary would later have reason to recall. The speaker that night was thirty-year-old Andrew Crosse, who had devised a variety of instruments for experimenting with electricity. These instruments were located at his home in Somerset, and were too cumbersome to be transported. Nonetheless, he described how he had captured electricity during a thunderstorm, à la Franklin, and conducted it through wires into his laboratory, where he preserved it in Leyden jars. Some of Crosse's claims were clearly exaggerated; for example, he claimed that when he passed electricity through a stone, living insects emerged from it. But Mary, who had received little education in science from her father, was fascinated. The connection between electricity and the generation of life was not lost on her.

In November, Thomas Jefferson Hogg reappeared in Shelley's life, bringing desperately needed financial help. Since their Oxford days, Hogg had been emotionally dependent on Shelley and always wooed Shelley's female companions; it was almost as though he could strengthen his relationship with Shelley by sharing his women. Shelley, seeing an opportunity to expand the circle of people living out his radical philosophy, had invited Hogg to visit, curious to see if a bond would form between him and Mary. Afterward, Shelley noted in the mutual journal for Mary to read, "He was pleased with Mary.— this was the test by which I had previously determined to judge his character." Shelley tacitly encouraged Mary to sleep with his friend, often taking Clara Jane for walks so the other two could be alone. Mary resisted the pressure; she seems to have befriended Hogg only to please Shelley. At first she noted in her journal that Hogg was intellectually inferior: ". . . get into an argument about virtue in which Hogg makes a sad bungle," she wrote, adding, "quite muddle[d] on the point I perceive." A few days later, she argued with him about free will and wrote, "he quite wrong but quite puzzled — his arguments are very weak." Hogg's greatest virtue was persistence; he doggedly paid court to Mary much as he had done earlier to Harriet Westbrook and, even earlier, to Shelley's sister Elizabeth. Mary adroitly used her pregnancy to avoid physical intimacy.

Was Shelley's attempt to bring Mary and Hogg together intended to serve as an excuse for him to enjoy Clara Jane? Given the pages missing from the journals of the principals at crucial times, it is impossible to say. Shelley may have been motivated more by his utopian idea of establishing a free-love commune than by sheer physical attraction to Clara Jane, but it is clear that after this time, Mary saw her stepsister in a new light. Henceforth, she regarded Clara Jane as a threat.

In November, when Clara Jane was spending much time with Percy, she announced that henceforth she wished to be known only as Clara — later she would choose the name Claire (which is how we will refer to her from this point). The name change was possibly a declaration of independence, but it would have escaped none of the threesome that Claire is the name of the lively dark friend of the lovers in Rousseau's *Julie, ou La Nouvelle Héloise,* one of Shelley's favorite books. He described it as "an overflowing . . . of sublimest genius, and more than human sensibility," and Claire may well have adopted the name to bring herself closer to him.

Mary felt that her pregnancy and resulting health problems should have prompted Shelley's sympathy, but in fact they probably made her less sexually attractive, and Shelley never believed in exclusive relationships. There were also, of course, *two* women expecting babies fathered by Shelley. Harriet's impending delivery was another source of anxiety for Mary, even though Harriet herself had no illusions that the event would win back her husband. She wrote to a friend on November 20: "Next month I shall be confined. He will not be near me. No, he cares not for me now. He never asks after me or sends me word how he is going on." The child, a boy, was born prematurely November 30, and named Charles Bysshe. Harriet described Shelley's reaction: "As to his tenderness for me, none remains. He said he was glad it was a boy, because he would make money cheaper. You see how that noble soul is debased. Money now, and not philosophy, is the grand spring of his actions."

Mary's attitude toward Harriet had been cruel; she had accepted all Shelley's rationalizations for leaving his wife. After the birth of Harriet's son, a note of worry enters Mary's journal, as she now seems uncertain that Percy will remain faithful to *her*. On December 6th she jotted down,

> *Very unwell.— Clary & Shelley walk out as usual to heaps of places . . . a letter from Hookham to say that Harriet has been brought to bed of a son and heir. S[helley] writes a number of circular letters on this event which ought to be ushered in with ringing of bells, etc. for it is the son of his* wife. *Hogg comes in the evening . . . a letter from Harriet confirming the news in a letter from a* deserted wife *& telling us that he has been born a week.*

Mary believed Shelley's story that he and Harriet had separated by mutual agreement — hence her sarcasm about the "deserted wife." Just as she could read Shelley's comments in their mutual journal, so this one was there for him to notice.

As Shelley spent more time with Claire, Mary in turn began to welcome Hogg's company. She wrote eleven platonic but coquettish love letters to him in the early months of 1815. "You love me you say —" she wrote on New Year's Day, "I wish I could return it with the passion you deserve." On January 24, calling him "Alexy," after the sensuous hero of Hogg's recently published novel (a hero obviously based on Shelley, who was the only person to review the book), she said, "I hope it will cheer your solitude to find this letter from me that you may read & kiss before you go to sleep. . . . I know how much how tenderly you love me and I rejoice to think that I am capable of constituting your happiness." But there is no reason to believe that Mary consummated the relationship with Hogg or that she was ever in love with him. Indeed she seems to have wanted to like him more than she actually did. She left no doubt that Shelley was her one true love.

As Mary's pregnancy advanced, it grew ever more troublesome. She suffered from bleeding and had to stay in bed for much of the time. That gave rise to one of Shelley's nicknames for her: the "Dormouse." (He also called her "Maie" and "Pecksie," the latter a name from a children's book; she sometimes used it to refer to herself in letters to Hogg and Shelley.) Mary must have been frightened, for she was only seventeen and must have remembered the tragic outcome of her own birth. Nonetheless, Shelley, like Mary's father, seemed incapable of responding to her emotional needs. By January Shelley was turning more and more of his attention to Claire, who took Mary's place on their daily walks. Mary let her annoyance show in her journal entries: one read, "Very ill all day. S and J. out all day hopping about the town."

The Godwins had long suspected what Mary now perceived: Claire too was smitten with Percy and used her freaky moments to help arouse his interest in her. The two shared a tendency to emotional excess and Shelley enjoyed his role as her intellectual mentor. It is quite possible that during the winter of 1814–15, Shelley and Claire became lovers. Percy had always been in favor of free love on principle. Mary obviously hoped that, following his betrayal of Harriet, it would remain a principle rather than a reality, but Claire later described Shelley as "the Man whom I have loved, and from whom I have suffered much."

One piece of good news, from their standpoint, was the death of Percy's grandfather Sir Bysshe on January 6, 1815. He divided his estate between his son and oldest male heirs. This enabled Percy to get one thousand pounds a year, of which one-fifth went to Harriet and the children. Learning of these events, Godwin promptly broke his frosty silence and asked Shelley to make good on his earlier promise to settle the older man's debts. Percy did send a generous sum of money but it was insufficient to bring about a permanent solution to Godwin's financial difficulties.

Shelley went to the family estate at Field Place for the reading of the will and took Claire with him, leaving Mary in London, with Hogg a frequent visitor. How frequent were his visits, and how passionate, is impossible to know, for all the pages in Mary's journal for this period, from January 14 to January 29, have been removed. After Shelley and Claire returned, Mary noted in the journal that Hogg now sometimes slept overnight at the apartment. Nothing was said, in the pages that remain, about her having sex with him, but in her condition it would have been improbable.

Mary gave birth to a baby girl on February 22, 1815, going into labor so suddenly that the infant arrived before the doctor. The night of the birth, Hogg stayed at the Shelleys', making himself as useful as he could and remaining through the next day. While Mary was still weak and in bed, Shelley complained of ill health (as he would each time Mary gave birth) and Claire took him several times to visit a doctor. The delivery had been an easy one because the baby was two months premature. Dr. John Clarke, the same physician who had attended Mary's own mother after her birth (and killed her with his ignorance of sanitary measures), told Mary that the child could not survive. But Mary refused to accept defeat: she put her baby to her breast and tried to suckle it. In two days it took milk and Mary nursed it, hoping that she could keep it alive.

For some reason, Shelley even chose this time to make another of their numerous changes in residence. Though they had just moved on February 8, Shelley found a place he liked better, requiring them to relocate on March 2. Mary had to carry her eight-day-old baby to their new home. Hogg continued to visit, spending all day with Mary on March 5, for Percy and Claire were again out. On the following day, Mary's journal begins, "find my baby dead," followed by a long dash. The night before, she had looked in on the infant, and found it sleeping in its crib. It had lived just eleven days, the same length of time Mary's mother had survived after Mary's birth. In both instances, Mary had been the survivor.

Significantly, Mary turned to Hogg for support. "My dearest Hogg," she wrote him, "my baby is dead — will you come as soon as you can? I wish to see you . . . you are so calm a creature & Shelley is afraid of a fever from the milk — for I am no longer a mother now." Shelley again was showing his obsession with breasts, and was further concerned (with himself) because a doctor had told him that he was dying of tuberculosis, a diagnosis that proved to be erroneous.

The death of her baby haunted Mary, and Percy's attitude hurt her deeply. Though never named, the infant had lived long enough for Mary to form a real attachment to her. After its death, Mary often daydreamed of her little girl, frequently referring to these thoughts in her journal. Almost every day, Shelley and Claire left the house, leaving Mary to her lonely grief. She asked herself if she could ever have another child. Could she be a mother and nurture another life? Could she create life and not death in those she loved? Was she a monster?

On Sunday, March 19, a vision came to Mary as she slept: "my little baby came to life again — that it had only been cold & that we rubbed it before the fire & it lived — I awake & find no baby — I think about the little thing all day — not in good spirits." In her depression, she wanted life to be as Shelley had led her to think it could be: that wishing for things made them true. Mary heard a story that the doctor who had attended her had earlier revived a sailor who had been comatose for seven months — in effect, bringing him back to life. Could that really be done? Could he, somehow, do it for her dead child?

Mary roused herself enough to bring a different order to her life. She began to demand that Claire leave the household. "I see plainly — what is to be done," Mary wrote. The others at first resisted. Claire said she could never return to the Godwins at Skinner Street, and Percy protested that he and Mary bore a responsibility for Claire since it was they who were responsible for her predicament. This time, however, Mary persisted. If Claire could not go to Skinner Street, then she must move somewhere else.

The decision was delayed, as usual. When feelers were put out to the Godwins, they declared they no longer wanted to take Claire back, explaining that the scandal was hurting Fanny's chances of obtaining a teaching post in a school that her aunts ran in Dublin. Shelley agreed to take financial responsibility for Claire — as well as to "form her mind" (one of the few responsibilities in his life that he would live up to). But Claire continued to live with the couple as Mary seethed.

In mid-April, Shelley and Mary suddenly went by themselves to stay at an inn at Salt Hill in Buckinghamshire, in the Thames valley northwest of London. It may have been intended as a holiday, but there is evidence that Shelley was dodging his creditors again. Several pages have been ripped out of Mary's journal during this period, covering all the time she spent with Shelley at Salt Hill. It seems very likely that she became pregnant on this trip. The security of Shelley all to herself at last completely changed her mood. In the four letters she wrote to Hogg during that time — urging him to come and join them — the bereaved mother was gone, and the coquette returned: "I am no doubt a very naughty Dormouse [here a drawing of a dormouse] but indeed you must forgive me. . . . Do you mean to come down to us — I suppose not Prince Prudent well as you please but remember I should be very happy to see you."

After three days, they returned to London, where Hogg had found them (yet again!) new lodgings, with room for him to stay there as well. To Mary's annoyance, Claire had moved in ahead of them. The degree of hostility in the household must have been high, for Shelley began reading the calming works of the Stoic philosopher Seneca to escape from the chaos around him. On May 12 Mary wrote icily in her journal that Shelley had gone out with "his friend" in the morning and "the lady" in the afternoon. In the evening he had a last talk with "his friend." All these are references to Claire.

The next day, the first thing Mary wrote was "Clary goes." That day's entry was the last in this volume of her journals. Though there were blank pages left to write on, Mary finished the book with, "I begin a new journal with our regeneration." However, the next volume has been lost, and we have only the letters written by her and Shelley to determine what happened between then and July of the following year, 1816. By that time, though Mary had hoped otherwise, her brief period of exclusivity with Shelley would be over.

Claire had gone to stay in Lynmouth, a village in Devon on the west coast of England. A friend of hers lived there, and Shelley paid for Claire's expenses. On the day of her departure, he escorted her to the place where she was to board a carriage, and when he did not return till late in the day, Mary became "very anxious," no doubt feeling that even now Shelley might choose Claire over her. Claire, on her part, felt relief at escaping the friction that had developed among the threesome. She wrote to her other stepsister, Fanny, from Lynmouth: "I am perfectly happy — After so much discontent, such violent scenes, such a turmoil of passion & hatred you will hardly believe how enraptured I am with this dear little quiet spot."

Lynmouth would prove to be too boring a place for Claire, who loved excitement, but for eight months Mary was free of her. The threesome became a twosome. Mary knew that she was again pregnant and Shelley constantly complained of his health, so they too spent much of the summer away from London, often staying in seacoast towns such as Clifton and Torquay. The resort village of Torquay was filled with visitors that summer, for Napoleon was temporarily held there aboard a British warship; tourists could see him walking the deck. To Mary and Percy, like many others, Napoleon's presence marked the disappointing end of a long period of idealism that the French Revolution had sparked, for even though Napoleon was more despot than liberator, his downfall signaled the restoration of a monarchy in France.

Even in these pleasant vacation spots, Shelley could not stay put for long. He went off to London to consult with doctors about his illnesses, which now included a serious abdominal complaint. He told Mary that while he was away he would look for a house where the two of them could live. That left Mary stranded in Clifton, a town near the seaport of Bristol, alone and pregnant (not to mention unmarried, though Shelley introduced her as "Mrs. Shelley" to avoid controversy). Mary constantly feared that he might be with Claire, for Lynmouth was not too far away.

Mary wrote Shelley a letter that shows how disturbed she was at this time; the tone veers between desperation and cuteness. "We ought not to be absent any longer indeed we ought not — I am not happy at it," she began,

> when I retire to my room no sweet Love — after dinner no Shelley. . . .
>
> Pray is Clary with you? for I have enquired several times . . . but seriously it would not in the least surprise me if you have written to her from London & let her know that you are there without me. . . .
>
> Tomorrow is the 28th of July [the anniversary of their elopement]— dearest ought we not to have been together on that day — indeed we ought my love. . . . Your Pecksie is a good girl & is quite well now again — except a headach[e] when she waits so a[n]xiously for her loves letters — dearest best Shelley pray come to me.

Mary knew that Shelley had abandoned Harriet even though she was his legal wife. She had only faith that her erratic lover would not repeat the scene with her. Nevertheless, Shelley did return to Mary by the end of the week. He had good news: Dr. William Lawrence, the eminent surgeon, had assured him that he need not worry. Shelley did not have consumption, nor was he on the edge of death.

That out of the way, it was time to move again. In August, Shelley found a place for the two of them to live near Windsor, west of London. It was a two-story house of red brick with a garden for Mary. There the summer and fall passed quite peacefully. It was the longest time in their relationship that they lived as a couple, with no additional members of the household. Thomas Peacock, who lived close by, was a regular visitor, and at the end of August he and Mary's stepbrother, Charles Clairmont, joined the lovers for a trip along the Thames. Shelley, as always entranced by water, proposed they row a boat up the river to its source. While the men rowed, Mary enjoyed the lovely scenery along the winding banks.

When the group reached Oxford, they disembarked so Shelley could show them his former rooms and the Bodleian Library. As Charles wrote to Claire in a letter about the trip, they saw "the very rooms where the two most noted infidels, Shelley and Hogg . . . pored, with the incessant . . . application of an alchemyst, over the artificial and natural boundaries of human knowledge."

The trip was a productive one for Shelley; the relief from anxiety over bill collectors, ill health, and quarrels between Mary and Claire prompted a surge of poetic works. Charles reported to Claire, "We have all felt the good effects of this jaunt; but in Shelley the change is quite remarkable; he has now the ruddy healthy complexion of the Autumn upon his countenance, & he is twice as fat as he used to be." Perhaps the real reason for Shelley's newly robust appearance was that Peacock had persuaded him to give up his vegetarian diet and eat some pork chops.

Mary gave birth to a son on January 24, 1816, finally able to give her father the gift she herself was supposed to have been. She named the child William, hoping that would soften her father's heart and persuade him to resume their relationship. Shelley wrote sarcastically to Godwin that it would make Fanny and Mrs. Godwin happy to know that Mary had given birth to a son and that both mother and child were healthy. Despite this, Godwin was not reconciled with his daughter, though for that day he noted in his journal, "William, *nepos,* born."

Mary's son proved to be healthy, and at long last she had a home where she did not have to share Shelley with anyone else. Such happiness could not last — and it didn't. Shelley funded a scheme that had sent Charles Clairmont and Claire off to Ireland to start a business. That did not pan out, and early in 1816, Claire had returned to London, where she finally was able to move back into the Skinner Street residence of the Godwins. Shelley's legal battles over his will and the settlement with Harriet frequently took him to London as well. Mary fretted that he and

Claire would resume their relationship, and Mary knew by this time that she did not want to share Shelley any more than she had wanted to share her father's love.

Claire, however, was about to make a literary catch of her own. She had written a letter to a man whose very presence, it was said, could make respectable women faint. It was Claire's ambition not just to meet Lord Byron, but to become his lover.

CHAPTER FIVE

THE MOST DANGEROUS MAN IN EUROPE

She walks in beauty, like the night
Of cloudless climes and starry skies;
And all that's best of dark and bright
Meet in her aspect and her eyes:
Thus mellow'd to that tender light
Which heaven to gaudy day denies.

— "She Walks in Beauty,"
Lord Byron, 1815

When Lord Byron wrote these famous lines, his inspiration was the sight of his lovely female cousin at a party in London, but he might as well have been describing himself. Byron was a legend in his own time, renowned as much for his physical beauty as for his poetry. He personified the Romantic movement, turning his own life and obsessions into art, just as his life became a topic of rumor and gossip throughout Europe and America. Byron became famous just as mass-market publications and mass-produced copperplate images were starting to appear. Through them, he became the first international celebrity.

At all times and places, beauty has been an asset, and Byron made the most of his striking features. Few who met him escaped his spell. Samuel Taylor Coleridge, the poet, described him in 1816, when Byron was twenty-eight: "so beautiful a countenance I scarcely ever saw — his eyes the open portals of the sun." The French author Stendhal, who saw him in Milan later that same year, remembered, "I was struck with Lord Byron's eyes. . . . I never in my life saw any thing more beautiful or more expressive. Even now, when I think of the expression which a great painter should give to genius, I always have before me that magnificent head." Shelley's cousin Thomas Medwin met Byron five years later and wrote: "His . . . lips and chin had that curved and definite outline which distinguishes Grecian beauty. His forehead was high, and his temples broad; and he had a paleness in his complexion, almost to wanness. . . . [His eyes] were of a greyish brown, but of a peculiar clearness, and when animated possessed a fire which seemed to look through and penetrate the thoughts of others." Caroline Lamb, who lost her dignity, reputation, and finally her sanity over Byron, summed up his allure for women: "That beautiful pale face is my fate."

Byron worked hard to maintain his looks. He adopted a special way of walking on his toes to increase his height (5'8") and to conceal the limp that resulted from a congenital birth defect. Careful to preserve his teeth, he used a special powder to brush them and had it sent to him whenever he left England. He wore gloves, even when indoors, to preserve the white skin of his notably small and shapely hands; he habitually wrote after midnight and slept through the morning to avoid exposure to sunlight. He was very proud of his soft chestnut hair. Scrope Davies, a close friend, once entered Byron's bedroom to catch him fast asleep wearing hair curl papers. Davies awoke him with the cry: "Sleeping Beauty!" Byron exploded into rage and Davies explained that he thought his hair curled naturally. "Yes, naturally every night," replied the poet; "but do not, my dear Scrope, let the cat out of the bag, for I am as vain of my curls as a girl of sixteen."

Byron continually exercised and dieted, and may even have been anorexic. He followed a lifelong regimen that alternated between binge eating and crash diets, for when he let himself go, he gained weight quickly. He measured his waist and wrists each morning and if he was not satisfied he would immediately take Epsom salts and a variety of patent medicines intended to purge him — the diet pills of the day. Along with his weight, his energy cycles varied from manic highs to moods of depression and paranoia. When he was in one of his lethargic periods he became "bloated and sallow," his knuckles "lost in fat." Reaching a manic period, he would become obsessed with his weight, eating nothing but vinegar, water, and a bit of rice. At a dinner party when he exasperated the hostess by refusing to eat the prepared meal, he was asked what he *did* eat and he replied: "Nothing but hard biscuits and soda water." Byron's weight obsession continued throughout his life. Not long before he died, he explained to a doctor in Greece: "I especially dread, in this world, two things, to which I have reason to believe I am equally predisposed — growing fat and growing mad; and it would be difficult for me to decide, were I forced to make a choice, which of these conditions I would choose in preference."

The one flaw in his physical perfection was his deformed foot. As a child he suffered agonies caused by devices intended to straighten it. (Some have described it as a club foot, but Byron's bootmaker claimed that the defect was that one foot was an inch and a half larger than the other and his ankles were very weak, which caused the foot to turn out too much.) Byron wore a very close-fitting, thin boot that he laced tightly for support. The calf of one leg was also weaker than the other, so he always wore long pants even when swimming. Thomas Medwin once mused that it might have been "a *cloven* foot."

Indeed, the defective foot affected Byron's gait only slightly, but because so much concern had been shown over it when he was young, its greatest effect was on Byron's sense of himself. He regarded it as the mark of Cain, one of his favorite Biblical characters and the subject of one of his great poems. He felt deeply ashamed of what he considered to be his lameness. Seated or standing, he always made an effort to conceal the flaw. At parties, he looked for a place to stand where he could hide the base of his leg behind a curtain or tablecloth. In his full-length portraits, the foot is always in shadows. When his lifelong friend John Cam Hobhouse was visiting him in Italy, Byron abruptly accused him of looking at his foot. Hobhouse replied: "My dear Byron, nobody thinks of or looks at anything but your head."

The "deformity" was one reason Byron saw himself as an outsider, and why he pushed himself so hard. Byron drove himself to excel in such sports as swimming, boxing, riding, and shooting — and of course lovemaking. He expressed the link between his lameness and his greatness in a poem:

Deformity is daring.
It is its essence to o'ertake mankind
By heart and soul, and make itself the equal —
Ay, the superior of the rest.

The poet he claimed to admire most was Alexander Pope, a hunchback.

Byron noted that he had developed sexually at a young age: "My passions were developed very early — so early — that few would believe me — if I were to state the period — and the facts which accompanied it," he once told a friend. Byron thought that these early sexual experiences had deprived him of an ordinary childhood, pushing him into premature aging. Later in life, he linked this precocious sexuality with his tendency to melancholy and depression.

Those childhood sexual experiences were both platonic and physical. When Byron was about seven and living in Aberdeen with his mother, he felt an intense love for his equally young cousin Mary Duff. "I recollect all we said to each other, all our caresses, her features, my restlessness, sleeplessness. . . . How the deuce did all this occur so early?" he wrote in his journal in 1813. "I certainly had no sexual ideas for years afterwards; and yet my misery, my love for that girl were so violent, that I sometimes doubt if I have ever really been attached since." Later when he heard of Mary's marriage to another, it "was like a thunder-stroke — it nearly choked me."

As to physical experience, Byron had been aroused as a young boy by a maid named May Gray. He told a friend she "used to come to bed with him and play tricks with his person." This behavior continued for two years until his mother found out and Gray was sacked. The experience warped Byron's feelings about women, often causing him to see them as nothing but sex objects. He later described his attitude: "Now my *beau ideal* would be a woman with talent enough to be able to understand and value mine, but not sufficient to be able to shine herself. All men with pretensions desire this, though few, if any, have courage to avow it."

Byron knew that he was a bisexual although there was no such word then (Coleridge coined it in the year of Byron's death), and the penalty for homosexual behavior was harsh. Indeed, convictions for sodomy could be punished with a death sentence. Though youthful experimentation with other boys was acceptable, adult homosexuality was not. Sodomy — defined as anal penetration and emission — was difficult to prove, but "assault with attempt to commit sodomy" was easier. Those convicted were exposed in the public pillory, where some were stoned to death by gawking crowds or pelted with mud and excrement. The new level of intolerance had led some homosexuals to flee England. One such was William Beckford, author of the Gothic novel *Vathek*, a favorite book of Byron's. The strong homophobia of the times made Byron's mixed feelings about his attraction to boys understandable.

The hero of Byron's poems was often an aristocrat haunted by sins of the past. That image came not only from his own life but from the tales of his ancestors on both sides. Their wild background, of which Byron was proud, dated back to the Norman Conquest. The Byruns, as the family name was spelled then, claimed they had come over with William the Conqueror in 1066 and their name is listed in the Domesday Book. Newstead Abbey, Byron's home in Nottinghamshire, came to the family during Tudor times after Henry VIII dissolved the monasteries and distributed their lands among those faithful to him.

The poet's grandfather John Byron, nicknamed "Foulweather Jack" for his ability to attract storms, was a vice admiral in the Royal Navy. After being shipwrecked off the coast of Patagonia, he survived by eating his dog, including the skin and paws. Later he was put in charge of an exploring expedition, but luck was still not with him, for he managed to circumnavigate the globe without finding a single new island. During the American Revolution, his bad luck caused a storm to blow up during a naval battle against French ships in the West Indies. His assignment ended in utter failure and he was relieved of his command.

Like his son and grandson, Foulweather Jack was a rake. His escapades with a chambermaid found their way into the scandal sheets of the time. When he died, the noble title and the estate passed to the poet's great-uncle William, known as the "Wicked Lord." William married an heiress and ran through her fortune; supposedly he was in the habit of throwing her into a lake on the estate when she displeased him. He murdered his cousin and neighbor William Chaworth; the event was so notorious that those who wanted to attend his trial had to purchase tickets. William was found guilty of manslaughter but set free. He spent much of his later years in isolation with his trained crickets, who reportedly left the crannies of the walls of Newstead Abbey on his command. At his death, the estate showed the signs of long neglect: its once-famous oaks had been cut down and the manor house was a wreck.

The poet's father —"Mad Jack," he was called — was also notorious. As a young Captain of the Guards, he had carried on a love affair with the married Marchioness of Carmarthen. They ran off together and wed after her husband divorced her. She died soon after, giving birth to a daughter named Augusta, who would become notorious as Byron's half sister — and lover. Mad Jack didn't have time to grieve for long, for with his wife's death, her (and his) annual income of four thousand pounds ended as well. He headed for Bath, the marriage-market of the day, looking for an heiress. Mad Jack's son would note that he was "a very handsome man, which goes a great way." To pay for his gambling debts, Jack was said to have charged wealthy women for his sexual services.

At Bath, Catherine Gordon, though she was fat, loud, and gawky, attracted his attention — as well she should have, for she was sole heiress to a large fortune. The Gordons held the estate of Gight in northern Scotland near Aberdeen. This noble family traced their lineage back to James I, king of Scotland from 1406 to 1437. The Gordons had produced a succession of Scottish lairds known for their violence and cunning until the last two generations, whose members suffered from melancholia. Catherine's father and grandfather had both committed suicide by drowning themselves. Jack had no trouble getting Catherine to fall in love with him, and they were married a few months later, in 1785. Nor did Jack have much difficulty running through her fortune, for he led an extravagant life and gambling was one of his many pleasures. With no parents to safeguard her, Catherine soon lost her castle, her wealth, and then her husband too.

All that Mad Jack left her was a son, born George Gordon Byron on January 22, 1788. He was born with a caul, a membrane over his head, which is often regarded as a positive omen. As part of the old superstition, the caul was kept for good luck, and later was sold to John Hanson, the family lawyer, who gave it to his brother, a captain in the Royal Navy. If it held any luck, Captain Hanson did not benefit, for his ship sank, leaving only one survivor (not Hanson).

Nor did the caul seem to presage good fortune for the infant, for young George's deformed foot indicated, at least to his father, that he would never walk. Byron later blamed the deformity on the fact that his mother had kept her corset tightly laced during her pregnancy. Though that couldn't have been the source of the problem, it did affect his feelings toward her. Meanwhile Mad Jack went to France, where he took up with his half-sister Fanny in an incestuous relationship that Jack's son would later imitate. Incest seemed truly to be a family affair for the Byrons.

One woman was never enough for Mad Jack (and besides, Fanny was married), and he wrote his sister-lover sexually explicit letters bragging of his other conquests. "I believe I have had one third of Valenciennes," he estimated in one missive. He died, possibly a suicide, when his son George was three. Jack had asked his sister to be his heir, but she shrewdly refused, knowing he would leave nothing but debts. She was right, and the debts now became, legally, the responsibility of his son.

Though Mad Jack had treated Catherine as badly as would seem possible, she grieved so loudly when she received news of his death that passers-by in the street heard her agonized cries. Byron himself — though he never really knew his father, having seen him on only a few occasions — tended to idealize him. Following Jack's death, his widow and son lived in genteel poverty in Aberdeen. They formed a close if turbulent bond, but though she sometimes doted on him, at other times she had fits of rage when she smashed crockery and called him names such as a "lame brat." Sometimes she accused him of being just like his father. She hit him when he bit his nails, a lifelong habit he could never break. Byron, embarrassed by his mother's girth, would stick pins into her fat arms as they sat in church. Despite everything, his mother was ambitious for him and made great personal sacrifices to keep up appearances, give him pride in his noble heritage, and encourage his love of reading.

An unexpected series of deaths among the heirs of Byron's uncle the "Wicked Lord" gave young George the family title. At the age of ten he inherited Newstead Abbey and became the sixth Lord Byron. When he came to school for the first time after his accession, the rector addressed him as "Georgius Dominus de Byron" and the other boys applauded. The new lord was so overcome that he burst into tears and tried to run away. The title would always mean a great deal to him.

When Byron and his mother visited Newstead Abbey, they found that it lacked a roof and there were cattle stabled in the great hall that had once been a drawing room. The only use for the abbey seemed to be as a setting for some of the popular Gothic novels of the time. The founder of the genre, Horace Walpole, had fallen in love with the ruins when he had visited Nottinghamshire in 1760, and the prolific and successful Ann Radcliffe had been inspired by the abbey when she was staying in the area while writing *The Romance of the Forest* (1791). She also featured the "Wicked Lord" in one of her books. To the ten-year-old Lord Byron, of course, the estate was enchanting. Because of its dilapidated condition, however, Byron and his mother lived in nearby Nottingham.

Byron entered the boarding school Harrow when he was thirteen. Though he was a small, fat boy with plastered-down hair, he adjusted well and recalled Harrow as "a home, a world, a paradise." He took part in sports, excelling in swimming, and he even played cricket, despite his foot, which he refused to allow to hinder him.

Byron discovered at Harrow how easily he could write poetry, and he began to reveal a vast ambition. He wrote his mother in 1804: "I will cut myself a path through the world or perish in the attempt. . . . I will carve myself the passage to Grandeur, but never with Dishonour. These Madam are my intentions." But the seeds of his destruction also sprouted here. He had his first crush on a boy when he met John Fitzgibbon, Earl of Clare, who was four years younger. (Indications are that their love was quite innocent, for Byron was shocked and disgusted when Lord Gray, a tenant who was occupying Newstead Abbey, made a pass at him.) Byron recalled years later: "My School friendships were with *me passions* (for I was always violent) but . . . that with Lord Clare began one of the earliest and lasted longest. . . . I never hear the word '*Clare*' without a beating of the heart — even *now*, and I write it with the feelings of 1803–4–5 — ad infinitum." It was also while at Harrow that Byron began to correspond for the first time with his half-sister, Augusta, who had been living with her maternal grandmother.

In 1805, when he was seventeen, Byron enrolled at Cambridge. Though Oxford had been his first choice — he could not go there because there were no vacant rooms at the college he preferred — Byron claimed that these years were the happiest time of his life. Many students of his social rank hardly cracked a book, but Byron read widely in the English classics and loved biographies and history as well as modern poetry. He found his own voice with his first published book of poetry, *Poems on Various Occasions.* While attending Cambridge, he met a young choirboy of humble birth named John Edleston. He gave Byron a heart made of carnelian quartz that Byron kept with him until he died. The young lord considered adopting Edleston and establishing a relationship that would "put 'the Ladies of Llangollen' to the blush." (The Ladies of Llangollen were two eccentric English aristocrats who lived together and dressed as men; they had actually inspired Mary Wollstonecraft's plans for her relationship with Fanny Blood.) Byron, however, had nothing like an exclusive relationship with Edleston, nor with anyone else. During his Cambridge years, he took mistresses, engaged in promiscuous sex, and fathered a son by his maid Lucy.

Byron was far from entirely studious, and he took full advantage of his aristocratic status, providing himself with a mistress, two manservants, and his own carriage emblazoned with the Byron coat of arms and the family motto *Crede Byron!* ("Trust Byron"). He also kept at the university three horses, a bear, and several dogs. Throughout his life he liked a menagerie around him. He sent his family lawyer a request for provisions: "I will be obliged to you to order me down 4 Dozen [bottles] of Wine, Port — Sherry — Claret, & Medeira, one Dozen of Each; I have got part of my Furniture in, & begin to *admire* a College Life." Byron always loved to dress up in costumes, and Cambridge provided plenty of opportunities. He wrote, "Yesterday my appearance in the Hall in my State Robes was *Superb,* but uncomfortable to my Diffidence." His noble title allowed him to eat with the dons at their table and to wear a richly embroidered gown with a gold-tasselled mortarboard. He enjoyed other perks of a peer of the realm: he did not have to go to lectures or take exams. It was easy, as a lord, to get credit from the local tradesmen and Byron fell into debt due to his high living. When his mother saw the bills, she wailed, "That boy will be the death of me, & drive me mad . . . he has behaved as ill as possible to me for years back, this bitter Truth I can no longer conceal, it is wrung from me by *heart rending agony*."

Byron had entered Cambridge weighing more than two hundred pounds, having been fat all his life. Here the ugly duckling changed into a beauty. He described his method of losing weight: "I wear *seven* Waistcoats, & a great Coat, run & play at Cricket in this Dress, till quite exhausted by excessive perspiration, use the hot Bath daily, eat only a quarter of [a] pound [of] Butchers meat in 24 hours, no Suppers, or Breakfast, only one meal a Day, drink no malt Liquor, little Wine, take physic occasionally, by these means . . . my Clothes, have been taken in nearly *half a yard*." Byron returned home so much lighter that many of his friends did not recognize him. His weight loss — to 147 pounds — changed his looks, and his face took on the chiseled features for which he became famous.

With no need actually to perform work to obtain a degree, Byron spent much of his time in London, where he took boxing lessons from "Gentleman John" Jackson, who had been champion of England. Rumor had it that Jackson and his partner, a fencing master, were homosexuals. Their "social club" was a gathering place for London's demimonde, a milieu that Byron enjoyed. He gambled, attended boxing matches, plays, and late-night clubs, and patronized teenage prostitutes, writing his Cambridge friend John Cam Hobhouse, "I am buried in an abyss of Sensuality." He also invited friends to join him at Newstead Abbey, where he planned to establish a new version of the notorious Hell-Fire Club of the previous century, whose members gathered for orgies of spectacular reputation. Byron amused his guests by firing pistols at the stone walls and serving wine in cups made from polished skulls that he had disinterred from the abbey's crypt.

On the surface, Byron seemed to be a feckless playboy. Part of his malaise during this period came from the fact that his one published book of poetry had garnered harshly critical reviews. Yet despite what appeared to be a dissipated life, Byron continued to write, now going on the counterattack and writing a poetic assault on reviewers and fellow poets, whose work he savagely ridiculed. Published anonymously in early 1809, *English Bards and Scotch Reviewers* was sharp enough to attract attention, and the ill-kept secret of Byron's authorship soon got out. Among its admirers were Mary Godwin and Percy Shelley.

That same year Byron turned twenty-one, and was entitled to take his seat in the House of Lords, a privilege he exercised almost at once. When the staid Earl of Eldon, Lord Chancellor of England and a leading Tory, or conservative, offered his hand in welcome to the newest member, Byron merely touched the elder man's palm — a calculated insult — and then sat on the left side of the hall, home to the opposition party. (Byron would not, however, speak before the Lords until 1812.)

Finished with Cambridge and bored, he decided to leave England. It was a tradition for young Englishmen of the upper classes to go on a grand tour of Europe to complete their education. Since the Napoleonic Wars made it impossible to visit some of the usual countries, Byron and his companion Hobhouse planned a different itinerary, through Portugal, Spain, Malta, Sicily, Albania, Greece, and the Ottoman Empire. Leaving in July 1809, Byron thought he might not return, expressing his feelings in *Childe Harold*, the poem that would result from the trip:

Adieu, adieu! my native shore
Fades o'er the waters blue;
The night-winds sigh, the breakers roar,
And shrieks the wild sea mew.
Yon Sun that sets upon the sea
We follow in his flight;
Farewell awhile to him and thee,
My native Land — Good Night.

For Byron, this journey was a life-shaping experience, in which he would begin constructing his own legend and developing the cultural horizon that would make him a great poet. Young and adventurous, he wanted to make his mark on the world. In Portugal, he tested his athletic prowess by swimming the Tagus River from Old Lisbon to the Terre de Belem, a grueling struggle against the tide that took him two hours. An

English officer stationed in Lisbon reported that Byron's charms did not go unnoticed, writing that he "became the idol of the women, and the lionising he underwent there might have made him exceedingly vain, for he was admired wherever he went."

Next, he and Hobhouse went on to Cadiz, in Spain, where they watched a bullfight from the governor's box, an experience that Byron turned into ten vivid stanzas in *Childe Harold:*

> *On foams the bull, but not unscathed he goes;*
> *Streams from his flank the crimson torrent clear:*
> *He flies, he wheels, distracted with his throes;*
> *Dart follows dart; lance, lance; loud bellowings speak his woes.*

While in Cadiz the two friends also attended the opera, where the unmarried daughter of the commander of the Spanish fleet flirted with Byron. He was surprised by her boldness, and reported to his mother, "If you make a proposal which in England would bring a box on the ear from the meekest of virgins, to a Spanish girl, she thanks you for the honour you intend her, and replies, 'wait till I am married & I shall be too happy.'"

Byron and Hobhouse made their first Greek landing at the port of Patras in September. They were now in the Ottoman Empire, for the Turks had controlled Greece and southeastern Europe for four hundred years. As they moved up the coast to Albania, they found themselves in an exotic land, a startling contrast to England. Turks wearing turbans sported pistols and daggers in their belts. Black-skinned slaves carried goods through the street markets. High-pitched voices from the soaring minarets of mosques called the faithful to prayer. Byron was particularly fascinated and impressed by the Albanian Christian soldiers called Suliotes, who reminded him in dress and spirit of the clans of northern Scotland. (One of Byron's most famous portraits would depict him wearing a Suliote outfit.)

Byron told a friend in later years that the air of Greece had made him a poet. It was, however, in Janina, Albania, that Byron began *Childe Harold* on October 31, 1810. He described his reaction to the region:

The scene was savage, but the scene was new;
This made the ceaseless toil of travel sweet.

Ali Pasha, ruler of Albania, welcomed the two English travelers and provided them with a military escort that safeguarded them through the mountains to his palace. (Though Byron thought this courtesy was merely his due as an English lord, there were political reasons for the hospitality; the English fleet had recently captured some Greek islands, and the wily pasha, a former bandit chief, was angling for a military alliance.) Ali was a grossly fat man, short by European standards, but with light blue eyes and a white beard. Byron, well turned out in a scarlet military uniform with glistening sword at his belt, made quite an impression; the pasha even appeared to flirt with him. Homosexuality was not regarded with the same disapproval in the Ottoman Empire as it was in England, and Byron found many new opportunities for sexual adventures. The public baths employed young and handsome men to wash customers in private rooms and provide extra services for those who could pay. Byron would later refer to the Turkish bath as "that marble paradise of sherbet and sodomy."

On Christmas Day Byron and Hobhouse arrived in Athens, a city that their classical education had prepared them to love. They explored the ruins of the Parthenon. It was at this time that Lord Elgin, the British attaché to the Ottoman Empire, stripped the building of the marble friezes and statues that are today displayed in the British Museum as the "Elgin marbles." Byron would attack the art-loving Elgin as a cultural thief. Even so, he and Hobhouse settled down and became part of an expatriate group that included Giovanni Battista Lusieri, whom Lord Elgin had employed to supervise the removal of the statues. Lusieri introduced Byron to his brother-in-law, Nicolo Giraud, a boy in his midteens who became Byron's Italian teacher, and then, lover.

Ever expansive in his erotic tastes, Byron also wrote that he was "dying for love" of the three daughters of his landlady, who ranged in age from twelve to fourteen. One of Byron's friends recalled him describing his "act of courtship often practiced in that country"— cutting himself across the chest with a dagger to impress one of the girls. Hobhouse, in his journal of the trip, noted another occasion when Byron was dressing in "female apparel & dancing with Demetrius."

After spending ten weeks in Athens, the two English travelers crossed the sea to the heart of the Ottoman Empire in Anatolia, today's Turkey. At the Dardanelles, the strait separating Europe and Asia, Byron recalled the mythical deed of the Greek Leander, who swam the strait to reach his beloved, the priestess Hero. Byron set out to imitate it. The strait is about four miles wide, with a strong tide. Byron swam while the water was still frigid from melting snow, wore long trousers to hide his deformity, and yet he succeeded in duplicating the epic feat. Of swimming the Hellespont he wrote, "I plume myself on this achievement more than I could possibly do on any kind of glory, political, poetical, or rhetorical." He was building his own legend.

In Constantinople, the capital of the empire, Byron absorbed all he saw, seemingly without the alienation that most would feel on first contact with such a foreign culture. He wrote to a friend: "I see not much difference between ourselves & the Turks, save that we have foreskins and they none, that they have long dresses and we short, and that we talk much and they little."

Hobhouse returned to England in July 1810, but Byron stayed on for almost a year longer, mainly in Greece, visiting Mount Olympus and other important classical sites. Byron made friends among the Greeks and learned how much they wanted to recover their long-lost independence. He would make their cause his own. On one occasion he intervened to save a young female slave just as soldiers were about to carry out a death sentence imposed on her by the local Turkish governor. The incident later became the basis for his poem *The Giaour*.

This was a happy time for him. Seeing a flock of eagles overhead while on the road to Delphi, Byron hoped — a young man's hope — that they were an augury that he would achieve fame. The day before, he had written these lines:

Oh, thou Parnassus! whom I now survey,
Not in the phrensy of a dreamer's eye,

Not in the fabled landscape of a lay,
But soaring snow-clad through thy native sky,
In the wild pomp of mountain majesty!

At Malta, on his return home in 1811, he wrote a note to himself: "At twenty three, the best of life is over and its bitters double." On his arrival in England in July, he learned that his mother was very ill. He did not reach her before her death. She was only forty-six, and despite their turbulent relationship, Byron was overcome with grief and guilt. Sitting beside her dead body, he said to her maid, "I had but one friend in the world, and she is gone!"

Before his mother was buried, Byron learned that a close Cambridge friend had drowned in the River Cam. "Some curse," he wrote on August 7, "hangs over me and mine. My mother lies a corpse in this house; one of my best friends is drowned in a ditch." By October Byron suffered another blow, hearing of the death of Edleston earlier in the year from consumption. It was a blow that brought down his spirits. Edleston was a person, he wrote, "whom I once loved more than I ever loved a living thing." He poured out his sorrow in a lament, camouflaging the sex of his beloved by titling it "To Thyrza." This poem was a favorite of Mary and Percy's.

Ours too the glance none saw beside;
The smile none else might understand;
The whisper'd thought of hearts allied,
The pressure of the thrilling hand;

The kiss, so guiltless and refined,
That Love each warmer wish forbore;
Those eyes proclaim'd so pure a mind,
Even Passion blush'd to plead for more.

The tone, that taught me to rejoice,
When prone, unlike thee, to repine;
The song, celestial from thy voice,
But sweet to me from none but thine;

The pledge we wore — I wear it still,
But where is thine?— Ah! where art thou?
Oft have I borne the weight of ill,
But never bent beneath till now!

In early 1812, Byron made his maiden speech in the House of Lords, in defense of clothworkers who had received death sentences for destroying spinning machines in factories. Nottingham, Byron's home, was a center of the Luddite movement, named for a man who had been thrown out of work by the mechanization of the cloth trade and who began smashing the machines in response. British soldiers used bayonets to control the Nottingham weavers who had broken into local factories. Despite the inherent drama of the clash, Byron's speech, though heartfelt, was not very impressive and he realized that he would probably be bored in a political career. He was spared that very soon.

Byron had turned the manuscript of *Childe Harold* over to a friend, who found a publisher for it: John Murray, who would publish all of the poet's work from then on. Byron did not want his name on the book, but he was persuaded to allow it to be sold as the work of "the author of *English Bards and Scotch Reviewers*," which was sufficient for anyone in the British literary world to know the poet's true identity. Against Byron's wishes, the publisher lined up good advance notices from critics, and the first printing of five hundred copies was sold out on the day of publication, March 10, 1812. The work was an immediate success. As Byron later recalled, "I awoke one morning and found myself famous."

The title character Childe Harold (a "childe" is a candidate for knighthood) was the first Byronic hero, establishing a pattern of fatal melancholy that provided an irresistible appeal for women. The Childe was "the gloomy wanderer," "the cold stranger," who carried his darkness and his secrets wherever he goes. The distinctive exoticism of the places where he wanders fascinated the public, who knew little about eastern Europeans and Turks. Particularly intriguing to women was the idea that the character was in fact Byron's alter ego. Byron always denied that, saying that Harold was the "child of imagination," but people would not be convinced.

Childe Harold, with its sometimes shocking subject matter, fit well the spirit of the time. King George III had been declared mad and his son appointed regent. The Regency era (1811–20) would be marked by scandals both high and low, and the misadventures of the prince regent, known as "Prinnie," and his wife, Caroline, provided fodder for savage cartoons and columns of irreverent gossip in London's sixteen daily newspapers.

Scandals at home contrasted with significant international and political events. In 1812, Napoleon unwisely invaded Russia and British forces scored important victories against French armies in Spain. The tide was turning against England's archenemy after a dozen years of French successes. Across the Atlantic, Britain's relations with the United States were deteriorating, and the British would go to war there as well. Internally Britain was seething with discontent over the new machines that threatened the livelihood of many artisans. In that same year, the prime minister, Spencer Perceval, was assassinated, the only time in English history this has ever happened. Yet even with all this to discuss, the two most notable events of the year, from the point of view of London society, were Byron's sudden fame and the introduction of a shocking new dance — the waltz.

Byron discovered that he was in demand among women of all ages and classes. Morals in Regency society were nonexistent, as long as one managed to be discreet. However, Byron became the target of one of the most indiscreet women in London: Lady Caroline Lamb, wife of William Lamb, a future prime minister of Britain. Their affair was notable even among the scandals of the day. Lady Caroline, three years older than Byron, was a moody woman with a hot temper, used to getting whatever she wanted. Her family had suspected she was mad when she was a child, but she grew up virtually unsupervised. She loved to shock people with her unconventional ways. When she first was introduced to Byron at a party, she turned her back on him, knowing that would pique his interest. But that night she wrote in her journal her now-famous words: that he was "mad, bad, and dangerous to know."

Once Lady Caroline caught Byron's attention, she pursued him openly, writing love letters, offering herself to him. They had a brief, very intense affair. Samuel Rogers, a poet and banker as well as an inveterate gossip, wrote:

> She absolutely besieged him. He showed me the first letter he received from her; in which she assured him that, if he was in any want of money, "all her jewels were at his service." They frequently had quarrels; and more than once, on coming home, I have found Lady C. walking in the garden, and waiting for me, to beg that I would reconcile them.— When she met Byron at a party, she would always, if possible, return home from it in *his* carriage, and accompanied by *him* . . . But such was the insanity of her passion for Byron, that sometimes, when not invited to a party where he was to be, she would wait for him in the street till it was over! One night, after a great party at Devonshire House, to which Lady Caroline had not been invited, I saw her — yes, saw her — talking to Byron, with half of her body thrust into the carriage which he had just entered.

Caroline quickly lost all sense of caution, at one point demanding to elope with Byron. Byron, with his many lovers, soon tired of her, but she refused to accept rejection. She sent him a clipping of her blond pubic hair, telling how she cut herself while trimming it and cautioning him not to hold the scissors too close when he returned the favor. When Byron ordered that she not be admitted to his house, Lady Caroline appeared disguised as a pageboy and Byron had to take a knife away from her, uncertain if she was threatening him or herself. Trying to convince her that her love was futile, Byron confided his homosexual feelings, an exciting piece of gossip that she later vengefully spread around London. Finally accepting defeat, she burned Byron in effigy and parodied his family motto by inscribing *Ne Crede Byron* ("Don't trust Byron") on her servants' buttons. Yet when she died in 1828, a rose and a carnation that Byron had given her were found dried and carefully preserved among her possessions.

Byron was the best-known poet of his time, achieving a celebrity that crossed boundaries and even continents. He possessed the kind of fame that only certain entertainment stars do today. Claire Clairmont, one of the many women who offered themselves to Byron — and one of those few who were accepted — recalled many years later, "In 1815, when I was a very young girl, Byron was the rage. When I say the rage, I mean what you people nowadays can perhaps hardly conceive. I suppose no man who ever lived has had the extraordinary celebrity of Lord Byron in such an intense, haunting, almost maddening degree. And this celebrity extended all over the Continent to as great an extent as in England; and remember, in those days there were no railways or telegraphs."

Much of Byron's fame came from his status as a Romantic hero — the product of his careful calculation and the conflation of his imagined characters with himself. The protagonists of his poems followed the Romantic ideal, expressed by painter Caspar David Friedrich: "Follow without hesitation the voice of your inner self." Readers entranced by the adventurous and tragic figures of Byron's poetry imagined that he was writing about himself — and he tried to live up to that image.

Byron had imbibed a sense of sin from the Scottish Calvinism in which he was raised. He sometimes saw himself as a fallen angel and became obsessed with the question of why evil exists. The most popular Byronic heroes were the cosmic rebels and fallen angels. Particularly appealing to women was the rogue who displayed his dark side, but who could be tamed by love and tenderness. In Jane Austen's novel *Persuasion,* written in 1818 when Byron was at the height of his fame, a group of young women discusses how to pronounce *The Giaour,* the title of Byron's poem about a Venetian nobleman who seeks to avenge the death of his lover, a slave executed by her Muslim master. That was thrilling stuff for the young women of the quiet English villages where Jane Austen and many other avid readers of Byron's poetry spent their lives.

Men too found Byron appealing — for his adventurous exploits and his sense of style. Byron's boxing skills and his feats as a swimmer added to his legend. Trying to find the secret of Byron's appeal for women, many young men imitated him in dress and grooming. Byron made his curly hair glisten with a preparation called "Macassar oil." When countless male swains did likewise, it became necessary for housewives to cover the upholstered backs of couches and chairs with a cloth, so that the oil didn't leave a stain. This was the origin of the "antimacassar," a decorative item in homes that survived long after the fad for Macassar oil faded.

The early 1800s had seen a revolution in men's fashion, in which eighteenth-century knee breeches were discarded, and long pants adopted. The brightly colored silk suits of the past, along with powdered wigs, became unfashionable. The renowned dandy Beau Brummel, the fashion arbiter of the time, called for simplicity and elegance, with an emphasis on restraint rather than flamboyance. He popularized wearing black evening clothes. Byron's obsession with his weight meshed perfectly with this new style, which emphasized a smooth line from top to bottom. Here too he set the mode that was ardently imitated throughout much of Europe and America. Before his time, a slim figure was regarded as a sign of ill health or poverty; since then, it has remained the ideal.

Poet, adventurer, fashion leader — Byron was all these, but that was not enough for his ambitions. His travels had inspired him to side with the nationalistic struggles of such people as the Italians and Greeks, who were ruled by outsiders. As one of the first "citizens of the world," Byron spoke out against tyranny wherever he saw it. In an age that recalled the initial enthusiasm inspired by the French Revolution, Byron seemed to be one of the few who still carried the torch for freedom. Such advocacy got attention for the cause, and for Byron.

The Romantics espoused the "great man" theory of history, admiring both the great man of politics and the genius of art and literature for their own sake — they were above national or political allegiances. Byron, whose greatest poems seemed to be about himself, or at least the public persona he cultivated, saw himself as the literary version of the emperor, living up to his soubriquet, "the Napoleon of rhyme." Byron and Napoleon shared world-conquering dreams. Lady Blessington, who spoke to the poet in the last years of his life, wrote: "Byron had two points of ambition — the one to be thought the greatest poet of his day, and the other a nobleman and man of fashion, who could have arrived at distinction without the aid of his poetical genius."

Oddly enough, Byron's affair with Caroline Lamb brought him his closest female confidante: the mother of Caroline's husband, Lady Melbourne.

Lady Melbourne had never liked her daughter-in-law. Known as "the Spider" for her deviousness, she provided Byron an entrée into the highest ranks of society. In 1812, she was over sixty but still attractive with beautiful eyes and a sharp mind, a grande dame of cynical charms. She kept her own counsel and enjoyed being the intimate of powerful men. "No man is safe with another's secrets, no woman with her own," she once remarked. At nineteen, she had married a man for whom she had little feeling and during their marriage she had a string of affairs, including one with the prince regent. It was commonly believed that all six of her children were illegitimate.

Lady Melbourne felt that Byron should be married, and she knew a suitable woman: her niece, Annabella Milbanke. Annabella was a pretty, level-headed, clever, but naive girl, the only child of doting parents. Well educated (as Caroline had not been), Annabella had a talent for mathematics, having taught herself geometry by reading Euclid. The only problem was that Byron did not like "blues" — short for bluestockings — as he called educated women. "I should like her more if she were less perfect," Byron wrote. Annabella first saw Byron at Lady Melbourne's house, but did not speak to him. She noted to her mother that "all the women were absurdly courting him and trying to deserve the lash of his Satire. I thought *inoffensiveness* was the most secure conduct, as I am not desirous of a place in his lays [songs] . . . I made no offering at the shrine of Childe Harold, though I shall not refuse the acquaintance if it comes my way."

Women who did not at once succumb to Byron's charms were often irresistible to him, and he consciously tried to present the "good angel" side of his personality to Annabella at their next meeting. When they did begin to converse, she confronted him on equal terms and did not play the role of adoring fan. She talked of goodness and genius, and whether genius made one happy; she in fact ventured to suggest that he was *not* happy. Seldom had anyone spoken to Byron in this vein, and he found her sincerity attractive. Though Byron did not love her, he was touched by her character and wanted to settle down. In October 1812, he proposed, but she rejected him. When he saw her again the following spring, he blushed furiously. This brought forth a long letter from Annabella, the start of a more conventional courtship correspondence.

But another, deeper relationship was to destroy the possibility of Byron's ever leading a "normal" life with Annabella. After the death of his mother, Byron drew closer to his half-sister, Augusta. Now his only living relative, Augusta was married to her cousin Captain George Leigh, who spent most of his time gambling and drinking. Four years older than Byron, Augusta, with her chestnut hair and large eyes, was said to resemble a female version of him. Separated as children, they became closer as they grew older, and Byron formed a deep attachment for her. In June of 1813, she arrived in London to ask him for help because her husband's gambling debts had put her home in danger of being seized by bailiffs.

Byron himself was in financial difficulty, and had been forced to put Newstead Abbey up for sale, Nonetheless, he was glad to see Augusta and included her in his social rounds. He escorted her to a dinner given by Sir Humphry Davy's wife in honor of the famous French intellectual Madame de Staël. Byron was pleased to see Augusta blossom socially, but increasingly he began to feel an unbrotherly desire for her. Augusta was unorthodox as well. She said of herself, "Of what consequence was one's behaviour, provided that it made nobody else unhappy?" Like Byron she was amoral. They shared the same wild family heritage; to him the blood tie only made her more attractive. The two of them seemed to understand each other effortlessly, and with her he could be as free as a child again, for he trusted her completely. By August 1813, they were deeply involved and Byron planned to take her to Sicily where they could live together.

Byron told Lady Melbourne of his plans to elope, shocking even her. Eventually Augusta reconsidered, for she had a child, and they gave up the idea of running off. Nevertheless, Byron told Lady Melbourne that he was more in love with Augusta than ever. She warned him against his desires, predicting that the relationship would raise a scandal that would destroy him.

Byron explored his incestuous feelings in *The Bride of Abydos,* 1,200 lines of poetry that he claimed to have written in four nights. Though set in Turkey, it told of a love between cousins who had been raised together as brother and sister. (In his original draft, the lovers had actually been brother and sister.) Byron portrays Zuleika's passionate love for her cousin Selim in words that shocked his readers.

Thy cheek, thine eyes, thy lips to kiss,
Like this — and this — no more than this,
For, Allah! sure thy lips are flame,
What fever in thy veins is flushing?
My own have nearly caught the same,
At least I feel my cheek, too, blushing.

In the winter of January 1814, Byron and Augusta traveled together to Newstead Abbey, spending three weeks there alone. It was the harshest winter in a generation and they were snowbound, sharing the cold stone rooms with only the ghosts of mad and wicked Byrons of the past. They celebrated Byron's twenty-sixth birthday together, "a very pretty age if it would always last," he wrote. He confided in a letter to Lady Melbourne: "I am much afraid that that perverse passion was my deepest after all."

Despite his passion for Augusta, Byron still sporadically wrote to Annabella. After she had turned down his proposal, Annabella had had a change of heart. She started to believe that her love could change the dark side of Byron. He seems to have tried to give Annabella warnings about his true nature. "The great object of life is sensation," he wrote, "to feel that we exist, even though in pain. It is the 'craving void' which drives us to Gaming, to Battle, to Travel — to intemperate but keenly felt pursuits of every description whose principal attraction is the agitation inseparable from their accomplishment." But while she was said to be level-headed, Annabella was as susceptible as anyone to the blindness caused by love.

Despite inner qualms, Byron proposed a second time in September 1814. Perhaps he felt it was the only way to avoid the doom of his relationship with Augusta. This time Annabella accepted.

They were married on January 2, 1815, in a small ceremony at the home of the bride's parents at Durham in the north of England. Byron had arrived only the day before, after keeping his bride and her relatives waiting for two weeks, during which time he found excuses to delay. John Cam Hobhouse, the best man, recalled that after he saw the newlyweds off in a coach, "I felt as if I had buried a friend." Byron wrote to Lady Melbourne: "We were married yesterday . . . so there's an end of that matter and the beginning of many others . . . the kneeling was rather tedious — and the cushions hard — but upon the whole it did vastly well." These words are hardly those of a smitten man.

Byron and his bride spent their honeymoon in the Milbankes' Yorkshire estate of Halnaby, a dark and dreary place. The setting matched Byron's lack of romantic feelings. "[H]ad Lady B on the sofa before dinner," was the inelegant way that he described his wedding night. Returning from the honeymoon, he took his bride to visit Augusta. The thinly veiled joking between the half-siblings led Annabella to suspect what their real relationship was. Byron wrote to his friend Thomas Moore that "the treaclemoon is over."

The relationship went from bad to worse. Byron quarreled with Annabella's parents and refused to attend her birthday party. He also made clear his disappointment that Annabella did not seem to have as much money as he had hoped. Annabella, on her part, thought her husband's sometimes violent behavior was a sign of insanity. Worst of all, Augusta spent a great deal of time in their flat in London, ostensibly to assist now that Annabella was pregnant. Annabella studied medical journals to try to understand the man she had married, for she deeply wanted to help. But nothing could save their marriage, for Byron and Augusta were unable to keep their secret while living in such close proximity. Byron, now drinking heavily, apparently also confessed his homosexual escapades to Annabella.

In January 1816, a month after giving birth to Byron's daughter, significantly named Augusta Ada, Annabella left him and returned to her parents' house. (The daughter, always called Ada by her mother's family, would grow up to be a mathematics prodigy who helped develop an early form of the computer; she also lost a fortune gambling on horses, convinced she could devise a foolproof system of betting.) Byron professed to be shocked when his wife left him, even though he had been openly hostile to her for some time. Byron wrote to his half-sister: "She — or rather — the separation — has broken my heart — I feel as if an Elephant has trodden on it — I am convinced I shall never get over it — but I try." He added, "I breathe lead."

Despite the chaos in his personal life, he still managed to write. In 1815 he published *Hebrew Melodies,* which contains what are perhaps his most famous lines: "She walks in beauty . . ." *The Bride of Abydos* was snapped up by the reading public because no one could miss the parallel between its tale of the doomed love between two cousins and the gossip about Byron and his sister that was starting to make the rounds. Annabella never publicly gave her reasons for leaving Byron. Her father had no such scruples, and he spread the news of the young lord's scandalous relationship with his half-sister. Byron, who had been the toast of the town only a little while before, was now universally reviled. He appeared at a reception given by Lady Jersey — astonishingly, bringing Augusta along as his companion — where most of the guests turned their backs on him. (Not all his sex appeal had evaporated, however; one former admirer stepped forward to tell him, "You had better have married *me.*") Socially, Byron became virtually a pariah. Now just a curiosity, when he went out in public, people followed him with telescopes and opera glasses. His debts were piling up as well. Byron agreed to a legal separation from Annabella and decided to leave England.

This, then, was the man to whom Claire Clairmont, seventeen and inexperienced, wrote a letter asking him to accept her love. Claire, having only recently returned to London from her "exile," wanted to make a conquest that could surpass Mary's. In Claire's eyes, there could be no bigger catch than Byron. So it was that she sent him this appeal:

> An utter stranger takes the liberty of addressing you. It is earnestly requested that for one moment you pardon the intrusion, & laying aside every remembrance of who & what you are, listen with a friendly ear. . . . It may seem a strange assertion, but it is not the less true that I place my happiness in your hands. . . .
>
> If you feel . . . tempted to read no more, or to cast with levity into the fire, what has been written by me with so much fearful

> inquietude, check your hand: my folly may be great, but the Creator ought not to destroy his Creature. If you shall condescend to answer the following question you will at least be rewarded by the gratitude I shall feel.
>
> If a woman, whose reputation has yet remained unstained, if without either guardian or husband to control she should throw herself upon your mercy, if with a beating heart she should confess the love she has borne you many years, if she should secure to you secrisy [*sic*] & safety, if she should return your kindness with fond affection & unbounded devotion could you betray her, or would you be silent as the grave?

The message was signed with a false name, though Claire soon revealed her true one.

Byron did not respond. He received many such requests from young women, though few as determined as Claire. She wrote him several more such letters, including one that informed him, "I have called twice on you but your Servants declare you to be out of town." She claimed to need his advice: "I am now wavering between the adoption of a literary life or of a theatrical career." She tried to impress him by quoting Dante in the original Italian, "Lasciate ogni speranza, voi ch'entrate" [abandon all hope, ye who enter here]," and commenting, "I think it is a most admirable description of marriage."

Only the letters she wrote him still exist, but it is evident from them that at some point he began to write her back. Why he did so is unclear. Her sheer persistence may have impressed him — she says he called her "a little fiend" (a name that he also used for Caroline Lamb). In one letter, Claire sent him some of Shelley's poems, her way of letting Byron know that she was Shelley's companion. Claire asked Byron to give Shelley advice: "If you think ill of his compositions I hope you will speak — he may improve by your remarks." As it happened, Shelley himself had earlier sent Byron a copy of *Queen Mab,* and Byron had been impressed.

The Shelley reference may have been Claire's trump card, for Byron had heard of Shelley's running away with "the daughters of Godwin," and Byron too was known as an admirer of Godwin. At any rate, he agreed to meet Claire, not at his home, but at a room at the Drury Lane Theatre, where he was a "literary advisor." Dante's warning should have been on her mind, because she was entering the world of the man whose charm and beauty made him, as mothers warned their daughters, "the most dangerous man in Europe."

Claire used the meeting to expand the relationship. Now she sent him requests to come to his house. Byron apparently expressed some interest in meeting Mary, and Claire responded, "I will bring her to you whenever you shall appoint." In a later letter, however, she started to set down conditions: "Will you be so good as to prepare your servants for the visit, for she [Mary] is accustomed to be surrounded by her own circle who treat her with the greatest politeness." The meeting went well, and Claire wrote to Byron afterward, slipping in a request that indicates she knew of his plans to leave England: "Mary is delighted with you as I knew she would be; she entreats me in private to obtain your address abroad that we may, if possible, have again the pleasure of seeing you. She perpetually exclaims, 'How mild he is! how gentle! So different from what I expected.'"

But the affair was not moving quickly enough for Claire, and she cast aside any feigned delicacy to take the initiative. She sent Byron a letter that plainly offered him her sexual favors: "Have you then any objection to the following plan? On Thursday Evening we may go out of town together by some stage or mail about the distance of 10 or 12 miles. there we shall be free & unknown; we can return early the next morning. I have arranged every thing here so that the slightest suspicion may not be excited." Many years later, Claire explained her actions:

> I was young, and vain, and poor. He was famous beyond all precedent, so famous that people, and especially young people, hardly considered him as a man at all, but rather as a god. His beauty was haunting as his fame, and he was all-powerful in the direction in which my ambition turned. It seems to me almost needless to say that the attentions of a man like this, with all London at his feet, very quickly completely turned the head of a girl in my position; and when you recollect that I was brought up to consider marriage

> not only as a useless but as an absolutely sinful custom, that only bigotry made necessary, you will scarcely wonder at the result, which you know.

It was not very difficult to get into Byron's bed, and Claire soon found herself his mistress. Or as Byron later described the affair, "if a girl of eighteen comes prancing to you at all hours, there is but one way . . ." It meant little to Byron — he insisted to Augusta, "I am not in love — nor have any love left for any." But to Claire it was a transforming experience. Years later she called the sexual experience perfect. She scribbled on a note to Byron: "God bless you — I *never* was so happy." In old age, however, she would have another view of the situation. "I am unhappily the victim of a *happy passion;* I had one like all things perfect in its kind, it was fleeting and mine lasted ten minutes but these ten minutes have discomposed the rest of my life."

In fact her involvement with Byron in England was more like two months than ten minutes. Toward the end of it, she asked more and more insistently what his address overseas would be. "I assure you," she wrote, "nothing shall tempt me to come to Geneva by myself since you disapprove of it [and] as I cannot but feel that such conduct would be highly indelicate." In the end, he gave her only the address, "Geneva, Poste Restante," the equivalent of general delivery. That would not deter Claire, who proved even more persistent than Caroline Lamb, and had another trump card to play: she was pregnant, a secret she would keep until the summer.

Byron, though deeply in debt, had a coach specially built for his travels in Europe — an exact replica of the one Napoleon had used. Virtually a palace on wheels, it was large enough to hold his bed, a traveling library, and a chest with a complete dinner service for two. It required four to six horses to pull it, and drew crowds wherever Byron traveled. The bill for it was five hundred pounds. It was characteristic of Byron that he never paid it. He fled England in April 1816. A mob of creditors descended on his London home almost immediately, stripping it of everything of value.

CHAPTER SIX

THE SUMMER OF DARKNESS

I busied myself to think of a story.— a story to rival those which had excited us to this task. One which would speak to the mysterious fears of our nature, and awaken thrilling horror — one to make the reader dread to look around, to curdle the blood, and quicken the beatings of the heart. If I did not accomplish these things, my ghost story would be unworthy of its name.

— Mary Shelley, introduction to *Frankenstein*, 1831

MARY SHELLEY WROTE the words above some fifteen years after the "haunted summer" of 1816 on Lake Geneva. Her journals for that crucial summer, along with all but two letters, are lost — possibly destroyed intentionally in the image-cleansing effort that she and her daughter-in-law undertook later. Their absence leaves a gap in our knowledge, and requires us to accept Mary's explanation for the source of her inspiration.

The forces that brought together the five young people who met at Byron's villa are clear enough. Byron himself was fleeing England and the scandal that enveloped his name. He intended to spend the summer relaxing, but not so far away that friends from England could not visit him. France was less appealing to him now that the monarchy had been restored, and so he chose Switzerland as a base. Claire, of course, *had* to pursue Byron because he was her love-trophy and the father of the child growing within her. Claire had disclosed the latter fact to no one else as yet; instead, she enlisted Shelley and Mary as her companions by revealing only the first of her secrets: she had become Byron's lover.

But, still, why did Mary agree to go? It must have seemed like a repetition of her original elopement with Shelley, in which Claire tagged along. Moreover, Mary now was nursing a five-month-old son, William, and that could not have made traveling any easier. Shelley, still complaining of illness, had wanted to go to sunny Italy that summer, but — intrigued by the possibility of meeting Byron — his intentions changed after Claire's announcement. So Mary had to follow him, even if reluctantly, unaware that she was heading toward her destiny, but perhaps sensing that Byron could help her accomplish what she had to do.

The spectre of her mother always hung over Mary, reminding her that she had an obligation to live up to her heritage, to prove herself a worthy daughter. Now that Mary had incurred the displeasure of her revered father, it seemed even more important for her to achieve something momentous, as her parents had. Living, studying, reading with Shelley had taught Mary a great deal, and she was conscious of her ripening talents. Would it not be possible, she may have asked herself, that she could learn even more from Byron, a man renowned for his creative genius?

The act of creation and the supremacy of imagination were, of course, of central concern to all the Romantic writers. From her girlhood, Mary had listened to discussions of creativity among the visitors at her father's home. Samuel Coleridge had written that imagination is an "echo of the Infinite." William Blake believed that man could become divine through love and imagination, and he combined poetry and art to tap the deepest resources of the human psyche. Mary's own creation, a man who hoped to assume divine powers as the father of a brand-new race of humans, would be right in line with this creative tradition.

During that fateful summer in Geneva, nature showed the full force of its power. Byron, Shelley, and Mary all wrote letters about the unusual weather. Byron complained, "We have had lately such stupid mists — fogs — rains — and perpetual density — that one would think Castlereagh [a British Tory foreign minister hated by Byron] had the foreign affairs of the kingdom of Heaven also — upon his hands." Not since the year of Mary's birth had the weather been this bad. Unknown to them, the frightening natural phenomena were the result of a catastrophic volcanic eruption in the Dutch East Indies (now Indonesia) the year before. The cataclysm literally tore the top off Mount Tambora, reducing its height by 3,600 feet and sending some thirty-five cubic *miles* of debris into the air — the greatest such disaster in recorded history. The dust particles dispersed in the atmosphere and eventually circled the globe, cutting off the light of the sun, cooling air temperatures, and causing frequent storms.

Thunderstorms punctuate Mary's novel just as they did her summer, and in the most prosaic of ways a storm played a part in the novel's creation: it forced the five friends indoors, where the contest began. Many years later on a return trip to Geneva with her son, Mary would see her achievement as part of her time in Switzerland "when first I stepped out from childhood into life." Viewed in isolation, her novel appeared with all the unpredictable brilliance of a jagged bolt of lightning. But the emotions surrounding that summer had come from a long-brewing storm that at long last liberated Mary's creativity. She blossomed with a masterpiece that made her Mary Wollstonecraft's true daughter.

On May 2, 1816, the Shelley party — Percy, Mary, Claire and little William — set out from England. They retraced the route of their elopement trip two years earlier, but this time had more money and could travel in style by closed carriage. Mary's spirits rose, for she was leaving behind her disapproving father as well as the melancholy she had felt on the anniversary of the death of her first child.

When they reached France, Claire sent a note to Byron's Geneva address, using Mary as bait: "you will I suppose wish to see Mary who talks & looks at you with admiration; you will, I dare say, fall in love with her; she is very handsome & very amiable & you will no doubt be blest in your attachment; nothing could afford me more pleasure."

The travelers moved through France to the border with Switzerland, where they had to ascend a steep pass over the Jura Mountains. Riding in a carriage drawn by four horses, with ten men walking alongside to steady it on the treacherous mountain road, they left the town of Les Rousses just as night was falling. While snow pelted the windows and the men outside yelled commands at each other, the carriage struggled up the rugged terrain. Mary, peering out, was thrilled by the awesome scenery, finding it "desolate" yet "sublime."

On May 14, the Shelley party descended from the peaks to the shore of Lake Geneva. They took a suite of rooms at the Hotel d'Angleterre in

Secheron, a suburb on the outskirts of Geneva. Mary was energized by the beauty of the snow-capped Alps that hovered around them, "the majestic Mont Blanc, highest and queen of all." Three days after their arrival, she wrote to Fanny in exhilaration, "I feel as happy as a new-fledged bird, and hardly care what twig I fly to, so that I may try my new-found wings." She and Shelley rented a small sailboat and took it out on the lake. Mary treasured those happy moments, when if the weather permitted they often stayed out till ten o'clock in the evening and on their return were "saluted by the delightful scent of flowers and new mown grass, and the chirp of grasshoppers, and the song of the evening birds." She and Shelley continued their literary pursuits, reading and writing all morning long. Mary started to write a children's book that she later gave to her father to publish. The couple also began to translate Godwin's *Political Justice* into French as another gift to the greedy philosopher, who sent Shelley a letter with the exciting news that Godwin had found someone willing to purchase some of Shelley's property, so that Shelley could give Godwin more money.

Like other tourists, they explored. The area around Geneva had many literary associations. Such people as John Milton, Voltaire, the historian Edward Gibbon, and — for them, best of all — Rousseau had been born nearby or had lived in temporary homes along the lake by the city. That summer, the well-known writer Madame de Staël, former participant in the French Revolution (who had fled during the Terror), lived nearby, as usual hosting both intellectuals and the socially prominent at her salon. It was a bracing atmosphere.

Meanwhile, Claire was anxious because Byron, who had left England before them, had not yet arrived. She visited the post office and saw, uncollected, the letter she had sent him from Paris. She now left a second one, saying, "I leave this for you that you may write me a little note when you do arrive."

Byron was taking his time. His huge Napoleonic carriage (with the initials L. B. prominently painted on the sides) attracted attention, and crowds gathered round it to catch a glimpse of the most notorious man in Europe. His estranged wife, Annabella, who received news of him regularly, learned that "the curiosity to see him was so great that many ladies accoutred themselves as chambermaids for the purpose of obtaining under that disguise a nearer inspection."

Byron was accompanied by his longtime valet, Fletcher, and his personal physician, the young, handsome, and earnest John Polidori. Polidori was as much interested in a literary career as a medical one, and unknown to Byron, the doctor had been promised five hundred pounds by Byron's own publisher to write an account of the poet's European tour. When they left England, Polidori began a journal to use as a source. Like other literary "evidence" about the group, it does not exist in original form. It begins on April 24 and continues to the end of the year, but there is a significant and frustrating gap from June 30 to September 16. In addition, the diary was later copied and edited by Polidori's sister, who burned the original after removing passages she found improper — and because her brother was traveling with Byron, they must have been numerous.

Polidori was from a distinguished literary family. His Italian grandfather, Agostino Ansano Polidori, had combined literature with medicine by writing a long poem in *ottava rima* on the human skeleton, titled *Osteologia*. John's father, Gaetano, studied law, but went on to become a secretary for Vittorio Alfieri, the Italian Romantic poet. He remained with Alfieri for four years and nursed him through a near-fatal illness, but it was rumored that the poet was jealous of his assistant's good looks, which attracted women. After parting ways with Alfieri, Gaetano went to England, where he met and married Anna Maria Pierce, a governess. John William, the oldest of their four sons, was born on September 7, 1795. Though Gaetano himself was not a devout Catholic, he raised his sons to be Roman Catholics, while the couple's four daughters were brought up in the Anglican Church. Catholics in England had freedom to worship in their faith at this time, but they still lacked political rights. (Byron had spoken out for Catholic emancipation in the House of Lords.)

Young John went to Catholic schools and excelled at his studies. His religious education left a mark on the boy, whose first choice for a career was to be a priest. His father, however, urged him to study medicine, and John always did what his father wanted even when he resented it. At the age of fifteen, Polidori entered the University of Edinburgh, one of the most highly regarded medical schools in Europe. Here he studied all aspects of medicine — anatomy, surgery, chemistry, pharmacy — and one extracurricular activity necessitated by the serious shortage of cadavers for anatomical study: along with other students, Polidori dabbled in grave-robbing, an activity that certainly helped foster a Gothic imagination.

Polidori always had ambivalent feelings about medical school. At one point, he wrote home and expressed the desire to go fight for Italian independence. His father responded that he was "a madman fit for a strait waistcoat." He advised his son to cool down and finish his degree. John obeyed but showed his feelings in a letter to his father: "You wound my heart by blaming me for what I cannot prevent. . . . The first part of your letter is nothing but a thorn, which pierces me the more as I always wait for your letters in the hope of something pleasant."

With his soft, dark eyes and curly hair, Polidori, like Lord Byron, was physically gorgeous, but his father's bullying had humiliated him many times and he never established a sense of confidence. In addition, high expectations had put relentless pressure on him. All of this left him moody and overly sensitive, traits that made him difficult to deal with. He took up writing poetry to console himself, composing *Ximenes,* a tale of revenge and seduction. It also featured a suicide, perhaps the beginning of Polidori's obsession with that topic.

Polidori always seemed to be searching for a father figure who would approve of him. One of the first was William Taylor, a Norwich intellectual. Taylor was a scholar and translator but he had a dark side: he was fascinated with suicide and nightmares. Taylor helped John write the dissertation for his medical degree. Polidori had become interested in sleepwalking from reading fiction about it, and in the dissertation, he described a case of somnambulism (or as he termed it, oneirodynia) that his uncle Luigi, himself a fine doctor, had treated. The patient was a ten-year-old boy who did everything in his sleep — not only walked but used the chamber pot, attacked a servant, talked, and prayed. Polidori showed his literary bent by prefacing the dissertation with the sleepwalking scene from *Macbeth.* It earned him his degree at the age of nineteen, though he still did not particularly want to practice medicine.

Instead, Polidori tried his hand at writing for several British literary and political journals, and became involved with the fight against capital punishment, publishing an article, "On the Punishment of Death." Sir Henry Halford, a distinguished London physician, became interested in the young man and introduced him to Byron. It seemed like a good match; Byron needed a physician to travel with, because his frequent crash diets sometimes endangered his health. For Polidori, the poet was another potential father figure, who could help him achieve his aspirations for a writing career. Moreover, Polidori spoke Italian and French as well as English, which would be useful in traveling on the Continent.

Of course, it would likely have been better if Byron and Polidori had taken time to become better acquainted, but the poet hired Polidori just two days before he was about to leave England. It soon became clear that their personalities did not mesh well. Polidori continually tried to find some way of impressing Byron, but as with his father, he failed miserably. Byron quickly took a dislike to him, dubbing him "Polly Dolly," and making him a frequent target of his often-vicious wit.

It was probably just as well that Polidori was able to keep his journal out of Byron's hands, for the poet would have laughed at its prose. Polidori described their crossing the English Channel:

> The sea dashed over us, and all wore an aspect of grief . . . The stars shedding merely a twilight enabled me to see the phosphoric light of the broken foam in all its splendour. But the most beautiful moment was that of its first appearance: no sound around save the sullen rushing of the vessel, and the hoarse cries of the heaving sailor; no light save a melancholy twilight, which soothed the mind into forgetfulness of its grief for a while — a beautiful streak following the lead through the waves.

They landed at Ostend in Belgium. There, Polidori wrote breathlessly, "As soon as he reached his room, Lord Byron fell like a thunderbolt upon the chambermaid."

In more restrained language, Polidori wrote his sister Frances on May 2: "I am very pleased with Lord Byron. I am with him on the footing of an equal, everything alike: at present here we have a suite of rooms between us. I have my sitting-room at one end, he at the other. He has not shown any passion; though we have had nothing but a series of mishaps that have put *me* out of temper though they have not ruffled his." Polidori was too optimistic in describing the status of his relationship with the poet. Once, when they were in a hotel overlooking the Rhine, Byron set him straight. Polidori had boldly asked what Byron could do better than he, aside from writing poetry. Byron responded, "First . . . I can hit with a pistol the keyhole of that door. Secondly, I can swim across that river. . . . And thirdly, I can give you a d——d good thrashing."

Byron enjoyed visiting the sites of famous battles. While in Belgium, he and Polidori went to Waterloo, where only a year before, Napoleon had suffered his final defeat at the hands of a coalition led by England's Duke of Wellington. Though forty thousand men had died there, Byron wrote Hobhouse that the battlefield was "not much after Marathon & Troy" (both of which he had earlier seen), and because he admired Napoleon added, "I detest the cause & the victors — & the victory." Avoiding France, the travelers crossed Germany to Switzerland, stopping at Morat, the scene of a fifteenth-century battle where the Swiss had defeated the Burgundians in a bloody fight. Byron raided an ossuary, taking some bones as souvenirs. Writing to Hobhouse, he reported, "I brought away the leg and wing of a Burgundian."

Unlike Shelley, Byron did not like the Swiss. He called their country "a curst selfish, swinish country of brutes, placed in the most romantic region of the world. I never could bear the inhabitants, and still less their English visitors." Still, he was looking forward to his summer at one of the world's most beautiful locations. As Byron and Polidori were crossing the Jura, they tried to determine where the "clouds were mountains or the mountains clouds." When he saw the lake, which he called by its French name, Byron reported, "Lake Leman woos me with its crystal face."

On May 25, Byron and his party checked into the Hotel d'Angleterre, where the Shelley party was also staying. Signing the hotel register, the poet put down his age as one hundred, apparently because the journey had been so exhausting. The ever-vigilant Claire soon spotted his signature and sent a note: "I am sorry you are grown so old, indeed I suspected you were 200, from the slowness of your journey. I suppose your venerable age could not bear quicker travelling . . . I am so happy." Byron ignored her.

The day after he arrived, Byron received a letter from his friend Hobhouse informing him of Caroline Lamb's revenge. She had just published a bestselling novel titled *Glenarvon* — a wildly fictionalized account of her affair with Byron. The book was currently the talk of London, but Hobhouse noted loyally that it had only hurt Caroline's reputation further. He added,

> You will hardly believe it but there is not the least merit in the book in any way except in a letter beginning "I love you no more" which I suspect to be your's — Indeed she had the impudence to send a paragraph to some paper hinting that the whole novel is from the pen of Lord B.— I do not like to contradict it for fear of selling the book by propagating the lie — Her family are in a great quandry [*sic*] and know not what to do. I presume she is actually a personal terror to them.

Caroline even had the effrontery to lift two lines from Byron's own poem, *The Corsair,* to use as the epigraph for her book: "He left a name to all succeeding times, / Link'd with one virtue and a thousand crimes." Later in the year, when Byron read the book, he commented, "It seems to me that, if the authoress had written the *truth,* and nothing but the truth — the whole truth — the romance would not only have been more *romantic,* but more entertaining. As for the likeness, the picture can't be good. I did not sit long enough."

Byron had another woman, closer to hand, to worry about. He had not responded to Claire's letters, but since they were all staying in the same hotel, it was impossible to avoid her. Two days after Byron's arrival, Claire saw him and Polidori take a boat onto the lake; by the time they returned, she had brought reinforcements, Mary and Shelley, to the quay, where she introduced them. Shelley, she knew, was intensely curious about Byron, and fortunately Byron took to him at once. Byron extended an invitation to Shelley to dine that evening with him — pointedly excluding Claire and Mary.

Polidori managed to insinuate himself into the dinner, but he wasn't a very good listener, for his journal entry for that date includes a description of Shelley that manages to be wrong on several counts: "the author of *Queen Mab*, came; bashful, shy, consumptive [incorrect diagnosis]; twenty-six [Shelley was twenty-three]; separated from his wife; keeps the two daughters of Godwin [Claire wasn't Godwin's], who practice his theories." Polidori seemed to be under the impression that Claire and Shelley were lovers, although he realized that she was, or had been, Byron's as well.

A few days later, Polidori breakfasted with the group he thought of as "the Shelleys." Percy told a self-justifying story about his marriage to Harriet, claiming that when they met he had believed he was dying and married her only so she would benefit from his estate when he passed on. Shelley also told Polidori that his father had tried to consign him to a mental institution and that he was only saved from that horrible fate by Dr. Lind, his favorite teacher at Eton. This seems to have been self-dramatization on Percy's part.

The five young people, greatly talented but each terribly flawed, quickly drew closer together. Byron and Shelley, who could be standoffish with strangers, found themselves to be kindred spirits and soon began boating together. They had long conversations about all the subjects they were interested in — including art, literature, science, politics, and philosophy. It was the beginning of a lifelong friendship.

Byron also took up with Claire, who had refused to be ignored. She wrote him: "I have been in this weary hotel this fortnight & it seems so unkind, so cruel, of you to treat me with such marked indifference. Will you go straight up to the top of the house this evening at half past seven & I will infallibly be on the landing place & shew you the room."

He gave in. As he wrote Augusta later that summer: "Now — don't scold — but what could I do?— a foolish girl — in spite of all I could say or do — would come after me — or rather went before me — for I found her here. . . . I could not exactly play the Stoic with a woman — who had scrambled eight hundred miles to unphilosophize me."

Before long, the two parties became dissatisfied with the hotel and decided to find places to live on the opposite side of the lake. On June 1, the Shelley group became the first to leave, moving into the Maison Chapuis, a small waterside cottage by a cove on the southern shore where the two poets would keep a sailboat. The majesty of the scenery became even more awesome when the thunder and lightning raged and the Shelleys watched from their windows as the storms became "grander and more terrific." Mary wrote: "We watch them [the thunderstorms] as they approach from the opposite side of the lake, observing the lightning play among the clouds in various parts of the heavens, and dart in jagged figures upon the piny heights of Jura, dark with the shadow of the overhanging cloud, while perhaps the sun is shining cheerily upon us. One night we *enjoyed* a finer storm than I had ever before beheld."

Sometimes, as a storm was blowing up outside, Mary heard the sound of singing from the direction of the water. This was Byron's way of battling the winds, as he boldly crossed the lake in a small open boat in spite of the weather. Each evening he came to visit them and afterward, even as late as midnight, he would go back to the hotel in Secheron. Polidori, who avoided these trips, said that they were made "often whilst the storms were raging in the circling summits of the mountains around." The oarsman who rowed Byron's boat recalled that on one occasion, he warned the poet that they were in danger of sinking, and Byron stripped, ready to attempt to swim ashore if the boat foundered. At this time Byron was working on the third canto of *Childe Harold,* and it is clear from some of its stanzas that the strange weather provided inspiration for him:

The sky is changed!— and such a change! Oh night,
And storm, and darkness, ye are wondrous strong,
Yet lovely in your strength, as is the light
Of a dark eye in woman! Far along,
From peak to peak, the rattling crags among
Leaps the live thunder! Not from one lone cloud,
But every mountain now hath found a tongue,
And Jura answers, through her misty shroud,
Back to the joyous Alps, who call to her aloud!

And this is in the night: — Most glorious night!
Thou wert not sent for slumber! let me be
A sharer in thy fierce and far delight, —
A portion of the tempest and of thee!
How the lit lake shines, a phosphoric sea,
And the big rain comes dancing to the earth!
And now again 'tis black,— and now, the glee
Of the loud hills shakes with its mountain-mirth,
As if they did rejoice o'er a young earthquake's birth.

On the tenth of June, Byron rented the much larger Villa Diodati, "the prettiest place on all the Lake," he recalled, just a ten-minute walk from Shelley's new dwelling. From its second-floor balcony there was a stunning view of the water and the mountains beyond, but the house also attracted Byron because it had associations with John Milton, a poet he particularly admired. It had been the property of the Diodati family, one of whose members was Charles Diodati, Milton's schoolmate and only close friend. Their personalities had been opposites: Diodati was carefree and adventurous, Milton bookish and almost antisocial. Milton had spent some time at Lake Geneva with Diodati before the present villa house was built. Tragically, Diodati was destined to die young. In the elegy Milton had written for him, the poet said that they were "most intimate friends from childhood on." Their loving relationship had a deep resonance for Byron.

The new residences did not, however, guarantee privacy. Byron's reputation had preceded him, and the news that he was now involved with one or more of the Shelley group — famous in their own right — set the local rumor mills churning. English tourists could keep up to date with the news from home by reading the gossipy *Galignani's Messenger,* so they knew all about Byron, Caroline, Augusta, and Annabella. The chitchat about him was to be a continual nightmare for Byron. Jacques Dejean, the hotel proprietor, rented telescopes to his guests so they could watch the comings and goings at Villa Diodati. Some oglers mistook tablecloths hanging to dry over the balcony for petticoats — starting the story that the women took them off when they visited Byron. The poet remembered it bitterly: "There is no story so absurd that they did not invent it at my cost. I was watched by glasses [telescopes] on the opposite shore of the Lake, and by glasses too that must have had very distorted optics. I was waylaid in my evening drives — I was accused of corrupting all the *grisettes* [young girls] in the Rue Basse. I believe that they looked upon me as a man-monster." Unfortunately for those who hoped to glimpse a spicy scene through their telescopes, "it proved a wet, ungenial summer, and incessant rain often confined us for days to the house," as Mary recalled. Despite — or perhaps because of — this, many now believed that Byron was sleeping with both of the Godwin stepsisters. The Lutheran clergyman John Pye Smith, traveling in Switzerland that summer, wrote that on August 9, "at about a mile & a half from the town, we passed the house in which Lord Byron lives, in a sullen & disgraceful seclusion. Besides his servants, his only companions are two wicked women. He sees no company; and Mr. Ferriere told us that no person of respectability would visit him." The poet Robert Southey repeated some of these rumors and added that Byron and Shelley had formed a "League of Incest." Byron never forgave him for it, though he later pointed out reasonably that since none of them were actually blood kin to any of the others, incest could not have entered into their relations.

Lord Glenbie, another visitor to Geneva that summer, noted in his Swiss travel diary that Byron was being "cut" by everyone. Byron summed up the downside of fame in the lines:

With false Ambition what had I to do?
Little with love, and least of all with Fame!
And yet they came unsought, and with me grew,
And made me all which they can make — a Name.

Because the Villa Diodati was larger than the Shelley cottage, it became the favored place for the five young people to gather. Claire, who still had not revealed her pregnancy to anyone, hoped to put her relationship with Byron on a sounder basis — if nothing else, to persuade him to acknowledge her as his mistress. The only way she knew how to do this was pursue him.

Byron evidently used Polidori as a kind of chaperone to make it difficult for Claire to catch him alone. Polidori, meanwhile, developed a crush on Mary and sought to impress her with his knowledge of literature and science. Byron noticed this, and on one occasion prompted Polidori to make a fool of himself. Early one afternoon, as the two men stood on the second-floor balcony of the Villa Diodati, they saw Mary stroll up the hill toward the villa. Rain had made the ground slick and she was having a little difficulty. Byron told Polidori, "Now you who wish to be gallant ought to jump down this small height, and offer your arm." At once, Polidori swung himself over the balcony rail, but when he dropped to the ground, he slipped badly and sprained his ankle. Byron could not stifle his laughter, even though he helped carry Polidori inside and gave him a pillow for his foot. It turned out to be a serious injury that hobbled Polidori for the rest of the year.

Polidori got his revenge. While the group was out boating, whether by design or accident, Polidori struck Lord Byron with an oar on his knee. The blow was hard enough to cause Byron to turn his head away to hide the pain. As reported by Thomas Moore, Byron's friend and biographer:

> After a moment he [Lord Byron] said, "Be so kind, Polidori, another time, to take more care, for you hurt me very much."—"I am glad of it," answered the other; "I am glad to see you can suffer pain." In a calm suppressed tone, Lord Byron replied, "Let me advise you, Polidori, when you, another time, hurt any one, not to express your satisfaction. People don't like to be told that those who give them pain are glad of it; and they cannot always command their anger. It was with some difficulty that I refrained from throwing you into the water; and, but for Mrs. Shelley's presence, I should probably have done some such rash thing." This was said without ill temper, and the cloud soon passed away.

Byron did much of his best work late at night — he went to bed at dawn and did not get up until the afternoon — and the four others adjusted to his schedule. For Shelley and Mary, this gave them the mornings to study and read and sail. Mary happily had Shelley to herself: they had hired a twenty-one-year-old Swiss woman called Elise to help take care of William, and Claire was distracted by her desperate pursuit of Byron.

Mary did, however, have a new rival for Shelley's attention. Everything exotic and strange attracted Byron, and Shelley fell into that category. When Byron finally rose from his bed, he often went sailing with Shelley in the boat the two of them had purchased.

Byron was intensely stimulated by Shelley's ideas and it showed in the outpouring of work he accomplished that summer — he completed the third canto of *Childe Harold*, wrote *The Prisoner of Chillon*, and began *Manfred*. Their friendship had less influence on Shelley's poetry; Byron may even have had an inhibiting influence on the younger man, who later said, "I despair of rivalling Lord Byron, and there is no other with whom it is worth contending."

Mary was not unaware of Byron's handsome profile. She would later write of him, "Beauty sat on his countenance and power beamed from his eye." He and Shelley were such opposites: one fair, the other dark; the younger man frail and neurasthenic, the elder robust and athletic. Shelley's voice was high-pitched, while Byron's was deep and dramatic. Nonetheless, for Mary, Byron's intellect was his true attraction. She was flattered by any signs that he admired her opinions.

The two men had contrasting attitudes toward women. Shelley wanted intellectual companions as well as lovers, whereas Byron held women in low esteem and, with the exception of his sister, did not take them seriously. That attitude certainly extended to Claire, who was merely a sex object to him.

When storms drove the five inside, they read aloud to one another or simply talked late into the night. Mary described those wet evenings to Thomas Moore: "We often sat up in conversation till the morning light. There was never a lack of subjects, and grave or gay, we were always interested." Byron usually chose the topic of conversation and directed his remarks at Shelley, showing that he didn't care to hear the others' views. Mary the Dormouse listened intently as Byron and Shelley discussed art, literature, science, politics, and philosophy. The two men were fundamentally different in their view of humankind. Byron believed that people were born with a set nature and they could choose only to deal with, protest, or endure their human conditions. Shelley felt that people were more plastic — that they could succeed in perfecting themselves and overcome anything.

One night, the conversation turned to what Mary called "the nature of the principle of life." The theory of vitalism, popular among the Romantics' contemporaries, held that an élan vital, or life force, distinguished living things from nonliving things. Some thought that there was a connection between the élan vital and electricity. Byron, Shelley, and Polidori had heard of Luigi Galvani, an Italian scientist, who had shown in 1786 that he could produce muscular contractions in dead frogs by touching them with a pair of scissors during an electrical storm. In so doing, Galvani conjectured the existence of an "animal electricity" that produced life. Galvani's nephew, Giovanni Aldini, carried the work a step farther. In 1803 Aldini performed experiments on human corpses, using a Leyden jar. He claimed that by applying electricity, he could make dead bodies sit up, raise their arms, clench their fists, and blow out candles placed before their mouths. Stories had circulated in Europe that dead bodies had even been brought back to life.

Seated quietly to the side, sometimes making clear copies of Byron's poems that could be sent to his publisher (Byron hated this kind of tedious work, which both Mary and Claire did for him), Mary filed away everything she heard. She was not completely ignorant of modern science, though her father had not made it a part of her education. As a girl, she might have heard Humphry Davy discuss his experiments with light, heat, and gases at her father's house, although Godwin indicated what he thought of science when, referring to Davy, he said, "What a pity such a man should degrade his vast talents to Chemistry." But living with Shelley, a science enthusiast from boyhood, had broadened Mary's knowledge.

What Mary brought to the summer was a lifetime of reading. Just during 1815 and the summer of 1816, she read works by Goethe, Schiller, Calderon, Dante, Tasso, Ariosto, Alfieri, Shakespeare, Milton, Coleridge, Matthew "Monk" Lewis, as well as Byron and Shelley. Many novels, most of them in the popular Gothic genre, were also on her reading lists — as indeed they were for the other members of the group as well. The Romantic writers and thinkers did not view the genre with disdain, but rather embraced it as part of their revolt against eighteenth-century rationalism. Gothic authors, they felt, were tapping into deep, primal feelings.

On June 16, the weather was particularly dramatic and as the five huddled around the fireplace of the Villa Diodati, Byron selected a volume of German ghost stories (called "flutter" stories because of their effect on the hearts of readers) translated into French. The book was *Fantasmagoriana, ou Recueil d'histoires d'apparitions de spectres, revenants, fantomes, etc.* The word *fantasmagorie* describes the theatrical art of making ghosts and other phenomena appear through optical illusions. The spectacle was invented in 1798 when the Belgian Étienne Gaspard Roberts staged a show using lanterns and transparent slides to project images. The shows frightened and delighted audiences with visions of disembodied heads, skeletons, and spectral figures. Mary and Shelley had in fact attended one of these spectacles in London on December 28, 1814, at the same performance where they had heard Andrew Crosse's lecture on electricity. Mary must have remembered that occasion when Byron read the title of the book, for she was fond of words, and she had noted "phantasmagoria" in her journal eighteen months earlier.

The tales in the book Byron now read from were written in the same spirit as Roberts's show. Byron obviously chose them for the effects he could create, reading in his sonorous, emotional voice. Anyone who has ever been in an isolated house during a storm knows the feelings the imagination can produce in that situation. Every lightning flash and thunderclap made Byron's listeners jump. Each movement of the shadows thrown by the candles added to the nervous tension.

One of the stories in the collection concerned twin sisters, one of whom had died. A young duke arrives at the castle of the dead girl's father; he relates that he has recently seen her in Paris. The girl's father has her grave opened because he wonders if she may have been "re-animated." The body is still there, but a year after the girl's death, it has remained uncorrupted. At the climax of the story, at the surviving girl's wedding, the dead sister appears and takes her place as the lover of the groom. Mary could not have helped noting the comparison between herself and Claire, who had competed with her for Shelley earlier, and had now returned to intrude again. But before Mary had much time to ponder any parallels, Byron began another tale, one that he must certainly have known spookily mirrored Mary and Percy's own situation. This was "La Revenant," about a girl who defies her father by marrying someone he does not approve of; later she loses her baby and then is abandoned by her husband. Through it all, thunder cracked and the moaning of winds provided a sort of lamenting chorus.

Recalling that fateful evening years later, Mary did not describe herself as being particularly disturbed by the tales. Instead, she said they "excited in us a playful desire of imitation." Byron, pleased with their reaction, suggested that each of them write a ghost story. To Mary, for some reason, he gave added encouragement. "You and I," he told her "will publish ours together." Byron was not in the habit of putting himself on an equal basis with a woman, and certainly not from the standpoint of writing ability, so he may very well have said this simply to annoy Claire or Polidori, who clearly would have liked to publish something as Byron's equal. But once said, a die was cast. (Mary herself ignored Claire's role in the contest when she wrote later, "There were four of us.")

Those few words of encouragement from Byron were sufficient to spur Mary. "I busied myself," she wrote "*to think of a story,* — a story to rival those which had excited us to this task. One which would speak to the mysterious fears of our nature, and awaken thrilling horror." But as creative people know, the Muse resists when commanded to speak. Frustratingly, Mary had trouble getting started.

Polidori, eager at the chance to please Byron, struggled as well. He noted in his journal on the next day, "The ghost-stories begun by all but me." Byron, of course, had no difficulties, for he always had a topic: himself. The hero of his piece was an aristocrat, Augustus Darvell, who was traveling in Turkey. The story's narrator, his companion, realizes that Darvell is possessed by some mysterious secret. Darvell even makes the narrator promise to bury him after his death and tell no one where. But after eight manuscript pages, Byron grew bored with the effort and quit. He felt more at home in verse than he did in prose. (Even his letters are series of thoughts separated by dashes, as if he were writing lines of poetry.)

For his part, Shelley began a story that Mary later said was "founded on the experiences of his early life," but like Byron he soon gave up the effort. Ever-loyal Mary explained that Shelley was "more apt to embody ideas and sentiments in the radiance of brilliant imagery, and in the music of the most melodious verse that adorns our language, than to invent the machinery of a story." Apparently he had lost the ability that had enabled him to write two Gothic novels while still a teenager.

Polidori, laid up with his injured ankle, finally came up with something. Fifteen years later, Mary remembered Polidori's story with words that were less than admiring:

> Poor Polidori had some terrible idea about a skull-headed lady, who was so punished for peeping through a key-hole — what to see I forget — something very shocking and wrong of course; but when she was reduced to a worse condition than the renowned Tom of Coventry ["Peeping Tom," who was blinded because he looked at Lady Godiva during her famous ride], he did not know what to do with her, and was obliged to despatch her to the tomb of the Capulets, the only place for which she was fitted.

Perhaps as a result of Mary's lack of enthusiasm, Polidori abandoned this effort. But eventually another idea came to him, different from the one she describes, and he would develop it into a figure of horror whose only rival was her own creation.

Vampires were among the topics discussed by the circle of five at Byron's villa that summer. The hidden secret of the hero of Byron's aborted ghost story was that he was actually one of those frightening undead creatures that are found in the myths of many cultures. The idea that life could be extended, even to the extent of immortality, by consuming the blood of others was an old one — and of course it fit right in with the overriding question of the summer: what was the source of the élan vital that distinguished living things from nonliving? Romantic writers — including Byron, who had referred to vampires in his poem *The Giaour* — found the image of beings who fed on the lifeblood of others an appealing metaphor. And that metaphor was sometimes applied to the brutally self-centered poets themselves. When Shelley had abandoned his pregnant wife for Mary, Harriet had written a friend, "In short, the man I once loved is dead. This is a vampire." She was not the only one to think of Shelley, or Byron, in such terms.

The rains continued, and the group still gathered nightly at Byron's villa. Shelley was very fond of tea, and Byron had it served even late at night. Once more, around midnight of June 17–18, the group started to tell ghost stories. This time Byron showed them a poem he had received just before leaving England. It was "Christabel," by Samuel Taylor Coleridge, whom Byron had mocked in *English Bards and Scotch Reviewers*. The older poet bore no grudge, and now wanted Byron's help in getting a new book of poetry published. Mary, of course, knew Coleridge well; all her life she remembered the thrill of hiding behind the sofa with Claire, listening to him read *The Rime of the Ancient Mariner* to her father and a group of his friends. More recently, Byron had been similarly entranced, as Coleridge had recited for him one of his new poems, "Kubla Khan," written under the influence of opium. The once-critical Byron had been overcome with the magnificence of Coleridge's voice and words, and was more than willing to help by sending "Kubla Khan" and "Christabel" to his publisher, John Murray.

"Christabel" fit right in with the group's other readings at the villa. It was about a female vampire, Geraldine, who sucks the strength from the pure maiden Christabel. The stanza in which Geraldine undresses and exposes her true nature to Christabel reads:

Then drawing in her breath aloud,
Like one that shuddered, she unbound
The cincture from beneath her breast;
Her silken robe, and inner vest,
Dropt to her feet, and full in view,
Behold! her bosom and half her side —

A sight to dream of, not to tell!
Oh shield her! shield sweet Christabel.

At that point Byron paused for dramatic effect. The silence was broken by a shriek; Shelley stood up, put his hand to his head, and ran out of the room screaming. Polidori and Byron followed, and the doctor calmed Shelley by throwing water in his face and administering some ether. Polidori described the incident:

> *. . . his lordship having recited the beginning of Christabel . . . the whole took so strong a hold of Mr. Shelly's [sic] mind, that he suddenly started up and ran out of the room. The physician and Lord Byron followed, and discovered him leaning against a mantel-piece, with cold drops of perspiration trickling down his face . . . enquiring into the cause of his alarm, they found that his wild imagination having pictured to him the bosom of one of the ladies with eyes . . . he was obliged to leave the room in order to destroy the impression.*

Shelley had long shown an obsession with breasts, and he harbored decidedly complicated feelings about them. (His bizarre attempt to breast-feed Harriet's baby had been but one manifestation of this.) He had been looking at Mary just before his hysterics began. Was he thinking that it was *her* breasts that had eyes, and if so, what secrets did they perceive when they looked at him? Whatever the case, Byron was shocked at Shelley's behavior, for as he noted in a letter to a friend, Shelley did not lack courage.

Mary might have used the incident as a spur to her own creativity, but still her Muse was not speaking. As she came down to breakfast each morning, the others asked her, "Have you thought of a story?" and, she recalled, "each morning I was forced to reply with a mortifying negative." She wanted so much to achieve something great, to compete with people whom she respected. In some ways, the summer had been happy, but many concerns dragged at her spirits, distracting her from what she wanted to do. Though she was not yet nineteen, she had experienced the death of one child and now had an infant to care for. She was, still, an unmarried mother in an age when that was far more disgraceful than today. The father of her children had turned out to be more mercurial than she had bargained for, and now complained of ill health though he had not yet turned twenty-four. Claire's presence was a constant reminder that Percy might at any time decide to take up with another woman. Despite all the philosophical reasons for regarding marriage as slavery and prostitution, Mary yearned for exclusivity. Not having it hurt her self-confidence; she blamed herself for looking for unconditional love from people — Godwin and Shelley — unable to give it. Finally, her beloved father was not speaking to her, even though Mary had presented him with a grandson named William. She had to do more than that to win back his affection.

Writers are often asked the question, "Where do you get your ideas?" Fifteen years later, Mary remembered quite specifically how the idea of *Frankenstein* had come to her. On June 22, Byron and Shelley were planning to go on a long trip around the lake together. Though Mary made no objection to being left behind, it was another reminder that the men preferred to discuss intellectual matters with each other, rather than with her. That night, perhaps for the last time in a week or so, the group gathered again at the Villa Diodati, but instead of ghost stories, Byron and Shelley resumed their discussions of great things —"various philosophical doctrines"— while Mary, the daughter of a philosopher, remained "a devout but nearly silent listener."

According to Mary, one of the topics that night was "the nature of the principle of life, and whether there was any probability of its ever being discovered and communicated." Of particular interest was an experiment said to have been performed by Erasmus Darwin. Darwin, someone said during the discussion at Villa Diodati, had "preserved a piece of vermicelli in a glass case, till by some extraordinary means it began to move with voluntary motion." It isn't clear just what might have impelled Darwin to try to preserve pasta in a glass case, or what the "extraordinary means" were that caused it to move. Mary seemed aware of possible doubts when she wrote later about that evening, for she inserted the remark, "I speak not of what the Doctor really did, or said that he did, but, as more to my purpose, of what was then spoken of as having been done by him."

Listening to the conversation, Mary slipped into one of those silent reveries that took her deep within herself. "Perhaps," she recalled thinking, "a corpse would be re-animated." Galvanism had indicated such things were possible. Then she carried her speculations to the next level, where art began to grow. "Perhaps," she mused, "the component parts of a creature might be manufactured, brought together, and endued with vital warmth."

The conversation at the villa continued long into the night, "and even the witching hour had gone by, before we retired to rest," wrote Mary. But late as it was, she could not sleep. "My imagination, unbidden, possessed and guided me, gifting the successive images that arose in my mind with a vividness far beyond the usual bounds of reverie." Though the room was pitch black, she closed her eyes tightly. That did not shut out her "mental vision," and she saw the figure of a man, a "pale student of unhallowed arts," whose name she did not yet know, "kneeling beside the thing he had put together. I saw the hideous phantasm of a man stretched out, and then, on the working of some powerful engine, show signs of life, and stir with an uneasy, half vital motion." It lived.

In Mary's vision, the "artist" responsible for this creation was terrified by "his odious handywork." He fled, hoping that the process he had set in motion would cease by itself, that "the slight spark of life which he had communicated would fade . . . that the silence of the grave would quench for ever the transient existence of the hideous corpse." Like Mary, the creator of the monster retreated to bed. Unlike her, he found refuge in sleep, "but he is awakened; he opens his eyes; behold the horrid thing stands at his bedside, opening his curtains, and looking on him with yellow, watery, but speculative eyes."

Just the thought of it startled her and as she opened her own eyes, terror-stricken, Mary half expected to find the monstrous creature standing over her. She looked around the darkened room where she slept, trying to fasten on something real. "I wished to exchange the ghastly image of my fancy for the realities around," she recalled fifteen years later. "I see them still; the very room, the dark *parquet,* the closed shutters, with the moonlight struggling through, and the sense I had that the glassy lake and white high Alps were beyond." But the "hideous phantom" would not leave her mind. She tried to think of something else . . . "my tiresome unlucky ghost story! O! if I could only contrive one which would frighten my reader as I myself had been frightened that night."

Then she realized what had happened: "I have found it!" she exclaimed to the darkness.

Frankenstein.

CHAPTER SEVEN

"A HIDEOUS PHANTOM"

Did I request thee, Maker, from my clay
To mould me man? Did I solicit thee
From darkness to promote me?

— *Paradise Lost,* John Milton, 1667

THE MORNING AFTER her "waking vision," Mary was able to announce that she had "*thought of a story.*" She needed no further inspiration, but promptly sat down at her work table and started to write. "It was on a dreary night of November," were her first words (in the voice of Victor Frankenstein), "that I beheld the accomplishment of my toils." (This would eventually be the opening of chapter 4 in the 1818 edition and chapter 5 of the 1831 revised version of Mary's *Frankenstein.*) In character as Victor, she described the creation of the monster in terms similar to her vision.

> With an anxiety that almost amounted to agony, I collected the instruments of life around me, that I might infuse a spark of being into the lifeless thing that lay at my feet. It was already one in the morning; the rain pattered dismally against the panes, and my candle was nearly burnt out, when, by the glimmer of the half-extinguished light, I saw the dull yellow eye of the creature open; it breathed hard, and a convulsive motion agitated its limbs.

The agelong dream of humanity has been realized, and death has been conquered. Yet Victor realizes almost at once that his creation is a "catastrophe."

He had gathered human parts from dissecting rooms and charnel houses with the intention of producing a perfect creature — and now it is evident that he has desperately failed. It is, he tells the reader, beyond his ability to describe

> the wretch whom with such infinite pains and care I had endeavoured to form. His limbs were in proportion, and I had selected his features as beautiful. Beautiful! — Great God! His yellow skin scarcely covered the work of muscles and arteries beneath; his hair was of a lustrous black, and flowing; his teeth of a more pearly whiteness; but these luxuriances only formed a more horrid contrast with his watery eyes, that seemed almost the same colour as the dun white sockets in which they were set, his shrivelled complexion, and straight black lips.

The words flowed easily. Mary had formed the basic idea of her story, and at this point she intended that it be only a short one. The scientist Victor Frankenstein discovers the mystery of life, the secret of animation. He constructs and brings to life a creature of immense size, but the nameless monster's distorted features and terrifying proportions isolate the creature from the rest of the world. People see only his ugliness and do not realize that he has tender inner feelings. Frankenstein himself is revolted by his creation, and rejects it, leaving it to his own devices. The creature goes out into the world, seeking love from his fellow creatures but doomed not to find it.

The eighteen-year-old author, in her first attempt at fiction, had just created two characters that would be more enduring than any other fictional creations of her time.

Shelley was off boating with Byron while Mary was writing the first pages of her book. From June 22 to 30, the two poets toured Lake Geneva and its surrounding villages, seeing the literary sites and discussing poetry. Byron wanted to see the places that appeared in his favorite Rousseau novel, *Julie, ou la Nouvelle Héloïse.* The book was written in epistolatory form, in this case a series of passionate love letters. Rousseau's heroine, Julie, was seduced by her tutor Saint-Preux. Pregnant, the young girl is given in marriage to a friend of her father. Her new husband is generous enough to invite the tutor to come live with them in a ménage à trois. One can see why Shelley, who was reading the novel on this trip, liked this book. The existence of the happy threesome, living at the chateau of Clarens, is ended by Julie's death from pleurisy, which she contracted while saving her children from drowning. The book had an enormous popular success throughout Europe; like Byron, its author was suspected of portraying scenes from his own life (as the tutor) in his work.

Polidori, still hobbled by his ankle injury, was left behind. Byron was glad to be rid of both him and Claire, whom he now found to be a tremendous nuisance. (Byron had even tried unsuccessfully to bar Claire from the villa.) There was, of course, no thought of inviting Mary on the trip: the great men were sharing great thoughts.

The two poets had much in common. Both were rebels from the English upper class who had gone to the best schools. They both denounced the English government of the time as reactionary and felt that they had been driven into exile by the rumors of scandal in their lives. But the differences between them were even more stark. Byron was a peer of the realm who had a seat in the House of Lords. Shelley was of the landed gentry, and thus not as distinguished. But while Shelley cared little for his social position, Byron really did. He was, after all, *Lord* Byron. The more embarrassing difference for Shelley was that he had published only two obscure poems (even *Queen Mab* was little known), while Byron was the most renowned poet in the world at the time. Though Byron flouted convention, he was in favor of its continued existence, while Shelley believed that the world could — and should — really be changed. Shelley wrote to his friend Thomas Love Peacock that Lord Byron "is an exceedingly interesting person and as such is it not to be regretted that he is a slave to the vilest and most vulgar prejudices, and as mad as the winds." Being called "mad" by Shelley was a distinction indeed.

Shelley and Byron stopped at Clarens and saw through the window of the novel's inn the famous grove *(le bosquet de Julie)* where Julie read her love letters. Byron complained that the monks had cut down the trees, forgetting that it had been an incident from a novel rather than reality. Before arriving there, the poets had experienced a real-life danger that could have come straight from Rousseau's novel. They were on a boat near Meillerie, on the south shore of the lake, when waves broke the rudder, causing the boat nearly to capsize. According to Shelley it was "precisely in the spot where Julie and her lover were nearly overset, and St. Preux was tempted to plunge with her into the lake." Shelley, though he loved boats, could not swim, so Byron offered to bring him to shore, which was not far away. But Shelley refused, responding to a crisis as he customarily did — with passive acceptance. According to a later account, he seated "himself quietly upon a locker, and grasping the rings at each end firmly in his hands, declared his determination to go down in that position, without a struggle." The wind finally did blow their boat to shore, but Shelley felt ashamed at his helplessness and by Byron's generosity. "I knew that my companion would have attempted to save me," he wrote Peacock, "and I was overcome with humiliation."

The incident only added to Shelley's blue mood. He was having a very dry spell creatively and had hoped this trip might unblock him. He found inspiration when the two poets reached Montreux and visited the Castle of Chillon, originally built in the ninth century. Descending into its dungeons, no longer used, Shelley and Byron saw on the walls "a multitude of names," scrawled by prisoners "of whom now no memory remains," Shelley wrote. He also noticed "a beam, now black and rotten, on which prisoners were hung in secret. I never saw a monument more terrible of that cold and inhuman tyranny, which it has been the delight of man to exercise over man." The thought of prisoners struggling to preserve their lost identities stuck with Shelley, and Mary later wrote that he conceived the idea for his poem "Hymn to Intellectual Beauty" while on this trip. In it, Shelley reminisces about his decision to become a poet. Almost as if reassuring himself, he wrote,

I vowed that I would dedicate my powers
To thee and thine — have I not kept the vow?
With beating heart and streaming eyes, even now
I call the phantoms of a thousand hours
Each from his voiceless grave . . .

Probably the last portrait of Mary Wollstonecraft, this image was painted by her friend John Opie in 1797, just months before the birth of her daughter, an event that led to Wollstonecraft's death eleven days later.
National Portrait Gallery, London

William Godwin, the idealistic yet personally cold philosopher who was Mary Shelley's father. This portrait was painted by James Northcote, one of Godwin's admirers.
National Portrait Gallery, London

Mary Shelley was forty-two when Richard Rothwell made this portrait of her. She shows the strain of the tragic events that dogged her life.

National Portrait Gallery, London

Painted by Amelia Curran when the Shelleys were in Rome in 1819, this portait of Percy Shelley gives something of the ethereal quality of the poet.
National Portrait Gallery, London

Through reproductions of images like this portrait of Lord Byron, the poet's handsome face became known throughout Europe and North America. He has been called the first international celebrity.

National Portrait Gallery, London

This is the only known portrait of Mary Shelley's stepsister, Claire Clairmont. It was painted in 1819 by Amelia Curran. Claire is said not to have liked it.

City of Nottingham Museums: Newstead Abbey

John Polidori, Byron's young doctor, as he appeared in the summer of 1816 at Lake Geneva. Byron cruelly ridiculed Polidori's literary pretensions, but the story Polidori wrote in response to Byron's challenge has had a lasting influence.

National Portrait Gallery, London

William Blake made this illustration for a 1791 edition of Mary Wollstonecraft's *Original Stories*. Her daughter certainly saw it during her childhood, and to many it bears a resemblance to the scene that inspired her to write *Frankenstein*.
From the authors' collection

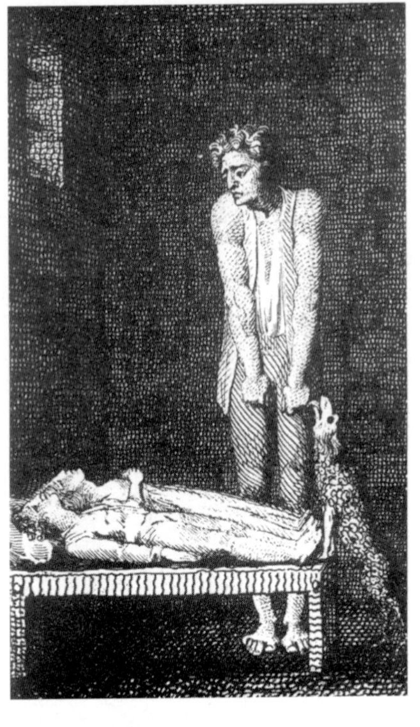

The frontispiece for the 1831 edition of *Frankenstein,* in which Mary made key revisions from her original 1818 work.
British Museum, 1153.a.9.(1)

William Shelley, the first son of Mary and Percy, as he was depicted by Amelia Curran shortly before his death in Rome in June 1819. Mary's description of Victor Frankenstein's younger brother William (who is strangled by the monster) is hauntingly similar to that of her real-life son.

The Carl H. Pforzheimer Collection of Shelley and His Circle, the New York Public Library, Astor, Lenox, and Tilden Foundations

Allegra, the daughter of Claire Clairmont and Lord Byron, as she looked at the age of eighteen months. Discarded by Byron in a convent school after he had taken her from Claire, the little girl died suddenly at the age of five. Claire never forgave Byron.

John Murray Collection

The Nightmare, the painting by Mary Wollstonecraft's lover Henry Fuseli, which attracted wide attention when it was exhibited. The woman's body is in the same position as Victor Frankenstein's bride after she was killed by the monster on her wedding bed.

The Nightmare, *1781, Henry Fuseli, Founders Society Purchase with funds from Mr. and Mrs. Bert L. Smokler and Mr. and Mrs. Lawrence A. Fleischman, photograph © 1997 The Detroit Institute of Arts*

Byron had no problem finding inspiration, and in his fashion he seized directly on what he had seen and experienced. One of those who had been imprisoned at the castle in the sixteenth century was the Swiss patriot François Bonivard. In a hotel where he and Shelley were staying, Byron tossed off a sonnet in tribute to him, and for good measure wrote *The Prisoner of Chillon*, a poem nearly four hundred lines long. No wonder Shelley felt intimidated.

The poets returned to Lake Geneva on June 30. Mary showed Percy what she had written, and he encouraged her to continue. During the next three weeks, she further developed her characters and plot. Many of the names that she gave her characters were taken from her own family, friends, or other associations. Percy had used Victor as a nom de plume for some of his youthful poems, and "the Victor" with a capital *V*, is also frequently used in Milton's *Paradise Lost* to refer to God. The name Frankenstein had possibly come from the castle that Mary may have seen on her elopement trip two years earlier. She may also have been inspired by Benjamin Franklin, whose experiments with electricity were well known. Strikingly, Mary chose to call Victor Frankenstein's younger brother William, a name charged with emotions for her. Victor Frankenstein's cousin, whom he marries, was called Elizabeth — the name of both Shelley's favorite sister and his mother.

In the novel, Victor is the son of Adolphus Frankenstein, a government official in Geneva; Adolphus's wife, Caroline, is a much younger woman who had been the daughter of one of Adolphus's friends. (Like several of the relationships in the book, this one had uncomfortable undertones of incest.) When Victor is three, his family takes in a young, orphaned cousin named Elizabeth, who his parents hope will be Victor's future wife. They grow up feeling like brother and sister. Victor's mother then dies as a result of nursing Elizabeth through an illness, which she herself contracts.

Like Percy, the young Victor becomes interested in the works of such alchemists as Cornelius Agrippa, Albertus Magnus, and Paracelsus. The traditional quest of alchemy was to find the philosopher's stone — a substance that would turn base metals into gold, and the alchemists' scientific pursuits included what today would be called chemistry. One day, when Victor is fifteen, he sees lightning strike a beautiful old oak tree during a terrible thunderstorm, much like those Mary had experienced that summer. The sudden destruction of this huge and powerful object draws Victor's attention to the forces that modern science might unshackle. "I eagerly inquired of my father the nature and origin of thunder and lightning." Victor says. "He replied, 'Electricity;' describing at the same time the various effects of that power. He constructed a small electrical machine, and exhibited a few experiments; he made also a kite, with a wire and string, which drew down that fluid from the clouds." From this point, Victor Frankenstein will devote all his energies toward studying electricity and other natural forces.

When Victor is seventeen, he goes to study at the university at Ingolstadt. Mary's choice of this city was significant: it was known for being the center of the Illuminati, a secret society dedicated to revolution and improvement of the human race. It was rumored that the members carried out experiments intended to discover the secret of immortality. Young Percy Shelley had read of the Illuminati in his "blue books" of Gothic lore and adventure. Both he and Mary had also read Godwin's novel *St. Leon,* set near Ingolstadt, about an alchemist who receives not only the philosopher's stone but an elixir of immortality.

At Ingolstadt, Victor too becomes fascinated with the forces that generate life, and he throws himself into his studies so completely that he loses interest in everything else. Though his mother, on her deathbed, had joined Elizabeth's and Victor's hands together as a sign they should marry, Victor makes no effort to return to Geneva to see his family or his fiancée. Uncovering the mystery of life subsumes all his other desires.

In creating Victor, Mary was borrowing a stock figure from folklore and Gothic novels — the sorcerer or alchemist who relentlessly seeks knowledge that should best remain hidden. Her innovation, however, was to turn the man of magic into a man of science, employing the brilliant insight that both magic and science promised the same things. "Whence, I often asked myself," Victor recalls, "did the principle of life proceed?" To answer this question he begins to study decay and death, "forced to spend days and nights in vaults and charnel houses." Victor exhausts himself in

> examining and analysing all the minutiae of causation, as exemplified in the change from life to death, and death to life, until from the midst of this darkness a sudden light broke in upon me — a light so brilliant and wondrous, yet so simple, that . . . I became dizzy with the immensity of the prospect which it illustrated. . . . After days and nights of incredible labour and fatigue, I succeeded in discovering the cause of generation and life; nay, more, I became myself capable of bestowing animation upon lifeless matter.

Deftly, Mary avoids the problem of explaining what this "cause of generation" is; sufficient to state in suitably ornate prose that Victor has found it.

Armed with this knowledge, Victor sets out to build a creature of parts before animating it. He flatters himself that he is working for the good of humanity rather than his own glory. Impatience, however, sows the seeds of his failure. "As the minuteness of the parts formed a great hindrance to my speed, I resolved, contrary to my first intention, to make the being of a gigantic stature; that is to say, about eight feet in height, and proportionately large."

Soon he has collected enough parts to arrange into a body. His egotism shows again as he describes his expectations: "A new species would bless me as its creator and source; many happy and excellent natures would owe their being to me. No father could claim the gratitude of his child so completely as I should deserve theirs.

"Pursuing these reflections," Victor continues, "I thought, that if I could bestow animation upon lifeless matter, I might in process of time (although I now found it impossible) renew life where death had apparently devoted the body to corruption." Here, Mary takes Victor's dream a step farther to pursue one of her *own* fantasies: the idea that her first baby could — even now — be brought to life again.

All of Victor's research is done in the utmost secrecy; this, along with the language Mary used to describe his work, indicated that there is something shameful about his experiment. Victor asks,

> Who shall conceive the horrors of my secret toil as I dabbled among the unhallowed damps of the grave, or tortured the living animal to animate the lifeless clay? . . . I collected bones from charnel houses; and disturbed, with profane fingers, the tremendous secrets of the human frame. In a solitary chamber, or rather a cell, at the very top of the house, and separated from all the other apartments by a gallery and staircase, I kept my workshop of filthy creation. . . . The dissecting room and the slaughterhouse furnished many of my materials; and often did my human nature turn with loathing from my occupation, whilst still urged on by an eagerness which perpetually increased. I brought my work near to a conclusion.

Secrecy about a shameful matter must have been much on Mary's mind that summer. Just before Shelley and Byron left on their boat trip, Claire apparently confessed to Shelley the secret of her pregnancy, and who the father was. Shelley, as Claire hoped, conveyed the news to Byron. Byron's reaction can only be guessed at, but while on that same trip Shelley took the time to change his will, leaving some twelve thousand pounds to Claire and "any person she may name." Mary had apparently not been informed of Claire's condition (though one wonders if she might not have guessed the truth), and later Byron, Shelley, and Claire would gather to discuss the custody and care of the child — pointedly excluding Mary.

We now come to the "dreary night of November." The "dull yellow eye of the creature" opens, and after two years of work, Victor sees the results of his labor and runs away. In doing so, he utterly fails in his role as the creator, the parent, of the monster. Victor runs from his laboratory to his bedroom and throws himself on his bed, where he has a most disturbing dream. "I thought I saw Elizabeth, in the bloom of health, walking in the streets of Ingolstadt. Delighted and surprised, I embraced her; but as I imprinted the first kiss on her lips, they became livid with the hue of death; her features appeared to change, and I thought that I held the corpse of my dead mother in my arms; a shroud enveloped her form, and I saw the grave-worms crawling in the folds of the flannel." This image was directly inspired by one of the ghost stories Byron had read earlier, but Mary heightened it to include the incestuous angle and the transformation of one's beloved. Creation and death are linked in Frankenstein's dream, in Mary's novel, and in Mary's life. Her own birth accompanied the death of her mother, and her own motherhood accompanied the death of her child.

In the novel, it is just at this moment that Victor opens his eyes and sees the creature holding up the curtain of the bed. Here Mary was adapting an image that she could have seen often in her childhood, for the scene almost duplicates an illustration that William Blake did for one of Mary Wollstonecraft's children's books. In Blake's copperplate engraving, there are two people lying on the bed — the children of the male figure who looks down on them. Living with him in debtor's prison, they have caught a fever and died. Earlier, the man's wife and other children had also perished in morbid circumstances. In the engraving, the man's dog — his only remaining companion — licks at his hand. Later, the dog is shot by a passing gentleman whose horse was frightened by it. It was not a happy story, and the illustration must have stuck in Mary's mind.

Again Victor responds to the creature's mute appeal for affection by running away. Ironically, at the culmination of his research, the moment of his triumph, all Victor's pleasure in life ends. He becomes sick and never again is gratified by anything. Instead the product of his knowledge — his creation — leads to the deaths of those he loves. The monster disappears from Victor's account at this point in the story, and Victor tries to forget him, although of course the reader turns the pages waiting for his return.

Victor is nursed back to health by his good friend Henry Clerval, also a student at Ingolstadt. Clerval, the better side of Shelley, is generous and clear-eyed. "[H]is conversation was full of imagination," Victor relates, "and very often, in imitation of the Persian and Arabic writers, he invented tales of wonderful fancy and passion." After several months of recovery, Victor receives a letter from his cousin Elizabeth, who persuades him to return home to Geneva. Before he can do so, however, a letter from his father informs him of the murder of Victor's younger brother

William, strangled in Plainpalais Park, the place where revolutionaries had held executions in Geneva.

Readers must ask why Mary gave the first victim in her novel a name that had so many references for her. William was, first of all, the name of her beloved father, her original teacher. It was the name she herself would have borne, had she been the boy her parents expected. Later, that name went to her half-brother, the son her despised stepmother was able to give to Mary's father. Finally, and most astonishing, it was the name of Mary's own baby, then nursing at her breast. The William in the novel is even described as looking the same way Mary's son looked: "with sweet laughing blue eyes, dark eye-lashes, and curling hair. When he smiles, two little dimples appear on each cheek, which are rosy with health." Which of these Williams did Mary have in mind as she envisioned the monster's huge, powerful hands closing around his throat, choking the life out of him? Whatever the answer (and it may be all four), the fictional moment certainly reflects the intensity of Mary's emotional conflicts.

Victor starts for home to grieve with his family. As he is approaching Geneva, flashes of lightning signal the onset of a storm over the Jura mountains. "While I watched the storm," Victor says,

> so beautiful yet terrific, I wandered on with a hasty step. This noble war in the sky elevated my spirits; I clasped my hands, and exclaimed aloud, "William, dear angel! this is thy funeral, this thy dirge!" As I said these words, I perceived in the gloom a figure which stole from behind a clump of trees near me; I stood fixed, gazing intently; I could not be mistaken. A flash of lightning illuminated the object, and discovered its shape plainly to me; its gigantic stature, and the deformity of its aspect, more hideous than belongs to humanity, instantly informed me that it was the wretch, the filthy daemon to whom I had given life. What did he there? Could he be (I shuddered at the conception) the murderer of my brother? No sooner did that idea cross my imagination, than I was forced to lean against a tree for support. The figure passed me quickly, and I lost it in the gloom. Nothing in human shape could have destroyed that fair child. *He* was the murderer! I could not doubt it.

Victor realizes something else too: he shared the guilt of murdering his innocent younger brother. "I considered the being whom I had cast among mankind, and endowed with the will and power to effect purposes of horror, such as the deed which he had now done, nearly in the light of my own vampire, my own spirit let loose from the grave, and forced to destroy all that was dear to me." With these words, Victor Frankenstein realizes that the creature is his doppelgänger — an insight that seems to have extended to readers and audiences, for today the name "Frankenstein" is popularly applied not only to the creator, but to the monster, who is never named in the book.

The full title of Mary's novel was to be *Frankenstein: Or, the Modern Prometheus.* The figure of Prometheus, the rebellious Titan who stole fire to help humankind and then was punished by the gods, preoccupied all the writers that summer in Geneva. One of the books the Godwins had published when Mary was a child was a collection of classical myths; Mary's favorite had been the Prometheus story, a variant of which had the Titan molding a man from clay and using fire to breathe life into his creation. Shelley had been reading aloud from Aeschylus's *Prometheus Bound,* translating from the Greek as he went along. Two years later, he would begin writing his continuation of the story, *Prometheus Unbound,* in which Prometheus — a figure Shelley identified with — is freed from the punishment to which Zeus has condemned him and is hailed as the savior of the human race.

Byron's much shorter poem, "Prometheus," written in the summer of 1816, was probably inspired by Percy's reading of the Aeschylus play. His attitude is one of defiant resignation to fate:

Thou art a symbol and a sign
To Mortals of their fate and force;
Like thee, Man is in part divine,
A troubled stream from a pure source;
And Man in portions can foresee
His own funereal destiny;
His wretchedness, and his resistance,
And his sad unallied existence:

To which his Spirit may oppose
Itself — and equal to all woes,
And a firm will, and a deep sense,
Which even in torture can descry
Its own concenter'd recompense,
Triumphant where it dares defy,
And making Death a Victory.

Mary was interested in yet another interpretation of Prometheus — the myth as told by Ovid in his *Metamorphoses,* which she had read the year before. Prometheus here was a figure who brought humans into life:

Whether with particles of heavenly fire,
The God of Nature did his soul inspire;
Or Earth, but new divided from the sky,
And, pliant, still retain'd th' ethereal energy;
Which wise Prometheus temper'd into paste,
And mix't with living streams, the godlike image cast . . .
From such rude principles our form began;
And earth was metamorphosed into Man.

Here, Prometheus forms a man from clay and animal parts and stirs it into life with "particles of heavenly fire" he has stolen from the chariot of the sun. In *Frankenstein,* Mary would employ the vocabulary of science, but the spark of life would effectively remain the same.

In late July, Mary, Percy, and Claire decided to go on a trip to Chamonix to view the spectacular scenery of mountains and glaciers. (Byron turned down their invitation, apparently not wishing to give Claire the opportunity to put him in a compromising position.) The trip had all the hallmarks of a Shelley brainstorm, because it was certain to be dangerous, and completely unsuitable for the pregnant Claire to embark on. The rainy weather had swelled the Arve river, which they would cross, to the point of flooding. Many of the roads in the region were washed out and there was an ever-present danger of avalanches because of wide temperature swings. At dusk the local residents built bonfires to protect their crops because even though it was late July, the nighttime temperature dropped close to freezing — all part of the odd weather that summer.

The threesome set out on July 21 on horseback. Baby William, at least, was spared the journey, remaining at home with his nursemaid. Shelley wrote, "The day was cloudless & exceedingly hot, the Alps are perpetually in sight, & as we advance, the mountains which form their outskirts closed in around us. We passed a bridge over a river which discharges itself into the Arve. The Arve itself much swollen by the rains, flows constantly on the right of the road." They passed through some little towns and the scenery became more "savage" and "colossal."

The next day they switched to mules, for they were heading into ever-higher regions. Mary wrote, "[T]his appeared the most beautiful part of our journey — the river foamed far below & the rocks & glaciers towered above — the mighty pines filled the vale & sometimes obstructed our view. We then entered the Valley of Chamounix [*sic*] which was much wider than that we had just left." There, they had their first sight of a glacier, the Glacier des Bossons, and Mary commented on the strange shapes the vast ice sheet took. "[A]s we went along," she added, "we heard a sound like the rolling of distant thunder & beheld an avelanche [*sic*] rush down the ravine of the rock." Everything she was seeing would be both inspiration and material for the book she was writing.

Signing the register at the inn where they stayed that night, Shelley wrote "atheist" in Greek after his name; for good measure, he listed his destination as "l'enfer," or hell. A later traveler, an English clergyman, noted this "horrid avowal of atheism," and mentioned it in a book he wrote about his trip through the region in the same month. Later yet, Byron was accused of having written the damning identifications, and a literary hubbub ensued, with accusations and corrections filling the pages of English magazines. People did not take such things lightly.

As they proceeded up the slopes of Montanvert ("Green Mountain," something of a misnomer that summer), they saw signs of nature's destructive power. "Nothing can be more desolate than the ascent of this mountain," wrote Mary. "[T]he trees in many places have been torn away by avelanches [*sic*] and some half leaning over others intermingled with stones present the appearance of vast & dreadful desolation." The rain fell in torrents, soaking them to the skin, and they decided to turn back. On the way, Shelley fell, hurt his knee, and fainted. Finally they managed to stagger back to the inn, where Mary took the opportunity to work on her novel. On July 24 she noted, "I . . . write my story," the first reference to *Frankenstein* in her journal.

The next day was even more fruitful for literary inspiration. They reached the summit of Montanvert, from which they looked down on the Mer de Glace ("Sea of Ice"), an immense glacier. As Mary described it: "This is the most desolate place in the world — iced mountains surround it — no sign of vegetation appears except on the place from which [we] view the scene — we went on the ice — It is traversed by irregular crevices whose sides of ice appear blue while the surface is of a dirty white." Mary recorded that she was "pleased and astonish[ed]" by the lonely, barren spot. It matched her mood, for it was in this "world of ice" that she would set the confrontation between Victor Frankenstein and his creature. Here the monster, as emotionally desolate as the landscape, would force his creator to listen to the story of his struggle to become loved.

Heavy rains made the travelers decide to return to their lakeside villa. Two days later, on July 27, they reached the Villa Diodati, talked till midnight with Byron, and then returned to their own cottage. Mary wrote, "kiss our babe & go to bed."

The following day, Mary noted that it had been exactly two years "since Shelley's & my union." This anniversary may have prompted Mary to add a detail that advanced the plot of her book and gave new insight into the monster: He demands that Victor Frankenstein create a mate for him to end his isolation.

Mary also was getting ready for Percy's birthday. On the first of August she made him a balloon, presumably from cloth or paper. Shelley was fond of such toys; he and Harriet had once used small hot-air balloons to randomly distribute copies of one of his revolutionary tracts. The next day, Mary went to Geneva with Percy to buy him another present, a telescope. On August 4, Shelley turned twenty-four. He and Mary went out in the boat and she read to him the fourth book of Virgil's *Aeneid* — an interesting choice, for it tells the story of Dido, whose love for Aeneas is doomed because he leaves her. A high wind ruined the balloon launch; the source of the hot air that was intended to cause it to rise instead set the balloon on fire.

That was symbolic of the general mood, for two days earlier several things had happened that would cast a pall over the rest of the summer. First, a letter arrived with the unwelcome news that Sir Timothy Shelley was making it difficult for his son to receive money that Percy had expected as part of the settlement of his grandfather's will. This meant Mary, Claire, and Percy would soon have to return to England, instead of continuing on the extensive European tour they had planned.

The same day, Byron called Claire and Percy to a meeting at the Villa Diodati. It was made clear that Mary was not included in the invitation, as noted in her journal. Byron's purpose was to declare that his affair with Claire was over. He accused her of not being sexually passionate and he appears also to have been annoyed by her Godwinian beliefs. These were obviously pretexts; the truth was, he was tired of her and because, unlike Lady Caroline Lamb, Claire had no powerful friends, he could dismiss her easily.

Except, of course, for the fact that she was carrying his child, and that was the topic of the discussion. Byron wanted to put the child in someone else's care — he suggested his half-sister Augusta, of all people — but Claire persuaded him to promise to raise the child himself, implicitly acknowledging it as his own. Its birth was to remain secret so that Claire would escape the disgrace. Particularly important to Claire was the need to conceal the illegitimate baby from her mother. Byron agreed that the child should stay with him at least until it was seven. Claire could visit as the "aunt" of the child, which would not hurt her reputation, but it was understood that Claire would never be part of the Byron household.

Percy and Claire could no longer keep the situation a secret from Mary, who could not have been pleased, for the new agreement with Byron entrapped the others, as Claire could not be left alone during her pregnancy. Nevertheless, they decided to remain at the lake a while longer before starting back to England. Mary took the opportunity to continue working on her novel. In the evenings they still often went to Byron's. On August 13, however, something happened to change that. Mary wrote in her journal ". . . afterwards we all go up to Diodati," and then underneath she added the single word "war." She never again went to Byron's villa, though Shelley and Claire did. What happened is impossible to say, but there was clearly some argument that alienated her.

Byron was expecting other guests. On the eighteenth, Shelley went to the villa and met Matthew Gregory Lewis, popularly known as "Monk" from the title of his most famous novel. *The Monk,* written when the author was only nineteen, featured the sensational sexual adventures of a Capuchin monk, who initially loses his virginity to a young novice, actually a woman disguised as a man. The book continues through rape, matricide, and incest, until finally the monk sells his soul to the devil, who as usual gets the better of the bargain. Even for a Gothic novel, *The Monk* was unusually lurid; in one of its most famous scenes, the central character rapes a virgin who turns out to be his sister while they are in a vault surrounded by rotting bodies.

Lewis was an heir to a West Indian fortune and traveled with a large retinue of Jamaican servants in livery. At times Byron was less than charitable about him, characterizing him as "a good man — a clever man — but a bore." Nevertheless, he had invited Lewis to visit, partially because he was nearly as notorious as Byron himself, though he lacked Byron's sublime talent.

At Diodati Lewis recited for them his own translation of portions of Johann Wolfgang Goethe's drama *Faust.* Shelley also recorded that he, Lewis, and Byron discussed ghosts, and whether they were real. Shelley was the only one who believed in the spectral, though the other two pointed out to him "that none could believe in Ghosts without also believing in God." Shelley refused to recognize the conflict with his atheism. Lewis then told five ghost stories, which Shelley summarized in the journal he and Mary were keeping. Though all were interesting tales, it does not appear that Mary drew inspiration for her novel from them.

Mary was hard at work, now creating her monster, one of the loneliest characters in literature. Not long after the publication of *Frankenstein,* a stage production of the story appeared in London. Setting a precedent that most have followed in adapting it for stage and screen since then, the monster is given no lines. He never speaks. In the novel, however, he is one of the three narrators who tell parts of the story from their own viewpoints, a complex structure that foreshadows modern artistic experiments. The monster has a chance to explain himself in the way Mary knew best: with words. That such a young writer could construct such a sophisticated narrative was, in retrospect, unsurprising. Copying Byron's manuscripts, though a tedious chore, had brought Mary very close to the elements that he forged into great poetry, and the poem that was Byron's primary focus — the third canto of *Childe Harold* — was one of his finest works. Mary also brought to her own writing an enormous body of reading and contacts with some of the leading minds of the British Isles. Her active life since eloping with Shelley two years earlier had stimulated her intellectually while raising deep questions and insecurities in her psyche. Her writing gained power and maturity in the process.

And of course, though by nature quiet and retiring, Mary brought to her work a ferocious ambition to succeed. She had known for a long time that she wanted to be a writer like her parents. Shelley, whatever else his faults, had encouraged her in that goal; as Mary wrote, Shelley "was, from the first, very anxious that I should prove myself worthy of my parentage, and enrol myself on the page of fame."

The novel's power stems from the monster's ability to make the reader understand and sympathize with its plight. Mary knew its feelings well, for its life story parallels her own. First, the creature has no mother. Victor has eliminated women from the creation process, substituting the forces of science. The creature's first experience is thus not the tender touch and nurturing breast of a mother, but instead Victor's horror and rejection. Born with an adult body but the mind of an infant, the creature resembles Rousseau's natural man — he is naturally good. He commits evil acts because of bad nurturing, just as in Godwin's analysis of society. Now, Mary is saying through her fiction what she could not possibly have said to her father: *she* was a victim of bad nurturing as well. Abandoned at birth, the creature says, "No father had watched my infant days, no mother had blessed me with smiles and caresses." Through her creation, the monster, Mary is expressing her own fears and rages.

In the novel, the monster educates himself by hiding in a shed attached to a cabin in Germany, where a French-speaking family named De Lacey is living — a blind man and his two grown children, Felix and

Agatha. The monster learns to speak and even to read from watching and listening to the De Laceys through cracks in the wall. In the same way, Mary had learned by listening to the intellectual conversations in her father's house. Later, Percy read whole books to her. Listening became her style of learning; most recently she had employed it when sitting quietly while Shelley and Byron talked.

The monster, from his hiding place, discovers the power of speech: it can produce emotions — happiness, joy, love. The emotions were positive ones, because the De Laceys were a happy family, despite their poverty. In much the same way, Mary had witnessed a secure and happy home life during the two years when she visited the Baxters in Scotland, also as an outsider.

One day, a new person enters the scene: Safie, an Arabian woman who is apparently to become Felix's wife. Felix teaches her to speak French, increasing the monster's verbal skills at the same time. He reads and explains to her the Comte de Volney's *The Ruins of Empires,* a kind of world tour of civilization. Profoundly antireligious, Volney's work had been a major influence on Shelley's composition of *Queen Mab.* (Godwin, for some reason, disliked the book.) By chance, the monster finds in the woods a case containing three other books: Plutarch's *Lives,* Milton's *Paradise Lost,* and Goethe's *The Sorrows of Young Werther.* The creature reads them, learning about civilization, sentiment, and morality from books. These are crucial texts, for they had a vital influence on Romanticism, on Mary, and on the monster himself. The creature admits later that he believed *Paradise Lost,* Milton's great poem (some, including Byron, ranked it above Shakespeare's plays) to be "a true history." He comprehends that he was intended to be like Milton's Adam, "but his state," he says, "was far different from mine. . . . He had come forth from the hands of God a perfect creature . . . but I was wretched, helpless, and alone." Instead, he turns to Satan, "for often, like him, when I viewed the bliss of my protectors, the bitter gall of envy rose in me."

In similar fashion, he learns about such concepts as honor, justice, and correct behavior from Plutarch's *Lives* — a series of biographies of great figures from Greece and Rome. Finally, the monster arrives at his understanding of passion and emotion from *The Sorrows of Young Werther,*

Goethe's wildly popular 1774 novel that inspired a wave of suicides by young people, emulating the book's hero, who shoots himself because of a tragic love affair. The books fire the monster with certainty that he knows how life should be lived, but as he proceeds through the world he finds that these ideals do not always conform with reality. Books alone were not adequate preparation for life — as Mary was herself discovering. And by pointing this out, she was pointing a finger at those, like her father and Shelley, who sometimes insisted otherwise.

Mary used a quote from *Paradise Lost* as the epigraph of the novel, a question that Adam asks God in Milton's poem; implicitly, Victor's creature asks it of *his* creator in Mary's novel:

> *Did I request thee, Maker, from my clay*
> *To mould me man? Did I solicit thee*
> *From darkness to promote me?*

On the next page, Mary wrote "To William Godwin."

The monster now reads some notes he took from Victor's laboratory when he left Ingolstadt. They describe the process of his creation and the monstrous nature of his looks. He is filled with hatred for his creator — "the minutest description of my odious and loathsome person is given, in language which painted your own horrors. . . . I sickened as I read. 'Hateful day when I received life!' I exclaimed in agony. 'Cursed creator! Why did you form a monster so hideous that even you turned from me in disgust?'" As a child, Mary too had read her father's memorial to her mother, and thus knew much about their courtship and perhaps even her own conception — intimate, personal details that are kept from most children. In portraying the monster's anger, she made the same judgment that critics of Godwin's intended tribute did: some things are better kept secret.

When the three younger members of the De Lacey household go out for a walk, the monster decides to attempt human contact. He knows that he is ugly, but since the father of the De Lacey family cannot see, that will not matter. Given this handicap, the old man experiences the "real" monster, the one who is a thinking, sensitive being. They converse, and the monster tries to convey his secret. Unfortunately, the three sighted members of the household return and drive him away because they are horrified by the way he looks. Mary knew that her identity as the child of Godwin and Wollstonecraft had also often masked her individuality. Even Shelley, she must have suspected, loved her not for who she was but for who her parents were.

Shattered, the monster returns to his creator with a demand: he wants Victor to make him a female counterpart, someone who will love and cherish him. Victor begins the project, but before he finishes, thinks better of it and destroys the female creature. He hears the sound of footsteps where he is working and the monster appears. He threatens Victor: "Remember, I shall be with you on your wedding night." Egocentric Victor imagines this to be a threat against himself.

The monster gets his revenge by killing those Victor loves — just as Victor has destroyed the female that the monster would have loved. First he brings about the death of Victor's friend, Henry Clerval. Victor now makes the mistake of thinking that he will be the creature's next target. On his wedding night, he leaves his bride Elizabeth alone while he searches for the monster. He misses the obvious: that Elizabeth is the intended victim. He hears her scream, and rushes back to their room: "She was there, lifeless and inanimate, thrown across the bed, her head hanging down, and her pale and distorted features half covered by her hair. Every where I turn I see the same figure — her bloodless arms and relaxed form flung by the murderer on its bridal bier."

Victor faints (as Shelley was in the habit of doing in times of stress), but then recovers to see a new, horrifying vision:

> While I still hung over her in the agony of despair, I happened to look up. The windows of the room had before been darkened; and I felt a kind of panic on seeing the pale yellow light of the moon illuminate the chamber. The shutters had been thrown back; and with a sensation of horror not to be described, I saw at the open window a figure of the most hideous and abhorred. A grin was on the face of the monster; he seemed to jeer, as with his fiendish finger he pointed towards the corpse of my wife.

The scene strongly recalls *Nightmare,* the painting by Henry Fuseli, Mary's mother's lover, with the creature playing the role the horse had in the picture.

Victor now devotes himself to the destruction of the monster he has created. In some ways, the rest of Mary's story resembles Godwin's own, most famous, novel, *Caleb Williams.* In that book two men, master and servant, alternately pursue and flee each other in a life-and-death struggle. At the core of the conflict in *Frankenstein* is a cri de coeur by the monster. "All men hate the wretched," he says, "how then must I be hated, who are miserable beyond all living things! Yet you my creator, detest and spurn me, thy creature." As William Godwin was currently spurning his daughter.

On August 28, Byron and Shelley had a final sail together and a long walk along the harbor. Byron gave Shelley the printer's copies of his poems, collected in a red leather quarto volume, which Shelley promised to deliver to Byron's publisher. They included some of his finest poetry — canto 3 of *Childe Harold,* "Darkness," "Prometheus," *The Prisoner of Chillon,* "The Dream," "Monody on the Death of Sheridan," and "Stanzas to Augusta." The next day the Shelley household packed up and was off to Geneva and the trip home.

Claire left a letter for Byron, writing, "My dreadful fear is lest you quite forget me." She cautions him as a wife might have, "One thing I do entreat you to remember & beware of any excess in wine," but then returns to her wounded mode, "now don't laugh or smile in your little proud way for it is very wrong for you to read this merrily which I write in tears. . . . I shall love you to the end of my life."

When the travelers reached the port of Le Havre, Mary must have reflected that this was the birthplace of her half-sister. Here it was that Mary Wollstonecraft had given birth to Fanny Imlay, had hoped to find happiness with Gilbert Imlay. A melancholy thought to return home on. Mary's summer of creative inspiration was over.

CHAPTER EIGHT

"I SHALL BE NO MORE . . ."

He sprung from the cabin-window . . . upon the ice-raft which lay close to the vessel. He was soon borne away by the waves, and lost in darkness and distance.

— *Frankenstein,* Mary Shelley, 1818

WITH THE WORDS ABOVE, Mary ended her masterpiece. Her monster disappears into the Arctic mists, his ultimate fate unexplained. The creature had promised to do himself in, saying,

> Do not think that I shall be slow to perform this sacrifice. I shall . . . seek the most northern extremity of the globe; I shall collect my funeral pile, and consume to ashes this miserable frame, that its remains may afford no light to any curious and unhallowed wretch, who would create such another as I have been. I shall die. I shall no longer feel the agonies which now consume me, or be the prey of feelings unsatisfied, yet unquenched.

But he still might be out there.

The ending the monster chose — the one Mary chose for him — echoed Mary's life in the four months after she, Percy, and Claire returned to England. Two suicides weeks apart shattered Mary's peace of mind, and the family's reaction to both was oddly inappropriate. The first death was kept as secret as possible; the note left behind indicated a wish to be forgotten, and that was granted to the extent that even the body was abandoned. The second death resulted in what should otherwise have been a joyous occasion; in almost obscene haste, Mary and Percy would celebrate their wedding.

By allowing the readers of her novel to think that the monster might still be alive, continuing his lonely search for love and understanding, Mary permitted herself to think that perhaps those who had willingly left life behind also — somewhere, somehow — lived. She had, as challenged, written a ghost story after all.

The Shelley party arrived back in England on September 8, 1816, landing at Portsmouth instead of London via the Thames — for Claire, now showing her pregnancy, could not risk appearing in London. (Victor Frankenstein would also leave the British Isles from this port, avoiding London because he cannot bear recalling the times that he shared there with the now-murdered Henry Clerval.) Shelley went on to London to try to clear up his financial affairs. Claire and Mary set out for Bath, a fashionable resort town where the pregnant Claire would be among strangers. She assumed the title "Mrs." when they found lodgings.

Soon Percy joined them. Even from a distance he tried to get Byron to assume financial responsibility for Claire, but without success. Mary was disturbed that Shelley and Claire had kept from her the secret of Claire's pregnancy for so long. Feeling shunted into the position of outsider, Mary would include secrecy among the sins that Victor Frankenstein committed in his pursuit of forbidden knowledge.

In Bath, Mary took art lessons and started reading the novels of Samuel Richardson — *Pamela, Clarissa,* and *Sir Charles Grandison.* She was considering ways to lengthen *Frankenstein* so that it could be published as a novel and these epistolatory novels, told in the form of a series of letters, probably influenced her. In *Clarissa,* Richardson presents events from multiple points of view, and Mary would frame her novel in a similar way, adding not only length but additional complexity and nuance. Another book from Mary's September reading was *Glenarvon,* Lady Caroline Lamb's novel. It must have been fun to read for anyone, like Mary, who knew Byron.

Mary and Claire had informed the Godwins they were staying at Bath for Claire's health. Fanny — quiet, melancholy eldest child of the family, who seemed always to blend into the background — had written Mary two letters in late September and October. In one, she urged her half-sister to persuade Shelley to give more money to Godwin, for "it is of the utmost consequence for *his own* [Godwin's] and the *world's* sake that he should *finish his novel* and is it not your and Shelley's duty to consider these things?" Godwin had already been informed that the money Shelley expected to get from his grandfather's estate was being held up, and Mary noted in her journal, "stupid letter from F."

Fanny was the only child in the Godwin household with no natural parent living there, and although Godwin had treated her as his own, she often felt lonely and isolated. She also suffered because she was caught in her position of emissary between the Godwins and the runaways Mary and Claire. On October 9, a depressed Fanny left London and went to Bristol, which was not far from Bath. From here she wrote two letters. One, to Godwin, read in part, "I depart immediately to the spot from which I hope never to remove." This worried Godwin enough that it actually propelled him into action: he went to Bristol to look for her. At the same time, Mary and Percy received another letter, which has been destroyed. Mary wrote in her journal, "In the evening a very alarming letter comes from Fanny — Shelley goes immediately to Bristol — we sit up for him until two in the morning when he returns but brings no particular news." Later inserted in the same day's entry are the grim words "Fanny died this night."

In a seaside hotel at Swansea, Fanny had taken an overdose of laudanum, the poison of choice of her mother. She left a suicide note on the table next to her body, which read, "I have long determined that the best thing I could do was to put an end to the existence of a being whose birth was unfortunate, and whose life has only been a series of pain to those persons who hurt their health in endeavouring to promote her welfare. Perhaps to hear of my death will give you pain, but you will soon have the blessing of forgetting that such a creature ever existed as . . . [here the signature was torn off]." There would be eerie echoes of this note in Mary's novel. In the monster's final speech, he tells of his intended suicide with the words, "when I shall be no more, the very remembrance of us both will speedily vanish."

The suicide of "a respectable-looking female" was reported in the Swansea newspaper for October 12. Among her effects were a gold watch (a present that Percy and Mary had brought her from Geneva). The newspaper noted that the corpse's stockings were marked with the letter "G" and her stays with the initials "M.W."

Fanny's motives for killing herself remain unclear. The most likely suggestion is that she was despondent at being denied the chance to go to Ireland and teach at the school operated by her aunts, Mary Wollstonecraft's sisters. Her aunt Everina had recently come to London to discuss the possibility, but turned Fanny down.

Another possible motive was that Fanny maintained a secret, hopeless love for Percy Shelley. A Godwin family friend, Maria Gisborne, wrote in her journal in 1820: "Mr. G. told me that the three girls were all equally in love with ———, and that the eldest put an end to her existance [*sic*] owing to the preference given to her younger sister." That it was Godwin's suggestion throws some doubt on this theory, for he made up a number of stories trying to conceal Fanny's suicide altogether. Indeed, Godwin acted abominably. Fear of disgrace led him to abandon Fanny in death. He never went to claim the body and forbade the rest of his family to do so as well. He wrote to Mary on October 13, "Go not to Swansea; disturb not the silent dead; do nothing to destroy the obscurity she so much desired that now rests upon the event." Mary and Shelley wanted to claim Fanny's body to make sure it received a proper burial but honored Godwin's wishes. As a result, no member of the family was present at the pauper's funeral. No one knows whether Fanny was buried in a potter's-field grave or if, as sometimes happened with other unclaimed bodies, hers was acquired by a Frankenstein-like medical experimenter.

Godwin, trying to account for her absence, told others that Fanny died a natural death. He wrote a friend in May of the following year:

> From the fatal day of Mary's elopement, Fanny's mind had been unsettled, her duty kept her with us; but I am afraid her affections were with them. Last autumn she went to a friend in Wales — and there was a plan settled about her going from thence to spend a short time with her aunts in Dublin, but she was seized

> with a cold in Wales which speedily turned to an inflammatory fever which carried her off.

This from a man whose philosophical teaching said lying was wrong even when it was meant to save people's feelings. Fanny's stepbrother Charles was not even informed of her passing until much later, and he continued to send her letters as late as August of the following year.

The news hit Mary hard, and she wore mourning clothes for some time. She and Fanny had shared the distinction of being the children of a fearless pioneer of sexual freedom. The words "unfortunate birth" in Fanny's suicide note hit home, for Mary had already given birth to two children to whom that phrase could apply, and Claire was pregnant with another. Mary inevitably asked herself if she could have done something more for Fanny, even wondering if she should have invited Fanny to move in with the already extended "family" around Shelley. Later Percy himself would memorialize Fanny's death with these lines:

Her voice did quiver as we parted,
Yet knew I not that heart was broken
From which it came, and I departed
Heeding not the words then spoken.
Misery — O misery,
This world is all too wide for thee.

As always, Mary found solace in reading and work. In her journal entry for October 28, she noted that she was reading the Humphry Davy pamphlet *A Discourse, Introductory to a Course of Lectures on Chemistry*. She spent several days with it, so there is no doubt it was of great interest to her. In it, Davy celebrated the accomplishments of the modern chemist, particularly "his" ability to "modify and change the beings surrounding him, and by his experiments to interrogate nature with power, not simply as a scholar, passive and seeming only to understand her operations, but rather [as] a master, active with his own instruments." Davy sounds here, with his idea of mastering nature, much like Victor Frankenstein.

Mary also read Lord George Anson's *A Voyage Around the World*, which familiarized her with the ongoing process of mapping the regions of the world. Nowhere, of course, was the map so incomplete as in the polar areas, which were subjects of intense speculation. Magnetism was another of the forces of nature that scientists of the time were investigating, and they wondered what polar property might be attracting compass needles to point in that direction. Also on Mary's reading list was John Locke's *Essay Concerning Human Understanding*. She used much of its observations on learning and sensation to describe her creature's intellectual development. Her conscientious research on what must have been difficult topics show Mary's serious purpose: this was not to be a Gothic potboiler, but a novel that posed — and perhaps answered — serious questions.

In addition, unlike the Gothic novelists, Mary didn't intend to create horror from magic, superstition, or fantasy, but from the fear of modern science. The "mad scientist" whose experiments spin out of control may be a cliché today, but in Mary's time it was brand new, and she was ahead of her time in imagining that scientific discoveries could be as scary as the witchcraft and sorcery of the past. She recognized that the "gift" that the scientist Victor Frankenstein gave to the world was as much a threat as a blessing, anticipating the fears of a scientist as notable as Albert Einstein, who wrote about the unintended consequences of the search for knowledge, "By painful experience we have learned that rational thinking does not suffice to solve the problems of our social life. Penetrating research and keen scientific work have often had tragic implications for mankind."

To lengthen and enrich her tale, Mary filled in details, now writing a subplot about the unjust accusation made against the Frankenstein family's servant Justine, who is framed for William's murder when the monster leaves incriminating evidence on her sleeping form. Although Victor's cousin/fiancée Elizabeth stoutly defends Justine at her trial, Victor himself — who knows the truth — fails to testify in her behalf. He leaves the courtroom because he fears the shame of admitting it was his creation that has killed his brother. Victor's inaction is clearly analogous to Godwin's attempts to deny Fanny's suicide, in which he considered only his own reputation. Soon Mary would see an example of that kind of dishonesty in the other man in her life.

Harriet had never recovered emotionally after Shelley abandoned her and their two children, Ianthe and Charles. As her hopes for a reconciliation dwindled, Harriet's depression deepened. In a letter to a friend in Ireland, she asked, "Is it wrong, do you think, to put an end to all one's sorrows? I often think of it — all is so gloomy and desolate. Shall I find repose in another world? Oh grave, why do you not tell us what is beyond thee?"

On November 9, Harriet left her lodgings in London and was never seen alive again. She wrote to her elder sister Eliza, revealing that she planned to kill herself and asking her forgiveness. As for her husband, "I have not written to Bysshe. Oh, no, what would it avail, my wishes or my prayers would not be attended to by him, and yet should he receive this, perhaps he might grant my request to let Ianthe remain with you always. Dear lovely child, with you she will enjoy much happiness, with him none. My dear Bysshe, let me conjure you by the remembrance of our days of happiness to grant my last wish." Her desperate, pathetic tone should have moved even the hardest heart: "Do not refuse my last request, I never could refuse you and if you had never left me I might have lived, but as it is I freely forgive you and may you enjoy that happiness which you have deprived me of." If there was a reason for suicide, the letter expressed it: "Too wretched to exert myself, lowered in the opinion of everyone, why should I drag on a miserable existence? embittered by past recollections & not one ray of hope to reason on for the future."

Harriet's body was discovered on December 10, floating in the Serpentine in Hyde Park in London. She had been living by herself under the name Harriet Smith, and a coroner's jury looking into her death brought down the verdict "found drowned." Mary and Shelley did not receive the news for five days, and then only secondhand through a friend of theirs.

Harriet's suicide brought out the worst in Shelley, as Fanny's had in Godwin. The *Times* printed a brief notice of the coroner's trial, noting that the deceased had been "far advanced in pregnancy." Shelley, who had gone to London after he heard the news, wrote Mary that Harriet had become a prostitute. He denied any responsibility for her death, instead choosing to blame her family, the Westbrooks. He wrote,

> It seems that this poor woman — the most innocent of her abhorred & unnatural family — was driven from her father's house, & descended the steps of prostitution until she lived with a groom of the name of Smith, who deserting her, she killed herself.— There can be no question that the beastly viper her sister, unable to gain profit from her connexion with me — has secured to herself the fortune of the old man — who is now dying — by the murder of this poor creature.

These lies only indicate Shelley's inability to face up to the consequences of his own actions.

Many years later, Claire Clairmont told a different story. She described Harriet's lover, presumably the father of her unborn child, as a soldier who had been ordered abroad. His letters did not reach her and she became depressed that she had been abandoned a second time by a man she had loved. She had remarked to her sister, "I don't think I am made to inspire love, and you know my husband abandoned me." So on a gloomy, rainy day Harriet acted on the suicidal impulses that she had entertained for a long time.

This suicide would haunt Mary, for in her mind Harriet's fate was linked to her own. It hit her even harder than Fanny's death had, for she could more seriously blame herself for Harriet's despair, and she felt keenly the guilt that Shelley repressed or denied. Indeed, Mary would come to believe that this lonely death marked the beginning of a series of tragedies. Harriet became Mary's own personal ghost who returned to haunt her whenever she was at a low ebb, leading to Mary's belief that her happiness always came at the expense of someone else. In her journal in 1839, twenty-three years later, she would write, "Poor Harriet to whose sad fate I attribute so many of my own heavy sorrows as the atonement claimed by fate for her death." An attempt to cross out the last nine words was made later, in a different color ink.

Shelley now filed suit to gain custody of his children, who were with Harriet's sister, but Harriet's family took steps to block him. Shelley's lawyer suggested that his case for regaining the children would be stronger if he were a married man, so on December 30, less than a month after the discovery of Harriet's suicide, Mary and Percy pledged their vows in a London church. The unseemly haste with which this was done was also a result of pressure by the Godwins. Mrs. Godwin had told Percy that her husband would commit suicide if they did not marry.

Shelley presented the idea of marriage to Mary in a letter containing probably the least romantic proposal in history — certainly by a great poet: "[Y]our nominal union with me . . . a mere form appertaining to you will not be barren of good." According to Mrs. Godwin — not necessarily a reliable source, but she should have her say too — Mary told Percy, "Of course you are free to do what you please . . . [but] if you do not marry me . . . I will destroy myself and my child with me." In any event, the knot was speedily tied. Percy wrote to Lord Byron that his marriage to Mary "was a change, (if it be a change) which had principally her feeling in respect to Godwin for its object. I need not inform you that this is simply with us a measure of convenience." Claire was unable to appear at the wedding, for her advanced pregnancy was now impossible to conceal.

Godwin was by his account the happiest person at the ceremony. He wrote to his brother,

> The piece of news I have to tell, however, is that I went to church with this tall girl some little time ago to be married. Her husband is the eldest son of Sir Timothy Shelley, of Field Place, in the county of Sussex, Baronet. So that, according to the vulgar ideas of the world, she is well married, and I have great hopes the young man will make her a good husband. You will wonder, I daresay, how a girl without a penny of fortune should meet with so good a match. But such are the ups and downs of this world. For my part I care but little, comparatively, about wealth, so that it should be her destiny in life to be respectable, virtuous, and contented.

Butter wouldn't melt in his mouth.

As for the happy bride, she wrote a few lines in her journal summarizing everything that happened between December 16 and the end of the month. Cryptically, she mentions "a marriage takes place on the 29th," even getting the date wrong. Two weeks later, she wrote Byron,

> Another incident has also occurred which will surprise you, perhaps; It is a little piece of egotism in me to mention it — but it allows me to sign myself — in assuring you of my esteem and sincere friendship — *Mary W. Shelley*

So Mary had chosen to take the name from the tombstone rather than that of the father who had raised and educated her. Ever after, she would call herself "Mary Wollstonecraft Shelley." Even Godwin referred to her in his journals as "MWS."

The greater part of the letter Mary sent Byron in January was concerned with another event. On January 12, 1817, Claire gave birth to a girl she called Alba. The Shelley group's nickname for Byron had been Albé (for L. B.). Claire had written Byron at least four letters since she last saw him, typically alternating between teasing (she quoted from *Glenarvon*) and appealing for his love. It was Claire's hope that the birth of the child would bring her and Byron back together. Mary's letter informed him that Claire "sends her affectionate love to you." As with the letters he had received from Claire, Byron did not respond to this one. Through Shelley, however, he made a request that Claire change Alba's name. The child was later baptized Clare Allegra Byron, and she would become known as Allegra.

Byron wrote to a friend giving his opinion about the affair with Claire.

> You know . . . that odd-headed girl — who introduced herself to me shortly before I left England. . . . I never loved nor pretended to love her — but a man is a man —& if a girl of eighteen comes prancing to you at all hours — there is but one way — the suite of all this is that she was with *child* — & returned to England to assist in peopling that desolate island. . . . The next question is the brat *mine*? I have reason to think so — for I know as much as one can know such a thing.

Before their wedding, Mary had begged Shelley for "a house with a lawn a river or lake — noble trees & divine mountains that should be our little mouse hole to retire to — But never mind this — give me a garden & *absentia Clariae* ["the absence of Claire"] and I will thank my love for many favours." She would get the house, but not the absence.

The Shelleys took a lease on a house in Marlow, up the Thames River just far enough from London so that it had a rural feeling. It had a large room that Shelley used as a library, and a backyard garden where Mary could putter. Life at Marlow was not the private, quiet existence Mary had yearned for. Because they were so close to London, many friends and acquaintances came to visit. The house was often filled with guests like Leigh Hunt, his wife, and their many children. Hunt and his brother John had been imprisoned for two years for publishing attacks on the prince regent in their journal. Shelley had donated money for their defense, and Hunt became an early enthusiast of Shelley's poetry. Another regular visitor was Shelley's old friend Thomas Love Peacock, who lived nearby with his mother. Peacock and Mary did not like each other very much, for he felt loyal to Harriet, whom he had known first. (Peacock was so attracted to Claire, on the other hand, that he proposed to her. Claire turned him down; all her hopes were still on Byron.)

The Shelleys also went to literary gatherings at Peacock's mother's house and the home of the Hunts, where Shelley first met John Keats, then also struggling to make his reputation as a poet. William Hazlitt, critic, essayist, and friend of Godwin's, described Shelley at this time as a man with "a fire in his eye, a fever in his blood, a maggot in his brain, a hectic flutter in his speech, which mark out the philosophic fanatic . . . there is a slenderness of constitutional *stamina,* which renders the flesh no match for the spirit."

Though their friends knew the truth, the Shelleys kept up the pretense that Claire's baby belonged to someone else. "Claire has reassumed her maiden character," Shelley wrote Byron, as if posing as such made it so. When the Godwins came to visit, Allegra was presented as a cousin of the Hunts that Claire was helping to care for. She was a beautiful child, quite like her parents. Shelley told Byron, "Her eyes are the most intelligent I ever saw in so young an infant. Her hair is black, her eyes deeply blue, and her mouth exquisitely shaped."

Claire was fiercely proud of the infant. She wrote to Byron:

> My affections are few & therefore strong — the extreme solitude in which I live has concentrated them to one point and that point is my lovely child. I study her pleasure all day long — she is so fond of me that I hold her in my arms till I am nearly falling on purpose to delight her. We sleep together and if you knew the extreme happiness I feel when she nestles closer to me, when in listening to our regular breathing together, I could tear my flesh in twenty thousand different directions to ensure her good.

Claire's happiness increased when Percy bought her a piano at the end of April. She would play and sing by candlelight in the evenings, and Percy liked to sit and listen. Percy — as Byron had earlier — wrote a lyric poem celebrating Claire's voice. Contrary to his usual procedure, Shelley did not show the poem to Mary but sent it to the *Oxford Herald* to be published under a pseudonym. Even the title, "To Constantia," was intended to conceal the identity of the author and his subject. Marriage did not end the secrets that existed between Mary and Shelley.

Those secrets may have been easier to keep since Mary had many distractions. She was working hard to finish her novel, she had a young child, and now she found herself pregnant again as well. The eldest Hunt son, Thornton Leigh Hunt, years later described his youthful impressions of Mary at this time:

> Shelley's fullness of vitality did not at that time seem to be shared by the partner of his life . . . she did not do justice to herself either in her aspect or in the tone of her conversation. . . . With a figure that needed to be set off, she was careless in her dress; and the decision of purpose which ultimately gained her the playful title of "Wilful Woman" then appeared . . . her temper being easily crossed, and her resentments taking a somewhat querulous and peevish tone.

Peacock, perhaps more perceptively, drew a literary portrait of the relationship between Mary and Percy (who was thinly disguised as Scythrop in Peacock's novel *Nightmare Abbey*). Of Mary: "She loved Scythrop, she hardly knew why . . . she felt her fondness increase or diminish in an inverse ratio to his. . . . Thus, when his love was flowing, hers was ebbing; when his was ebbing, hers was flowing. Now and then there were moments of level tide, when reciprocal affection seemed to promise imperturbable harmony."

Mary's work on *Frankenstein* may have accounted for the "peevishness" that young Thornton Hunt noticed in her. On March 5, 1817, she had a significant dream that she mentioned to Leigh Hunt. She explained the abrupt ending of the letter she sent him by writing, "I had a dream tonight of the dead being alive which has affected my spirits." It had been exactly two years since the death of her first child, and Mary was still haunted by the desire to bring her daughter back to life.

Mary came up with a new structure for her book; it now became a story within a story within a story. One reason for this was to pad the manuscript to novel length, but it was also a way to distance herself from the emotions at the heart of the tale. The book has three narrators — all male. Captain Robert Walton, who serves as a neutral observer, begins the tale in letters to his sister, Margaret Walton Saville, a woman with the same initials as Mary Wollstonecraft Shelley. The recipient of the letters never appears or takes a role in the action; the reader only assumes she received the letters her brother writes. Mary drew her model from both Goethe's *The Sorrows of Young Werther,* and Rousseau's *Julie,* as well as Samuel Richardson's works. At the time, the epistolatory form was thought to add to a novel's verisimilitude. Goethe was frequently asked whether the letters that make up his novel were real.

Robert Walton is an explorer seeking to reach the North Pole. Much like Victor Frankenstein, he is ambitious to achieve a great discovery that will benefit humanity. He reminds the reader of Shelley too, when he writes, "My life might have been passed in ease and luxury; but I preferred glory to every enticement that wealth placed in my path."

In Walton's second letter, he expresses the loneliness of his quest, a trait that the reader will later discover he shares with the monster. "I shall commit my thoughts to paper," Walton writes his sister, ". . . but that is a poor medium for the communication of feeling. I desire the company of a man who could sympathize with me; whose eyes would reply to mine. You may deem me romantic, my dear sister, but I bitterly feel the want of a friend." The twin themes of overweening ambition and personal loneliness pervade the novel. Mary was witness to the former, and victim of the latter.

Polar exploration was of high interest at the time Mary was writing. In 1774, Captain James Cook had sailed to the edge of the ice sheet that covers Antarctica. He wrote in his journal: "[My] ambition leads me not only farther than any other man has been before me, but as far as I think it is possible for man to go. . . ." Yet people still wanted to know what lay beyond, at the very points — north and south — on which the earth rotates on its axis. In 1818 the British government established a prize for the discovery of the long-sought Northwest Passage, a sea route above North America to Asia. Earlier expeditions searching for the passage had turned back because of the icy, frigid seas.

Because the polar regions were terra incognita, their nature was open to wild speculation. It was commonly believed that the sun never set at the North Pole and therefore the region around it would experience continually warm temperatures. In the first letter to his sister, Robert Walton describes what he might find at the Pole. "There, Margaret," he wrote, "the sun is for ever visible; its broad disk just skirting the horizon, and diffusing a perpetual splendour. There — for with your leave, my sister, I will put some trust in preceding navigators — there snow and frost are banished; and sailing over a calm sea, we may be wafted to a land surpassing in wonders and in beauty every region hitherto discovered on the habitable globe. . . . What may not be expected in a country of eternal light?" Like Godwin and Shelley, Walton was seeking no less than a paradise on earth.

Instead of paradise, Walton finds a starving and desperate Victor, who has pursued the monster all the way to the Arctic. Victor warns Walton of the danger, not of the monster but of the quest for knowledge that created him: "Learn from me, if not by my precepts, at least by my example, how dangerous is the acquirement of knowledge, and how much happier that man is who believes his native town to be the world, than he who aspires to become greater than his nature will allow."

Both Walton and Frankenstein disguise their lust for power by pursuing seemingly altruistic quests, and in Promethean fashion, they are both undone by their ambitions. At the end of the book, Walton faces the mutiny of his crew and fails in his quest. Victor Frankenstein, after witnessing the deaths of those closest to him, loses his life in the attempt to destroy his greatest creation. Mary had real-life models for these characters: both her father and her husband assumed the roles of teachers, not only toward her, but toward all humanity. They justified their actions by their lofty goals, but at the very time Mary was writing she witnessed the terrible consequences of their arrogance: the abandonment of children and lovers, the suicides of Fanny and Harriet.

Many Gothic novels, particularly those written by women, have a female heroine rather than a hero. *Frankenstein* is a novel of male voices. There are no major female characters to provide a counterweight of love and tenderness to the males' ambitions and desire for power. A modern feminist critic has declared that *Frankenstein* is the story of what happens when a man tries to have a baby without a woman. The result in the book, of course, is disastrous. There can be no doubt that Mary was inspired by her own upbringing, with its overwhelming father figure.

Most of the book is set in the Alps and the Arctic — where the cold and ice symbolize the creature's isolation and friendlessness, and perhaps the cold, unfeeling personalities of Walton and Frankenstein. The setting also echoes Mary's favorite poem, Coleridge's *The Rime of the Ancient Mariner,* which was set in the Antarctic. There would be specific references to that poem throughout *Frankenstein,* and several characters quote from it, including the creature.

The three narrators spiral the reader downward into the heart of the book, and from there outward again to its climax. After meeting Victor Frankenstein, Walton serves as the recorder of Victor's narrative. But Victor retains his desire for control. As Walton relates later, "Frankenstein discovered that I made notes concerning his history; he asked to see them, and then himself corrected and augmented them in many places; but principally in giving the life and spirit to the conversations he held with his enemy. 'Since you have preserved my narration,' said he, 'I would not that a mutilated one should go down to posterity.'" Walton says that Frankenstein's "eloquence is forcible and touching; nor can I hear him, when he relates a pathetic incident, or endeavors to move the passions of pity or love, without tears." Significantly, the monster will also use words to persuade Victor — and the reader — of his humanity, even though his story reaches the reader thirdhand, contained within Victor's narrative that is in turn reported by Walton.

Indeed, the creature is much the most eloquent of all the narrators. "Listen to my tale," the monster says to Frankenstein, "when you have heard that, abandon or commiserate me, as you shall judge that I deserve." Victor confesses to Walton that the creature did have remarkable powers of persuasion, "even power over my heart." Here the novel expresses one of Mary's deepest wishes: that she would have the ability to move the hearts of her father and her husband, that she could make them understand her needs.

After the creature tells his story and flees, Victor's narrative resumes. He destroys his scientific instruments, is unjustly imprisoned for Clerval's murder, and marries Elizabeth only to find her murdered on their wedding night. He dedicates his life to the destruction of the monster and pursues him to the Arctic. After Frankenstein is found by the sailors, Walton then takes up the narrative again. His ship is now immobilized in ice, frozen and immovable. The crew demands that Walton turn back. Frankenstein, hearing this, scolds them, calling them unworthy of the great task on which they have embarked. "The ice," he tells them, "is not made of such stuff as your hearts might be; it is mutable, cannot withstand you, if you say that it shall not." It was a line that could have been uttered by Shelley, confident that a truly determined man need not be stopped by the forces of nature.

When Walton nonetheless accedes to the crew's demands, Frankenstein tries to rise from his bed and resume the chase on his own. But he is too weak; in fact, he is dying. Frankenstein has a moment when he realizes his own folly and says to Walton, "I am a blasted tree; the bolt has entered my soul." Thus the sense of the power of lightning, which Victor first experienced in his youth when he witnessed the destruction of the tree, has become internalized. He thought to harness that power, but it has destroyed him.

Yet Mary apparently had trouble passing a final judgment on his quest. Frankenstein appears to show repentance when he advises Walton, "Seek happiness in tranquillity, and avoid ambition." Then he seems to have a change of heart as he adds with his last words, "Yet why do I say this? I have myself been blasted in these hopes, yet another may succeed." Mary cannot quite allow him to admit that the quest has been wrong from the beginning, has always been futile.

The next day, Walton finds the monster in the room where Frankenstein's corpse lies. Walton must close his eyes because the creature's ugliness is so overpowering, but calls on him to remain. The creature wants to find forgiveness for his sins, but his creator can no longer give it: he is silent and cold. Walton summons up the courage to scold the "demon" for failing to listen to "the voice of conscience." The creature protests that he was mistreated and that far from lacking remorse, he suffered more than Victor did. His self-hatred was greater than the contempt anyone may have felt for him.

Walton tries to quell the sympathy he feels for the monster, remembering Victor's warning that it could be eloquent and persuasive. He again chides the giant creature, who begins a long speech in which he compares himself to a "fallen angel," like Satan in John Milton's *Paradise Lost.* "Yet," he adds, "even that enemy of God and man had friends and associates in his desolation; I am quite alone." As much a Romantic figure as any of Byron's heroes, the creature announces his intention to go to the North Pole and take his own life. "I shall ascend my funeral pile triumphantly, and exult in the agony of the torturing flames," he declares. Then, in Walton's words, "He sprung from the cabin-window, as he said this, upon the ice-raft which lay close to the vessel. He was soon borne away by the waves, and lost in darkness and distance." Mary cannot let the reader watch him die, as she herself never saw the bodies of Fanny or Harriet. She thus leaves us with the impression that the monster might still be alive, wandering somewhere.

* * *

Mary finished *Frankenstein* in May 1817. In writing it, she had faced issues that she had a difficult time confronting in real life — a cold father, a manipulative husband, a dead child, and a thicket of emotional problems in her relationships. The book depicted characters with enormous ambitions that they sought to attain without consideration of the cost to others. Mary ventured to suggest that even people of good intentions and genius — as both Godwin and Shelley considered themselves — can go wrong. But to criticize these two titanic figures, quite literally the gods of her life, she had to disguise herself as a monster.

Nineteen years old, Mary had paid a high price for her quest for love. Eloping with Shelley had damaged her relationship with her father and had been the cause of Harriet's suicide. Now Mary realized, and resented, that Percy was attached as much to Claire as herself. Pregnant for the third time, Mary was responsible for the care of her own child as well as Claire's, and had a husband who constantly complained of his health. It was amazing that she could write anything at all.

Mary read again the third canto of *Childe Harold* at the end of May and it brought back memories of that magical, haunted summer just a year earlier. Byron, in his absence, had grown into a romantic figure for her. Mary wrote in her journal on May 28, "How very vividly does each verse of his poem recall some scene of this kind to my memory — This time will soon also be a recollection — We may see him again & again — enjoy his society but the time will also arrive when that which is now an anticipation will be only in the memory — death will at length come and in the last moment all will be a dream."

Toward the end of the month, Shelley and Mary went to London with the manuscript and submitted it to John Murray. Mary's hopes rose when she heard that Murray himself had liked it. But William Gifford, the editor of the Tory *Quarterly Review* and a literary advisor to the publisher, did not — regarding the book as too radical in its social and political implications. The idea of creating a human being without divine help (considered much more important than the female contribution) was anathema in those reactionary times. Following Gifford's advice, Murray passed.

A second publisher rejected the novel with what Mary thought was insulting swiftness. In late August, another publisher, Lackington's, expressed interest in the book, and with Shelley negotiating the contractual details, the novel was accepted. In dealing with Lackington's, Shelley did not reveal the author's name and insisted that the book should be published anonymously — a not uncommon practice at the time. Shelley took over the task of shepherding *Frankenstein* through the publication process, editing and checking galley proofs. He also urged the publisher to advertise the book, which had never been done for his own works.

There has long been controversy about Shelley's role in writing the novel. He made a few changes in the manuscript, but does not seem to have made any major alterations in the story; indeed, Shelley's editorial comments tended to be minor and condescending. When Mary wrote "igmatic" Percy corrected her in pencil in the margin: "enigmatic o you pretty Pecksie!" He used similar endearments in other parts of the editing, acting more as a mentor than a co-author. Mary accepted almost all of Shelley's changes, showing her insecurity as an author who had never been published. As a rule, Mary favored simple Anglo-Saxon words and straightforward or conversational sentences. Shelley had a more ornate style of writing and favored polysyllabic words; for example, he substituted "converse" for "talk." In only a few places did Shelley subtly change the meaning of the text. To Percy, the monster was like a traditional Gothic horror figure. For example, when the female monster is destroyed, Mary has the creature withdraw "with a howl of devilish despair." Percy added, "and revenge." Such changes took away some of the monster's humanity. Percy also introduced the word "abortion" to refer to the creature. Mary always saw him as completely human, though monstrous in behavior.

Percy's changes to the manuscript also tended to justify Dr. Frankenstein's behavior and portray him as the victim, rather than the creator of the evil. This reflected not only Shelley's lack of awareness but also his very similarity to Victor. Mary Shelley always saw that Frankenstein was deluding himself. So too was her husband.

The most important change that Shelley made was in the last line of the novel. Mary's original was, "He sprung from the cabin window as he said this upon an ice raft that lay close to the vessel & pushing himself off he was carried away by the waves and I soon lost sight of him in the darkness and distance." Percy changed this to "He sprung from the cabin-window, as he said this, upon the ice-raft which lay close to the vessel. He was soon borne away by the waves, and lost in darkness and distance." Mary's "lost sight of" more strongly maintained the possibility that the monster was still alive.

That summer Shelley's hypochondria flared up again; he obsessively checked his legs for signs of the dreaded elephantiasis. Meanwhile he had started what was to become one of his major works, a poem called *Laon and Cythna.* It was a defense of the ideals of the French Revolution, but a central feature of the plot was sexual love between brother and sister.

Shelley's unconventional ideas on marriage and "free love" made some people suspect that Allegra might be *his* child. That rumor did not help Shelley in his attempt to gain custody of his children by Harriet. In August 1817, the court awarded both Ianthe and Charles to a guardian named by Harriet's relatives. Just a month later, on September 2, 1817, Mary gave birth to another child, a girl she named Clara Everina. Mary chose the second name after her mother's sister; the first obviously was meant to honor Claire.

Mary had a hard month after the birth of her daughter, for in addition to the usual cares of a new mother, she had to worry about Shelley's financial condition and his complaints of ill health. Again, Mary's giving birth had prompted Shelley to develop symptoms of illness. "My health has been materially worse," Percy told Godwin.

> My feelings at intervals are of a deadly & torpid kind, or awakened to such a state of unnatural & keen excitement that, only to instance the organ of sight, I find the very blades of grass & the boughs of distant trees present themselves to me with microscopical distinctness. Towards evening I sink into a state of lethargy & inanimation, & often remain for hours on the sofa between sleep & waking, a prey to the most painful irritability of thought. Such, with little intermission, is my condition.

The first proofs for *Frankenstein* arrived at the end of September. Percy went to London to supervise the different publishing projects of the family, to consult Dr. Lawrence, and to raise money. (Claire too had a novel that Percy tried to find a publisher for, but to no avail. No trace of the book survives, but it may have been Claire's "entry" in Byron's ghost story contest.) Mary wrote to him, "I am just now surrounded by babes. Alba is scratching and crowing — William amusing himself with wrapping a shawl round him and Miss Clara staring at the fire. . . . Adieu — dear love."

Mary was unable to supply enough of her own milk to satisfy her newborn, so cow's milk was obtained, but that upset little Clara's stomach. Feeling depressed, Mary wrote to Percy that she no longer had the energy to work on the *Frankenstein* revisions. She sent him a batch of proofs with the notation, "I am tired and not very clear headed so I give you carte blanche to make what alterations you please."

Shelley informed Mary that the doctor in London had said he must go either to the English seacoast or to Italy for his health, and asked her to decide. Though she dreaded being uprooted again, Mary chose Italy. One of her reasons was to make sure that Byron accepted the responsibility of caring for Allegra. Claire's love for the child had made her reluctant to take steps to send her to Byron, and Byron refused to come to England to fetch her. He was now living in Venice in a large house on the Grand Canal overlooking the Rialto Bridge. Claire, always hopeful of a reconciliation with Byron, wrote him, speculating on what Allegra's life with him would be like, "Poor little angel! in your great house, left perhaps to servants while you are drowning sense and feeling in wine."

Mary was worried about what her father would say when he heard they were leaving. Worse, Percy had promised to give Godwin more money, but now found he could not supply it. Mary wrote a letter to Percy in October that shows the deep attachment she would always have for her father, "I know not whether it is early habit or affection but the idea of his silent quiet disapprobation makes me weep as it did in the days of my childhood. I am called away by the cries of Clara . . . God knows when I shall see you — Claire is forever wearying with her idle & childish complaints." At Percy's suggestion, they concealed from Godwin their plans for going abroad.

As it turned out, *Frankenstein* would not be Mary's first published book. While she was putting the finishing touches on the novel, she combined some of her letters and journal entries to produce a book about her elopement trip in 1814. *History of a Six Weeks' Tour* was published anonymously in December, shortly before *Frankenstein* was due to appear. Such travel accounts were popular in an era without movies, television, or even photography, and Mary clearly wanted to do her part to raise some money for the household.

The end of 1817 was a fertile period for the family publishing industry. William Godwin's novel *Mandeville* — the book Fanny had thought should be completed for the world's sake, even as she contemplated suicide — was published. Some readers, including Shelley, thought it was Godwin's best work in years. But Peacock, in his novel *Nightmare Abbey,* has a character flip through what is obviously intended to be Godwin's book, remarking, "Devilman, [*Mandeville*] a novel. Hm. Hatred, revenge, misanthropy, and quotations from the Bible. Hm. This is the morbid anatomy of black bile."

Mary was gratified with the warm reception that greeted *History of a Six Weeks' Tour.* Thomas Moore praised it, guessing who the author was, and Percy told him, "Mrs. Shelley, tho' sorry that her secret is discovered, is exceedingly delighted to hear that you have derived any amusement from our book.— Let me say in her defence that the Journal of the Six Weeks Tour was written before she was seventeen, and that she has another literary secret which I will in a short time ask you to *keep* in return for having *discovered* this."

Percy himself was hardly idle. The publisher of *Laon and Cythna* had withdrawn all copies of the book from sale because of its inflammatory contents, but allowed Shelley to tone it down and republish it under the title *The Revolt of Islam.* In December he also wrote the sonnet that has proved to be his most enduring work, "Ozymandias."

Mary received her first bound copy of the three-volume *Frankenstein* on the last day of 1817. Percy had written a preface in the author's voice. He assured readers that "The event on which this fiction is founded has been supposed, by Dr. Darwin, and some of the physiological writers of Germany, as not of impossible occurrence." He then went on to describe the origin of the book in "casual conversation" and in the setting of the book around Geneva. "The season was cold and rainy, and in the evenings we crowded around a blazing wood fire, and occasionally amused ourselves with some German stories of ghosts, which happened to fall into our hands. These tales excited in us a playful desire of imitation." This story, he said, was the only one completed. He declared that the book was a psychological study that "affords a point of view to the imagination for the delineating of human passions more comprehensive and commanding than any which the ordinary relations of existing events can yield." It is doubtful that Mary herself would be immodest enough to make such a claim.

The first edition consisted of five hundred copies. It would eventually sell out, but after the publisher deducted his expenses, Mary was left with proceeds of only twenty-eight pounds (the equivalent of about $3,000 in 2005 dollars). Mary braced herself for bad reviews — just the book's dedication was sufficient to garner several. After reading *Mandeville,* Mary had decided to dedicate her own novel to her father, and reviewers, seeing this, suspected that Percy was the author of *Frankenstein.* In the Tory *Quarterly Review,* John Wilson Croker wrote:

> [*Frankenstein*] is piously dedicated to Mr. Godwin and is written in the spirit of his school. The dreams of insanity are embodied in the strong and striking language of the insane, and the author, notwithstanding the rationality of his preface, often leaves us in doubt whether he is not as mad as his hero. Mr. Godwin is the patriarch of a literary family, whose chief skill is in delineating the wanderings of the intellect, and which strangely delights in the most afflicting and humiliating of human miseries. His disciples are a kind of *out-pensioners of Bedlam,* and like "Mad Bess" or "Mad Tom," are occasionally visited with paroxysms of genius and fits of expression, which make sober-minded people wonder and shudder.

Croker was a prominent opponent of Romantic poetry (his later review of John Keats's *Endymion* was so savage that it is said to have hastened Keats's death), but he wasn't alone in disliking *Frankenstein.* William Beckford, a fellow Gothic novelist and author of *Vathek,* a Byron favorite, noted in the flyleaf of his copy of Mary's novel, "perhaps the foulest toadstool that has yet sprung up from the reeking dunghill of the present times." Samuel Johnson's muse Hester Thrale Piozzi, now an old lady, wrote, "Nothing attracts us but what terrifies, and is within — if within — a hairbreadth of positive disgust . . . some of the strange things they write remind me of Squire Richard's visit to the Tower Menagerie, when he says 'They are *pure* grim devils,'— particularly a wild and hideous tale called Frankenstein."

Shelley had personally sent a copy of the novel to Sir Walter Scott, one of the most popular and respected writers of the time. Scott responded by writing a generally favorable review in *Edinburgh Magazine* in the March 1818 issue, "It is no slight merit in our eyes," he wrote, "that the tale [*Frankenstein*], though wild in incident, is written in plain and forcible English, without exhibiting that mixture of hyperbolical Germanism with which tales of wonder are usually told, as if it were necessary that the language should be extravagant as the fiction." Scott also commented favorably about the descriptions of landscape, as having "freshness, precision and beauty." He found some parts of the plot improbable — the monster's ability to learn how to speak and read through a hole in the wall, for example — but he enjoyed the book. "Upon the whole, the work impresses us with a high idea of the author's original genius and happy power of expression. We . . . congratulate our readers upon a novel which excites new reflections and untried sources of emotion."

Those closest to Mary naturally praised the book, though she must have been particularly gratified by her father's reaction. Godwin wrote proudly of it as "the most wonderful work to have been written at twenty years of age that I ever heard of." Even Byron commented that Mary's novel was "a wonderful work for a Girl of nineteen — *not* nineteen indeed at that time." Claire, who had irritated Mary in so many other ways, was openly generous in her estimation of the book. She wrote in a letter to Byron,

> Mary has just published her first work . . . It is a most wonderful performance full of genius . . . as no one would imagine could have been written by so young a person. I am delighted & whatever

> private feelings of envy I may have at not being able to do so well myself yet all yields when I consider that she is a woman & will prove in time an ornament to us & an argument in our favour. How I delight in a lovely woman of strong and cultivated intellect. How I delight to hear all the intricacies of mind & argument hanging on her lips.

She was praising women's intellect to the wrong person.

Shelley also wrote a review that he planned, unsuccessfully, to publish anonymously to publicize the novel. He praised the book's moral nature and the emotions it evoked, summing up the meaning of the work as, "Treat a person ill, and he will become wicked. Requite affection with scorn . . . for whatever cause, as the refuse of his kind — divide him, a social being from society, and you impose upon him the irresistible obligations — malevolence and selfishness." This interpretation linked the book's moral to Godwin's philosophy, indicating that Percy missed much of the point.

Mary had not seen any of the published reviews for her book by the time she and Shelley left England. When they had moved into their house in Marlow, Shelley had taken out a twenty-one-year lease on it. In reality, they stayed there for just a little less than a year, though that was a long stretch by Shelley's standards. Since they were traveling for Shelley's health, Mary had no idea how long they might stay in Italy. She selected a hundred books to be shipped to their destination, and a smaller number to carry in their luggage. In early February, she closed up the house and joined the rest of the party in London.

For the next month, Mary shopped and enjoyed company. They went to the British Museum to see the Elgin Marbles, which had just been put on display. They stocked up on writing materials and paper. They went to the theater and opera — Mary in a strapless gown and Shelley in a formal coat. Hunt described Shelley as "a thin patrician-looking young cosmopolite yearning out upon us," and Mary as a "sedate-faced young lady bending in a similar direction with her great tablet of a forehead, & her white shoulders unconscious of a crimson gown."

Before they were able to depart, more unpleasantness with the Godwins arose. Claire had never told her mother about Byron and the child, but rumors had reached the Godwins that Allegra was Claire's child and Shelley was the father. When confronted, Claire told them about her love affair with Byron. Her mother was horrified and blamed her daughter's downfall on Mary, whom she bad-mouthed for the rest of her life. In point of fact, the Godwins never believed that Byron was truly the father of Claire's child, which made Mary's father even more resolute in trying to collect what he felt was his monetary due from Shelley.

On March 11, the same day that *Frankenstein* had its official publication, Mary, Percy, and Claire, along with William, Clara, Allegra, and two nursemaids, set out on the road to Dover. Here they lodged for the night because no boats were leaving the port. The remnant of a tremendous storm that had passed over England spreading ruin in its wake was still producing high winds and rain. As in Mary's novel, the bad weather was an ominous sign. They left England on March 12. Four of the travelers, including the three youngest, would never return.

CHAPTER NINE

THE GHOSTS' REVENGE

Who telleth a tale of unspeaking death?
  Who lifteth the veil of what is to come?
Who painteth the shadows that are beneath
  The wide-winding caves of the peopled tomb?
Or uniteth the hopes of what shall be
  With the fears and the love for that which we see?

— "On Death," Percy Shelley, 1815

THE STORM BLEW the Shelley entourage across the Dover Strait to Calais in less than three hours. Though speedy, the trip was rough; one of the frightened passengers recited the Lord's Prayer constantly. Shelley, as always, was happiest when he traveled. He wrote to Leigh Hunt, "We are all very well & in excellent spirits, Motion has always this effect upon the blood, even when the mind knows that there are causes for dejection." Before the summer was out, Shelley's love of motion, abrupt and nearly incessant, would turn deadly.

For their third trip through France, for novelty's sake, they chose a different route, skipping Paris this time. They were disappointed; on the first day Mary wrote in her journal that "The country is uninteresting but the weather is delightful." After a week they arrived at Lyons and hired another carriage to get them to Italy. Mary wrote with excited anticipation, "we can see from here Jura and Mont Blanc & the whole scene reminds me of Geneva."

By the twenty-eighth of March they were approaching the Alps. Mary was thrilled to see the sun rise on their snowy peaks, so reminiscent of her 1816 summer. Their carriage followed a winding river, where the scenery was gorgeous. Then they began to ascend the heights that they would have to cross. "The snows encroach upon the road," Mary wrote, and she found it "dreadful" as they made their way along the edge of a precipice, where a thousand-foot fall was only inches away from the carriage wheels. Taking the new road that Napoleon had built though the Cenis Pass, they entered Italy.

They stayed in Milan for three weeks, possibly to please Claire, who wanted to keep as long as possible her beloved Allegra, now fifteen months old and developing a personality. Claire, whose singing voice had been celebrated by both Byron and Shelley, also loved attending the operas and ballets at La Scala. Late in the evenings, after the nurses had put the children to bed, Claire played chess with Percy. The growing closeness between the two of them disturbed Mary but she could do nothing about it. There is little reason to think that Shelley would hesitate to have sex with Claire, for he always opposed "exclusive" sexual possession — by husbands or wives. Claire was, in this, even more an ardent disciple than Mary. Events later made the precise relationship between Shelley and Claire at this time important.

On April 13, Shelley wrote to Byron, ". . . to inform you that your little girl has arrived here in excellent health and spirits, with eyes as blue as the sky over our heads." They thought they could lure Byron to join them and re-create the atmosphere of the 1816 summer, but their hopes were dashed when Byron refused to pick up his daughter. He made it abundantly clear that he did not want to see Claire "for fear that the consequence might be an addition to the family." Claire's letters made it clear that she still hoped Byron might again become attracted to her.

Apparently Byron also suggested that Claire should not visit her child after she gave it up. Percy, ever solicitous of Claire, replied to Byron on April 22, "You write as if from the instant of its departure all future intercourse were to cease between Claire and her child. This I cannot think you ought to have expected, or even to have desired. . . . What should we think of a woman who should resign her infant child with no prospect of ever seeing it again, even to a father in whose tenderness she entirely confided? . . . Surely it is better if we err, to err on the side of kindness than of rigour."

But there was little kindness in Byron's letter to his friend John Cam Hobhouse in England. "Shelley has got to Milan with the bastard & it's mother — but won't send the shild [*sic*] — unless I will go & see the mother — I have sent a messenger for the Shild [*sic*] — but I can't leave my quarters."

Shelley, sensing Byron's new attitude, warned Claire that it might be better if she raised the child herself. Claire disagreed, arguing that Allegra would have greater opportunities in life if she were brought up by Byron. Claire still hoped that Allegra could be her entry back into Byron's life — that the little girl would melt the heart of the heartless lord. She wrote Byron a letter agreeing to give up Allegra, but asking him to send a lock of his hair so that she might put it with Allegra's in a locket. "Remember that I am wretched how wretched," she wrote, "and for the smallest word of kindness from you I will bless & honour you." Having made up her mind, Claire kept Allegra until her own twentieth birthday, on the twenty-seventh of April. The next day, the child's nursemaid Elise Duvilliard took Allegra to Venice.

On May 1, the Shelleys, with their two children and Claire, went on to Pisa. There they received a letter from Elise, telling them that Byron was delighted with the pretty child with her blond hair and blue eyes. At Byron's villa, she wrote, "they dress her in little trousers trimmed with lace and treat her like a little princess."

The Shelleys were still looking for a place to settle down, but though they visited Pisa's famous Leaning Tower and the university, they decided the city was not for them. Mary was disturbed by the sight of chained criminals working in the streets. "I could never walk in the streets except in misery," she wrote, for "you could get into no street but you heard the clanking of their chains."

They went south to Leghorn (Livorno) where a small colony of English emigrés lived. The Shelleys had a letter of introduction to Maria Gisborne, the grande dame of English society there — and onetime babysitter for Mary. Gisborne had led an adventurous life. As a child, she had lived with her father, who was an English merchant in Constantinople; they later moved to Rome, where Maria met and married her first husband, William Reveley. With him she returned to England, becoming friends with William Godwin and Mary Wollstonecraft. Maria Reveley had taken the infant Mary Godwin and her sister Fanny Imlay into her home and cared for them in the days following the death of Mary Wollstonecraft. Widowed soon after, Maria had received several proposals of marriage from Godwin — by letter — but turned him down, instead marrying John Gisborne, a businessman. They moved to Rome in 1801 and had lived in Italy ever since. Shelley described the Gisbornes to Peacock, "Mrs. Gisborne is a sufficiently amiable & very accomplished woman . . . Her husband a man with little thin lips receding forehead & a prodigious nose is an excessive bore."

Mary found Maria Gisborne to be a sympathetic listener, perhaps the first she had encountered since eloping with Shelley. In time, Maria would almost resume her role as surrogate mother, and would be one of the few people Mary reached out to when tragedy struck.

Despite the hospitality shown them by the Gisbornes, the Shelleys were not happy with Livorno. Maria suggested that they might like Bagni di Lucca, a spa town sixty miles north, where they went early in June. They settled in a little house called Casa Bertini, surrounded by mountains and woods. Mary was pleased for "we have a small garden and at the end of it is an arbour of laurel trees so thick that the sun does not penetrate it." They also acquired a new Italian servant, Paolo Foggi, who would cause them considerable trouble in the future.

While at Casa Bertini, the Shelleys received the March issue of *Blackwood's Magazine* that contained Sir Walter Scott's review of *Frankenstein.* Mary was thrilled to read his praise, but a bit taken aback that Scott thought Shelley had written the book. She sent a letter of appreciation to Scott, revealing herself as the author.

Byron refused to respond to Claire's letters, so she kept in touch with her child through Elise, who had stayed on as Allegra's nursemaid. Two letters from Elise in August set in motion a tragedy that would begin the destruction of Mary's happiness. When Claire heard that her daughter was in ill health, she wanted to rush to her. Shelley learned upon inquiry that Byron had, for the time being, turned Allegra over to the British consul at Venice, Richard Hoppner. Claire, more worried than events would prove justified, persuaded Percy to take her to Venice to see Allegra.

They departed on August 17, leaving Mary at Bagni di Lucca with her two children.

Shelley and Claire arrived at the Hoppners' house on August 23, finding Allegra was well and in good spirits. Claire rejoiced at the sight of her daughter, whom she had not seen for two and a half months. Shelley wrote Mary that the girl was "as beautiful as ever," but taller and paler. Hoppner took him aside and advised him not to tell Byron that Claire was in the city, for Byron often expressed his "extreme horror" of meeting her again.

Shelley went to see Byron at his palazzo on the Grand Canal at three in the afternoon, when he was sure he would be out of bed. It was clear why Byron refused to go anywhere to meet friends or former lovers; he had gained weight and looked much older. Another visitor that year reported that Byron's "face had become pale, bloated, and sallow. He had grown very fat, his shoulders broad and round, and the knuckles were lost in fat." Byron was living a dissolute life about which tongues were wagging even outside of Venice. Shelley wrote of him, "He associates with wretches who . . . do not scruple to avow practices which are not only not named, but I believe seldom even conceived in England." Byron's sexual escapades were the talk of Venice and he immortalized them in these verses:

So we'll go no more a-roving
So late into the night,
Though the heart be still as loving,
And the moon be still as bright.

For the sword outwears its sheath,
And the soul wears out the breast,
And the heart must pause to breathe,
And love itself have rest.

Though the night was made for loving,
And the day returned too soon,
Yet we'll go no more a-roving
By the light of the moon.

Despite the way Byron looked, he was happy to see Shelley again. They discussed the Claire and Allegra situation. Shelley led Byron to believe that Claire and Mary and the other children were all in nearby Padua and then brought up his plan for Allegra to visit them. Byron turned down the idea, instead offering to let Claire as well as the Shelleys stay with Allegra at Byron's summer house in Este. To Shelley this was a welcome surprise, one that would be sure to please Claire.

The two poets found once again that they enjoyed each other's company. Byron, who was all image, was fascinated by Shelley, who never cared what people thought of him. Shelley, for his part, found Byron's facility with words irresistible. The two took a gondola to the Lido, Venice's seaside resort. It was one of Byron's favorite spots, and he kept horses there. He and Shelley rode along the beach and talked about literature, life, and the meaning of their lives.

The ride became the basis for Shelley's poem *Julian and Maddalo: A Conversation,* written in 1819. In its prose preface, Shelley described the Venetian nobleman Count Maddalo (Byron): "He is a person of the most consummate genius. . . . But it is his weakness to be proud: he derives, from a comparison of his own extraordinary mind with the dwarfish intellects that surround him, an intense apprehension of the nothingness of human life. . . . His ambition preys upon itself, for want of objects which it can consider worthy of exertion."

About Julian, the figure who represents himself, Shelley wrote he was "passionately attached to those philosophical notions which assert the power of man over his own mind, and the immense improvements of which, by the extinction of certain moral superstitions, human society may yet be susceptible . . . Maddalo takes a wicked pleasure in drawing out his taunts against religion. What Maddalo thinks on these matters is not exactly known." As night fell, the two poets returned to Byron's palazzo and talked until five in the morning before Shelley returned to Claire.

Shelley was now in a dilemma; he felt he had to produce Mary at Byron's villa at Este as quickly as possible so Byron would not suspect his deception. He sent a letter explaining the situation to Mary and asked her to leave Bagni di Lucca at once. He gave her specific instructions for the journey so that she could make the trip in five days, and told her to bring Paolo Foggi. "I have done for the best — and my own beloved Mary, you must soon come & scold me if I have done wrong, & kiss me if I have done right."

Shelley's request came at the worst possible time, for it was now the height of the Italian summer, and the heat was affecting Clara's health. On the twenty-first of August Mary noted in her journal that Clara was "not well." The notation was repeated the next two days. On the twenty-eighth of August, just as Mary was enjoying a visit from the Gisbornes, Shelley's letter arrived, summoning her to Este. Two days later, while still packing for the journey, she celebrated her twenty-first birthday. She set out the next day with her two children, three-year-old William and Clara, just shy of her first birthday. Clara was continually crying, for she was cutting her teeth. In the suffocating heat of the journey, she contracted dysentery, a very common ailment of the time for infants.

By the time they reached Byron's villa at Este, Clara was dehydrated and suffered from mild convulsions. Mary wrote to Mrs. Gisborne,

> . . . we have arrived safe and yet I can hardly call it safe since the fatigue has given my poor Ca an attack of dysentery and although she is now some what recovered from that disorder she is still in a frightful state of weakness and fever as [*and*] is reduced to be so thin in this short time that you would hardly know her again — the physician of Este is a stupid fellow but there is one come from Padua & who appears clever — so I hope under his care she will soon get well, although we are still in great anxiety concerning her.

Over the next two weeks, Clara improved only slightly.

Meanwhile, Shelley was bothered by ailments of his own, suffering from a severe stomachache, which he believed was a result of being poisoned by some Italian cakes. Claire too complained of health problems that summer. The two of them went to Padua to consult a doctor on September 22. They arrived too late to see him and Shelley decided to go on to Venice by himself to meet Byron. He sent Claire back to Este with a note telling Mary to bring little Clara to the doctor in Padua on September 24 at 8 a.m. and that he would meet her there. This meant Mary and her child had to leave Este at 3:30 in the morning and also required taking Clara on yet another uncomfortable journey.

On the appointed day, Mary did as Shelley had asked. By the time she met him at Padua, Clara's condition had grown worse. Shelley insisted that they take her on to Venice, where Byron had told him of a better physician, a Dr. Alietti. Maddeningly, they were detained at Fusina, on the coast opposite Venice, when Austrian soldiers demanded their passports, which the Shelleys had forgotten. (Italy was not yet a nation, and parts of it belonged to the Austrian empire.) Percy finally managed to talk their way through. While they were crossing the lagoon from the mainland to Venice by gondola, the baby started to go into convulsions. Mary carried her to an inn while Shelley searched for the doctor, who was not at home. Clara Everina died in her mother's arms on September 24. Mary wrote that day in her journal (in which the deaths of Fanny Godwin and Harriet Shelley were also recorded), "This is the Journal book of [my] misfortunes." The child was buried on the Lido beach with no memorial stone. Mary could not bear to attend the service.

She spent the next four days in Venice. During that time she saw Byron, who commiserated with her and then gave her two of his new poems to transcribe for the printer. Perhaps this was not as cold as it sounds; her friends may have wanted to take her mind off her loss, for Mary also records that at this time Mrs. Hoppner took her to the library, an art gallery, and shopping.

Percy sent a letter to Claire describing the death of Clara, and added, "All this is miserable enough — is it not? but must be borne [*one line is here erased*] — And above all, my dear girl, take care of yourself." He wrote to Peacock as well in early October, "I have not been without events to disturb & distract me, amongst which is the death of my little girl. She died of a disorder peculia[r] to the climate." He then went on to describe his interest in Byron's new poem *Don Juan* and mentioned that he himself was starting to write a poetic drama that would be called *Prometheus Unbound.*

Mary, not easily consoled, blamed Percy's carelessness and Claire's selfishness for the tragedy. She resented the fact that Percy acted for Claire's welfare at the expense of their own child. Mary also suspected that her husband did not feel the loss of their little girl as keenly as she did, for his favorite was William, affectionately called Willmouse.

If Mary looked for sympathy from her father, she was disappointed as usual. Godwin, after receiving the news in a letter from Mary, criticized her for her excessive grief: "I sincerely sympathize with you in the affliction which forms the subject of your letter, and which I may consider as the first severe trial of your constancy and the firmness of your temper that has occurred to you in the course of your life. You should, however, recollect that it is only persons of a very ordinary sort, and of a pusillanimous disposition, that sink long under a calamity of this nature."

They spent the next two months at Byron's villa, where the sight of Claire playing with Allegra must have bitterly reminded Mary of her own loss. At the end of October, Claire returned Allegra to the Hoppners, but she continued to travel with Mary and Percy. They visited Rome, and then settled in Naples, where they planned to stay for the winter.

Mary sank into a deep depression. The ghost of the past in the form of Harriet came back to haunt her and cast a pall over her marriage. For a time Mary found it difficult to have sexual relations with Shelley. Shelley, in his turn, was starting to believe that Mary was a disappointment. Sometimes it appeared that he found Claire to be a more lively personality and a more enthusiastic student of his principles. He caught the mood in a poem titled "The Past" that seemed directed at Mary:

Wilt thou forget the happy hours
Which we buried in Love's sweet bowers
Heaping over their corpses cold
Blossoms and leaves, instead of mould?
Blossoms which were the joys that fell,
And leaves, the hopes that yet remain.

Forget the dead, the past? Oh, yet
There are ghosts that may take revenge for it,

Memories that make the heart a tomb,
Regrets which glide through the spirit's gloom,
And with ghastly whispers tell
That joy, once lost, is pain.

The winter of 1818–19 brought another potentially dangerous secret into Percy and Mary's relationship. On February 27, 1819, Percy went to a courthouse in Naples and registered the birth of a daughter, Elena Adelaide Shelley, whose birthdate he gave as December 27, 1818. He listed himself and Mary as parents, although the "mother" was not present to sign the certificate; two witnesses, a barber and a cheese merchant, attested to the fact that Mary had given birth to the child. Little is known for sure about the baby, except that Mary was definitely *not* the mother.

Literary historians still argue over the parentage of Elena Adelaide. Mary's journal makes no mention of her, nor did Mary seem otherwise to be aware of her existence. Elena Adelaide was turned over to foster parents and never entered the Shelley household. Mary did note in her journal that Claire was "not well" on December 27, the date that the mysterious child had been born. Elise Duvilliard, the nursemaid who was again traveling with the Shelleys, later claimed that Claire had given birth to the child, and that its father was Percy. However, her testimony is colored by the fact that in January 1819, when the Shelleys discovered Elise herself was pregnant, by Paolo Foggi, both servants were dismissed. Shelley's ideas of sexual freedom evidently had some limits. Unfortunately, Claire's journal between April 1818 and March 1819 is — like so many other crucial records — missing. It would be possible to tell her condition during this time because she marked the onset of her menstrual periods with a cross.

If the true parents of the child were Percy and Claire, she would have had to have become pregnant either during their final days in England or the first days in Europe. On the other hand, if the baby was indeed Claire's child, would she have been willing to give it up, so soon after losing possession of Allegra? It could be argued that Claire might have agreed to this arrangement because a second child would have weakened her position with Byron, but she clearly enjoyed being a mother.

Another theory is that the child was a foundling that Shelley wanted to adopt as a replacement for Clara Everina and restore Mary's happiness. If so, it would not be the first time Shelley had such a harebrained idea. As a little boy, he had wanted his family to adopt a Gypsy child, and on the elopement trip through France with Mary, he had actually offered to take a French child as his own, but the parents refused. If that were the case, however, why didn't he bring this child home to Mary?

In any event, the baby, to whom Shelley referred as his "Neapolitan charge," died June 9, 1820, when it was a mere fifteen months old — one more casualty left behind in Shelley's wake. Registering the child's birth had been Shelley's last act in Naples. He was on the move again, taking his loved ones wherever his whims commanded. Mary's journal for February 28, 1819, has the notation: "A most tremendous fuss." Six days later, on March 5, they arrived in Rome. Here they met Amelia Curran, the daughter of an Irish politician, who had come to Italy to study painting. In Rome, she made a portrait of Shelley; more important, she painted the only known portraits of Claire and little William. William appeared positively angelic in Curran's painting — much the way his counterpart is described in *Frankenstein:* "with sweet laughing blue eyes, dark eyelashes, and curling hair. When he smiles, two little dimples appear on each cheek, which are rosy with health."

Mary regained some of her spirits, and evidently her relationship with Shelley improved, for in March, she became pregnant again. But the ghosts were not finished. Three-year-old Willmouse was the delight of his parents. He was talking now, chattering away in three languages — English, Italian, and French. On May 25, William fell ill; the doctor diagnosed an attack of worms and prescribed laxatives. Three days later, the boy appeared to be convalescing, but the doctor advised the Shelleys to leave Rome, for the oppressive summer heat could be dangerous for him. Actually, the Tiber marshes near the city were breeding grounds for mosquitoes that spread malaria, but the connection was not yet realized.

For once, Shelley did not seize the opportunity to run off to another location — a lack of action that may have killed his son. On June 2, Willmouse fell ill with a high fever and the sweats and chills of malaria. Mary was frantic at the thought of losing another child, and she and

Claire sat up with the boy during his restless, sleepless nights. The Shelleys enlisted the help of John Bell, an expatriate English doctor, who was the physician of Pauline Borghese, sister of Napoleon. Mary anxiously watched for any sign of improvement. On June 3, she recorded hopefully, "William is very ill but gets better towards the evening — . . ."

But the next day William suffered convulsions that left him exhausted and weak. By June 5, his condition was critical. For Mary, it was a repetition of the nightmare she had endured with Clara Everina. She wrote a frantic note to Maria Gisborne, "William is in the greatest danger — We do not quite despair yet we have the least possible reason to hope — Yesterday he was in the convulsions of death and he was saved from them — Yet we dare not must not hope — . . . The misery of these hours is beyond calculation — The hopes of my life are bound up in him."

Mary's journal stops after she wrote the date for the fourth of June. By then she must have known that the doctor could not save her son. Little Willmouse died at noon on June 7, a victim of the malaria epidemic that was sweeping Rome. Mary may have thought of the lines she wrote in *Frankenstein*: "William is dead!— that sweet child, whose smiles delighted and warmed my heart, who was so gentle, yet so gay." He was buried in the Protestant Cemetery at Rome. Amelia Curran was asked to set a small stone pyramid over William's grave — but even that tender gesture would bring another more crushing revelation to Mary three years later.

With Willmouse's death, Mary felt her happiness had ended. They soon left Rome for Leghorn with Mary clutching the painting of William that Amelia Curran had made. She wrote to Amelia on June 27, saying that she could think of nothing else but her dead child. "I am going to write another stupid letter to you — yet what can I do — I no sooner take up my pen than my thoughts run away with me —& I cannot guide it except about *one* subject & that I must avoid." Mary asked about the tomb for William that Amelia had promised to decorate: "near which I shall lie one day & care not — for my own sake — how soon — I shall never recover [from] that blow — I feel it more now than at Rome — the thought never leaves me for a single moment — Everything on earth has lost its interest to me."

On June 29, Mary wrote to Leigh Hunt's wife, Marianne: "I never know one moments ease from the wretchedness & despair that possesses me.... I feel that I am no[t] fit for any thing & therefore not fit to live... William was so good so beautiful so entirely attached to me — To the last moment almost he was in such abounding health & spirits."

Percy also mourned his son. He wrote to Thomas Peacock on June 8, "Yesterday after an illness of only a few days my little William died. There was no hope from the moment of the attack. You will be kind enough to tell all my friends, so that I need not write to them — It is a great exertion to me to write this & it seems to me as if, hunted by calamity as I have been, that I should neve[r] recover any cheerfulness again —." He more easily found expression for his grief in poetry.

My lost William, thou in whom
Some bright spirit lived, and did
That decaying robe consume
Which its lustre faintly hid, —
Here its ashes find a tomb,
But beneath this pyramid
Thou art not — if a thing divine
Like thee can die, thy funeral shrine
Is thy mother's grief and mine.

Where are thou, my gentle child?
Let me think thy spirit feeds,
With its life intense and mild,
The love of living leaves and weeds
Among these tombs and ruins wild;—
Let me think that through low seeds
Of sweet flowers and sunny grass
Into their hues and scents may pass
A portion —

William's death plunged Mary into such sorrow and depression that it destroyed some of her feelings toward her husband. She withdrew emotionally and transformed her grief into anger against him — a silent, separating coldness that reflected the way Godwin had punished her. Percy's carelessness and egotism, which had once marked him as a poet unlike other men, now seemed merely cruel and selfish to her. Mary found it hard to be interested in lovemaking at such a time.

Her depression may have, on the other hand, actually increased Percy's ardor. In a poem he wrote — keeping it secret from her — he described her "Mourning in thy robe of pride, / Desolation — deified!" He urged her to make the most of the moment in sensual delight:

Ha! thy frozen pulses flutter
With a love thou darest not utter,
. . . Kiss me;— oh! thy lips are cold;
Round my neck thine arms enfold —
They are soft, but chill and dead;
And thy tears upon my head
Burn like points of frozen lead.

Yet he never addressed Mary's needs and the causes of her sorrow, and in another poem he wrote — this one specifically for her eyes — he complained about them.

My dearest Mary, wherefore hast thou gone,
And left me in this dreary world alone?
Thy form is here indeed — a lovely one —
But thou art fled, gone down the dreary road,
That leads to Sorrow's most obscure abode;
Thou sittest on the hearth of pale despair,
Where
For thine own sake I cannot follow thee.

It is almost superfluous to say that William Godwin acted at his worst during this, the saddest moment of his daughter's life. Despite her tragedy, he was determined to manipulate her to get money out of her husband. On learning of William's death, Godwin wrote Mary two letters; the first is lost; Shelley may have destroyed it. But we can gauge its contents by a reference to it in a letter Percy sent to Leigh Hunt:

> We cannot yet come home. Poor Mary's spirits continue dreadfully depressed. And I cannot expose her to Godwin in this state. I wrote to this hard-hearted person, (the first letter I had written for a year), on account of the terrible state of her mind, and to entreat him to try to soothe her in his next letter. The very next letter, received yesterday, and addressed to her, called her husband (me) "a disgraceful and flagrant person" tried to persuade her that I was under great engagements to give him *more* money (after having given him £4,700), and urged her if she ever wished a connection to continue between him and her to force me to get money for him.— He cannot persuade her that I am what I am not, nor place a shade of enmity between her and me — but he heaps on her misery, still misery.— I have not yet shewn her the letter — but I must.

After Godwin heard about Mary's depression, he wrote her that if she persisted in her "selfishness and ill humour," those people close to her "will finally cease to love" her. Once again, Godwin threatened what she always feared most, the same punishment he had used in her childhood: the withdrawal of love.

The kindest view of Godwin is that he was appealing to Mary's higher nature, urging her to assuage her grief through stoicism. It is difficult, however, to find any sensitivity in his words when he scolds her, "I had thought you to be ranked among those noble spirits that do honour to our nature. Oh! what a falling off is here! . . . you have lost a child; and all the rest of the world, all that is beautiful, and all that has a claim upon your kindness, is nothing, because a child of three years old is dead!"

A year later Percy would warn Godwin about the effect his letters had on Mary: "Your letters," he wrote, "from their style and spirit . . . never fail to produce an appalling effect on her frame."

The summer of 1819 was one of the lowest points in Mary's life. Although only twenty-two, she had experienced enough tragedy and loss for a lifetime. Her experiences led to thoughts of suicide, and probably only the fact that she was again pregnant kept her going. News of the success of *Frankenstein* may have raised her spirits a bit. In August, five months after the publication of the book, Thomas Love Peacock wrote Shelley, "I went to the Egham races. I met on the course a great number of my old acquaintance, by the reading portion of whom I was asked a multitude of questions concerning *Frankenstein* and its author. It seems to be universally known and read. The criticism of the *Quarterly,* though unfriendly, contained many admissions of its merit, and must on the whole have done it service." As a postscript to a letter Percy sent to Peacock in July, Mary asked, "What has been the fate of the 2 vessels that sailed for the north pole?" indicating that her curiosity about the scientific background of her novel was still alive.

Mary began to deal with her grief the only way she was able to — by writing. On the fourth of August, she began two new projects. One was a new journal, in a new book. "I begin my journal on Shelley's birthday," she wrote. "We have now lived five years together & if all the events of the five years were blotted out I might be happy — but to have won & then cruelly have lost the associations of four years is not an accident that the human mind can bend without much suffering."

At the top of the page, Mary had written from memory a Shelley poem that seemed to reflect her awareness that she needed to put the past behind her:

That time is gone for ever — child —
Those hours are frozen forever
We look on the past, & stare aghast
On the ghosts with aspects strange & wild
Of the hopes whom thou & I beguiled
To death in life's dark river.

The waves we gazed on then rolled by
Their stream is unreturning
We two yet stand, in a lonely land,
Like tombs to mark the memory
Of joys & griefs that fade & flee
In the light of life's dim morning.

Willmouse had died but perhaps even worse, the original William, Mary's father, threatened to withhold his love from her. So, on the same day that Mary began a new journal, she started to write a novel in which she would reclaim that love. In something like five weeks, she completed *Mathilda,* her most personal book. It dealt with the topic of father-daughter incest. Perhaps she was inspired by Shelley, who was putting the finishing touches on a play, *The Cenci,* about a historical Italian family that had practiced incest. He had originally heard the story while they were visiting the Gisbornes; at the time Percy suggested Mary write a novel on the subject. Then in April, in a museum in Rome, the Shelleys and Claire had seen a portrait of the daughter of the Cenci family, Beatrice. Claire, who probably knew of Byron's affair with his half-sister, wrote Byron, "I am sorely afraid to say that in the elder Cenci [the father] you may behold yourself in twenty years hence but if I live Allegra shall never be a Beatrice." So the topic was much on everyone's mind.

Mary's new novel was again told by a first-person narrator. Mathilda was a woman whose mother had died "a few days after my birth." Her father, overcome with grief, left Mathilda to be raised by her cold, unfeeling aunt. The theme of abandonment is here as in *Frankenstein,* for it resonated with the deepest feelings of Mary's own life. Mary skewers Godwin with this description of the father in the novel:

> He was a sincere and sympathizing friend — but he had met with none who superior or equal to himself could aid him in unfolding his mind, or make him seek for fresh stores of thought by exhausting the old ones. He felt himself superior in quickness of judgement to those around him . . . he became at the same time dogmatic and yet fearful of not coinciding with the only sentiments he could consider orthodox . . . at the same time that he strode with a triumphant stride over the rest of the world, he cowered, with self disguised lowliness, to his own party.

Mathilda's father returns sixteen years later and finds that his daughter is willing to forgive him. They move to London, but when a young man courts Mathilda, her father discovers, to his horror, his own attraction to her — a sexual rather than a paternal love. At first he treats her coldly, trying to suppress his desires, but she is shattered by his abrupt change in attitude. When Mathilda confronts him, he confesses what his true feelings are. She is horrified: "One idea rushed on my mind: never, never may I speak to him again." (The worst punishment she could imagine, obviously.) In shame, the father leaves a very long suicide note ("... rise from under my blighting influence as no flower so sweet ever did rise from beneath so much evil"). He then drowns himself.

Mathilda goes to Scotland, where she lives for two years in virtual isolation, feeling suicidal. Then she meets a young man, a Poet with a capital P, named Woodville, who encourages her to have a more positive approach to life. Woodville, clearly modeled after Shelley, is depicted as if Mary were trying to remind herself why she originally loved the man who was her husband:

> His genius was transcendant [*sic*], and when it rose as a bright star in the east all eyes were turned towards it in admiration ... He was glorious from his youth. Every one loved him; no shadow of envy or hate cast even from the meanest mind ever fell upon him. ... His heart was simple like a child, unstained by arrogance or vanity ... To bestow on your fellow men is a Godlike attribute — So indeed it is and as such not one fit for mortality;— the giver like Adam and Prometheus, must pay the penalty of rising above his nature by being the martyr to his own excellence.

Woodville's fiancée has died a few months earlier, but after meeting Mathilda his spirits rise. "He soon took great interest in me, and sometimes forgot his own grief to sit beside me and endeavour to cheer me." Being with him is good for Mathilda too: "Woodville for ever tried to lead me to the contemplation of what is beautiful and happy in the world." In a spasm of despondency, however, she proposes to him one day that they commit suicide together — she even prepares the laudanum. He explains to her all the reasons for living, persuading her that they must do so. Some of these sound like arguments Mary must have made to herself during her periods of depression.

While Woodville is away nursing his sick mother, Mathilda contracts tuberculosis. Knowing she has only a short time to live, she devotes her last energies to writing the manuscript that is this novel. The pain of Mary's own life emerges. Mathilda writes as she prepares to die: "I am alone . . . the blight of misfortune has passed over me and withered me; I know that I am about to die and I feel happy — joyous.— I feel my pulse; it beats fast; I place my thin hand on my cheek; it burns; there is a slight, quick spirit within me that is now emitting its last sparks. I shall never see the snows of another winter." As the book ends, the dying Mathilda's thoughts return to her father. "I go from this world where he is no longer and soon I shall meet him in another."

Mary sent the manuscript to Godwin in 1820. Maria Gisborne, who brought it to him, told Mary that he had found the subject "disgusting and detestable." Though his daughter had sent it to him to publish, Godwin put the manuscript away — a gesture made all the more remarkable because he would have been sure to make money on the book's publication, given the success of *Frankenstein*. It is, however, hard to see how Godwin could have reacted otherwise. The only question that remains is how conscious Mary was of the feelings toward Godwin that prompted her to write *Mathilda*. Those emotions were clear enough to others; no one in the Shelley family ever attempted to publish this work, and though Mary was to write and publish several more novels during her lifetime, it took *Mathilda* almost 150 years to see print.

Percy was also hard at work. In Rome, he had spent much of his energies writing a poem that would retell the Prometheus myth from a more optimistic perspective, one that would reflect the Godwinian vision of humankind continually progressing. Shelley's *Prometheus Unbound* is a very long verse play that deals with the triumph of good and love over evil, his attempt to write a work comparable to *Paradise Lost*. Though Percy chose the same model as Mary did in her book, the two Shelleys came to completely different interpretations of the myth. Percy persisted in his vision of a society ever moving toward greater and greater perfection, foretelling a future utopian society that was brought about by Prometheus's sacrifices. Mary had come to a different conclusion, one which grew stronger over the years. She saw the folly of man's attempts at immortality and overweening ambition and found them to be destructive rather than constructive urges. The Promethean figure in her work — Dr. Frankenstein — destroys himself and those he loves while failing in his quest to help humanity. In arriving at that insight, Mary was intellectually outgrowing both her models for Dr. Frankenstein: her father and her husband.

As the time drew near for Mary to give birth, the Shelleys traveled to Florence so that she could have the best possible medical care. Dr. Bell was to be there and Mary wanted to make sure that she had a safe delivery. But when her time came, Bell was sick and unavailable. On November 12, Mary had an easy two-hour labor before her "small but healthy, and pretty" baby appeared. The son was named Percy Florence Shelley; just as Mary had given her first son her father's name, she named this one after her husband. He was baptized in a church — this must have been at Mary's insistence — and his middle name came from the city where he was born.

For Mary the arrival of another son brought a small end to her suffering, but she never completely recovered from the deaths of Clara and William. She still avoided emotional commitment with her husband and even to a degree with her new baby because of her strong fear that he would be taken from her as well. She expressed these feelings to Marianne Hunt: "he is my only one and although he is so healthy and promising that for the life of me I cannot fear yet it is a bitter thought that all should be risked on one, yet how much sweeter than to be childless as I was for 5 hateful months." Mary's fear of losing a child was so great that she blistered her feet by walking vigorously to encourage her milk production so that she could nourish the infant. Percy wrote that his wife's life, "after the frightful events of the last two years . . . seems wholly to be bound up" in her new son's. Mary watched over Percy Florence for hours, even while he was sleeping.

In Florence Shelley wrote perhaps his most popular poem, *Ode to the West Wind,* which indicates that he too was trying to come out of his misery.

> *O Wild West Wind, thou breath of Autumn's being,*
> *Thou, from whose unseen presence the leaves dead*
> *Are driven, like ghosts from an enchanter fleeing.*

The poem ends with the immortal lines

> *The trumpet of a prophecy! O Wind,*
> *If Winter comes, can Spring be far behind?*

That optimistic spirit of the poem would prove to be misplaced.

CHAPTER TEN

A DOSE FOR POOR POLIDORI

Lord Ruthven had disappeared, and Aubrey's sister had glutted the thirst of a VAMPYRE!

— *The Vampyre,* Dr. John Polidori, 1819

THE SAME YEAR that Mary lost her two children, 1819, saw the publication of Dr. John Polidori's tale *The Vampyre,* the second of the modern myths created at the Villa Diodati in the haunted summer of 1816. The vampire figure was not new. It had long been the subject of legends and folklore before it was used in fiction in the nineteenth century. The belief that some dead people rose from the grave and fed on the blood of the living was widespread; such stories are found in Chinese and Japanese traditions as well. Nor was belief in vampires limited only to the ignorant. Rousseau, who did not believe in them, nevertheless had written, "If there is in this world a well-attested account, it is that of the vampires. Nothing is lacking: official reports, affidavits of well-known people, of surgeons, of priests, of magistrates; the judicial proof is most complete. And with all that, who is there who believes in vampires?" The Roman Catholic Church had recognized the existence of vampires in the fifteenth century.

The editor who wrote an introduction to the original publication of Polidori's book noted that the *London Journal* of 1732 printed an account of a case of vampirism in Hungary. A man named Arnold Paul (or Arnod Paole), who had served in the army on the borders of Turkish Serbia, complained that while there he had been tormented by a vampire. He had found a way to counter the threat by eating some of the dirt from the vampire's grave and rubbing himself with its blood. However, Paul himself, after returning to his home village, fell off a hay wagon and broke his neck. After his burial, he himself became a vampire, and many people complained of being tormented by him. A local magistrate gave permission to open Paul's grave. When his corpse was disinterred, it was found to be uncorrupted. A stake was driven through its heart, upon which a shower of blood spurted from the body and Paul cried out as if alive. Similar sightings and stories about vampires were recorded throughout the eighteenth century.

The editor also noted that in many parts of Greece, the transformation into vampire form is thought to be some kind of punishment after death. That belief, the editor speculated, may have inspired certain lines from Byron's poem *The Giaour:*

But first, on earth as Vampyre sent,
Thy corse shall from its tomb be rent;
Then ghastly haunt thy native place,
And suck the blood of all thy race;
There from thy daughter, sister, wife,
At midnight drain the stream of life;
Yet loathe the banquet which perforce
Must feed thy livid living corse,
Thy victims ere they yet expire,
Shall know the demon for their sire;
As cursing thee, thou cursing them,
Thy flowers are withered on the stem.
. . . .
Wet with thine own best blood shall drip
Thy gnashing tooth and haggard lip;
Then stalking to thy sullen grave —
Go — and with Gouls and Afrits rave;
Till these in horror shrink away
From spectre more accursed than they!

Polidori's monster, however, had modern touches that would influence all future vampire tale-tellers from Bram Stoker to Anne Rice. His vampire, Lord Ruthven, was an aristocrat, not a peasant or outcast as folkloric vampires were. Second, the vampire really is Ruthven and not a spirit that inhabits his body. Third, Ruthven is a traveler, a wanderer through the world. Finally, he is a seducer who preys on innocent victims; women, rather than being repelled, are attracted to him. All these elements were innovations introduced by Polidori — and of course all were inspired by none other than Lord Byron.

Byron had been the first to start writing a ghost story in response to his famous challenge. Writing came easily to him, and when he got down to work was capable of producing hundreds of lines of poetry in a night. However, prose did not seem to be his métier, for after writing only a few pages, he gave up the effort. What he did complete was intriguing. Told from the point of view of a young man, it describes the narrator's acquaintance and travels with Augustus Darvell, "a man of considerable fortune and ancient family." As in many of Byron's epic poems, the narrator and Darvell travel to the East, exploring Greek ruins near Ephesus. Darvell shows a familiarity with the area that indicates he has been there before. He tells the narrator that he has returned to die. He has one last request: giving the narrator his ring, he makes him swear to throw it into a certain spring near the Bay of Eleusis. Afterward, he must go to the temple of Ceres and wait one hour. Darvell refuses to explain what will happen next.

This is, of course, a hook calculated to draw the reader into the story, and shows Byron's narrative skill. Unfortunately, readers were destined to be disappointed, for after describing Darvell's sudden death, and the rapid decomposition of his body ("his countenance in a few minutes became nearly black"), Byron left his task, never completing the story.

The sudden darkening of the face after death was commonly held to be one of the attributes of vampires. It is obvious that the event the narrator will observe if he follows Darvell's instructions is the reappearance of his friend. If Byron had decided to continue, he would have told his own vampire story, which would have been a logical outgrowth of the discussions that inspired Mary Shelley to write *Frankenstein*. Both deal, in a sense, with immortality. Mary envisions it achieved through science;

Byron, through supernatural means. Byron's vision is thus closer to the traditional Gothic tales; Mary rises above them.

Byron dated his fragment June 17, 1816. At that time Polidori was still floundering with the hackneyed effort Mary described in her 1831 introduction to *Frankenstein*. He eventually incorporated it into another story, but must not have gotten very far with it in the summer of 1816, for it is never mentioned again in anyone's journals or letters.

After the Shelleys and Claire left Lake Geneva, Byron had less need for Polidori. At the beginning of the 1816 trip, Byron had been taking large amounts of laxatives to keep his weight down, and required a doctor's presence to ensure he didn't damage his health. Now he allowed himself to relax as old friends such as John Cam Hobhouse came to visit him at Villa Diodati. Hobhouse reported to Byron's sister, "A considerable change has taken place in his health; no brandy, no very late hours, no quarts of magnesia, nor deluges of soda water."

Polidori became not only superfluous, but also a burden, since he required emotional tending. Once, thinking that he was going to be fired, he had gone to his room with the intention of committing suicide. Byron appeared at the door and offered his hand as a "sign of reconciliation." On another occasion, Polidori got into an argument with a local apothecary about the quality of the magnesia he was supplying. Incensed at the man's "impudent" tone, Polidori struck him, breaking his eyeglasses. He was hauled into court and ordered to pay for the damage. Byron could not have been pleased at attracting further notoriety. All in all, as Byron explained in a letter to his sister, "I had no use for [Polidori] & his temper & habits were not good."

Byron eventually found some way of dismissing Polidori without putting him into a suicidal depression. In a letter to his father, Polidori put the best face on things, perhaps parroting whatever Byron had told him: "We have parted, finding that our tempers did not agree. he [*sic*] propos[ed] it & it was settled. there was no immediate cause, but a continued series of slight quarrels. I believe the fault, if any, has been on my part, I am not accustomed to have a master, & there fore my conduct was not free & easy."

Polidori was not ready to return to England, and decided to travel to

Italy, the land of his forebears. Shipping his trunks ahead to Milan, he set out on foot from Geneva. It was an ambitious trek, and his travel journal reveals only that he suffered from ill-fitting shoes and sore feet. It took him fifteen days, and when he arrived, he found waiting for him another letter of rebuke from his father: "your letter produced in me a twofold and opposite sensation: gratification at your having quitted a man so discredited in public opinion, and sorrow at seeing you almost a vagrant, and at the uncertainty at your lot." In other words, not only did his father disapprove of what Polidori had been doing, he also disapproved of his not doing it any longer.

Byron had been generous with severance pay, and Polidori could for the time being enjoy some of the finer things in life. He spent some evenings at La Scala, where he met a well-known literary priest, Father Ludovico di Breme, author of an Italian work on Romanticism. At Father di Breme's box, Polidori was introduced to prominent visitors such as Marie-Henri Beyle, better known by his pen name Stendhal. One evening Byron appeared as well, and Stendhal misunderstood the relationship between the two men, later recalling that Polidori was Byron's "pimp."

Even here, Polidori managed to make a spectacle of himself that rivaled the one on stage. One night an Austrian officer who wore a large fur hat was blocking Polidori's view of the stage. Polidori asked him to remove it, and the officer took offense. He asked Polidori to step outside, and Polidori, expecting a duel, willingly did so. However, the officer merely wanted to arrest him without a fuss. Byron, feeling that he was honor-bound as an Englishman to come to Polidori's defense, rushed to the local guardhouse with some friends. Stendhal, who had followed out of curiosity, described the incident: "There were fifteen or twenty of us gathered around the prisoner. Everybody was talking at once. M. Polidori was beside himself and red as a beet. Lord Byron, who on the contrary was very pale, was having great difficulty containing his rage." Finally, one of Byron's friends suggested that those without titles leave the room. That left Byron and some others, who guaranteed Polidori's good behavior by writing their names on a card. Impressed, the Austrians released Polidori, but the next day he was unceremoniously expelled from Milan.

Still on foot, traveling in the midst of a thunderstorm, he made his way to the town of Arezzo, where his uncle Luigi Polidori lived. The uncle wrote to his brother in England praising his nephew but sounding a note of alarm about his gambling and problems with money. Polidori hatched a plan to go to Brazil as medical advisor to the Danish consul. He sought his former employer's assistance, and Byron wrote to John Murray asking if he could get Polidori some letters of recommendation from friends in the British government. But the Brazil venture did not come to pass.

Polidori practiced medicine in Italy for a while, and traveled with an English family, the Guilfords, whose father had died while they visited Pisa. Apparently Polidori supervised his embalming and now prepared to take the body back to England. He bid a final farewell to Byron at Venice, where the poet gave him some books for Murray and two miniatures of himself for Byron's sister. Byron could not help ridiculing Polidori's efforts. In a letter to another friend, he wrote, "The Doctor Polidori is here on his way to England with the present Lord Guilford — having actually embowelled the last at Pisa & spiced & pickled him for his rancid ancestors.— The said Doctor has had several invalids under his proscriptions — but now has no more patients — because his patients are no more."

In the spring of 1817, Polidori settled in Norwich, opening a medical practice. He did not prosper, possibly because he had few connections in the community, but also because his religion made him something of an outsider as well. He was continually forced to borrow money from his father and godfather — always a terrible and humiliating experience. Both made him beg and offered advice as if he were still a child. His father wrote in a letter, "It is, however, time for you to put your head to work, for if you did not start using your judgement at the age you have now reached, I despair of your ever making use of it. Independence is what every sage and prudent man must aspire to, but it cannot be obtained by one who does not know how to limit his expenses to the means that he can readily obtain."

Bad luck stalked Polidori. In September, he suffered a brain concussion when his carriage struck a tree. Polidori lay unconscious for several days, and faced a long convalescence. For the rest of his life, he experienced aftereffects of the injury, and it seemed to affect his speech.

Polidori had not given up on writing. As Byron later said, "Instead of making out prescriptions, he took to writing romances; a very unprofitable and fatal exchange, as it turned out." A month before the carriage accident, Polidori had completed a verse play, *Ximenes,* and submitted it to John Murray. Murray was apparently embarrassed at having to turn it down and appealed to Byron to write a "*delicate* declension of it, which I engage faithfully to copy. I am truly sorry that he will employ himself in a way so ill-suited to his genius; for he is not without literary talents." Byron let his sadistic tendencies get the better of him and responded with one of the cleverest, yet cruelest, rejection letters ever written.

Dear Doctor — I have read your play
Which is a good one in its way
Purges the eyes & moves the bowels
And drenches handkerchiefs like towels
With tears that in a flux of Grief
Afford hysterical relief
To shatter'd nerves & quickened pulses
Which your catastrophe convulses.
I like your moral & machinery
Your plot too has such scope for Scenery!
Your dialogue is apt & smart
The play's concoction full of art —
Your hero raves — your heroine cries
All stab —& every body dies;
In short your tragedy would be
The very thing to hear & see —
And for a piece of publication
If I decline on this occasion
It is not that I am not sensible
To merits in themselves ostensible
But — and I grieve to speak it — plays
Are drugs — mere drugs, Sir, nowadays —

It goes on for sixty-eight more lines, with witty references to Murray's other authors, including Byron himself. If Murray had actually sent it to Polidori, the young man would certainly have been crushed, since the style made it unmistakable that Byron wrote it. In any case, the combination of a rejection (even a dull, polite one from Murray) and his serious head injury must have depressed him deeply.

He was like many young people whose parents have pushed them to achieve goals set by the parents. Once the degree has been earned, the medals won, the mountain climbed, they are then unsure what they really want to do with their lives. Those with artistic leanings find that the Muse does not always smile on people who spend long hours hard at work. Polidori had hoped that by traveling with Byron he would learn to write like Byron — but nothing can teach anyone how to become a genius.

However, living with Byron gave Polidori a subject, one that was sure to attract an audience, for it was the same subject that the poet used for his own wildly popular work: the image Byron had created of himself. In Polidori's work, however, Byron would be transformed from the dashing hero tormented by a mysterious secret in his past. He would become the malicious Byron that Polidori hated.

Just when Polidori wrote *The Vampyre* is not known for certain. Much about its composition remains shrouded in mystery, for he claimed it was published without his permission. It first appeared in the *New Monthly Magazine* on April 1, 1819. Accompanying the tale was an "Extract of a Letter to the Editor from Geneva," which purported to explain the circumstances under which the story had been written. Whoever penned the letter certainly knew of the events of the summer of 1816 at Villa Diodati. He (or she) described in detail the evening when Byron challenged his guests to write "a tale depending on some supernatural agency." The letter-writer even acknowledged that "Miss M. W. Godwin" had written *Frankenstein* as a result. This fact was still not generally known at the time, and many people believed Shelley or Godwin had been the actual author. Most surprising, however, was the letter-writer's assertion that this new work, *The Vampyre,* was Byron's "entry" in the contest.

Byron first heard about it later in the month through a letter from John Murray, in which Murray gave his version of events:

> [Here is] a copy of a thing called The Vampire, which Mr. Colburn [Henry Colburn, owner/publisher of the journal] has had the temerity to publish with your name as its author. It was first printed in the New Monthly Magazine, from which I have taken the copy which I now enclose. The Editor of that Journal has quarrelled with the publisher, and has called this morning to exculpate himself from the baseness of the transaction. He says that he received it from Dr. Polidori for a small sum, Polidori saying that the whole plan of it was yours, and that it was merely written out by him. The Editor inserted it with a short statement to this effect; but to his astonishment Colburn cancelled the leaf [page] on the day previous to its publication . . . fearing that this statement would prevent the sale of this work in a separate form, which was subsequently done. He informs me that Polidori, finding that the sale exceeded his expectation, and that he had sold it too cheap, went to the Editor, and declared that he would deny it.

Some critics have felt that Polidori intentionally put Byron's name on the story to increase its sales, but surviving letters and documents show that Polidori was horrified at the work's publication, which apparently was a surprise to him. When Byron's friend John Cam Hobhouse, who knew Polidori, insisted that he publicly explain the origin of the manuscript, Polidori wrote the editor of the *New Monthly Magazine* in May:

> As the person referred to in the Letter from Geneva, prefixed to the Tale of The Vampyre in your last Number, I beg leave to state, that your correspondent has been mistaken in attributing that tale, *in its present form,* to Lord Byron. The fact is, that though the *groundwork* is certainly Lord Byron's, its developement is mine, produced at the request of a lady, who denied the possibility of any thing being drawn from the materials which Lord Byron had said he intended to have employed in the formation of his Ghost story.

In other words, Polidori had merely written it as a response to a second challenge, by an unnamed woman who wanted to see what he could make of the story Byron had begun. This mysterious woman — possibly his one-time lover Madame Brélaz, whom he had met in Switzerland — was presumably the source of the manuscript that appeared in the *New Monthly*.

Byron chimed in with a letter, published in a rival magazine, airily denying authorship of *The Vampyre*. "If the book is clever it would be base to deprive the real writer — whoever he may be — of his honours — and if stupid — I desire the responsibility of nobody's dullness but my own. . . . I have besides a personal dislike to 'Vampires,' and the little acquaintance I have with them would by no means induce me to divulge their secrets." Despite these letters of denial, when *The Vampyre* was published in book form, readers still believed that the tale had been written by Lord Byron. His name guaranteed a big sale; this was not the first time someone had tried to pass off work as Byron's.

Worse yet, *The Vampyre* had been registered by the book publisher, meaning that Polidori had lost the copyright. Polidori protested the unauthorized use of his work and threatened a lawsuit, but in the end received a token payment of only thirty pounds. It must have been galling to him, because the book became a bestseller.

Polidori's tale is a reworking of Byron's own failed attempt to meet his Diodati challenge, with a different setting and name. In the eight-page fragment Byron completed, his vampire, Augustus Darvell, had been a wanderer who ends up in a Muslim graveyard rotting from an inner corruption. Polidori changed the name of the character to Lord Ruthven, who is "killed" by a bandit's bullet, and he changed the locale of some parts of the story from the Near East to London. Lord Ruthven, not by coincidence, is the name of the Lord Byron character in Lady Caroline Lamb's novel, *Glenarvon*.

Polidori cast himself as the innocent Aubrey who is destroyed by Lord Ruthven. Ruthven appears as a striking and mysterious figure in the fashionable drawing rooms of London, attracting the attention of all the ladies. Of course, Polidori had seen the real-life Byron draw similar reactions when he visited the salons of Geneva. Aubrey, despite his observations of the Count's "deadly hue" and "dead grey eye," is also drawn to him. Like Polidori himself, Aubrey eagerly joins his new friend on a tour of the Continent. Along the way, however, Aubrey sees additional evidence of Ruthven's vicious character, becomes disillusioned, and leaves him. Aubrey heads for Greece to study antiquities and there falls in love with a young Greek woman named Ianthe. Ianthe had been a dream maiden in Shelley's *Queen Mab*, a poem that Polidori read and admired during the summer of 1816.

Ianthe and her parents warn Aubrey not to go to a certain place after dark, because it is the haunt of vampires. He disregards their advice, and hears the cries of a woman coming from a hut. When he tries to rescue her, he is set upon in the darkness by "one whose strength seemed superhuman." Aubrey breaks free, and then villagers with torches arrive to save him. They find the body of Ianthe, with the marks of a vampire on her neck.

Aubrey falls ill from a fever, and lies in a half-conscious state for some time; in his delirium he imagines that it is Lord Ruthven who has killed Ianthe. But when he awakens, he finds that he has in fact been tended by Lord Ruthven, who arrived in Athens and came to his aid. The two men begin to travel together again, and are set upon by bandits in the mountains. Ruthven is mortally wounded, but as he lies dying he makes Aubrey promise to "conceal all you know of me," in order to protect his reputation. Aubrey swears an oath to comply with his friend's last wish.

Aubrey returns to London, where his younger sister is about to be presented into society. At the reception, Aubrey hears someone say in his ear, "Remember your oath!" He turns to find that Lord Ruthven has returned. Aubrey becomes aware that Ruthven intends to court his sister, but feels honor bound not to reveal what he knows about the mysterious nobleman. The conflict drives Aubrey nearly to madness, and again he spends a long time convalescing. When he becomes lucid, he learns that his sister is preparing to be married to Lord Ruthven. Aubrey struggles to persuade her not to go through with the wedding, but he is regarded as deranged. He ruptures a blood vessel and dies, but not before he finally breaks his oath and tells the whole story to his sister's guardians. They rush to rescue her, but are too late. The last sentence of the story reads,

"Lord Ruthven had disappeared, and Aubrey's sister had glutted the thirst of a VAMPYRE!"

The power of the story is clearly related to the way it plumbs Polidori's own tortured relationship with Byron, which was always an unequal one. Polidori desperately wanted to be in the first rank of artists but he was forever overshadowed by the talent of others. His anxiety about his artistic ability was magnified by Byron's sadistic teasing. Byron could not control his contempt for Polidori for the same reason he could not bring himself to love Claire: both desired him too much — they were *needy*. Yet like Claire, Polidori not only resented, and even hated, Byron but was also attracted to him, a duality that must have caused self-loathing. Polidori's vampire story shows his fascination with the dark sexuality of the seducer and his fear of being seduced. In *The Vampyre,* Ruthven dominates Aubrey just as Byron dominated Polidori. Polidori gained some revenge by depicting Byron as a vampire, a monstrous and evil being who sucks the lifeblood from people who cannot resist his charms. Yet when the story later appeared in a book version, the name of the central character was changed from Ruthven to Strongmore, possibly because the publisher (or Polidori) feared a lawsuit.

Despite all of Aubrey's efforts, evil triumphs completely at the end of *The Vampyre,* and in that too lies some of the tale's peculiar power that has enabled its central character to survive several incarnations over the two centuries since. *Frankenstein* is more conventional in that sense, for in the end, Victor is punished for his hubris, Captain Walton decides to abandon his reckless quest, and the monster repents. Lord Ruthven never repents; he conquers, and will apparently continue to do so. Mary's monster is ultimately a good person with an ugly exterior; the vampire Lord Ruthven has a fascinating appearance that masks the evil within.

There were other differences. Lord Ruthven is obsessed with sexuality while Victor avoids — even flees from — the sexual, regarding it as a distraction from his work. His whole project is, in many ways, an effort to excise women — and sex — from procreation. Victor's ideals may have been noble (though the results are not), whereas Ruthven is truly wicked, but it is hard to know who is the more alien — and alienated. Ruthven is a supernatural being; he can rise from the dead and reappear elsewhere.

(When Aubrey considers trying to kill him, Polidori wrote, "death, he remembered, had been already mocked.") Victor Frankenstein, on the other hand, attempts to control the powers of nature and use scientific means to "mock death." But both, equally obsessed with harnessing the élan vital, end up remarkably inhuman.

Annoyed that *The Vampyre* was being passed off as his own work, Byron sent the fragmentary beginning of his own vampire story to John Murray, who printed it at the end of Byron's poem *Mazeppa.* That still did not prevent many people from believing that Byron was the true author of *The Vampyre,* and Polidori's story became popular, particularly on the Continent. Goethe reportedly felt it was Byron's finest work. Not long after its publication, plays and operas of the story attracted audiences.

Polidori's tale would inspire others. Thomas Peckett Prest, a prolific English writer who is best known today as the originator of the character who later became Sweeney Todd, the Demon Barber of Fleet Street, published in 1847 *Varney the Vampire or The Feast of Blood.* This 868-page blockbuster seems to have been the first novel to introduce the idea that the vampire could change form into a batlike creature and fly (the better to appear at the windows of young women's bedrooms) — but he still had the aristocratic background and the other characteristics of Lord Ruthven.

Polidori left Norwich and moved to London, where he entered the literary world. He succeeded in finding a publisher for *Ximenes,* the play that John Murray had turned down, and found work reviewing books for one of the city's many journals. In 1819 he published the book that *he* claimed was the result of the challenge Lord Byron had thrown down to his friends on a stormy night in June 1816. This was *Ernestus Berchtold: The Modern Oedipus,* the title an obvious parallel to Mary's *Frankenstein: The Modern Prometheus.* In a preface to the novel, Polidori claimed, "The tale here presented to the public is the one I began at Coligny, when Frankenstein was planned."

Polidori's novel included a supernatural spirit who makes short peripheral appearances, but its plot really revolves around incest, as the subtitle implies. It too is a tale told primarily in the first person, by the title character. Ernestus, a young man who was raised from infancy by a village pastor in Switzerland, relates that his mother died giving birth to twins —

Ernestus and a sister. The man who had apparently been their father died earlier of wounds he had suffered before they arrived in the village. Ernestus grows to adulthood and falls in love with a wealthy young woman named Louisa Doni. Louisa's brother, a Byron-like figure named Olivieri, seduces Ernestus's sister, causing her to flee. When Ernestus finds her, dying along with her newborn infant, she tells him that the Doni family patriarch, Count Filiberto, has a dark secret: he can summon up an evil spirit to do his bidding. Olivieri is soon punished: unexpectedly discovered to be the leader of a band of robbers, he is arrested and dies in jail.

Nevertheless, Ernestus marries Louisa. To decorate their rooms in Count Filiberto's palatial house, they hang a portrait of the Count next to one of Ernestus's mother. When the Count sees the latter image, he is violently disturbed. A few days later he dies, followed shortly by Louisa herself, who had suffered from consumption. Ernestus finds a manuscript that Count Filiberto had written in his last days, and this completes the book. In it, the count confesses that as a young man he and a friend traveled to Asia in pursuit of wealth. Both he and his companion loved the same woman, Matilda. Count Filiberto learned from a dying Arab the secret of summoning up an evil spirit who would grant his wishes. The spirit says, however, that each time the count is granted a wish, some disaster will befall those close to him. Heedless of the danger, the count agrees to the bargain and does become rich, although his friend dies. Returning home, he marries Matilda but becomes jealous because he suspects that his friend has somehow returned from the dead and is seducing her. He chases a carriage in which he believes they are fleeing, fires at it, and hears Matilda scream. He learns later that the man in the carriage with her was not her lover, but her father. The count presumed that he had killed her, but on seeing the portrait of Ernestus's mother, he recognized it as Matilda. She had survived, only to die giving birth to the twins, of which the count was the father. The count realized that his two children by a later wife have committed incest with Ernestus and his sister. Ernestus is left alone and despairing, the self-portrait of Polidori, who frequently noted his own loneliness in his journal.

The copies of *Ernestus Berchtold* that went on sale were lonely too: only 199 were sold, and the publisher offered the rest to Polidori at a cut rate.

Persevering, Polidori wrote other works, but they too failed to find many readers. Finally, the brilliant but hapless Polidori turned to yet another profession: the law. He was admitted to Lincoln's Inn in November 1820 and gave his mother's maiden name, Pierce, on the register. Pierce had a nice English sound which would be better for business than an Italian one. Rejecting his father's name may also, of course, have been Polidori's way of asserting his independence.

In August 1821, Polidori went to the seaside resort of Brighton with a friend. Apparently they spent their time at the gambling tables. Polidori was in desperate need of money, and had evidently forgotten what happened to the eager young men who played at faro with Lord Ruthven: "In every town, he left the formerly affluent youth, torn from the circle he adorned, cursing, in the solitude of a dungeon, the fate that had drawn him within the reach of this fiend." Polidori had no better luck, and when he returned to London, friends noticed that he seemed distracted and upset. He had lost far more money than he could pay; his only recourse would have been to ask his father once again to lend him money. That was too humiliating, and Polidori found another solution.

Polidori was living in his family's London house. John Deagostini, his godfather, had an apartment upstairs and on the evening of August 23, 1821, the two had dinner together. Deagostini recalled that the young man was acting strangely, but assumed it was the aftereffects of the head injury Polidori had suffered two years earlier. Retiring to his room, Polidori asked Charlotte Reed, a servant, to leave him a glass, explaining that he was ill; Reed assumed he intended to take medicine. Polidori told her that he might sleep late, so that if he did not arise before noon, she should not worry. Nevertheless, Reed later testified, she went to his room about ten minutes before twelve to open the shutters. (Not even the family servants respected him enough to follow his instructions.) The sunlight revealed Polidori lying on his bed, seemingly "very ill." Suspecting the worst, Reed told Deagostini what she had seen, and he sent her for a doctor. Two of them arrived. The first found signs of life and attempted to pump Polidori's stomach, but it was too late. He died a few minutes later, just a month short of his twenty-sixth birthday.

Deagostini later testified that one of the doctors drank some of the liquid left in the glass, to show that it was not poison. However, there had been a considerable period of time when Deagostini was left alone with the body, and the family had an interest in averting a coroner's verdict of suicide since that would mean Polidori could not be buried in consecrated ground. The coroner's jury was sympathetic, ruling that Polidori had "departed this Life in a natural way by the visitation of God." The body was interred on the twenty-ninth of August, 1821, in Old St. Pancras Churchyard, the same burial ground where Mary Wollstonecraft rested, and where Shelley and Mary had declared their love for each other.

Gaetano, his father, professed to be heartbroken. "I have been left miserable and unhappy for the rest of my life," he wrote a friend in December. "The idea of not seeing him again, of not hearing his voice any more, compared to those times when I used to see and hear him, accompanies me continuously, and if I did not have other children who need my help, I do not know what would have happened to me." He survived his son by thirty-two years; his grandchildren recalled being told never to mention John Polidori's name in his presence.

Of the five people who agreed to write a ghost story in the summer of 1816, Polidori was the first to die. Byron received the news from John Murray, who seems to have reached a different conclusion than the jury had about the cause of death. Byron told a friend,

> I was convinced something very unpleasant hung over me last night: I expected to hear that somebody I knew was dead — so it turns out — poor Polidori is gone! When he was my physician, he was always talking of Prussic acid, oil of amber, blowing into veins, suffocating by charcoal, and compounding poisons . . . he has prescribed a dose for himself . . . whose effect, Murray says, was so instantaneous that he went off without a spasm or struggle. It seems that disappointment was the cause of this rash act.

The journal in which Polidori recorded his anguish, his hopes, and his version of reality survived, but — as with so many other documents in this story — in a form revised by other hands. Polidori's sister Frances married Gabriele Rossetti, an Italian exile who taught Italian at King's

College. They were the parents of several talented children, including the poet Christina, the poet and painter Dante Gabriel Rossetti, and William Michael Rossetti, an art critic and editor. William published his uncle's journal in 1911, when he himself was in his eighties, but reported that years before his mother had removed all elements from it that she did not think were appropriate to print. This left, needless to say, considerably less than modern readers would hope for.

More than forty years after Polidori's death, William Rossetti recorded a contact with his deceased uncle during a séance. By the rules of this séance the spirit responded to questions by rapping on the table — once for yes, twice for no. For more elaborate messages, the participants would go through the alphabet and when they reached the right letter the spirit would rap. William Rossetti's séance diary for November 25, 1865, recorded that a spirit gave his name as "Uncle John." The person conducting the séance had no uncle of that name. Rossetti spoke up:

> I then said: "Is it my Uncle John?"— Yes. I asked for the surname, by the alphabet, but could not get it. Then: Is it an English surname? — No. — Foreign? — Yes. — Spanish, German, etc., etc., Italian? — Yes. — I then called over five or six Italian names, coming to Polidori. — Yes. — Will you tell me truly how you died? — Yes. — How? — Killed. — Who killed you? — I. — There was a celebrated poet with whom you were connected: what was his name? — Bro. This was twice repeated, or something close to it the second time. At a third attempt, "Byron." — There was a certain book you wrote, attributed to Byron: can you give me its title? — Yes. — I tried to get this title [*The Vampyre*] several times, but wholly failed. — Are you happy? — Two raps, meaning not exactly."

CHAPTER ELEVEN

THE LITTLEST VICTIM

I am ashes where once I was fire,
And the bard in my bosom is dead;
What I loved I now merely admire,
And my heart is as grey as my head.

My life is not dated by years —
There are moments which act as a plough;
And there is not a furrow appears
But is deep in my soul as my brow.

Let the young and the brilliant aspire
To sing what I gaze on in vain;
For sorrow has torn from my lyre
The string which was worthy the strain.

— "To the Countess of Blessington,"
Lord Byron, 1823

IN ALL THE books that resulted from Byron's challenge — *Frankenstein, The Vampyre,* and *Ernestus Berchtold,* the first victims are the innocents, those most loved by the protagonists. So it was in the lives of those who had received his challenge, as well as those around them. Mary's half-sister, then Shelley's first wife, gentle souls who could not stand up to the ruthless blows that life delivered them, had killed themselves. Next little Clara and Willmouse became victims of their frenetic father's inability to consider the needs of others before his own desires. All four of these deaths, in one way or another, were caused by the two men who had inspired the character Victor Frankenstein: Godwin and Shelley.

Now, the man who sat for the portrait of the Vampyre was to claim his own.

Allegra's nursemaid Elise brought the child back to Byron's house in Venice after she had spent the summer of 1818 with Claire and the Shelleys. Byron was living a wilder, more dissolute life than ever. He was writing the first canto of a long poem, *Don Juan,* which would be his most outrageous work, so far beyond the bounds of propriety that his closest friends urged him not to publish it. Having seen, and been inspired by, Mozart's opera *Don Giovanni,* Byron knew of the "catalog aria" in which Leporello ticks off the names of his master's conquests. In similar fashion, Byron replied to his friend Hobhouse, who had told him that a recent visitor to Venice had returned to England with the news that Byron had taken a lover. Byron asked, "Which 'piece' does he mean? — since last year I have run the Gauntlet; — is it the Tarruscelli — the Da Mosti — the Spineda . . ." and so on through the names of twenty-three mistresses "cum multis aliis" [with many others] that he had during 1818, "and thrice as many to boot since 1817. . . . Some of them are Countesses — & some of them Cobblers wives — some noble — some middling — some low — & all whores."

Even Byron realized this was not a suitable atmosphere for little Allegra, so he again palmed her off on the Hoppners, who in turn tried to interest other families in taking her. "She was not by any means an amiable child," wrote Richard Hoppner, "nor was Mrs. Hoppner or I particularly fond of her." Isabella Hoppner wrote to Mary Shelley complaining that Allegra was a backward and unlively creature who suffered in the Venice winter as her feet were always blocks of ice. She frequently wet the bed. The Hoppners suggested that she be brought up in Switzerland where the climate would suit her better.

A wealthy English widow, learning of Allegra's background, offered to adopt her if Byron would renounce his parental claim. Claire learned about the proposal and wrote to him, "My first wish is that my child should be with myself — that cannot be at present . . . next I should wish her to be with you — but that cannot be." She had heard of his numerous mistresses. However, she reminded him, there might come a time when he would choose to lead a "steady" life and "live so that Allegra may be with you & both be happy & make you happy . . . therefore before you do any thing . . . think and do not throw away the greatest treasure you have to strangers." Byron turned down the widow's offer.

By the middle of the summer of 1819, he had to do something, for the Hoppners had made plans to leave Venice for Switzerland. Without asking Byron, they had fired Elise, the only stable figure in Allegra's brief life. Mrs. Hoppner informed Byron that they would leave Allegra with their servant Antonio who, they assured Byron, had fine manners. Allegra did spend some time with this Antonio and his family, where four Italian girls fussed over her before she was turned over to the wife of the Danish ambassador.

Finally, in August 1819, Byron took responsibility for his daughter. "I wish to see my child — & have her with *me,*" he declared, ordering the two-year-old to be brought to him. It was all part of Byron's cycle of concern and neglect. He found that the Hoppners had done little for his daughter. She did not speak a word of English, nor even formal Italian because she had always been with servants, not the family. At first, the child charmed Byron. "Baby B" (as he called her) was beautiful and lively, and she could twist him around her little finger. In September, Byron wrote to Augusta, his half-sister, telling her that he saw the Byron traits in Allegra. He noted that she spoke nothing but Venetian and was "very droll — and has a good deal of the Byron — can't articulate the letter *r* at all [the Byrons had a Scottish accent] — frowns and pouts quite in our way — blue eyes — light hair growing *darker* daily — and a dimple in the chin — a scowl on the brow — white skin — sweet voice — and a particular liking of Music — and of her own way in every thing — is not that B. all over?" Of course, the musical talent marked Allegra even more strongly as her mother's child.

One reason why Byron may have decided to resume caring for Allegra was that in April he had met a woman who, for the first time since he left England, made him consider the joys of a "steady" life. Countess Teresa Guiccioli was nineteen, and married to a man of fifty-eight. Though lovely, she was not renowned for her beauty. A later English traveler, who had heard of her affair with Byron, wrote, "I was rather disappointed with her personal appearance . . . she gave one more the idea of a healthy, rosy, jolly-looking milkmaid, than a heroine of romance." Byron was attending a soirée when his hostess asked if he would like to be introduced to the young countess. At first he refused, but after some persuasion he let himself be led across the room. Teresa later recalled the moment in detail in her autobiography, and at her telling, she was overwhelmed by this "celestial apparition whom it seemed to her she had already seen and loved before, having seen him in her imagination."

It was no surprise that a young woman found the sight of Byron irresistible; the mystery was that Byron himself felt an attraction that was more than physical. They talked, that evening, of Italian poetry, a subject she was well versed in, having grown up in Ravenna, where Dante is buried. The discussion continued for far longer than politeness demanded. Teresa wrote, "already the subject of the conversation had become an accessory — already the important thing was to converse — was the development of that mysterious sympathy which grew with each word from the one and the other — and that had already rendered them insensible to what was happening around them." Her husband finally came to reclaim his wife. "She rose as if she were coming out of a dream," Teresa wrote of herself.

The next afternoon, when Count Guiccioli customarily took a nap, an elderly gondolier arrived at his palazzo with a note for his wife. Naturally, it was from Byron, and the boatman took her to a *casino,* a little house that Byron used for personal matters. "I was strong enough to resist at that first encounter," Teresa recalled, "but was so imprudent as to repeat it the next day, when my strength gave way — for B. was not a man to confine himself to sentiment. And, the first step taken, there was no further obstacle in the following days."

Byron was serious about Teresa, as he had not been about a woman in years. He wrote to Hobhouse, "I am in love — and tired of promiscuous concubinage — & have now an opportunity of settling for life." There *was* in fact the possibility of a permanent relationship, if Byron had been willing to accept its conditions. The countess turned down Byron's impulsive suggestion that they flee to South America; instead, she offered him the role of *cavalier servente,* publicly an escort and protector. It was understood that lovemaking might be part of the *cavalier servente*'s role, but only if done with complete discretion. Byron scorned this at first, ridiculing the duties. He wrote Hoppner, "I am drilling very hard to learn how to double a Shawl, and should succeed to admiration — if I did not always double it the wrong side out. . . . A man actually becomes a piece of female property."

The count assented to this arrangement. He was not the kind of man who would let his wife's infidelities go unnoticed; he had already had two wives, and rumors said he had poisoned the first one because she objected to his taking as a mistress the woman who would become the second. (He went to the theater the night the second one died.) However, he not only agreed to Byron's publicly accompanying Teresa to the theater and opera, he even invited the English *cavalier servente* to live with them at the Palazzo Guiccioli in Ravenna. The fact that Byron proved liberal with money was one factor in the count's apparent willingness to allow such a notorious rake near his wife. The count had asked Byron for a sizable loan, and Byron gave it to him. The "rent" on Byron's apartment in the Palazzo Guiccioli was deducted from what the count owed.

Though Ravenna was regarded as something of a backwater, compared to cosmopolitan Venice, Byron willingly moved in, along with little Allegra, whom Byron called Allegrina when he was paying attention to her. His apartment, separate from the family's living quarters, must have been quite extensive, for Shelley later reported that Byron's household included ten horses, eight large dogs (no lapdogs for Byron), three monkeys, five cats, five peacocks, an eagle, a crow, a falcon, two guinea hens, and an Egyptian crane. All except the horses walked, or flew, freely about the rooms. Allegra must have felt somewhat insignificant competing with this menagerie.

Byron of course had other interests — making love to Teresa when her husband was away ("by the clock," he complained), extending *Don Juan* through another three cantos, and attending the clandestine meetings of a murky group called the Carbonari, who were plotting the overthrow of Italy's foreign rulers. Through his friendship with Teresa's family, the Gambas, Byron had been initiated into the group with the rank of *capo*. (The Carbonari took their name from the workers who made charcoal in the forests, where their own secret meetings often took place.)

Neither by personality nor lifestyle was Byron a natural father, and he soon became bored or irritated with the demands of having a small child around. At times, Byron complained that she reminded him of her mother, Claire, though almost everyone else saw the temperamental similarities between the father and his daughter. The servants all doted on Allegra, something Byron attributed in part to her fair skin, "which shines among their dusky children like the milky way."

Allegra's mother started to make demands, something Byron never responded to graciously. Claire, now living with the Shelleys in Pisa, wrote to Byron in March 1820, pointing out that it had been nearly a year and a half since she had seen Allegra, even though Byron had promised she could visit the child regularly. She warned Byron that Allegra might suffer from Ravenna's unhealthy climate and asked him to allow the child to visit her and the Shelleys again that summer. When he failed to reply, she wrote a second time, suggesting that he send Allegra to meet her and the Shelleys in Bologna in May. Percy's health, unfortunately, was too frail to allow him to travel to Ravenna.

Byron was not about to give in to Claire. Though he enjoyed discussing poetry with Shelley, he distrusted his ideas about raising children. He wrote Thomas Hoppner, "I so totally disapprove of the mode of Children's treatment in their family — that I should look upon the Child [Allegra] as going into a hospital. [The word then meant a home for the indigent or orphans.] — Is it not so? Have they *reared* one?" That was indeed a low blow, implicitly blaming the Shelleys for the deaths of their children.

Byron continued, protesting that Allegra was receiving good care: "Her health here has hitherto been excellent — and her temper not bad — she is sometimes vain and obstinate — but always clean and cheerful — and . . . in a year or two I shall either send her to England — or put her in a Convent for education. . . . But the child shall not quit me again — to perish of Starvation, and green fruit — or to be taught to believe that there is no Deity." He was, of course, referring to Shelley's vegetarianism and atheism. Mrs. Hoppner conveyed Byron's remarks to Claire, who wrote with some irritation in her journal, "A letter from Mad[ame]. Hoppner concerning green fruit and God — strange Jumble." She wrote to Byron yet again, offering to make sure Allegra received the same food she had been accustomed to and assuring him, "she shall be taught to worship God." He could not have cared less.

Selfishly and obstinately, Byron kept Allegra. And sure enough, the child's first Ravenna summer, with its intense heat, did not agree with her. She came down with malarial fever and Byron had to move to a villa in the countryside for her sake. It took her quite a while to recover. Teresa sent the girl some toys, but she was annoyed when Byron hired a nurse that she considered too pretty. (Byron reassured her, "The woman is as ugly as an ogre.")

Claire may have found out about Allegra's illness, and if so surely wrote Byron an angry letter, although none from her during this time have survived. However, in August Byron told Shelley, "I must decline all correspondence with Claire who merely tries to be as irrational and provoking as she can be."

Not put off so easily when her daughter's welfare was at stake, Claire apparently persisted. Byron wrote Hoppner in September,

> Clare [*sic*] writes me the most insolent letters about Allegra — see what a man gets by taking care of natural children! — Were it not for the poor little child's sake — I am most tempted to send her back to her atheistical mother — but that would be too bad; — you cannot conceive the excess of her insolence and I know not why — for I have been at great care and expense — taking a house in the country on purpose of her — she has *two* maids & every possible attention. — If Clare thinks that she shall ever interfere with the child's morals or education — she mistakes — she never shall — The girl shall be a Christian and a married woman — if possible. — As to seeing her — she may see her — under proper restrictions — but She is not to throw every thing into confusion with her Bedlam behaviour. — To express it delicately — I think Madame Clare is a damned bitch — what think you?

Byron's allusion to Claire's morals, besides being stunningly hypocritical considering his own record, had been stoked by the Hoppners' repeating to him the story that in 1819 Claire had given birth to Shelley's child in Naples. They had heard it from the former nursemaid Elise, whose husband Paolo had tried unsuccessfully to blackmail Shelley by threatening to spread the tale. Meanwhile, Byron himself was anything but discreet, and the countess's ardor carried her away as well. The count apparently caught them in a compromising position in the family quarters of the palazzo, and while he could tolerate his wife's taking a lover, he could not accept such a brazen insult to his honor. Byron, seriously worried that the count was trying to have him assassinated, began to carry a brace of pistols wherever he went. Remarkably, he continued living in the count's palazzo — although he was no longer permitted in the family quarters.

Surprisingly, Teresa's father, Count Ruggero Gamba, who had considered his daughter's marriage to Count Guiccioli a good match, now worked to obtain an annulment. Count Ruggero and Byron had discovered their mutual interest in Italian nationalism — Ruggero was also part of the local Carbonari — and that may have won the count's favor. In a short time, the pope granted a decree of separation, although the terms of it demanded that Teresa live in her father's home in Ravenna. For a time, that would put a crimp in the romance between Byron and Teresa.

By this time, Allegra had ceased to be amusing to Byron, and became an uncomfortable reminder of his foolish love affair. Years later Teresa claimed that just the sight of her could at times be unbearable to Byron. "Each time she came into her father's presence, he used to turn away in disgust and exclaim, 'Enlevez la; elle ressemble trop à sa mère!' [*'Take her away; she looks too much like her mother!'*]" Byron had long thought that a convent education would be best for Allegra. He considered this a practical solution that would in time increase her chances of making a good marriage. (He had once even discussed a prearranged marriage between her and Count Guiccioli's son.) Moreover, he claimed to admire the Roman Catholic Church, and wished his daughter to be brought up in that faith. If Allegra were sent to England, Byron feared that her illegitimate birth would be a social handicap. In Italy, a hefty dowry counted as much as birth, and Byron had changed his will to leave Allegra five thousand pounds. Money was easier to give than affection.

On March 1, 1821, Byron enrolled Allegra in the convent boarding school of San Giovanni Battista at Bagnacavallo, twelve miles from Ravenna. She was just four years old and by far the youngest girl in the school. Byron did not think this was cruel: Allegra was precocious and Teresa herself had entered a convent school at five. From a material standpoint, Allegra was well equipped. She came to the convent with her own bed, chest of drawers, many pretty dresses, and her beautiful dolls, which were as gorgeously dressed as she herself was. Byron wrote his half-sister that he wanted Allegra "to become a good Catholic — & (it may be) a *Nun* being a character somewhat wanted in our family."

Later in the month, when Claire learned what Byron had done, she was furious. For her it was a disaster, and she wrote Byron a harsh letter, accusing him of breaking the promise he had made to her at the Villa Diodati that Allegra would always remain with one of her parents. She added an attack on convents and convent education, parroting Shelley's hostility to religion and its effect on Italian women. She claimed that such schooling was responsible for "the state of ignorance & profligacy of Italian women, all pupils of Convents. They are bad wives & most unnatural mothers, licentious & ignorant they are the dishonour & unhappiness of society." She accused Byron of condemning Allegra "to a life of ignorance & degradation," depriving her of the advantages of "belonging to the most enlightened country in the world." (She meant England, though as Byron was certainly aware, Parliament had just passed the Six Acts, designed to stamp out freedom of the press and political dissent.) Claire entreated Byron to let Allegra enter an English boarding school, offering to pay for it herself. Ironically, considering that Claire herself would convert to Roman Catholicism in her old age, she also accused Byron of having Allegra adopt a different religion in order to cut her off from her own mother and her friends.

Byron forwarded Claire's attack to Hoppner, with the notation, "The moral part of this letter upon the *Italians* &c. comes with an excellent grace from the writer [who] planted a child in the N [Naples] *foundling* &c." He was referring to the story that Claire and Shelley abandoned the child of their union to an orphanage in Naples. As for the charges Claire made against Catholicism, they only goaded Byron into stubbornness. He would write to Thomas Moore in March 1822, "I am no enemy of religion, but the contrary. As a proof, I am educating my natural daughter a strict Catholic in a convent of Romagna; for I think people can never have *enough* of religion, if they are to have any. I incline, myself, very much to the Catholic doctrines." This sounds very much like Byron professing mock piety merely for effect — as he himself was aware, for in a similar letter a few days later, he added, "I am afraid that this sounds flippant, but I don't mean it to be so. . . . Still, I do assure you that I am a very good Christian."

Hoppner, for one, approved of Byron's decision, writing him,

> Whether the convent in which you have placed her be well conducted or not, we of course . . . cannot be supposed competent to judge; but if we may form any opinion of the merits of a boarding school education in England from what we know of the child's Mama, I can have little hesitation in saying the convent is not likely to be worse. On the other question of religion it is one on which there naturally must be a diversity of opinion.

At the beginning of August, Shelley's health had improved enough so that he set out to visit Byron in Ravenna and to check on Allegra. Shelley had sent Byron a copy of a new poem, *Adonais,* his memorial to John Keats, who had died in April at the age of twenty-six, three years younger than Shelley. Shelley attached a note in which he belittled his own work in comparison to Byron's: "I send you — as Diomed gave Glaucus his brazen arms for those of gold — some verses I wrote on the death of Keats." In the poem, Shelley blamed bad reviews for Keats's untimely death. Byron was not an admirer of Keats's poetry, but of course he loathed reviewers, who had savaged the first two cantos of *Don Juan.* (*The British Critic:* "a narrative of degrading debauchery in doggrel rhyme." *The Eclectic Review:* "poetry in which the deliberate purpose of the Author is to corrupt by inflaming the mind, to seduce to the love of evil which he has himself chosen as his good.")

On the way to Byron's, Shelley stopped at Livorno, where Claire had gone to bathe in the sea to cure an attack of what was said to be scrofula, a form of tuberculosis. Shelley arrived late in the evening of August 3. He spent the next day, his twenty-ninth birthday, with Claire. Her journal entry read: "Saturday August 4th. S's Birthday 29 yrs. Rise at five — Row in the Harbour with S — Then call upon the Countess Tolomei. Then we sail into the sea. A very fine warm day. the white sails of ships upon the horizon looked like doves stooping over the water. Dine at the Giardinetto. S — goes at two." Shelley kept this detour a secret from both Mary and Byron.

When Shelley arrived at Ravenna, Byron showed him a letter he had received from Hoppner about a year before. This was the source of Byron's belief that Claire had given birth to Shelley's child in Naples; that Shelley abandoned it in the foundling hospital; that Shelley had previously tried to get an abortion for Claire and had kept Mary in the dark about the whole matter. The Hoppners had learned this from Elise and believed it. Byron tended to believe the story, but was not sure that Elise was a credible witness.

Shelley wrote to Mary and asked her to deny the story "which you only can effectually rebut." Though Mary was in no position to refute or confirm it, she wrote a long letter, claiming that Elise's story was a malicious lie. She explained that Elise had been put up to this slur by her husband, Paolo Foggi. Mary passionately asserted that her marriage had "ever been undisturbed." Neither her letter nor the one Shelley sent to her mentioned the origin of the baby Elena herself. There is no record of whether Claire was informed about this exchange. Byron kept Mary's letter and may not have shown it to the Hoppners, who afterward kept the story in circulation.

Aside from that matter, Byron cheered Shelley up and imposed his routine on him for the next ten days. Byron arose at midday and the two talked until six; afterward they went riding and sat up all night in conversation. Shelley wrote to Peacock complaining about the sense of inferiority he felt when he was with Byron. "I write nothing, and probably shall write no more. It offends me to see my name classed among those who have no name. If I cannot be something better, I had rather be nothing."

Percy visited Allegra in the convent before he left Ravenna. He went alone; never once did Byron visit his daughter there, although the Countess

Guiccioli did. Percy had always loved Allegra, seeing her as part of his family, and he spent three hours at the convent. He brought her a gift of a gold chain and some sweets, noticing that she shared the sweets with a friend and the nuns, "not much like the old Allegra." Discipline was supposedly strict at the convent, but Shelley saw no evidence that it was severe. "Her light & airy figure & her graceful motions were a striking contrast to the other children there — she seemed a thing of a finer race & a higher order," he wrote. After overcoming Allegra's initial shyness, he was soon running and skipping with her through the garden. "Before I went away," he wrote Mary, "she made me run all over the convent, like a mad thing." The nuns were apparently retiring for their afternoon naps, and mischievously Allegra began ringing the large bell that was the signal for them to assemble. Shelley noted that "it required all the efforts of the prioresses to prevent the spouses of God to render themselves dressed or undressed to the accustomed signal. Nobody scolded her for these *scappature* [escapades]: so I suppose that she is well treated as far as temper is concerned."

He did have some criticisms, blaming Allegra's paleness on the fact that the convent did not serve vegetarian meals, and the religious atmosphere, of course, was not to his liking. He noted that Allegra "knows certain orazioni by heart & talks & *dreams* of Paradise & angels & all sorts of things — and has a prodigious list of saints — and is always talking of the Bambino. This *fuora* will do her no harm — but the idea of bringing up so sweet a creature in the midst of such trash till sixteen!" When Shelley asked Allegra whether she had a message for her father, the girl answered that he should come and visit her and bring "la *mammina* with him." She was referring to Teresa. Shelley never told Claire that her daughter had virtually forgotten her.

Shelley had made the trip to Ravenna with more than Allegra in mind. Both he and Byron had felt the sting of unfavorable reviews; now Shelley proposed they cooperate in a venture that would enable the two of them to strike back. They would invite Leigh Hunt to join them in Pisa and start a liberal political journal that would not be subject to the harsh restrictions on the press that were currently part of British law. Byron was thinking of leaving Ravenna in any case, for the Gambas, including Teresa, had been forced to flee after the Austrian authorities discovered a Carbonari plot.

On the way home, Shelley stopped at Florence, where he met the countess. Shelley described her as "a very pretty sentimental, innocent, superficial Italian, who has sacrifized [*sic*] an immense fortune to live for Lord Byron; and who, if I know any thing of my friend, of her, or of human nature will hereafter have plenty of leisure & opportunity to repent of her rashness." The countess, in turn, had her own impression of Shelley at this time:

> It was said that in his adolescence he was good-looking — but now he was no longer so. His features were delicate but not regular — except for his mouth which however was not good when he laughed, and was a little spoiled by his teeth, the shape of which was not in keeping with his refinement. . . . He was also extraordinary in his garb, for he normally wore a jacket like a young college boy's, never any gloves nor polish on his boots — and yet among a thousand he would always have seemed the most finished of gentlemans [*sic*]. His voice was shrill — even strident and nevertheless it was modulated by the drift of his thoughts with a grace, a gentleness, a delicacy that went to the heart. . . . Perhaps never did anyone ever see a man so deficient in beauty who could still produce an impression of it. . . . It was the fire, the enthusiasm, of his Intelligence that transformed his features.

Byron began making plans to move from the Palazzo Guiccioli (where he still resided, despite everything that had occurred) to Pisa. The mother superior of the convent, hearing of Byron's intended departure, invited him to visit Allegra before he left. The nun enclosed a note in Allegra's own childish handwriting (in Italian), showing how precocious she was, since she was not quite five:

> My Dear Papa —
>
> It being fair-time I should so much like a visit from my Papa, as I have many desires to satisfy; will you not please your Allegrina who loves you so?

Byron never answered the letter and did not visit. Instead, he passed Allegra's letter on to a friend, calling it "sincere enough but not very flattering — for she wants to see me because it 'is the fair' to get paternal Gingerbread — I suppose." On October 29, Byron left Ravenna. He left behind the more decrepit animals — a goat with a broken leg, a fish-eating heron, an old mutt, two ugly monkeys, and a badger on a chain. He also left behind unpaid bills and lastly, his four-year-old daughter in the convent, discarded as easily as the rest.

At the same time Byron arrived in Pisa, Claire was leaving the city for Florence, where she was to start a new life looking after someone else's children. "Just before Empoli," she wrote in her journal, "we passed Lord B — and his travelling train." It was hard to miss Byron's caravan, which consisted of his enormous carriage and several wagons carrying his personal possessions as well as the menagerie of animals he did bother to transport. He caused quite a stir as he passed through the villages along the road from Ravenna to Pisa. Byron did not see Claire, but through the window of the public coach in which she traveled, she caught a look at his pale, handsome face. She would never see him again.

In Pisa, Byron received the reviews of cantos 3, 4, and 5 of *Don Juan* — no better than the previous ones. *The British Critic:* "spawned in filth and darkness"; *The Edinburgh Magazine:* "poisoning the current of fine poetry . . . ribaldry and blasphemy."

By February of 1822, Claire was planning to take a job as a governess in Vienna, where her brother Charles now lived. This would mean she might not be able to see Allegra for a long time, so once again she pleaded with Byron, begging him to allow her to visit her daughter. "My dear Friend, I conjure you do not make the world dark to me, as if my Allegra were dead." Byron's refusal was a factor in changing Claire's mind: instead of going to Vienna, she remained in Florence.

In the early spring Claire's concern about Allegra increased. She even hatched a plan to remove the child from the convent with the aid of a forged letter. She tried to enlist the Shelleys in the plot, which had echoes in the past: Mary Wollstonecraft had kidnapped her sister from her husband; Shelley had wanted to rescue his own sister from school. For once,

Mary and Percy acted like grown-ups and turned down Claire's plan. Mary further tried to dissuade her by pointing out that Allegra was in a part of Italy that was relatively free of disease. She also warned Claire that it was unwise to irritate Byron, who was wealthy and had powerful friends. "L. B. would use any means to find you out," she wrote, and if Shelley were involved in the scheme, Byron might challenge him to a duel. "Another thing I mention," wrote Mary. "Spring is our unlucky season. No spring [since 1815] has passed for us without some piece of ill luck."

Shelley, of course, was hoping to establish the new literary journal with Byron, and needed his financial support. He did, however, go to Byron and ask him to make some gesture that would placate Claire. Claire, who heard about this after the fact, said Byron merely responded with "a shrug of impatience, and the exclamation that women could not live without making scenes."

Claire dropped the kidnapping plans, but on April 9, she wrote Mary again to express her fears: "I am truly uneasy for it seems to me some time since I have heard any news from Allegra. I fear she is sick." Claire's intuition was on target this time, for Allegra was indeed very ill. Four days later, Byron's Italian banker, who had recommended the convent school, was informed by the reverend mother that Allegra was suffering from a fever. A physician from Ravenna, Dr. Rasi, had been called in and feared that Allegra was suffering from typhus, which was raging in the area.

On April 16, Byron was informed that Allegra needed to be bled because the fever had attacked her chest, but the child was supposed to be out of danger. His banker wrote Byron that he had visited the convent and saw that Allegra was being attended by three physicians and all the nuns. "If there is any fault, it is of too much care," he said. Byron recommended a well-known doctor, saying he would pay for the man's services. He still did not realize that Allegra's sickness was life threatening, and did not mention her condition to anyone else.

The next message from the convent, on April 22, announced the death of Allegra. She had succumbed, probably to typhus, at ten in the morning on April 20. She was five years and three months old. The entry in the convent's record book said that Allegra's "extraordinary qualities of heart and of mind, her rare talents, and the lovableness of her character will cause her to be long remembered by all those who had the happiness to know her, and especially the nuns whose delight she was."

Teresa, now living in Pisa with her brother, was asked to break the sad news to Byron. She described his reaction: "A mortal paleness spread itself over his face, his strength failed him, and he sunk into a seat. . . . He remained immoveable in the same attitude for an hour, and no consolation . . . seemed to reach his ears, far less his heart." The next day, he had become somewhat reconciled, Teresa wrote. "'She is more fortunate than we are,' he said; 'besides her position in the world would scarcely have allowed her to be happy. It is God's will — let us mention it no more.' And from that day he would never pronounce her name." His reaction could indicate guilt as well as grief. Mary Shelley would later say that he "felt the loss, at first bitterly — he also felt remorse."

Byron's own description of his feelings was not so extreme. He passed on the news in a letter to Shelley, reporting that he was coping:

> The blow was stunning and unexpected; for I thought the danger over. . . . But I have borne up against it as I best can, and so far successfully, that I can go about the usual business of life with the same appearance of composure, and even greater. . . . I do not know that I have any thing to reproach in my conduct, and certainly nothing in my feelings and intentions toward the dead. But it is a moment when we are apt to think that, if this or that had been done, such event might have been prevented — though every day and hour shows us that they are the most natural and inevitable. I suppose that Time will do his usual work — Death has done his.

Godwin himself could hardly have put it better.

Percy and Mary worried what Claire's reaction would be. She was currently with friends in La Spezia on the coast, looking for summer housing for herself and the Shelleys. On her return to Pisa, Percy Shelley kept the news from her, waiting until they were settled in the house where they were to spend the summer. Even here, it was only after Claire guessed that something was wrong that she found out that her tragic premonitions had come true. On the evening of April 30, Claire overheard the name Bagnacavallo mentioned in the next room; when she appeared in the doorway, there was an abrupt silence in the conversation. Demanding to know the truth, she received the news with great dignity. She did not break down publicly, but wrote nothing at all in her journal for five months. Shelley feared that Claire might go mad with grief. Instead Claire returned to Florence to her job as a governess and kept on good enough terms with the Shelleys that she agreed to spend the summer with them. Mary was surprised that Claire managed to maintain her composure so well.

She was hiding what lay beneath the surface. Later, when Claire went through with her plans to go to Vienna, she wrote a friend that "I tried the whole journey to follow your advice and admire the scenery — dearest Lady it was all in vain . . . I only saw my lost darling." (When Claire was an old woman, she would cling to the belief that Allegra had not died and that Byron had sent a goat to England in a sealed coffin.)

Some of her wretched grief broke through in a cold and angry letter to Byron which he read and then sent to Shelley. The contents must have been horrible, for Shelley burned it and drafted his own letter to Byron on Claire's behalf:

> I will not describe her grief to you; you have already suffered too much; and, indeed, the only object of this letter is to convey her last requests to you, which, melancholy as one of them is, I could not refuse to ask, and I am sure you will readily grant. She wishes to see the coffin before it is sent to England, and I have ventured to assure her that this consolation, since she thinks it such, will not be denied her. . . . She also wished you would give her a portrait of Allegra, and if you have it, a lock of her hair, however small.

Byron did send Claire the portrait, a miniature that she kept until her death. Byron offered to make any funeral arrangements that Claire desired, but then complained at the high price of the embalming, claiming that it was the amount usually charged for an adult, and asking for a two-thirds discount. The Italian banker, who said, "I wish I had never met the noble Lord," footed the bill and later collected from Byron's estate.

The body was sent to England, where Byron wanted John Murray to make arrangements to have Allegra buried at Harrow, Byron's old school. He intended that she be interred inside the church with a memorial tablet reading,

In Memory of
Allegra
daughter of G. G. Lord Byron,
who died at Bagnacavallo,
in Italy, April 20th, 1822.
aged five years and three months
"I shall go to her, but she shall not return to me."
— 2nd Samuel, XII, 23.

The choice of this particular verse was odd, considering that Byron had never visited his daughter after sending her to the convent school. In any case, because Allegra was illegitimate, and to soothe the feelings of Lady Byron, who sometimes worshipped in the church, Allegra was buried under what one Byron biographer called "the present doormat," just inside the door, and the tablet was never erected. When he learned of the brouhaha about Allegra's burial, Byron wrote that it seemed "the epitome or miniature of the Story of my life." Byron, who knew he had been an inattentive father, later wrote of Allegra, "While she lived, her existence never seemed necessary to my happiness. But no sooner did I lose her, than it appeared to me as if I could not live without her."

The curse was now to claim another.

CHAPTER TWELVE

THE HATEFUL HOUSE

That time is dead for ever, child!
Drowned, frozen, dead for ever!
We look on the past,
And stare aghast
At the spectres wailing, pale and ghast,
Of hopes which thou and I beguiled
To death on life's dark river.

— "Lines," Percy Shelley, 1817, published 1824

After the birth of the Shelleys' latest child, Percy Florence, in November 1819, his father believed that things would return to normal, and Mary's depression would disappear. Now she had a baby again to make her happy. But Mary could not so easily forget the deaths of her children Clara and William, nor Shelley's open affection for other women. Mary's husband, like her father, had a blind spot for her emotional pain and was unable to deal with it except to complain how it affected him.

When she was younger, Mary tried to involve herself in the kind of community marriage her husband envisioned. She went through the motions with Thomas Jefferson Hogg, but there is no evidence their relationship was ever consummated, or that it was anything more than playacting on her side. Now she found that she had stronger feelings for order, religion, and domestic happiness.

Percy, of course, had not changed at all. He succeeded in keeping some of his affairs secret from Mary, who nevertheless suspected what was going on. And after the secret of his mysterious Neapolitan baby, Elena, suddenly emerged — when Byron showed Shelley the letter from the Hoppners at Ravenna — Percy had turned to Mary to bail him out, asking her to write a letter that exculpated him from blame.

Which she did. Outwardly, she was determined to remain loyal, to give him no cause to complain that she had ever been less than faithful. But the ghosts of their dead children hovered over their relationship, making her depressed and, Percy felt, emotionally cold to him. He himself withdrew into further secrets — furtively writing letters and concealing them from Mary, publishing a love poem to another woman and attributing it to an author Percy claimed was dead. Shelley reflected on his situation, "It seems as if the destruction that is consuming me were as an atmosphere which wrapt & infected everything connected with me." It was an assessment that proved prophetic.

The Shelleys had moved to Pisa in late January 1820, just a day after two-month-old Percy Florence had been baptized in the city whose name he bore. Pisa attracted them because of its cheaper housing and the presence of good doctors. As ever, Shelley could not control his restlessness. They had lived in three different Pisan residences by June.

Claire and Mary remained at odds. Claire pointedly wrote in her journal in February, "A bad wife is like Winter in a house." Later, she noted, "Heigh-ho, the Clare and the Ma / Find something to fight about every day." Mary clearly agreed, recording in her own journal that June 8 was "A better day than most days & good reason for it though Shelley is not well. C[laire] away at Pugnano."

Shelley was increasingly annoyed by Mary's jealousy, forgetting that she had justification for it. He wrote a friend in 1820:

> Claire is yet with us, and is reading Latin and Spanish with great resolution. Poor thing! She is an excellent girl. . . . Mary who, you know, is always wise, has been lately very good. I wish she were as wise now as she will be at 45, or as misfortune has made me. She would then live on very good terms with Claire. . . . Of course

> you will not suppose that Mary has seen . . . this . . . so take no notice of it in any letter intended for her inspection.

Percy was by now in the habit of asking his correspondents to reply to him through contacts in Pisa, in order to keep their communications secret.

Percy's anxiety grew when other problems presented themselves. In June, Paolo Foggi tried to blackmail Shelley with the rumor that Claire was the mother of Elena. Mary may not have known the specifics at this time, but she understood that Percy felt threatened. They consulted a lawyer to force Paolo to abandon his blackmail attempt.

Godwin, who always made matters worse, was again demanding money. Mary wrote her friends the Gisbornes, then visiting England, to ask them to "lend" Godwin four hundred pounds, which Shelley promised to repay. They did not. All of these threats and worries affected Mary's milk production, and the baby became ill. The problem appeared to be similar to that which had killed Clara, and Mary became so overwrought that she let Percy censor her mail to avoid any incoming messages that would upset her. Percy began warning Godwin and their friends not to write letters that would "disturb her quiet."

Mary got some relief when Claire left for Florence on October 20, 1820. There, she was to stay with a doctor who would introduce her to Florentine society so that she could obtain a job as a governess. Shelley accompanied Claire on the trip, returning with his cousin Tom Medwin, who had been living in Europe after military service in India.

Percy instructed Claire to send any letters to him at the Pisa post office, directed to the name Joe James. While she was in Florence, he in turn wrote her a letter that throws some light on their relationship: "I should be very glad to receive a confidential letter from you. . . . Do not think that my affection & anxiety for you ever cease, or that I ever love you less although that love has been & still must be a source of disquietude to me. . . ."

Medwin left an interesting description of Shelley at this time:

> It was nearly seven years since we had parted; but I should immediately have recognized him in a crowd. His figure was emaciated, and somewhat bent; owing to nearsightedness, and his being forced to

> lean over his books, with his eyes almost touching them, his hair, still profuse, and curling naturally, was partially interspersed with grey . . . but his appearance was youthful, and his countenance, whether grave or animated, strikingly intellectual. There was also a freshness and purity in his complexion that he never lost.

The Shelleys added new members to their circle of friends in Pisa. Mary began taking Greek lessons from an exile, Prince Alexander Mavrocordatos, who was involved in the Greek independence movement. Shelley dedicated his poem *Hellas* to Mavrocordatos, though he seems to have resented the attention the freedom fighter got from Mary. When the Greek left Italy to join his compatriots, Shelley wrote to Claire, "He is a great loss to Mary, and *therefore* to me — but not otherwise."

Shelley was more enthusiastic about Professor Francesco Pacchiani, a local "character" who had left the priesthood to write poetry and then had become a professor of chemistry at the University of Pisa. Mary wrote of him, "The poor people of Pisa think him mad and they tell many little stories about him, which make us believe that he is really somewhat odd or, as the English say, 'eccentric.' But he says — They believe me to be mad and it pleases me that they make this mistake; but perhaps the time will come when they will see that it is the madness of Brutus." Pacchiani's logic mirrored Shelley's opinion of himself, so it is not difficult to understand why the two got along so well, though Shelley later dropped Pacchiani when the professor showed a fondness for telling crude stories.

Pacchiani introduced the Shelleys to Countess Teresa Viviani, the nineteen-year-old daughter of the governor of Pisa. Emilia, as the Shelleys called her, was currently living in the convent of Saint Anna, "where she sees no one but the maids and the idiots," according to Mary. She was compelled to remain there until her parents arranged a suitable marriage for her, and Mary commented, "It is grievous to see this beautiful girl wearing out the best years of her life in an odious convent where both mind and body are sick from want of . . . exercise."

Nothing appealed to Percy more than a maiden in distress. He had "rescued" Harriet from her father in 1811, and repeated the performance with Mary in 1814. After he married the rescued maidens, unfortunately, they became less attractive to him. A friend, a poet manqué himself, who knew Percy in his last year of life commented, "He was inconstant in Love as men of vehement temperament are apt to be — his spirit hunting after new fancies; nothing real can equal the ideal. Poets and men of ardent imagination should not marry — marriage is only suitable to stupid people."

Shelley accordingly took Emilia under his wing, writing her what must have been a puzzling letter: "Here are we then, bound by a few days friendship, gathered together by some strange fortune from the ends of the earth to be perhaps a consolation to each other." A copy of this letter, and four others like it, were found, half-finished, in one of Shelley's notebooks. It would have been difficult for him to carry on a love affair with someone in as protected a position as Emilia, but of course for Shelley once a deed was imagined, it was as good as done in actuality.

Emilia became the inspiration for Shelley's poem *Epipsychidion* ("on the subject of the soul"), which he told a friend was "an idealized history of my life and feelings." He portrayed her as the incarnation of Venus, goddess of love:

I never thought before my death to see
Youth's vision thus made perfect. Emily,
I love thee. . . .

Claire appeared in the poem as a comet:

. . . O Comet beautiful and fierce,
Who drew the heart of this frail Universe
Towards thine own; till wreckt in that convulsion,
Alternating attraction and repulsion,
Thine went astray and that was rent in twain.

Mary was represented as the Moon, a cold figure who put the poet to sleep:

And all my being became bright or dim
As the Moon's image in a summer sea,
According as she smiled or frowned on me;
And there I lay, within a chaste cold bed:
Alas, I then was nor alive nor dead.

When Shelley sent *Epipsychidion* to his publisher, Charles Ollier, he asked that it be published anonymously. "I make its author a secret, to avoid the malignity of those who turn sweet food into poison." Obviously, he feared Mary's reaction. Stranger still, Shelley told Ollier that the poem was "a production of a portion of me already dead." He wrote a preface saying that the anonymous author "died at Florence, as he was preparing for a voyage to one of the wildest of the Sporades [Greek islands] . . . where it was his hope to have realised a scheme of life, suited perhaps to that happier and better world of which he is now an inhabitant, but hardly practicable in this."

Mary ultimately did learn of the poem, possibly having it in mind in 1839 when she wrote, "There are other verses I should well like to obliterate for ever." At the time, she was preparing an edition of Shelley's poems for publication. *Epipsychidion* was the only one of his long works that she printed without an introduction.

Two more people, Jane and Edward Williams, joined the Shelley circle in January 1821. Their relationship was as irregular as the Shelleys' had been in 1816. Edward Ellerker Williams had joined the English navy at the age of eleven and eventually served in India, where he met Jane, who was in an unhappy marriage. The two ran off together but were never formally married because Jane's husband refused to give her a divorce. Edward spent his time writing plays that were never produced, something Percy could sympathize with, and the two of them became fast friends. Jane, like Claire, had musical talents, but at the time Percy met the couple, he was still infatuated with Emilia, and described Jane as "an extremely pretty & gentle woman — apparently not *very* clever."

Mary's first impressions gave no indication that she found Jane a threat. "Jane is certainly very pretty," she wrote,

> but she wants animation and sense; her conversation is *nothing particular,* and she speaks in a slow monotonous voice: but she appears good tempered and tolerant. *Ned* seems the picture of good humour and obligingness, he is lively and possesses great talent in drawing so that with him one is never at a loss for subjects of conversation.

In March, Mary helped with the birth of the Williamses' second child and brought the news to Edward that he was now the father of a girl.

The following month, Percy, Edward Williams, and Henry Reveley, the son of Maria Gisborne, went on a sailing trip. When their boat capsized, Williams easily made his way to the shore, but only Reveley's quick assistance saved Shelley, who was helpless in the water. The threesome stayed at a local farmhouse for the night before making their way back to Pisa. Shelley's response seems bizarre. He wrote to Reveley on his return, "Our ducking last night has added fire instead of quenching the nautical ardour which produced it; and I consider it as a good omen in any enterprise that it begins in evil: as being more probable that it will end in good." Few people would have considered a narrow escape from drowning as "a good omen."

Byron joined the group in Pisa in November 1821. The Shelleys were now ensconced on the top floor of a villa on the Arno, with the Williams family living on the floor below. Byron settled on the opposite bank at the Palazzo Lanfranchi. Countess Teresa Guiccioli and her brother Pietro Gamba had a house just up the street, and Byron visited her daily. He loved his palazzo, a sixteenth-century building with dungeons in its cellar. His longtime valet, however, had misgivings. Byron wrote to John Murray that the palazzo "was so full of *Ghosts* that the learned Fletcher (my Valet) has begged leave to change his room — and then refused to occupy his *new* room — because there were more Ghosts there than in the other.— It is quite true;— that there are most extraordinary noises (as in all old buildings), which have terrified the servants so — as to incommode me extremely."

Shelley enjoyed the company and conversation of women, while Byron claimed to prefer the harem, where "they lock them up, and they are much happier. Give a woman a looking-glass and a few sugar-plums, and she will be satisfied." As a result, Byron's circle was always male-dominated. He liked to host stag dinners and take part in outdoor activities like shooting, riding, and boating. Even on Christmas Day the men all dined at the Casa Lanfranchi without the women. On these occasions Mary and Teresa looked to each other for companionship. Mary found Teresa a pretty and amiable woman, without pretensions.

The reason for Byron's arrival was ostensibly to begin preparations for the magazine that he, Shelley, and Leigh Hunt were to publish. However, this had to be delayed because Hunt's wife fell ill before they could leave England. The Hunts would not arrive in Italy until the spring of 1822.

In January 1822, the Shelley circle welcomed another member. Edward Trelawny was born the same year as Percy but he was a man of action rather than thought. Everyone recognized him as a romantic figure. Mary described Trelawny as "six feet high — raven black hair which curls thickly & shortly, like a Moor's . . . and a smile which expresses good nature and kindheartedness. . . . His company is delightful." He had, by his own account, a spectacularly checkered past, in which he left school at twelve after leading a mutiny in which the students flogged a cruel assistant headmaster. Trelawny enlisted in the British navy, from which he said he deserted to join a pirate band that roamed the sea from India to Malaysia. Finally he married an Arab woman whom he had rescued. He sounded exactly like a hero out of one of Byron's poems, and even Byron was taken in by the man's stories. After meeting Trelawny for the first time, Byron told Teresa that Trelawny was "the personification of my Corsair."

Edward Williams, who had known Trelawny in India, introduced him to the group, and Trelawny won acceptance with his tall tales. Mary liked his rakishness: "He tells strange stories of himself — horrific ones — so that they harrow one up . . . [with] simple yet strong language — he portrays the most frightful situations. . . . I believe them now I see the man. . . . I am glad to meet with one who among other valuable qualities has the rare merit of interesting my imagination."

In fact, though Trelawny had spent seven years in the navy, he never rose above the rank of midshipman and had an undistinguished record. He returned to England on a naval ship (not a pirate vessel) and made an unhappy marriage (not with an Arab) that ended in divorce. Most recently he had been living in Switzerland, supported by an allowance from his father. Trelawny had come to Italy specifically to meet Byron and Shelley, for he now fancied embarking on a literary career. Indeed, he made his relatively brief friendship with them his lifelong meal ticket.

Trelawny left a description of Mary at this time: "She brought us back from the ideal world Shelley had left us in, to the real one, welcomed me to Italy, and asked me the news of London and Paris, the new books, operas, and bonnets, marriages, murders, and other marvels." Like others, he was struck by "her calm, grey eyes." He described her as "rather under the English standard of women's height, very fair and light-haired, witty, social, and animated in the society of friends, though mournful in solitude."

Trelawny glimpsed some of the fault lines in the Shelleys' marriage during a day with the couple in the pine forest of Cascine outside Pisa. Mary became tired and rested beneath a tree while Trelawny found Shelley deep in the forest, daydreaming beside a deep pool. Shelley fantasized about the shapes of the rocks and trees. "We talked and laughed, and shrieked, and shouted, as we emerged from under the shadows of the melancholy pines," Trelawny wrote. When they rejoined Mary, Shelley's mood changed. He sighed, "Poor Mary! hers is a sad fate. Come along; she can't bear solitude, nor I society — the quick coupled with the dead."

Trelawny had brought with him the model of a schooner, which immediately captured Shelley's interest. He and Edward Williams decided to have a full-scale one built, under Trelawny's supervision. A year later, Mary was to recall, "Thus on that night — one of gaiety and thoughtlessness — Jane's and my miserable destiny was decided. We then said laughing each to the other, 'Our husbands decide without asking our consent . . . for, to tell you the truth, I hate this boat, though I say nothing.' How well I remember that night! How short-sighted we are!"

From the time she finished *Mathilda* Mary had been building a life of her own. She realized that Shelley could not be relied on and that his romantic ideas would never meet her need for a stable life. Increasingly, Mary turned to her friends and her mother's writing to enrich her existence. Her journal entries for February are introspective and searching — very different from the sort of notation previously offered. For example, on February 25, she wrote: "Let me in my fellow creatures love that which is & not fix my affections on a fair form endued with imaginary attributes . . . above all let me fearlessly descend into the remotest caverns of my own mind — carry the torch of self knowledge into its dimmest recesses — but too happy if I dislodge any evil spirit or enshrine a new deity in some hitherto uninhabited nook — Read Wrongs of Women [one of her mother's books]."

Looking within herself was Mary's only solace, for Percy had now fixated on the loveliness of Jane Williams. She had a fine singing voice and he bought her a guitar. He wrote her a series of love poems, cautioning, "I commit them to your secrecy." Shelley, however, showed them to Edward Williams, a liberal-minded husband like himself. In one poem, Percy summoned up another ménage à trois — he compares the three of them to characters from Shakespeare's *The Tempest:* Jane as Miranda, Edward as Ferdinand, and Percy as the ethereal spirit Ariel. He saw the Williamses' happy marriage as an ideal that contrasted with his own. Mary did not learn of the poems until after Shelley's death.

The death of Allegra gave a bad start to the summer, which only became worse as time went on. Mary had hoped Byron could join them in a repetition of 1816, but Byron had rented a large house up the coast at Livorno, where he was adding new cantos to his *Don Juan.* The Shelleys and the Williamses, along with three children and — as always — Claire, moved into a small house near a coastal village called San Terenzo. Casa Magni, which Mary had chosen reluctantly at Shelley's urging, turned out to be a hateful place for her. It was literally on the beach, almost trapped between the land and the bay. "The sea came up to the door [and] a steep hill sheltered it behind," Mary wrote. "The proprietor of the estate on which it was situated was insane." He had uprooted olive trees that had been growing on the hillside and planted hardwood trees, an act that to the local people was a glaring manifestation of his madness. But Shelley thought the new trees made the location seem like England, and praised the house's serenity and charm.

Mary recalled the location differently: "The gales and squalls that hailed our first arrival surrounded the bay with foam; the howling wind swept round our exposed house, and the sea roared unremittingly, so that we almost fancied ourselves on board ship." The ground floor of the house was uninhabitable because the earthen floors had never been paved, so the group lived in close quarters on the upper floor, where there were only four rooms and a terrace. They were forced to eat in the hallway between rooms.

The exterior environment was scarcely more comforting. Mary found the local residents primitive and frightening. "Our near neighbors," she wrote, "were more like savages than any people I ever before lived among. Many a night they passed on the beach, singing, or rather howling; the women dancing about among the waves that broke at their feet, the men leaning against the rocks and joining in their loud wild chorus. . . . Had we been wrecked on an island of the South Seas, we could scarcely have felt ourselves farther from civilization and comfort." All this was compounded by the fact that Mary had discovered she was pregnant, and in view of what she had already experienced, was nervous about being far from any medical assistance.

Percy was writing little. He wrote in a letter, "I have lived too long near Lord Byron and the sun has extinguished the glow-worm." When Byron had read him some of the new verses of *Don Juan,* Percy wrote to Mary: "I despair of rivalling Lord Byron . . . and there is no other with whom it is worth contending." He added, "The demon of mistrust & of pride lurks between two persons in our situation poisoning the freedom of their intercourse. This is a tax and a heavy one which we must pay for being human. I think the fault is not on my side; nor is it likely, I being the weaker. I hope that in the next world these things will be better managed."

With Trelawny along as his adviser, Shelley went to Genoa to take possession of the thirty-foot schooner he had ordered. Trelawny thought Shelley should learn to swim and had offered to give him lessons, but when Shelley stripped and jumped into a pool he had sunk to the bottom. Trelawny had to haul him out, and Shelley remarked, "I always find the bottom of the well, and they say Truth lies there. In another minute I should have found it, and you would have found an empty shell."

A man who had known Shelley at Eton saw him at Genoa sitting on the seashore eating bread and fruit. "Shelley was looking careworn and ill; and, as usual, was very carelessly dressed," the friend recalled. "He had on a large and wide straw hat, his long brown hair, already streaked with gray, flowing in large masses from under it, and presented a wild and strange appearance."

Trelawny arranged for the boat to be moved to Lerici, a town on the same bay where Casa Magni stood. As a prank, Trelawny had named the boat *Don Juan,* which irked Shelley. (It was particularly annoying because Mary had been busy with the tedious task of making a fair copy for the printer of Byron's great work.) Shelley tried to wash the name *Don Juan* off the sail where it had been painted, but eventually had to pay a local sailmaker to cut out the offending piece of cloth and sew in a new one. The name Shelley chose: *Ariel.* Shelley and Edward Williams began sailing immediately, assisted by a young English sailor named Charles Vivian. Shelley described his mood:

Less oft is peace in Shelley's mind
Than calm in water seen.

As usual Mary was having trouble during her pregnancy — ailments discounted by her husband, complaining to Claire, as "languor and hysterical affections." Emotionally Mary felt isolated, for Shelley was now constantly around Jane Williams. Mary turned her anger against the surroundings. "No words can tell you," she wrote to a friend, "how I hated our house & the country about it."

On June 16, Mary suffered a near-fatal miscarriage. She later recalled her very strong sense that she was about to die: "I had no fear — rather though I had no active wish — I had a passive satisfaction in death — Whether the nature of my illness — debility from the loss of blood without pain, caused this tranquility of soul, I cannot tell — but so it was — & it had this blessed effect that I have never since anticipated death with terror." This time Shelley rose to the occasion. With the help of Jane and Claire, he thrust Mary into a bath of freezing water and ice to stanch her bleeding. It worked and when a doctor arrived, he approved of the treatment. Shelley had saved her life.

Two days after Mary's miscarriage, Shelley wrote a letter to the Gisbornes, complaining that Mary did not understand him: "I only feel the want of those who can feel, and understand me. Whether from proximity and the continuity of domestic intercourse, Mary does not. . . . It is the curse of Tantalus, that a person possessing such excellent powers and so pure a mind as hers, should not excite the sympathy indispensable to their application to domestic life." He mentioned how pleasant it was to have

Jane Williams around, for she had "an elegance of form and motions that compensate in some degree for [her] lack of literary refinement." Mary's dawning awareness of Shelley's feeling toward the cheerful, fun-loving Jane only added to the depression she suffered as a result of the miscarriage.

From childhood Percy had been susceptible to visions and waking dreams. Mary herself had employed prophetic dreams in the plot of *Frankenstein;* now her husband's fate was presaged by a series of apparitions. Percy began to see ghosts.

The first appeared one clear evening while Shelley and Edward Williams were on the terrace of Casa Magni, enjoying the view of the moonlight on the water. Suddenly Shelley seized his friend's arm and stared out to sea. Alarmed, Williams asked if he were in pain. Shelley answered, "There it is again — there!" Williams looked but saw nothing. It took a while for Shelley to recover, but when he did he said he had seen a naked child rising from the sea, clapping her hands, and smiling at him. It was reminiscent of the last visit he had with Allegra, playing with her in the convent. Williams had to argue forcibly to convince Shelley that it was a hallucination. In his journal, Williams attributed the incident to Shelley's "ever wandering and lively imagination." Later Shelley told Mary that he had met himself, his doppelgänger, on the terrace of Casa Magni. It had stopped and asked him, "How long do you mean to be content?"

"Shelley had often seen these figures when ill," Mary wrote, but Jane Williams, of whom Mary remarked that she "has not much imagination & is not in the slightest degree nervous," also reported a vision of Shelley's double. From inside the house, she saw Percy walk past the window that opened onto the terrace, and a few seconds later, he crossed her view again, walking in the same direction. Jane was startled, because there was no way he could have done this without crossing back. (She actually thought Shelley might have jumped off the balcony to achieve what she had seen.) Later she discovered that Shelley had not even been at the house at the time this occurred. Even Byron told Thomas Moore that he had seen Shelley "walk into a little wood at Lerici," when (he discovered later) Shelley was at that time actually in some other place. Already he seemed to have become a disembodied spirit.

One night Shelley woke the entire household with his screams, resulting, he claimed, not from a nightmare but a "vision." As he lay in bed, ghostly figures of Edward and Jane had entered into his room, their bodies stained with blood and their bones sticking out. "They could hardly walk," Mary later recalled, and "Edward said —'Get up, Shelley, the sea is flooding the house, & it is all coming down.'" Percy said he had run to the window and seen the sea approaching. Then he had a second vision: he saw himself over Mary's bed, strangling her — a reprise of the scene from *Frankenstein* in which the monster kills Victor's bride.

Percy was so disturbed by these images that he asked Edward Trelawny to obtain some prussic acid — Polidori's poison of choice — for him. He told Trelawny that it would "be a comfort to me to hold in my possession that golden key to the chamber of perpetual rest."

Shelley's hallucinations and wild mood swings were reflected in the poem that he was working on just before he died: *The Triumph of Life*. In it, the unnamed Poet is guided by no less a figure than Jean-Jacques Rousseau, the philosopher who had inspired those who sparked and — like Wollstonecraft, Godwin, Mary, Percy, and Byron — admired the French Revolution. Rousseau, in the poem, says he has awakened from a long sleep:

> *Whether [my] life had been before that sleep*
> *The Heaven which I imagine, or a Hell*
> *Like this harsh world in which I wake to weep,*
> *I know not. . . .*

Shelley was disillusioned with his life, and in the poem he appears to be struggling to write for himself a rationale for existence. His only happy times at Casa Magni seem to have been listening to Jane Williams playing the guitar and sailing on his new boat.

In June, Leigh Hunt and his family finally arrived in Italy. Shelley and Edward Williams put to sea in the newly christened *Ariel*, planning to meet the Hunts at Livorno. On his desk, Shelley left his manuscript with the final words of an unfinished composition: "Then, what is life? I cried —"

The *Ariel* reached Livorno on the night of July 1. The next day Shelley greeted Hunt and his family, whom he had not seen in four years. He accompanied them to Pisa, where Byron had arranged for the new arrivals to stay at his palazzo. Shelley sent letters to both Mary and Jane Williams from Pisa — the last he would ever write. The one to Mary contains pessimistic news. Hunt's wife was not expected to live; Byron's interest in the magazine had waned because Teresa's father and brother had been exiled and now Byron wanted to leave Tuscany, taking Teresa with him to America, to Switzerland . . . he was not sure; finally, Hunt needed money to begin publication, and Percy would have to borrow it from Byron. "I have not a moments leisure — but will write by next post," he concluded, sounding the same as ever. To Jane Williams, Percy wrote a note more suitable for a beloved wife: "I fear you are solitary & melancholy at Villa Magni. . . . How soon those hours past, & how slowly they return to pass so soon again, & perhaps for ever, in which we have lived together so intimately so happily!— Adieu, my dearest friend — I only write these lines for the pleasure of tracing what will meet your eyes.— Mary will tell you all the news."

Percy returned to Livorno, where Trelawny was preparing to take Byron's new boat, the *Bolivar,* down the coast to Lerici. The plan was that they would all make the trip together, Shelley and Edward Williams in the *Ariel* and Trelawny in the larger vessel. However, the port authorities detained Trelawny because he did not have proper papers. Shelley and Williams decided to leave without him.

With only young Charles Vivian as crew, they set sail on the afternoon of July 8. As evening approached, a storm blew up. The crews of the Italian fishing fleet, seeing the ominous signs, made for port. One fisherman reported that he noticed the *Ariel* was having difficulty. He said he offered to take the passengers on board his own boat but they refused. He warned them to lower their sails but they paid no attention to this advice. The *Ariel* was never seen again.

Mary, still weak from her miscarriage, waited at the Casa Magni with Jane Williams. Each day they sat on the terrace, expecting the *Ariel*'s sails to come around the promontory to the north of the bay. Then a letter from Hunt arrived, addressed to Percy, asking whether he had gotten back safely, "for they say that you had bad weather after you sailed Monday and we are anxious." As she read those words, Mary dropped the letter. Jane picked it up, saw the contents, and cried, "Then it is all over!"

Mary pulled herself together, saying, "No, my dear Jane. It is not all over, but this suspense is dreadful — come with me, we will go to Leghorn [Livorno] . . . & learn our fate." They crossed the bay to Lerici and took the mail coach to Pisa. When they arrived, Mary's nervousness returned. She knew that the Hunts were at Byron's palazzo, but "the idea of seeing Hunt for the first time for four years under such circumstances, & asking him such a question was so terrific to me that it was with difficulty that I prevented myself from going into convulsions."

It was midnight by the time they arrived at Byron's. "I had risen almost from a bed of sickness for this journey," Mary recalled. "I had traveled all day." She was exhausted and terrified, and showed it. Byron recalled her appearance:

> I never can forget the night that [Shelley's] poor wife rushed into my room at Pisa, with a face pale as marble, and terror impressed on her brow, demanded with all the tragic impetuosity of grief and alarm, where was her husband! Vain were all our efforts to calm her; a desperate sort of courage seemed to give her energy to confront the horrible truth that awaited her; it was the courage of despair. I have seen nothing in tragedy on the stage so powerful, or so affecting, as her appearance, and it often presents itself to my memory. I knew nothing then of the catastrophe, but the vividness of her terror communicated itself to me, and I feared the worst.

Trelawny accompanied Mary and Jane back to Casa Magni, where they and Claire could only wait for news. They kept up their hopes by suggesting that Shelley and Williams might have only been blown off course. They sent messengers along the coast seeking information. Trelawny returned to Livorno, where he learned that two bodies had washed up on shore. They were virtually unrecognizable because they had been in the water ten days, and most of the flesh had been eaten by fish. Trelawny recognized the boots on Williams's corpse and found in a pocket on the other body two books Shelley had been reading: Keats's poetry and the plays of

Sophocles. The bodies were immediately buried on the beach, with quicklime sprinkled in the graves, because of Italian health regulations.

On the night of June 19, Trelawny returned to Casa Magni to break the news.

> I went up the stairs, and, unannounced, entered the room. I neither spoke, nor did they question me. Mrs. Shelley's large grey eyes were fixed on my face. I turned away. Unable to bear this horrid silence, with a convulsive effort she exclaimed: "Is there no hope?"
>
> I did not answer, but left the room, and sent the servant with the children to them. The next day I prevailed on them to return with me to Pisa. The misery of that night and the journey of the next day, and of many days and nights that followed, I can neither describe nor forget.

Grief left Mary virtually paralyzed, and Trelawny took charge of the funeral arrangements. The bodies were to be exhumed from their rough graves and cremated. Trelawny had a portable iron crematorium built, and brought frankincense, salt, wine, and oil to sprinkle on the bodies. On the fifteenth of August, he, Byron, and Hunt stood by as Edward Williams's corpse was disinterred. Byron was shocked by its appearance: "Are we to resemble that?" he exclaimed. "Why it might be the carcase of a sheep for all I can see."

The next day they dug up Shelley. His corpse was also badly decomposed, "a dark and ghastly indigo," but Trelawny consoled himself that the scenery, "lonely and grand," was so much like Shelley's poetry, "that I could imagine his spirit soaring over us." Byron asked Trelawny to save the skull for him, but Trelawny remembered the story that Byron had used a skull as a drinking cup, and put the entire body to the torch. The materials they sprinkled on the corpse made the flames glow with incandescence. Even so, Byron was so distressed by the smell that he stripped off his clothes and threw himself into the sea — the only place where his limp did not hinder him. He headed for his boat the *Bolivar,* anchored a mile and a half offshore. Leigh Hunt remained in the carriage, while

Trelawny watched the fire for four hours. In the open air, wine had to be added to the fire to coax it—"more wine," said Trelawny, "than he [Shelley] had consumed during his life. This with the oil and salt made the yellow flames glisten and quiver . . . the brains literally seethed, bubbled, and boiled as in a cauldron, for a very long time." After cooling the iron container in the sea, they gathered the ashes and found that the heart had remained intact. Byron had returned, and the three men set off to eat and drink. Hunt remembered, "We sang, we laughed, we shouted. I even felt a gaiety the more shocking, because it was real and a relief."

Byron described the scene to a friend: "We have been burning the bodies of Shelley and Williams on the sea-shore, to render them fit for removal and regular interment. You can have no idea what an extraordinary effect such a funeral pile has, on a desolate shore, with mountains in the background and the sea before, and the singular appearance the salt and frankincense gave to the flame. All of Shelley was consumed, except his *heart,* which would not take the flame, and is now preserved in spirits of wine."

Leigh Hunt took possession of the heart, and refused Mary's request that he turn it over to her; Jane Williams finally convinced Hunt to give it up. Mary would keep the badly charred object in a portable writing desk. The rest of Shelley's ashes, kept in a walnut case covered with black velvet, went on Byron's boat to Livorno and then to the home of the English consul in Rome. He was also a wine merchant so the ashes were stored in a wine cellar, awaiting a final decision on their disposition.

Just as her father could not bear to attend her mother's funeral, Mary herself stayed at home during the cremation. She spent the time writing a long letter to Maria Gisborne, telling everything that had happened since the beginning of the summer. To Mary, the act of writing was the beginning of expiation. She felt guilty because her relationship with Shelley was in tatters when he died. On the very day he left, they had quarreled, for she had felt his departure, at a time when she was still recovering from her miscarriage, was a desertion. She recalled that on that day, "I called him back two or three times, & told him that if I did not see him soon I would go to Pisa with the child."

In August, Byron wrote to Thomas Moore of Shelley: "There is thus another man gone, about whom the world was ill-naturedly, and ignorantly, and brutally mistaken. It will, perhaps, do him justice *now,* when he can be no better for it." He was overly optimistic.

The first public announcement of Shelley's death came from Leigh Hunt in the *Examiner* for August 4, 1822. He praised the poet: "Those who know a great mind when they meet it, and who have been delighted with the noble things in the works of MR. SHELLEY, will be shocked to hear that he has been cut off in the prime of his life and genius." Other publications noted Shelley's "fearless and independent spirit," his "estimable" character, and "highly cultivated genius."

Less flattering opinions appeared as well. The publication *John Bull* noted: "Mr. Byshe [*sic*] Shelley, the author of that abominable and blasphemous book called *Queen Mab,* was lately drowned in a storm." *The Gentleman's Magazine* wrote in an obituary, "Mr. Shelley is unfortunately too well known for his infamous novels and poems. He openly professed himself an atheist." Charles Lamb wrote to a friend that summer from France, "Shelley the great Atheist has gone down by water to eternal fire!" The response of Shelley's own father was cold and emotionless. "To lose an eldest son in his life time and the unfortunate manner of his losing that life," wrote Sir Timothy, "is truly melancholy to think of, but as it has pleas'd that great Author of our Being so to dispose of him I must make up my mind with resignation."

Reliable old Godwin put his own feelings above the need to comfort Mary. When news of Percy's death came via a letter from Hunt, he wrote his daughter,

> That you should be so overcome as not to be able to write is, perhaps, but too natural, but that Jane [Claire] could not write one line I could never have believed. . . . Leigh Hunt says you bear up under the shock better than could have been imagined; but appearances are not to be relied on. It would have been a great relief to me to have had a few lines from yourself. In a case like this, one lets one's imagination loose among the possibilities

> of things, and one is apt to rest upon what is most distressing and intolerable. I learned the news on Sunday. I was in hope to have my doubts and fears removed by a letter from yourself on Monday. I again entertained the same hope to-day, and am again disappointed. I shall hang in hope and fear on every post, knowing that you cannot neglect me for ever.

He recalled that he had not been speaking or writing to her; that had been for her own good, Mary's father explained. Now that she has experienced tragedy, they are again on the same, miserable level:

> All that I expressed to you about silence and not writing to you again is now put an end to in the most melancholy way. I looked on you as one of the daughters of prosperity, elevated in rank and fortune, and I thought it was criminal to intrude on you for ever the sorrows of an unfortunate old man and a beggar. You are now fallen to my own level; you are surrounded with adversity and with difficulty; and I shall no longer hold it sacrilege to trouble you with my adversities. We shall now truly sympathise with each other; and whatever misfortune or ruin falls upon me, I shall not now scruple to lay it fully before you.

He invited her to come and live with him and his wife and, of course, asked what financial provision Shelley had made for her.

Lord Byron told a friend after Shelley's death:

> He was the most gentle, most amiable, and *least* worldly-minded person I ever met; full of delicacy, disinterested beyond all other men, and possessing a degree of genius, joined to a simplicity, as rare as it is admirable. He had formed to himself a *beau ideal* of all that is fine, high-minded, and noble, and he acted up to this ideal even to the very letter. He had a most brilliant imagination, but a total want of worldly-wisdom. I have seen nothing like him, and never shall again, I am certain.

At the end of August, Mary wrote to Maria Gisborne describing the five weeks since she learned of Shelley's death:

> And so here I am! I continue to exist — to see one day succeed the other; to dread night; but more to dread morning & hail another cheerless day. . . . At times I feel an energy within me to combat with my destiny — but again I sink — I have but one hope for which I live — to render myself worthy to join him. . . . I can conceive but of one circumstance that could afford me the semblance of content — that is . . . in collecting His manuscripts — writing his life, and thus to go easily to my grave.

Mary would, in time, become the custodian of Shelley's memory and indeed place his reputation as a poet on a far higher level than he ever achieved during his lifetime. It would be Mary who ultimately made Percy a great man. In doing so, she carried out the words he wrote in "Ode to the West Wind":

> *Drive my dead thoughts over the universe*
> *Like withered leaves to quicken a new birth!*
> *And, by the incantation of this verse,*
> *Scatter, as from an unextinguished hearth*
> *Ashes and sparks, my words among mankind!*

CHAPTER THIRTEEN

GLORY AND DEATH

Now fierce remorse and unreplying death
Waken a chord within my heart, whose breath,
Thrilling and keen, in accents audible,
A tale of unrequited love doth tell.

— "The Choice," Mary Shelley, 1823

At percy's death, Mary was just twenty-four years old. Her identity had always been defined by those around her. First, she had been the daughter of Mary Wollstonecraft and William Godwin; then she became the companion and wife of Shelley. Now she would be known as the widow of Shelley. Like her creature, she had no name of her own.

Despite the difficulties of their marriage, Mary had loved Percy, and she depended on him in many ways. They had always been intellectual partners, and he had been her mentor from before the time she wrote *Frankenstein.* Literally her entire adult existence had been spent with him, and as bizarre as Percy's behavior had sometimes been, it was what Mary had come to experience as everyday life.

Unfortunately, Shelley had died at a low point in their relationship, and Mary would never be able to repair the rift, to say what needed to be said, to resurrect the warmth and intimacy they had formerly shared. As the initial shock of his passing wore off, however, Mary sought a way to resolve the conflicts between them. Words had been her refuge and now would be her tools. Just as her mother had once created ideal versions of her own life, Mary would use her writing skills to repair her marriage.

She would go farther than that: she would create an ideal version of Shelley himself.

Mary and Jane Williams, companions in grief, left the house at Lerici and moved back to Pisa, where Mary wrote lengthy and feverish letters that were novelistic in their description of Shelley's death and the events leading up to it. Mary now saw clearly the foreshadowings of disaster, visions showing the interrelationship of writing and reality.

In September 1822, Jane Williams went to London and Mary rented a large house in Genoa, where she was soon joined by the Hunts and their six children. Claire, after a brief love affair with Trelawny, headed off to Vienna to live with her brother Charles. Byron felt a certain obligation toward Mary, and paid her to make legible copies of his poems. He was writing more cantos of *Don Juan,* having received "permission" from his lover Teresa Guiccioli, who had felt that the earlier parts of the poem were too indelicate. Mary also wrote for the new journal, *The Liberal,* that Hunt edited with Byron's financial support. For the first issue she transcribed Shelley's poetical translation of Goethe's *Faust;* for the second she contributed a story of her own, "A Tale of the Passions, or the Death of Despina."

Meanwhile, Mary began what was to be a years-long task: editing Shelley's poems for publication. She wrote to people who might have copies, among them Percy's publisher Charles Ollier, Thomas Love Peacock, the Gisbornes, Hogg, and Godwin. Some of the work reopened wounds that had hardly begun to heal. At one point she asked Peacock for a desk from the Shelleys' former house at Marlow, in which she had kept letters. When it arrived in Italy, she found that reading the letters brought poignant memories of the ghosts of the past: "What a scene to recur to!" Mary reflected. "My William, Clara, Allegra are all talked of — They lived then — They breathed this air & their voices struck on my sense, their feet trod the earth beside me —& their hands were warm with blood & life when clasped in mine. Where are they all? This is too great an agony to be written about."

Nevertheless, working on Shelley's poems proved to be a tonic for Mary, and for the first time in the three months since his death, she began writing in her journal. The new journal, which Mary called her "Journal of Sorrow," began October 2, 1822. Her entries and letters made it clear that one of the few things that she lived for now was her three-year-old son, Percy Florence. "But [except] for my Child," she wrote, "it could not End too soon."

Mary felt the need to defend herself from the story being spread (unknown to Mary) by Jane Williams, that Percy had turned to Jane for companionship because Mary was so cold to him. (That had been why Hunt initially had refused to give Mary the heart of Percy after cremation.) Mary now used her journal to re-create a relationship with Percy — one that was "romantic beyond romance."

Hearing of these rumors, but not their source, she often tried to face her feelings honestly. "Oh my beloved Shelley," she wrote,

> *it is not true that this heart was cold to thee. Tell me, for now you know all things — did I not in the deepest solitude of thought repeat to myself my good fortune in possessing you? How often during those happy days, happy though chequered, I thought how superiorly gifted I had been in being united to one to whom I could unveil myself, & who could understand me. Well then, I am now reduced to these white pages which I am to blot with dark imagery.*

Other entries echoed the thoughts and feelings of the monster she had created in *Frankenstein:* "No one seems to understand or to sympathize with me. They all seem to look on me as one without affections — without any sensibility — my sufferings are thought a cypher —& I feel my self degraded before them."

That isolation increased with the passing days. A letter Mary wrote to Maria Gisborne in November begins, "No one ever writes to me. Each day, one like the other, passes on and if I were where I would that I were methinks I could not be more forgotten. I cannot write myself, for I cannot fill the paper always with the self same complaints — or if I write them, why send them, to cast the shadow of my misery on others." Mary confessed to Byron, "I would, like a dormouse, roll myself in cotton at the bottom of my cage, & never peep out." By the end of 1822, she was writing about herself as if she were the creature of her novel: "I am a lonely unloved thing.— Serious & absorbed — none cares to read my sorrow."

Mary forced herself to turn her attention to practical matters. She wrote to Percy's father, Sir Timothy, asking for an allowance for herself and her son. Byron, as co-executor (with Peacock) of Percy's estate, sent a letter supporting this request. Sir Timothy was unsympathetic; he blamed Mary for breaking up his son's first marriage to Harriet. He offered to help his grandson — but only if he could take control of his upbringing, as Sir Timothy had already done with Percy's first son, Charles. (Shelley's other child by Harriet, Ianthe, was in the custody of Harriet's father and her sister Eliza, whom Percy had so resented. Eliza had married a London bank clerk named Farthing Beauchamp, who had been left a fortune by an old lady on the condition that he change his name to Beauchamp.) Mary adamantly refused to surrender her son.

Shelley's ashes were still in the wine cellar of the English consul in Rome. The city's Protestant cemetery had refused to bury Shelley next to his son because there was no room, so Mary decided that William's body should be moved. When the grave was opened, however, it was discovered that it contained the skeleton of an adult. A ghastly mistake had been made, straight out of a Gothic novel. William's body was never found and a memorial tablet was erected to his memory, with no bones under it.

Finally, on January 21, 1823, an English chaplain buried the square wooden box containing Shelley's ashes in the New Enclosure of the Protestant Cemetery in Rome. Mary showed her growing religiosity in allowing such a service, for Percy died, as he lived, an avowed atheist.

The next month, Trelawny, just arrived in Rome, found what he considered a prettier spot, moved Percy's remains there, and even secured a plot next to it for himself. At Mary's request Trelawny put this quote from Shakespeare's *The Tempest* on the tombstone:

Nothing of him that doth fade,
But doth suffer a sea-change
Into something rich and strange.

Trying to support herself by literary efforts, Mary was hindered by constant bouts of depression. On March 30, 1823, she wrote: "I cannot write. Day after day I suffer the most tremendous agitation. I cannot write or read or think — there is a whirlwind within me that shakes every nerve. I take exercise & do every thing that may prevent my body from influencing evilly my mind; but it will not do. . . . I am a wreck."

Her depression was not helped by living with the Hunts. Their six children — compared by Byron to a "kraal" of savages — had been raised according to Rousseau's principles and were unruly and undisciplined. Mary was paying nearly half the rent of the huge house, and she was having trouble making ends meet. Byron even suggested that Mary accept Sir Timothy's offer, requiring her to abandon her son. (Byron himself showed he was not immune to the power of money when his wife's mother, known as Lady Noel, died and in her will left a large sum to Byron if he agreed to take her name. Accordingly, he began to sign himself "Noel Byron," although his knowing friends pointed out that this name change enabled him to use the initials "N. B."— the same as his idol Napoleon.)

For Mary, the only good news came from England, where *Frankenstein* was a success. Godwin, of all people, wrote Mary to express his pride. Whether he had suddenly developed paternal affection or was angling for money that Mary didn't have (Godwin would be forced into bankruptcy in the spring of 1825), he sounded sincere: "Frankenstein is universally known, and though it can never be a book for vulgar reading is everywhere respected . . . most fortunately you have pursued a course of reading, and cultivated your mind in the manner most admirably adapted to make you a great and successful author." Unconditional praise for his daughter from Godwin was rare indeed.

Mary's historical novel *Valperga* had been published in February 1823 to good reviews, although some critics were disappointed, for they had wanted another *Frankenstein.* She felt it was time to go home. She left Italy on July 25, 1823, and arrived in London with Percy Florence in August. At first they stayed with Godwin and his wife. A month later, Mary took up lodgings off Brunswick Square. For the first time in her life she had a room of her own.

Four days after her arrival, Mary attended a theatrical adaptation of *Frankenstein* and learned that her creature had acquired a kind of celebrity. From the beginning, people saw the dramatic possibilities in her novel, and onstage the characters took on new lives. The book's first transformation was Richard Brinsley Peake's 1823 play *Presumption; or, The Fate of Frankenstein,* which was staged at the English Opera House in the Strand. It introduced a new character, but one who would acquire permanent status in the Frankenstein canon: Fritz, Victor's bumbling assistant, who, in this version, sang a ditty to start the play.

Peake's Victor Frankenstein demonstrated the danger of misdirected intelligence and misuse of power, just as in the novel. He was an anguished person who turned inward and could not relate to others. Peake gave Victor a soliloquy on the nature of life and death near the end of the first scene. "To examine the causes of life — I have had recourse to death — I have seen how the fine form of man has been wasted and degraded — have beheld the corruption of death succeed to the blooming cheek of life!"

Mary attended the play with her father William, half-brother William, and Jane Williams; unfortunately their reaction to the scene in which William Frankenstein is taken and murdered by the monster was not recorded. The playwright made crucial changes in translating the novel to the stage. Even in this very first adaptation, the monster does not speak — setting a precedent for most of the subsequent dramatic renderings of it, including the 1931 motion picture that starred Boris Karloff. The novel's Arctic surroundings are ignored, as in most subsequent productions. Peake's play is set entirely in Geneva, and ends when an avalanche destroys both Victor and the monster.

Mary enjoyed the production in spite of the changes that had been made to her text. It was no doubt a thrill for her to see her characters brought to life in so public a form. She wrote, "I was much amused, & it appeared to excite a breathless eagerness in the audience." Mary particularly liked the fact that in the program, the role of the monster (who wore blue makeup) was represented only by a dash, showing that it had no name.

At least one London newspaper declared the stage production an "attack [on] the Christian faith" and a "burlesque [of] the resurrection of the dead." Handbills circulated in the streets warning people not to take their families to the play, mentioning that "The novel itself is of a decidedly immoral tendency; it treats of a subject which in nature cannot occur." But the moralists were apparently ineffective; that same year another dramatic version of the novel, titled *Frankenstein: or, The Demon of*

Switzerland, opened at a playhouse across the Thames. Two other London productions appeared not long afterward, and three years later, one in Paris. Mary received no payment for these adaptations of her work, but Godwin realized that the publicity generated by them made a new edition of the novel potentially profitable. He arranged for its publication, and for the first time Mary Shelley was listed as the author.

Encouraged by her fame, Mary now embarked on a new life earning a living in the only way she knew how — through writing. She also found a refuge in religion, a clear indication of her growing independence from both her father and her husband. Mary had a solid faith in an afterlife, many times expressing her belief that she would join Shelley after death, and she looked forward to her reunion with her "lost divinity." She wrote, "But were it not for the steady hope I entertain of joining him what a mockery all this would be. Without that hope I could not study or write, for fame & usefulness (except as far as regards my child) are nullities to me." She wrote to Jane Williams in December about their common loss. "God has still one blessing for you & me — the hope — the belief of seeing *them* again, & may that blessing be as entirely yours as it is mine."

Such letters were a sign that Mary felt a strong attraction to Jane Williams, even though they had been rivals for Shelley's affection. Mary's letters to Jane were indeed reminiscent of those her mother wrote to Fanny Blood, but Jane did not want that kind of relationship. She found a new love with Shelley's old friend Thomas Jefferson Hogg, whom Mary now found "queer, unamiable and strange." Mary watched curiously as the relationship grew between Jane and the man Shelley had wanted *her* to sleep with. In 1827, Jane entered into a common-law marriage with Hogg (she was still married to her original husband), and gave birth to his child. It was perhaps appropriate for Hogg to take Shelley's last love to be his own.

For her part, Mary was not yet seeking a new companion; she still lived with the ghosts of the past. "The wisest & best have loved me," she wrote. "The beautiful & glorious & noble have looked on me with the divine expression of love . . . those who might have been my lovers became my friends & I grew rich — till death the reaper carried to his overstocked barns my lamented harvest — But now I am not loved . . . Never o never more shall I love."

As she became more involved with collecting and editing Shelley's poems, her own work suffered — and she knew it. She wrote in her journal for January 1824: "I was worth something then in the catalogue of beings; I could have written something — been something. Now I am exiled from those beloved scenes. . . . I am imprisoned in a dreary town. . . . Writing has become a task — my studies irksome — my life dreary. . . . My imagination is dead — my genius lost — my energies sleep — I am not worth the bread I eat."

Painstakingly Mary tracked down Shelley's poems, some of which were written on scraps of paper. Even for Mary it took hours of patient work to decipher them. She knew that in order to rehabilitate Shelley's reputation she would have to play down his radicalism and stress his genius. She began the process in a preface to the collection of his poems she was planning, turning the tables and becoming Victor Frankenstein, reassembling her dead husband in perfect form. She described Percy as a poet who loved nature rather than as a radical atheist. "His life was spent in the contemplation of Nature, in arduous study, or in acts of kindness and affection," she wrote. Those who reviled Shelley misunderstood him: "His fearless enthusiasm in the cause which he considered the most sacred upon earth, the improvement of the moral and physical state of mankind, was the chief reason why he . . . was pursued by hatred and calumny. No man was ever more devoted than he to the endeavour of making those around him happy; no man ever possessed friends more unfeignedly attached to him."

Percy's unconventional ideas about marriage, which had hurt Mary so much, were never mentioned, and she described their final days together at the Casa Magni as happy ones: "I am convinced that the two months we passed there were the happiest he had ever known: his health even rapidly improved, and he was never better than when I last saw him, full of spirits and joy, embark for Leghorn."

In June 1824, Leigh Hunt and his brother John published Shelley's *Posthumous Poems* to fine reviews. Sales were good, though hardly Byronic. Before all the copies could be sold, however, Sir Timothy tried to extinguish his son's name and reputation as a poet. He insisted that the book be withdrawn, going so far as to halt the sale of the remaining 191 copies of the first printing. Sir Timothy threatened to cut off all financial aid to Mary and her son unless she agreed not to publish anything more by or about Shelley while Sir Timothy lived. An astonished Mary wrote, "Sir T. writhes under the fame of his incomparable son as if it were a most grievous injury done to him — & so perhaps after all it will prove." However, she agreed to comply with his demands, since Sir Timothy was over seventy; she assumed that by the time she had assembled enough materials for a biography of Percy, his father would be gone. However, Sir Timothy stubbornly lived on for twenty-one more years, during which time Mary continually chafed against the restrictions he had placed on the spirit and the work of his dead son.

The day before Mary had left Genoa for England, Byron departed Italy too. His destination was his destiny: Greece, where a war of independence against the Turks had begun in 1821. Byron had decided to join the fight; it matched his image of himself as a romantic hero who would roam the world fanning the flames of freedom. He was not content with poetry alone; as he had once told his wife in happier times, "All contemplative existence is bad. One should *do* something."

Byron had been moved by Shelley's death, for even though the younger poet felt intimidated by him, Byron admired Shelley's work. He had told Shelley's cousin Tom Medwin, "Shelley has more poetry in him than any man living; and if he were not so mystical, and would not write Utopias and set himself up as a Reformer, his right to rank as a poet, and very highly too, could not fail of being acknowledged." When Shelley died, Mary had turned to Byron for support and he had saved her dignity by giving her work, not simply handouts. Ever since Geneva, Byron had trusted Mary with his own poetry, letting her transcribe much of his masterpiece *Don Juan*. Sometimes he even wrote alternative endings to stanzas, letting Mary choose the one she liked better, and allowing her to remove verses she thought would not pass the delicacy test of Byron's lover, the Countess Guiccioli. Mary herself was no prude. She had read Byron's secret autobiography, which was reportedly scandalous, and it did not shock her.

Like most other women, Mary felt Byron's attraction. Her emotions were colored by the fact that she strongly associated him with Shelley and the magical summer of 1816. She wrote in her journal,

> I do not think that any person's voice has the same power of awakening melancholy in me as Albe's — I have been accustomed when hearing it, to listen & to speak little; — another voice, not mine, ever replied, a voice whose strings are broken; when Albe ceases to speak, I expect to hear *that other* voice, & when I hear another instead, it jars strangely . . . since incapacity & timidity always prevented my mingling in the nightly conversations of Diodati — they were as it were entirely tete-a-tete between my Shelley & Albe & thus . . . when Albe speaks & Shelley does not answer; it is as thunder without rain — the form of the sun without heat or light — as any familiar object might be, shorn of its dearest & best attribute — & I listen with an unspeakable melancholy — that yet is not all pain.

Tragically, the last time they saw each other, money caused a rift between Byron and Mary. When Mary requested that Byron send funds to Claire, who was said to be dangerously ill in Vienna, Byron told Mary to send the money and then he would repay her. As ever, he did not want to give Claire any reason to think they could be reunited. Byron did, however, want to help Mary when she decided to return to England. To salve her pride, he gave Leigh Hunt a thousand pounds, telling him to offer it to Mary as a "loan," but with the understanding that it would not have to be repaid. Hunt pocketed the money for himself. Moreover, Hunt viciously told Mary that Byron was bored by her and was paying for her voyage to England only because he didn't want her around.

Byron had been approached by the London Greek Committee, which had been formed to lend support to the Greek independence movement. Byron, like every English schoolboy, had been inculcated with the ideals of classical Greece. From the time of his first trip abroad as a young man, he had sympathized with the Greeks' desire to liberate themselves from the Ottoman Empire. He had written in the third canto of *Don Juan:*

Glory and Death

The isles of Greece, the isles of Greece!
Where burning Sappho loved and sung.
Where grew the arts of war and peace,
Where Delos rose, and Phoebus sprung!
Eternal summer gilds them yet,
But all, except their sun, is set.

Byron was feeling dissatisfied with his life, perhaps with life itself. *The Liberal* stopped publication after only four issues; it was neither a financial nor a critical success. The three-mile swim in the ocean Byron had made at Shelley's cremation caused his skin to blister and brought on a persistent fever. His hair was graying and he felt a decline in his physical powers. Drinking heavily and relying on purgative pills to control his weight did not help matters. He contributed money toward the cause of Greek independence, but the siren call of military glory drew him toward Greece itself.

Byron knew something of the difficulties he would face, but he wanted to rehabilitate his own reputation, at a low ebb in England because of *Don Juan*'s critical thrashing and lingering memories of the affair with his sister and the separation from his wife. (Byron had written a preface to the three newest cantos, charging his critics with "cant"— a word he enjoyed using, to mean the expression of conventionality and piety. Nonetheless, *Blackwood's* called the latest cantos "Garbage!" and *The Literary Gazette* termed them "moral vomit.")

In Italy, Byron remarked to another of his confidantes, Lady Blessington, "Yes! A grassy bed in Greece, and a grey stone to mark the spot, would please me more than a marble tomb in Westminster Abbey." Byron asked Trelawny to accompany him, and the make-believe adventurer was only too glad to agree. Countess Guiccioli was unhappy that Byron was leaving her, but her brother Pietro himself signed on and helped round up about fifty volunteers for the expedition. The *Bolivar* had been sold, but Byron chartered two boats, and procured enough medical supplies, he thought, to supply a thousand men for two years.

As always, Byron seized the opportunity to dress up in costume. He had tailors make him scarlet full-dress uniforms trimmed with gold lace, shoulder knots, and silver epaulets. Byron even commissioned several elaborate helmets modeled after those worn by Greeks of the Homeric era, and he had his family coat of arms and the motto of the Byrons embossed on the one he chose for himself. A decorative sword completed the outfit.

As Byron's fleet set sail from Genoa harbor on July 15, 1823, the men fired pistols into the air, sang patriotic songs, and shouted, "Tomorrow in Missolonghi." The next day, however, saw them back in Genoa, for a storm blew up that evening, forcing the ships back into port; it was not an auspicious beginning, but Byron told Pietro Gamba "that he considered a bad beginning a favourable omen"— a sentiment all too reminiscent of Shelley's optimism about his near-drowning.

Byron was aboard the *Hercules,* a small boat crammed with medical supplies, livestock, five horses, and chests stuffed with coins and banknotes. He was cash rich for the first time — from the sale of the family lands at Newstead — and Byron knew that spreading it around would ease his travels. Never without dogs, he brought a bulldog and a Newfoundland named Lyon. The mood on the voyage was light-hearted. Byron and Trelawny, along with the dogs, sometimes slipped overboard for a swim in the sea. Once, before going over the rail, the two friends donned the captain's scarlet waistcoat as a prank; he was so stout that it encompassed them both.

On August 3, Byron and his men landed at Argostoli in the Ionian Islands. Here Byron received his first reality check to the romantic view of the Greeks' struggle. There were many factions among the Greeks, and some were fighting each other rather than the Turks, who still controlled parts of Greece with heavily armed garrisons. The strongest rift was between those Greeks who had lived outside the country for many years, and those who had never left, having remained loyal to local chieftains called *klephts.* No matter which faction they belonged to, they all had a hand out for financial help from Byron.

His reaction was to retreat to the British-controlled island of Cephalonia and go into a funk. "I was a fool to come here," he wrote, "but being here I must see what is to be done." He fell in love for the last time — with a fifteen-year-old boy, Lukas Chalandritsanos. Byron made Lukas his "page" and bought him lavish presents — expensive clothes and a set of gold-plated pistols. Trelawny, who was eager for action, was disgusted and left to join a rebel leader named Odysseus, who reportedly lived in a cave.

On Cephalonia Byron thought mostly of the past, of what his life might have been. He would sometimes stare out to sea, wearing a cloak of Stewart tartan, reflecting his mother's claim that she had been related to Scottish royalty. He received letters from Augusta, his half-sister in England, reporting that Byron's seven-year-old daughter Ada suffered from headaches that were so severe they threatened her eyesight. He fretted that her mother, Lady Byron, was overtaxing her with a rigorous study schedule. Byron answered that he had had a similar condition when he was a child, but had bathed his head in cold water every morning to cure it. The letter made Byron recognize and regret how little he knew about his daughter. He wrote Augusta back asking, "Is the Girl imaginative? . . . I hope that the Gods have made her any thing save *poetical* — it is enough to have one such fool in a family."

On another day, Byron was startled to see the ghost of Shelley approach. In reality it was George Finlay, who bore a striking resemblance to the dead poet. Finlay, who would later write a history of the Greek war for independence, had come to Greece because he heard Byron was here, and wanted to join the fight. "Both [Byron's] character and his conduct presented unceasing contradictions," Finlay noted. "It seemed as if two different souls occupied his body alternately. One was feminine, and full of sympathy; the other masculine, and characterised by clear judgement. When one arrived the other departed. In company, his sympathetic soul was his tyrant. Alone, or with a single person, his masculine prudence displayed itself as his friend."

Byron finally made up his mind to join the Greek forces under Prince Alexander Mavrocordatos, the man who had taught Greek to Mary in Pisa. She had described Mavrocordatos as a cultivated and honest man, and Byron felt he was the potential George Washington among the Greek leaders. The prince's provisional government and headquarters were at the coastal town of Missolonghi and from there he wrote Byron, "Be assured, My Lord, that it depends only on yourself to secure the destiny of Greece." Byron's vanity could not resist such a summons.

Before he left, Byron was showing signs of ill health, probably brought on by the fierce heat of the Greek summer. He had brought one doctor with him from Italy; now a second, Julius Millingen, appeared, courtesy of the London Greek Committee. (It was Millingen who quoted Byron as saying, "I especially dread, in this world, two things, to which I have reason to believe I am equally predisposed — growing fat and growing mad.") Millingen tried unsuccessfully to dissuade Byron from the frequent use of weight-reducing pills and his heavy drinking.

Byron did not set off for the mainland till December 29. His little flotilla then maneuvered its way through the blockade of Turkish warships off the Greek coast. The larger of his two vessels, carrying Pietro Gamba and valuable supplies, was captured and briefly detained; by a coincidence Byron might have written in a fanciful poem, the captain of Gamba's ship had once saved the life of the Turkish commander, who accepted his story that Gamba was a traveler. However, it was an unpleasant reminder to Byron that there really was a war going on.

He landed at Missolonghi on January 5, and received a reception suitable for a conquering hero. Dressed in his scarlet uniform, he was greeted by a twenty-one-gun salute and a singing crowd of soldiers, priests, women holding up babies, and old people who wanted to catch a glimpse of him. News of his arrival had been rumored for weeks, and he was regarded as the savior of Greece. It was believed that Byron was capable of raising large amounts of money from English sources, organizing an army and navy to attack the Turkish stronghold of Lepanto, and settling the blood feuds among the Greek chieftains assembled at Mavrocordatos's headquarters. The prince himself turned out to be no George Washington: he was paralyzed with indecision and everyone now looked to Byron for leadership. The expectations for him were too great for anyone to fulfill.

Conditions were hardly what Byron was used to. The town, originally home to three thousand fishermen and their families, was in an unhealthy location next to a stagnant lagoon. Its muddy lanes were covered with human and animal excrement. Rain fell constantly, turning the place into a swamp where mosquitoes bred.

For the first time in his life, Byron was in a situation where he could not solve his problems with a clever turn of phrase or a flash of his rapier wit. The aristocrat who liked to sleep till noon now was besieged with requests and questions at all hours. Nothing could be done until Byron decided it must be done. He forced himself to rise by nine, receiving reports and issuing the orders of the day over breakfast. He personally inspected the supply accounts — guaranteeing payment for new supplies from his own accounts. Every day he met with the other leaders, who squabbled incessantly.

The London Greek Committee's assistance was often unhelpful. The committee's representative in Missolonghi, Colonel Leicester Stanhope, felt that the Greeks — of all people — needed to be educated in republican principles. He had ordered a printing press, which Byron had brought from Cephalonia, so that he could publish a newspaper, even though few Greeks outside the cities could read. The committee had also promised a drill instructor and artillery experts, but neither had yet arrived. The soldiers at Missolonghi included volunteers from many other countries, making communication difficult, though Byron attempted to train them himself (without great success).

Lady Blessington, his confidante in Italy, had observed that she could easily imagine Byron going courageously into battle, but not "enduring the tedious details, and submitting to the tiresome arrangements, of which as a chief, he must bear the weight." She was correct: Byron yearned for action. At his request, Mavrocordatos gave him the title Archistrategos, and "permission" to stage an attack on the fortress of Lepanto, still under Turkish control. Byron's plan may have been as much from historical consciousness as anything else, for Lepanto was the site of a famous victory over the Turks in 1471 by the combined forces of Spain and Venice.

Byron put himself at the head of a brigade of Suliotes, the Albanian warriors who had charmed him on his first trip to the Near East eleven years before. Unfortunately, he found them riotous and mutinous. When a ship brought needed supplies, Byron's Suliotes refused to carry them from the beach, because they had arrived on a saint's day. Enraged, Byron started the job himself until others finally joined him.

On his birthday, January 22, 1824, Byron was feeling depressed. Despite the favors he had shown to his beloved Lukas ("Luke")— even putting him in charge of a squad of thirty soldiers — the boy was greedy, arrogant, and worst of all, unloving to Byron. Byron emerged from his bedroom that morning to read a poem he had written especially for the occasion, titled "On This Day I Complete My Thirty-Sixth Year." The poem reveals a man obsessed by age and the loss of his youth — and along with it, his physical beauty and sexual power.

'Tis time this heart should be unmoved,
Since others it hath ceased to move;
Yet though I cannot be beloved
Still let me love!

My days are in the yellow leaf;
The flowers and fruits of love are gone;
The worm, the canker, and the grief
Are mine alone!

. . . .

Awake! (not Greece — she is awake!)
Awake, my spirit! Think through whom
Thy life-blood tracks its parent lake,
And then strike home!

Tread those reviving passions down,
Unworthy manhood! — unto thee
Indifferent should the smile or frown
Of beauty be.

If thou regrett'st thy youth, why live?
The land of honourable death
Is here: — up to the field and give
Away thy breath!

Seek out — less often sought than found —
A soldier's grave, for thee the best;
Then look around, and choose thy ground,
And take thy rest.

Byron knew by now that he was trapped. Any kind of military success seemed farther out of reach every day, yet he could not leave Greece, for the hopes of too many people rested on him. The disgrace he would suffer by departing would be monumental.

Despite the continual rains, Byron insisted on taking a horseback ride each day, accompanied by an honor guard of Suliotes, who kept up with him even though they were on foot. Many times he returned drenched to the skin, further undermining his uncertain health. The many years of alternating between starvation diets and wild living had undoubtedly weakened him physically. On February 15, he suffered a convulsive fit, probably the result of a high fever. Byron feared it was a symptom of epilepsy and allowed the doctors to treat him by applying leeches to his forehead. They overdid the treatment and had trouble stanching the flow of blood. Byron fainted. "It [the seizure] was very painful," he wrote in his journal, "and had it lasted a moment longer must have extinguished my mortality."

Over the next two months, Byron's health continued to deteriorate. His doctors, young men just out of medical school, continually advised bleeding by the application of leeches. It was then a standard treatment, but Byron resisted, declaring that more people died from being bled than were saved by it. Above all, he wished to keep his mental functioning as high as possible. Sometimes, to reassure himself that he was not losing his memory, Byron recited Latin verses from his school days. Someone reported that he held conversations with his Newfoundland dog: "Lyon, thou art an honest fellow, Lyon. Thou art more faithful than men, Lyon; I trust thee more."

Meanwhile, the rains kept coming — much as they had during the summer of 1816. When the sky cleared for a while on April 9, Byron went out riding with Pietro Gamba. They were caught in a sudden shower, and returned to the town sopping wet. Byron was shivering and feverish, but insisted on going out again the next day. In the evening, his doctor found him lying on a sofa. Byron "became pensive," and said that he had been thinking of a prediction "made to him, when a boy, by a famed fortune-teller in Scotland." He had warned Byron to beware of his thirty-seventh year — this year.

Byron continued his running dispute with the doctors as to the necessity of applying leeches to bring down his fever. In the end, the doctors won by arguing that if his illness progressed it would deprive Byron of his sanity. It was the only argument that would move him. Byron, who had inspired the image of the vampire, now began to give up his blood — two pounds of it the first day, according to the doctors' account. "Come," he told them, "you are, I see, a d——d set of butchers."

For the next three days, a weakened Byron drifted in and out of consciousness, delirious and shivering. "I fancy myself a Jew," he told someone sitting at his bedside, "a Mohamedan, and a christian of every profession of faith. Eternity and space are before me; but on this subject, thank God, I am happy and at ease." At other times he fell into the delusion that he had been cursed by an evil eye and commanded that the witches who had done this be brought to his bedside so he could confront them. Day after day the doctors drained his blood, at one point applying a dozen leeches to his temples. Byron retained one last shred of pride: when the doctors wanted to apply mustard plasters, he would not allow them to uncover his foot.

On the afternoon of Easter Sunday, Byron realized that he was dying and his thoughts turned to those dearest to him. He began calling out the names of his daughter Ada and of his much-loved sister Augusta. Knowing that death was near, he pleaded that his body not be chopped up or sent to England. On the evening of April 18, Byron opened his eyes a last time and said, "I want to sleep now." That night there was a violent thunderstorm. The Greek villagers knew what it meant: a great man was departing the earth. Byron died the next morning, virtually two years to the day from the death of Allegra in the convent at Bagnacavallo.

Despite Byron's request, the surgeons had not finished; they now cut him open for no good reason except possibly to find the source of his genius. They weighed the brain, reporting that it was much larger than an ordinary man's. Even the famous foot now lay exposed to the curious physicians who had killed their patient. Dr. Millingen wrote later of "the congenital malconformation of his left foot and leg," though those who knew and loved Byron always said it was his right foot.

At his funeral in Missolonghi, the chief mourner solemnly said, "All Greece is his sepulchre." Gamba described the scene: "The wretchedness and desolation of the place . . . the wild and half civilized warriors around us; their deep-felt, unaffected grief; the fond recollections; the disappointed hopes . . . all contributed to form a scene more moving, more truly affecting, than perhaps was ever before witnessed around the grave of a great man." A less sentimental view came from William Fletcher, Byron's faithful retainer, who wrote to Thomas Moore, "With great grief I inform you of the death of my late dear Master, my Lord, who died this morning at ten of the Clock of a rapid decline and slow fever, caused by anxiety, sea-bathing, women, and riding in the Sun against my advice." He ended the letter with a request for a job. No man is a hero to his valet.

Mary learned of Byron's death nearly a month later, on May 15. She had spent a miserable evening the night before, tormented by sad thoughts of Shelley and Italy. She wrote in her journal the next day:

> This [Byron's death] then was the "coming event" that cast its shadow on my last night's miserable thoughts. Byron has become one of the people of the grave — that innumerable conclave to which the beings I best loved belong. I knew him in the bright days of youth, when neither care or fear had visited me: before death had made me feel my mortality and the earth was the scene of my hopes — Can I forget our evening visits to Diodati — our excursions on the lake when he sang the Tyrolese hymn — and his voice was harmonized with winds and waves?— Can I forget his attentions & consolations to me during my deepest misery?— Never.
>
> Beauty sat on his countenance and power beamed from his eye — his faults being for the most part weaknesses induced one readily to pardon them. Albe — the dear capricious, fascinating Albe — has left this desart world! . . . God grant I may die young!

The Greeks wanted to bury Byron in their soil, but it was feared that if the Turks won the struggle, they would desecrate the body. An urn containing Byron's lungs was reportedly interred in a church in Missolonghi.

The rest of him was placed in a tin-lined box which was then submerged in a barrel of alcohol and sent to England. Byron's lifelong friend John Cam Hobhouse met the ship and noted that Byron's Newfoundland dog had remained by his master. On viewing the body, Hobhouse said the once-beautiful person was virtually unrecognizable —"not a vestige of what he was."

A closed coffin containing Byron's body was put on display in a London undertaker's. Admirers, enemies, and the merely curious filed through the room for seven days. On July 9, Mary Shelley went to see it, resting her hand on the casket for a moment as she passed. Hobhouse had requested a burial at Westminster Abbey; that was refused, so a funeral procession brought the body to the family church in Hucknall Torkard near Newstead. Mary wrote to Trelawny that "it went to my heart when the other day the hearse that contained his lifeless form, a form of beauty which in life I often delighted to behold, passed my window going up Highgate Hill on his last journey."

Hobhouse now took steps to protect Byron's "honor and fame." Byron had given a copy of his memoirs to Thomas Moore, telling him he could make some money by having it published, as long as he waited till after Byron's death. The Irish poet had in fact already deposited it with John Murray, in exchange for a loan of two thousand guineas, with the agreement that Moore might publish it. Hobhouse knew of this arrangement and worked hard to prevent the publication of the memoirs. He claimed that he did this to save the feelings of Byron's wife and half-sister, but Hobhouse, by this time a member of Parliament, might well have feared any revelations concerning the trip he and Byron had made to the Near East as young men. He prevailed, and on May 17, the manuscript of Byron's memoirs was burned in the fireplace of John Murray's house. Moore had protested that the others had not even read the manuscript, but they apparently saw no need to: the thought that Byron might have written a true account of his life was enough for them to feel it had to be destroyed.

Nowhere was Byron mourned more deeply than in Greece. He remains a national hero there today — statues of him are found throughout the peninsula, streets and squares are named for him. After his death poems and klephtic ballads celebrating his deeds became popular. Byron's modern biographer, Leslie Marchand, quoted from one of the ballads:

> *Missolonghi groaned and the Suliots cried*
> *For Lord Byron who came from London.*
> *He gathered the klephts and made them into an army. . . .*
> *The klephts gave to Byron the name of father*
> *because he loved the klephts of Roumele. . . .*
> *The woodlands weep, and the trees weep. . . .*
> *Because Byron lies dead at Missolonghi.*

In 1825, the Turks began a yearlong siege of Missolonghi. In the spring of the following year, some inhabitants tried to escape through enemy lines. Those too weak to flee stayed behind to burn the town to prevent the Turks from taking it. In the end, there were only a few survivors. But Missolonghi's sacrifice became an inspiration for the independence struggle, partly because of the town's association with Byron. The Greeks won in 1832, and Prince Mavrocordatos served several terms as the nation's prime minister.

Byron had been one of the most famous people in the world; his early death only increased his celebrity. As those who had known him began to publish their own recollections of his life and exploits, the Romantic hero that he personified grew to mythical status. Soon after his death, Thomas Medwin published his *Journal of the Conversations of Lord Byron at Pisa,* which most of Byron's longtime friends accused of distorting the poet's memory. Others, including Thomas Moore, tried to write his life, but Byron himself knew that no one would be able to get him down on paper. He told Lady Blessington a year before his death,

> People take for gospel all I say, and go away continually with false impressions. *Mais n'importe!* it will render the statements of my future biographers more amusing. . . . I am so changeable, being every thing by turns and nothing long,— I am a such a strange melange of good and evil, that it would be difficult to describe

> me. There are but two sentiments to which I am constant,— a strong love of liberty, and a detestation of cant, and neither is calculated to gain me friends.

Byron's personality was so powerful that people who had been only peripherally associated with him shared a part of his charisma. The young Benjamin Disraeli, who would one day be a novelist and then prime minister of Britain, was another of his admirers. He visited Lake Geneva in 1826 and wrote his father,

> I take a row on the lake every night with Maurice, Lord Byron's celebrated boatman. Maurice is very handsome and very vain, but he has been made so by the English, of whom he is the regular pet. He talks of nothing but Lord Byron, particularly if you shew the least interest in the subject. He told me that on the night of the famous storm [June 13] described in the third canto of *C[hilde] H[arold]*, had they been out five minutes more the boat must have been wrecked. He told Lord Byron at first of the danger of such a night voyage, and the only answer which B. made was stripping quite naked and folding around him a great *robe de chambre*, so that in case of wreck he was prepared to swim immediately. I asked him if [Byron] spoke. He said he seldom conversed with him or any one at any time.

Of Byron's female admirers, the Countess Guiccioli returned to her husband after writing, at the count's request, an account of her love affair with Byron. The most reckless of Byron's loves, Lady Caroline Lamb, continued her literary career, but never strayed far from her original subject. Her husband's family, who didn't want her scandalous behavior to ruin his political career, persuaded him to separate from her. He became prime minister, and Caroline spent her final years in an alcoholic haze, guarded by servants at a large country house. Her only companion was her mentally disabled son, whom Byron had been kind to. Lady Caroline's sister referred to the son as "Frankenstein."

The author of *Frankenstein* confided her deepest feelings about Byron to her journal, but even there was unable to express them frankly: "At the age of twenty six," Mary wrote,

> I am in the condition of an aged person — all my old friends are gone — I have no wish to form new — I cling to the few remaining — but they slide away & my heart fails when I think by how few ties I hold to the world — Albe, dearest Albe, was knit by long associations — Each day I repeat with bitterer feelings "Life is the desart and the solitude — how populous the grave," and that region to the dearer and best beloved beings which it has torn from me, now adds that resplendent Spirit, whom I loved whose departure leaves the dull earth dark as midnight.

Someone, using a different color ink, later crossed out the three words "whom I loved."

CHAPTER FOURTEEN

MARY ALONE

Alone — alone — all — all — alone
Upon the wide, wide sea —
And God will not take pity on
My soul in agony!

— a slightly revised quotation from Coleridge's *Rime of the Ancient Mariner,* as written in Mary Shelley's journal, 1841

FROM THE TIME Mary hid behind the family sofa and first heard Coleridge recite his great poem, it had moved her deeply. On April 16, 1841, nineteen years after Percy's death, Mary wrote a verse from it from memory — slightly misquoting — in her journal. Like the Ancient Mariner, Mary now felt herself isolated, friendless, and alone.

She had felt that way for a long time. By coincidence, the day before she learned of Byron's death in May 1824, she had begun a new novel, titled *The Last Man.* Like *Frankenstein,* it was what we would call a science fiction novel, though no such term existed then. The book's premise is that a plague wipes out the entire human race, except the eponymous last man. Mary felt herself well qualified to describe such a person, for as she wrote in her journal: "The last man! Yes I may well describe that solitary being's feelings, feeling myself as the last relic of a beloved race, my companions, extinct before me."

She often repeated those sentiments. On July 28, 1824, she wrote, "On this very day ten years ago, I went to France with my Shelley — how young heedless & happy & poor we were then —& now my sleeping boy

[Percy Florence] is all that is left to me of that time — my boy —& a thousand recollections which never sleep."

In October of the same year: "Tears fill my eyes — well may I weep — solitary girl!— the dead know you not — the living heed you not — you sit in your lone room, & the howling wind, gloomy prognostic of winter, gives not forth so despairing a tone as the unheard sighs your ill fated heart breathes. . . . I wonder why England should be called my country. I have not a friend in it — all those whom I have ever known here fly me."

Since her return from Europe, Mary had found that the unconventional life she had lived with Percy had barred her from a certain level of English polite society. She had borne Shelley's child out of wedlock and — many people believed — lured him away from his wife. And the rumors of her relationship with Byron did not help Mary's reputation. While her mother might have had the strength of personality to shrug off society's disapproval, Mary was different. She wrote to Trelawny, who was still in Greece, "I am under a cloud & cannot form new acquaintances among that class whose manners & modes of life are agreable [*sic*] to me —& I think myself fortunate in having one or two pleasing acquaintances among literary people."

Mary had initially set out to rehabilitate Shelley's reputation by creating a new version of him. Now she would do the same for herself: changing the story of their relationship, suppressing embarrassing or scandalous details. Acting once more as Dr. Frankenstein, this time she sought to create a perfect creature from her own parts. In the end, however, she could not escape that sense of alienation and loneliness that tormented her creature. As the years went by, the voice of the monster always returned to Mary's journal.

Mary was now the sole literary survivor of the Diodati circle. The poets' celebrity, however, did not die with them. Tourists could no longer view them through spyglasses, but the public's fascination with them lingered. In time, the details of the poets' lives blended with exaggerations and faulty memories to become myths. Byron and Shelley would forever remain young, and they left devotees who always associated them with their own youths. Fourteen-year-old Alfred Tennyson had run into the woods and carved Byron's name on a rock when he heard of his death. Ten years later, at the beginning of his own career as a great poet, Tennyson wrote, "Such writers as Byron and Shelley, however mistaken they may be, did yet give the world another heart and new pulses, and so are we kept going. Blessed be those that grease the wheels of the old world, insomuch as to move on is better than to stand still."

As one who had known both men, Mary was frequently pressed to describe her memories of them. (Claire was now in Russia, working as a governess, and thus out of reach of English scandal-mongers.) Usually Mary turned down these requests, once claiming that she was keeping a "vow I made never to make money of my acquaintance with Lord Byron — his ghost would certainly come and taunt me if I did."

Others had no such compunctions. Leigh Hunt, Thomas Jefferson Hogg, Thomas Medwin, Edward Trelawny, Thomas Love Peacock, as well as others, published their inside accounts. For the public, the two poets came to suggest opposites. Lord Byron's darker aspects were emphasized (he had once ironically termed himself "his Satanic Majesty"), which left Shelley to play the angel.

Mary broke her silence when Thomas Moore approached her for help on his biography of Byron. Mary had been horrified by Thomas Medwin's book, which purported to be a journal of conversations he had with Byron in 1821 and 1822. (Among other things, Medwin reported that Mary had gotten the idea for *Frankenstein* from Matthew "Monk" Lewis, while the notorious author was staying at the Villa Diodati. Mary had in fact not even met Lewis while he was there.) Mary called Medwin's book "a source of great pain to me, & will be of more — I argued against the propriety & morality of hurting the living by such gossip —& deprecated the mention of any of my connections — to what purpose, you see." Medwin had asked her to review his manuscript for errors and she refused, finding it "one mass of mistakes." Now, however, she realized she would have to tell someone her side of the story if only to counteract the lies that would inevitably appear.

After Byron himself, Moore was perhaps the most famous and popular poet of the time. Mary was eager to make his acquaintance, for she had read and enjoyed his works. Only days after Byron's funeral, they connected. Moore charmed Mary by showing his familiarity with Shelley's poetry, and later he told a friend that he found her "very gentle and feminine." She related anecdotes about Byron and brought with her a letter from Edward John Trelawny describing Byron's death in detail. (Trelawny, who was not actually there, had no trouble making up scenes as if he had been.) Moore reciprocated by singing for her; people said he had a fine Irish tenor.

Quickly, Mary developed a bit of a crush on Moore. She wrote in her journal that he was "very agreeable, and I never felt myself so perfectly at ease with anyone. I do not know why this is, he seems to understand and to like me. This is a new and unexpected pleasure." Moore was in fact a great philanderer and seems to have strung Mary along to get his information. In any case, she promised to help him by writing to Trelawny on his behalf, asking for more recollections of Byron. She would also persuade Countess Guiccioli to contribute her memories of her role in Byron's life.

When she met Moore again, three years later, Mary told the poet she had read the early portions of Byron's memoirs in Venice. Presumably so had Moore, but perhaps there had been differences in the manuscripts, so Mary agreed to write what she remembered of them. She also agreed to provide details of the 1816 summer and Shelley's death, as well as the story of Claire's love affair and Byron's child Allegra. Moore wrote in his journal after the meeting that Mary "seems to have known Byron thoroughly, and always winds up her account of his bad traits with 'but still he was very nice.'"

When the first volume of Moore's *Letters and Journals of Lord Byron: With Notices of his Life* was published in January 1830, he sent Mary an autographed copy. She approved of what she read. "The great charm of the work to me," she wrote John Murray, "and it will have the same for you, is that the Lord Byron I find there is our Lord Byron — the fascinating — faulty — childish — philosophical being — daring the world — docile to a private circle — impetuous and indolent — gloomy and yet more gay than any other. I live with him again in these pages."

Though Mary never remarried, she did occasionally seek love. Shunned by "proper" society in London, she nevertheless found friends among those who were outsiders. John Howard Payne, an American actor-playwright who wrote the lyrics to "Home, Sweet Home," became a friend. When he was manager of the Sadler's Wells Theatre, he sent Mary free tickets and began to appear regularly as her escort. He did not quite reach the point of proposing marriage, for she fended off a deeper relationship by asking him to convey her affection to his friend and sometime collaborator Washington Irving. The handsome Irving, author of "The Legend of Sleepy Hollow," had business interests that brought him to England, and Mary had made his acquaintance. Payne, feeling disappointed that he was to be a go-between and not a lover, broke off his courtship. For his part, Irving turned out not to be interested in Mary.

Mary still regarded Jane Williams as her strongest friend, once calling her "the hope and consolation of my life. . . . To her, for better or worse I am wedded — while she will have me & I continue in the love-lorn state that I have since I returned to this native country." Jane's adopting a form of marriage with Hogg, calling herself Mrs. Hogg, did not alter Mary's feelings. After learning Jane was pregnant Mary wrote, "Loveliest Janey — to thee tranquility and health!" In fact, Jane was not the friend Mary imagined she was, for she had continued to spread the story that Shelley had turned to her because of Mary's coldness. When Mary found this out, in July 1827, she wrote in her journal, "My friend has proved false & treacherous! Miserable discovery — for four years I was devoted to her — & I earned only ingratitude. . . . Am I not a fool! What deadly cold flows through my veins — my head weighed down — my limbs sink under me — I start at every sound as the messenger of fresh misery —& despair invests my soul with trembling horror — What hast thou done?"

Yet even then, Mary could not bear to break off her relationship with Jane — they had too much history together. Mary, sounding as plaintive as her monster, wrote in her journal, "I need companionship & sympathy only —& the only one I love can afford me so little. . . . I cannot live without loving and being loved — without sympathy — if this is denied to me I must die."

So Mary hid her pain and did not confront Jane until the following February when she wrote her: "Though I was conscious that having spoken of me as you did, you could not love me, I could not easily detach myself from the atmosphere of light & beauty that for ever surrounds you — I tried to keep you, feeling the while that I had lost you." Jane apparently showed some remorse, and the two women maintained their relationship until death divided them. Jane outlived Mary, dying in 1884.

Although Mary needed to write to make a living, her father-in-law's prohibition on using his son's name in print sometimes hindered her. Mary was now a Shelley too, so as an author, she had to become as nameless as her monster. When she published *The Last Man* in 1826, the title page declared only that it was the work of "the author of *Frankenstein*." Sir Timothy complained anyway, for the 1823 edition of *Frankenstein*, edited by Godwin, had claimed Mary Shelley as the author.

She continued to write novels, but none acquired the fame or popularity of her first. In each of her books, whether a novel of ideas or historical fiction, the characters are clearly drawn from the Diodati circle. Writing was her way of keeping them alive. In *The Last Man*, for example, two of the protagonists, Lord Raymond and Count Adrian, are depictions of Byron and Shelley. Raymond/Byron was "emphatically a man of the world." As for Adrian/Shelley: "his sensibility and courtesy fascinated everyone. His vivacity, intelligence, and active spirit of benevolence, completed the conquest. . . . In person, he hardly appeared of this world; his slight frame was overinformed by the soul that dwelt within."

In 1831, Mary had to fend off a proposal of marriage from Trelawny, along with his request for her help on another project. Seeing the success of Moore's book on Byron, Telawny decided to publish his own about Byron and Shelley. Mary refused to help him, and her letter makes it clear that she feared publicity about herself:

> You know me — or you do not, in which case I will tell you what I am — a silly goose — who far from wishing to stand forward to assert myself in any way, now than [*sic*] I am alone in the world, have but the desire to wrap night and the obscurity of

insignificance around me. This is weakness — but I cannot help it. . . . Shelley's life must be written — I hope one day to do it myself, but it must not be published now —

Her refusal irritated Trelawny, who pointed out she had helped Moore. But to Mary, contributing stories about Byron was one thing; talking about Shelley quite another. She wrote Trelawny, again trying to discourage him, "Shelley's life so far as the public had to do with it consisted of very few events and these are publicly known — The private events were sad and tragical — How could you relate them?" Trelawny took her advice, for the time being, and wrote an autobiography that Mary helped put in shape for publication. She even supplied the title — *Adventures of a Younger Son* — and helped him find a publisher. Trelawny played on what he portrayed as his close relationship with Shelley and Byron, using quotations from their works as chapter epigraphs. It reads as much like a Gothic novel as fact.

Mary was entrepreneurial. She wrote for *The Liberal* and *The Keepsake,* popular magazines of the time, and she provided biographies for Lardner's *Cabinet Cyclopedia,* among other projects. Mary worried about the quality of such work, because she had to churn out the words for money. "What a folly is it in me to write trash nobody will read," she wrote in her journal in 1825. Claire, the only other survivor of Diodati, sometimes reproached Mary with similar criticism. In the 1830s, Claire returned to Italy and took up residence in Florence, from which she wrote Mary regularly. (Many people fled the city during a cholera epidemic, but Claire remained, saying she would not desert the family she worked for; she survived.) Claire praised Mary's talents and chided her for being too modest. She was, moreover, disgusted that Byron appeared so often as a character in Mary's novels. "I stick to *Frankenstein,*" she once told Mary, "merely because that vile spirit [Byron] does not haunt its pages as it does in all your other novels, now as Castruccio, now as Raymond, now as Lodore. Good God to think a person of your genius . . . should think it a task befitting its powers to gild and embellish and pass off as beautiful what was the merest compound of Vanity, folly, and every miserable weakness that ever met together in one human Being!"

Claire added an exhortation to Mary that indicates how highly she regarded her:

> If you would but know your own value, and exert your powers you could give the men a most immense drubbing; you could write upon metaphysics, politics, jurisprudence, astronomy, mathematics, all those highest subjects which they taunt us so with our being incapable of treating, and surpass them; and what a consolation it would be, when they begin some of their prosy, lying but plausible attacks upon female inferiority, to stop their mouths in a moment with your name: and then to add, "and if women, whilst suffering the heaviest slavery could outdo you what would they not achieve were they free?"

Claire sounded more like the heir of Mary Wollstonecraft than her stepsister did.

To some extent we are all products of our time and place. Percy Shelley and Lord Byron had died still believing in the ideals that had sparked the French Revolution in their youths. Regency England, the time of their artistic flowering, had been characterized by a permissive morality and spirit. (Even so, both of them went well beyond it.) Mary had the misfortune of living longer than they, and had to adjust to different times, different mores. In 1830, King George IV, the former Prince Regent — who as "Prinny" had been a symbol of that lively age — died. His younger brother, William IV, took the throne, ushering in a new era. Though the future queen Victoria was then only twelve, the prudish and restrictive age that would bear her name had already begun.

Mary had changed as well. By the time she was in her thirties, she was a very different person from the teenager who had written *Frankenstein.* Shelley's ideals no longer appealed to her as they had when she ran off with him as a smitten sixteen-year-old. Deaths, betrayals, financial hardship, and despair had changed her outlook. She wanted respectability for her son and she needed the small stipends that Sir Timothy doled out — provided she didn't displease him. Mary, after all, had never really been as independent as her mother. When Leigh Hunt invited her to come back to Italy, Godwin told Mary that he had set his "heart and soul" on her staying in England. She told Hunt she must stay with her father, for "in this world it always seems one's duty to sacrifice one's own desires."

When Mary had the opportunity to revise the great novel of her youth, she took it. A publisher asked her to prepare a new edition of *Frankenstein* as part of a series called "Standard Novels." The inexpensively priced series gave the authors a chance to make editorial changes (improvements, in theory) and to write an introduction to their books. Mary's introduction contains an account of the events at Byron's Villa Diodati that led to the writing of *Frankenstein.* "And now, once again," she wrote, "I bid my hideous progeny go forth and prosper. I have an affection for it, for it was the offspring of happy days, when death and grief were but words, which found no true echo in my heart." Significantly, Mary herself was now willing to acknowledge her "hideous progeny"— the creature — as the true hero of the book, and not Victor Frankenstein, the title character.

Although Mary claimed that she made few changes from the original 1818 edition, some of her revisions reflect the differences in both herself and the times. She removed the dedication to William Godwin. Ernest, the middle son of the Frankenstein family, was made stronger and more robust. He was the only surviving Frankenstein in the book, and perhaps Mary associated him with her only living son, whose survival she wanted to ensure. She also eliminated the hint of incest in the original by changing cousin Elizabeth into an orphan of no relation to the Frankensteins. She wanted no reminders of the so-called league of incest in Geneva.

Just as Mary had revised her public accounts of Percy's life to make him a more respectable figure, now she also made changes in the man modeled after him: Victor Frankenstein. Victor is less manipulative in the 1831 edition and more the victim of circumstances. Though he is still overly ambitious and vain, the reader is told this is the result of a lack of parental guidance. "While I followed the routine of education in the schools of Geneva," Victor relates, "I was, to a great degree, self taught with regard to my favorite studies. My father was not scientific, and I was left to struggle with a child's blindness, added to a student's thirst for knowledge." Victor's need to teach himself without paternal oversight parallels the monster's similar self-education, by reading books he has found.

Some of Mary's 1831 additions are clearly prompted by bittersweet memories of Percy. When Walton describes Victor Frankenstein, this passage is new: "Even now, as I commence my task, his full-toned voice swells in my ears; his lustrous eyes dwell on me with all their melancholy sweetness; I see his thin hand raised in animation, while the lineaments of his face are irradiated by the soul within. Strange and harrowing must be his story; frightful the storm which embraced the gallant vessel on its course, and wrecked it — thus!"

The original version depicted Victor Frankenstein as a man making choices with free will — he could have abandoned his search for the "principle of life," but instead chose to pursue it to its destructive end. In the 1831 edition, however, he is the pawn of forces he does not control: "Destiny was too potent, and her immutable laws had decreed my utter and terrible destruction." The deaths of William Frankenstein and Justine are, in 1831, attributed to a curse imposed by "inexorable fate." Perhaps this change was prompted by Mary's inner guilt at killing off a character with the name William, now even more charged with painful memories than when she first wrote the book, at a time when her son William was safely at her breast. It also accompanied a shift in Mary's own viewpoint. She wrote to Jane Hogg in August 1827, "The power of Destiny I feel every day pressing more & more on me, & I yield myself a slave to it, in all except my moods of mind, which I endeavour to make independant [*sic*] of her, & thus to wreath a chaplet, where all is not cypress, in spite of the Eumenides."

Similarly, in 1831 Victor has a religious sensibility that was missing in 1818, and the passages relating to science and magic are now either excised or softened into "natural history," which the "new" Victor dismisses as "a deformed and abortive creation." When he attends Ingolstadt, his revived interest in science is portrayed as a regression to his childish enthusiasms.

Some changes in the revised version reflect timely new concerns. Imperialism enters the book when Victor's friend Clerval now announces his intention of joining the East India Company after his studies. "He came to the university with the design of making himself complete master of the oriental languages, as thus he should open a field for the plan of his life he had marked out for himself. Resolved to pursue no inglorious career, he turned his eyes toward the East, as affording scope for his spirit of enterprise." In the earlier edition, Clerval had loved learning, the arts, and nature for their own sake; now he, like Victor, is attracted to power. (Peacock, Shelley's real-life friend, was in fact a lifelong administrator for the East India Company.)

Mary also transformed herself. Writing about her own childhood in the introduction, she said, "I lived principally in the country as a girl, and passed a considerable time in Scotland. . . . It was beneath the trees of the grounds belonging to our house, or on the bleak sides of the woodless mountains near, that my true compositions, the airy flights of my imagination, were born and fostered." She is describing the Baxter home, not the Godwin family's crowded flat above the bookstore where Mary lived until she was fourteen. With the stroke of a pen, she wiped out Skinner Street, with its slaughterhouse stench, the mobs flocking to public executions, and even the despised stepmother. Mary was picking and choosing from the assembled parts of her past to create a better life.

Mary's ongoing project to rejuvenate her husband's reputation reflected her plans for the upbringing of her son Percy Florence. The radical educational ideas of Wollstonecraft, Godwin, and Shelley were dismissed, for above all, Mary intended Percy Florence to fit in. When a friend advised her to send her son to a school where he would learn to think creatively, she reportedly replied, "Teach him to think for himself? Oh, my God, teach him rather to think like other people!" That intention seemed to suit the boy's personality. He resembled his grandfather, Sir Timothy, more than his father, just as Percy Bysshe had resembled more *his* grandfather than his father.

Young Percy Florence's future suddenly looked brighter when his elder half-brother Charles, the son of Harriet, died of tuberculosis in 1826. Percy Florence was now the presumptive heir to the baronetcy, and the fortune that his father would have inherited. Sir Timothy took a greater interest in his grandson and even increased the allowance — slightly. He dangled the promise of even more aid, provided that the child be turned over to his care, an offer Mary again refused. A single mother scrounging to make ends meet from the little she received from Sir Timothy and her own literary earnings, she managed to give her son a fine education. She moved to the town of Harrow so that she could send him to its prestigious prep school as a day student.

Mary gave a motherly description of her son to Maria Gisborne in 1834, when the boy was fourteen and attending Harrow. "In person he is of a fair height & excessively fat — his chest would remind you of a Bacchus he has a florid complexion, blue eyes — like his father —& his looks & gestures & shape of his face would remind you of Shelley & his person before he grew fat — he is full of spirit & animation, but proud & reserved with strangers . . . he loves me more than he knows himself & would not displease me for the world." Mary related a story that reflected her own deepest fear: "One day I said to him —'Suppose when you grew to be a Man — you would leave me all alone'—'O Mamma,' he said, 'how do you think I could be so shabby:— that would be too bad!' To be *left all alone* [Mary's emphasis] seems to him the worst evil of all." As it was to her.

Later Percy Florence attended Trinity College, Cambridge, where he received his degree in 1841. He never showed any artistic promise, nor was he interested in poetry. He much preferred the theater. Leigh Hunt, who knew him as an adult, recalled, "When I mentioned Tennyson's poetry, Sir Percy said fellows had bored him a good deal with it at one time. He never read any of it of his own accord — saw no sense in it."

More deaths continued to shrink Mary's circle. In 1832, her half-brother William (the William she had not been), died of cholera. The following year, William Godwin, then seventy-seven and thinking himself forgotten, received a pleasant surprise when admirers (there were still some) obtained for him a sinecure government job as "Yeoman Usher" that provided him with a yearly stipend and an apartment for him and his wife. Ironically, the government Godwin had condemned would support him in his last years.

Three years later, in 1836, the eighty-year-old Godwin realized his end had come. Having prepared for this, as for all other vicissitudes, he pasted into his journal a valedictory message he had written just for the occasion. It warns, "Everything under the sun is uncertain. No provision can be a sufficient security against adverse and unexpected fortune, least of all to him who has not a stipulated income." He went to bed, where Mary watched over him during the next ten days, until he died.

At his request, Godwin was buried in St. Pancras Churchyard beside his first wife, though his second wife had been at his side for thirty-five years. Just as Godwin could not bear to attend Mary Wollstonecraft's funeral, so his daughter Mary was too distraught to come to his. Young Percy was the chief mourner and Trelawny showed up, ever ready to bask in greatness.

Godwin suffered in death the opposite fate of Percy Shelley. Percy had died before the scope of his achievement was widely known. Mary's father, by contrast, had reached the prime of his influence and fame early, and lived to see the diminution of his reputation. On his death, the *Gentleman's Magazine* printed a devastating estimate of Godwin: "In weighing well his merits with his moral imperfections, it is melancholy to discover how far the latter preponderated, and we are led to the very painful though certain conclusion, that it might have been better for mankind had he never existed." Thomas De Quincey, author of *Confessions of an English Opium-Eater,* wrote that "most people felt of Mr. Godwin with the same alienation and horror as of a ghoul, or a bloodless vampyre, or the monster created by Frankenstein."

The creator of Frankenstein, of course, had a different view, which she expressed in her journal.

> O my God — what a lot is mine — marked by tragedy & death — tracked by disappointment & unutterable wretchedness — blow after blow — my heart dies within me. I say "would I might die." that is wicked — but life is a struggle & a burthen beyond my strength. . . .
>
> I have lost my dear darling Father — What I then went through — watching alone his dying hours! . . .

> Thus is it — we struggle & storm but return to our task Master full soon.

Two years later, she had indeed returned to her task: "The great work of life goes on," she wrote. Pirated editions of Shelley's work had appeared, sometimes including poems that Shelley had not written, or corrupt versions of those he had. When trying to gain Sir Timothy's permission, Mary pointed to this as a reason to bring out an authorized edition. At long last, Sir Timothy consented, but only with the qualification that no biography of his son appear. Mary would get around this prohibition by attaching to each poem her own prefaces, which gave details of what was happening in Shelley's life at the time he wrote it. At the time, this was a new way to look at poetry, but it later became a standard critical method.

She also had to decide what precisely Percy had intended to be the final form of his poems. This was difficult, for his handwriting was notoriously illegible. Trelawny recalled, "It was a frightful scrawl; words smeared out with his finger, and one upon the other, over and over in tiers, and all run together in most 'admired disorder'; it might have been taken for a sketch of a marsh overgrown with bulrushes, and the blots for wild ducks." It was also painful work. Mary noted in her journal for February 12, 1839, "I almost think that my present occupation will end in a fit of illness. I am editing Shelley's poems & writing notes for them. . . . I am torn to pieces by Memory." Byron had trusted Mary to choose between alternate verses he had written; now she became a major force in shaping Shelley's work.

It was an auspicious time for all this, since Shelley's poetry had been taken up by the Chartists, a radical group that called for changes in Britain's electoral process that seem mild today, such as universal male suffrage, and vote by secret ballot. Mary herself resisted calls that she endorse the People's Charter, a petition asking Parliament to bring about these changes. She also turned down Trelawny when he asked her to write a pamphlet supporting women's rights, the cause that had been closest to her mother's heart. Mary felt her primary task now was to bring her husband's work into print; to do that she had to steer clear of any actions that would offend Sir Timothy. She also wanted to shelter her son from the storms of public abuse that had engulfed her parents and her husband. In her search for respectability, it was not just herself she was thinking of.

In any case, Mary's own views had changed; they were not the same as those of Wollstonecraft, Godwin, or Percy. She wrote in her journal in 1838 a defense of her refusal to speak out for liberal causes. For her it was a declaration of independence:

> In the first place, with regard to the "good Cause"— the cause of the advancement of freedom & knowledge — of the Rights of Women, &c.— I am not a person of Opinions. I have said elsewhere that human beings differ greatly in this — some have a passion for reforming the world; others do not cling to particular opinions. That my Parents and Shelley were of the former class, makes me respect it. . . . For myself, I earnestly desire the good & enlightenment of my fellow-creatures . . . but I am not for violent extremes which only bring on an injurious reaction. . . . Besides, I feel the counter arguments too strongly . . . on some topics (especially with regard to my own sex), I am far from making up my mind . . . and though many things need great amendment, I can by no means go so far as my friends would have me. When I feel that I can say what will benefit my fellow-creatures, I will speak,— not before. . . .

Mary's dilemma was that she craved the benefits of conventional ideas of womanhood, yet also wanted to fulfill the hopes of her unconventional parents and husband. She was always drawn in opposite directions, and she realized it.

In the suppressed 1824 edition of Percy's posthumous poems, Mary had written an introduction that gave a sanitized version of their marriage. She continued the process of making Shelley respectable in the prefaces she wrote for the publication of his collected poems in 1839. With Shelley no longer living, Mary could make him in death what he had not been in life. She had the opportunity to reverse roles with him as well. In their relationship, Shelley had been very much a mentor to her, but now she could act as the critic of *his* work. She wrote, for example, that he was often indiscriminate in his literary exploration. "His reading was not always well chosen; among them were the works of the French philosophers. . . . He was a lover of the wonderful and wild in literature, but had not fostered these tastes at their genuine sources — the romances and chivalry of the middle ages — but in the perusal of such German works as were current in those days."

The condemnation that critics had showered on Wollstonecraft's memory, once her unconventional life was revealed in Godwin's *Memoirs,* had obscured the messages of her writing. Mary did not want to be responsible for that happening to Shelley's work, so she never mentioned his atheism and ignored the fact that she and Percy were living together while he was still married to Harriet. Mary wrote out of Percy's (and her) life the marital crises, the revolutionary beliefs — and even Claire Clairmont. She gave her husband an honored poetic place in Victorian England. Most drastically, she dropped the parts of the notes to *Queen Mab* that made its irreligious subtext clear. She was in fact the real author of what Matthew Arnold would call "the beautiful and ineffectual angel" Shelley.

The four-volume edition of *The Poetical Works of Percy Bysshe Shelley* was published in the first months of 1839. Trelawny and Hogg, who fancied themselves custodians of Shelley's memory, promptly attacked Mary because of the cuts she had made to *Queen Mab*. A second edition of the *Poetical Works* appeared; it restored the cuts to *Queen Mab* and contained other new material. Shelley's reputation did in fact benefit from the publication of this authoritative collection; in time he would rival Byron in both popularity and critical esteem.

In 1840, Mary and her son, then twenty-one, took a summer trip to Switzerland and Italy. They visited the place where Percy had died, and the Villa Diodati, where Byron's challenge had sparked Mary to bring forth her monster twenty-four years earlier. Mary was touched by the sight of those familiar surroundings:

> The far Alps were hid; the wide lake looked drear. At length, I caught a glimpse of the scenes among which I had lived, when first I stepped out from childhood into life. . . . I could mark and recognise a thousand slight peculiarities, familiar objects then — forgotten since — now replete with recollections and associations. Was I the

> same person who had lived there, the companion of the dead? For all were gone; even my young child, whom I had looked upon as the joy of future years, had died in infancy — not one hope, then in fair bud, had opened into maturity; storm, and blight, and death, had passed over, and destroyed all.

Only the novel remained. Was it worth all the deaths, all the pain that had followed?

In April 1844, Sir Timothy Shelley finally died. Percy Florence inherited the fortune and the title of baronet that had been withheld from his father. Mary now had no constraints on her writing, but it had been seven years since she had written a novel, *Falkner,* and she no longer felt healthy enough to begin another one. For the first time she visited Field Place, the estate where her husband had grown up, and found it too dull to live in. Her son, now comparatively wealthy, purchased a boat, something that understandably made Mary uneasy.

In October, she made a last entry in her journal: "Preserve always a habit of giving (but still with discretion), however little, as a habit not to be lost. The first thing is justice. Whatever one gives ought to be from what one would otherwise spend, not from what one would otherwise pay. To spend little & give much, is the highest glory a man can aspire to." This was in fact a passage of advice from a letter Edmund Burke wrote to his son. Mary's mother had gained her first fame by replying to Burke's *Reflections on the Revolution in France* fifty-three years before. Mary had completed the circle.

Despite Mary's intention, expressed several times, to write the biographies of her father and her husband, she never did. Perhaps her creative energies were just no longer up to the task of doing any sustained work. It would have been emotionally wrenching to relive the past one more time. Most likely Mary could simply not deal directly with her feelings about the men who had been her mentors and shaped so much of her intellect and personality. In life they had both caused her great pain, yet she maintained a public devotion to them. Her true literary portrait of them was Victor Frankenstein. Perhaps that was enough.

Ever since her sojourn in Scotland during her early teens, Mary had yearned for a stable family life, as happy as the ones she portrayed in some of her books. Late in her life, like a heroine in a fairy tale, she got her wish. Mary did not wait passively for it: she seems to have arranged it herself. Living in London in 1847, she learned that a pretty young woman who admired Percy Shelley's poetry was visiting a relative nearby. Jane St. John had been widowed three years earlier at the age of twenty-four, the same age Mary had been when Shelley drowned. Fate was clearly knocking, and since Jane was too shy to approach Mary, Mary paid a call on her. As Jane recalled the scene a half century later:

> I had been resting one afternoon in my bedroom after having suffered from one of my bad headaches. Feeling better towards the late afternoon, I wandered down to the drawing-room to find my book, not knowing that the maids had let in a visitor. As I opened the door I started back in surprise, for some one was sitting on the sofa, and I said to myself, "Who are are you — you lovely being?" She must have seen my start of surprise, for, rising gently from the sofa, she came towards me and said very softly, "I am Mary Shelley." You ask what she was like. Well, she was tall and slim, and had the most beautiful deep-set eyes I have ever seen. They seemed to change in colour when she was animated and keen. She dressed as a rule in long soft grey material, simply and beautifully made. A more unselfish creature never lived.

Jane came from an unusual background that fit right in with the Godwin/Shelley tradition. She was one of nine illegitimate children of the banker Thomas Gibson. When she was twenty-one, she made a good marriage for herself: to Charles Robert St. John, the son of a viscount. Even Charles's titled family was checkered with illegitimacy, however. His father had fifteen children in all — only four legitimate, including Charles — by several women including his half-sister. (Shades of Byron.) Charles himself had earlier fathered an illegitimate son, who became Jane's ward when her husband died in 1844. (Mary Shelley called the young man a "relative" of Jane's former husband.) This irregular background made Jane, like Mary, yearn for respectability.

As it happened, Jane liked boating, as did Percy Florence. One thing led to another and they were married in June 1848, making Jane "Lady Shelley," a title she wore with pride until her death in 1899. The marriage was childless and yet happy — an oddly appropriate counterpoint to the link between creation and danger that existed in Mary's life and work. The association was in many ways another threesome, but one in which Mary was the centerpiece. They moved into Field Place, and Mary chose as her bedroom the very one her husband Percy had as a boy. Percy Florence was elected to Parliament and received a knighthood — respectability at last. As far as anybody knows, this son and grandson of four radical and creative individuals never had an original thought in his life.

Jane gave her mother-in-law the unconditional love Mary had yearned for but had failed to find as daughter, lover, and wife. Now Mary had a confidante and assistant in the work of reassembling a new, perfect creature from the parts of Percy Shelley. In service to this goal, there would be a few casualties. In the official version of Shelley and Mary's life together — issued by Jane in 1882 — poor first wife Harriet was defamed as unfaithful and crazy. Mary, it was alleged, had only agreed to run off with him (a tale too well known to be denied) *after* Percy and Harriet had agreed to a formal separation. Percy was turned into a kind of saint, with a room at Field Place furnished as a shrine devoted to him. It was a far cry from when Sir Timothy was alive and had forbidden Percy's name to be spoken in the house.

Documents that could reflect poorly on the family were hunted down, removed from archives, and destroyed. Mary's journal was combed through and the past revised. After a biographer of Henry Fuseli used the letters Mary Wollstonecraft had written her lover years before — the letters that Godwin had seen but not been allowed to read — Percy Florence Shelley purchased them; they are nowhere to be found today. Claire Clairmont's letters to Mary often refer to those Mary wrote in return, all now missing. The Shelleys initially cooperated with Hogg, who wanted to write a biography of his old friend, but when they saw how candid he planned to be, they withdrew their support. They also refused to cooperate with Trelawny, though he produced his book anyway; lack of facts was never a deterrent to his telling a good story.

Mary's happy life with her loving son and daughter-in-law lasted less than three years. She had long suffered from psychosomatic illnesses — headaches, nervous stomach, and depression. In December 1850 she began to experience a mysterious paralysis. The younger Shelleys wanted Mary to leave Field Place and move to Boscombe by the sea with them. However, she preferred to take up her old residence in London, where a doctor diagnosed a tumor of the brain. She died, her son and daughter-in-law at her bedside, on February 1, 1851, at the age of fifty-three. Years earlier Mary had written Maria Gisborne about Shelley, "Goodnight — I will go look at the stars, they are eternal; so is he — so am I." Now that was true.

The *Literary Gazette*'s obituary read, "It is not . . . as the authoress even of *Frankenstein* that she derives her most enduring and endearing title to our affection, but as the faithful and devoted wife of Percy Bysshe Shelley." Mary had attained the respectability that she so desperately desired — but at the cost of her own individuality and personal achievement. Her mother would have been horrified. Time has of course overturned this verdict. Today her creature and her creation are better known than any work by anyone else in the Diodati circle.

Mary wanted to be buried next to her parents, but Jane and Percy Florence felt St. Peter's Churchyard at Bournemouth was more pleasant, so they had the bodies of Godwin and Wollstonecraft moved there as well. There was a hitch when the rector of the church refused to allow the two notorious radicals to be buried in consecrated ground. Jane Shelley — *Lady* Shelley — appeared in a carriage, followed by two horse-drawn hearses, and announced she would wait there until the rector opened the gates. He did. Mary at last rested between her two famous parents, who, bound by the English earth, could no longer abandon their little girl.

Claire Clairmont moved from place to place, seldom returning to England, finding work as a governess or a companion. She never married, although men continued to be attracted to her — including Trelawny, who proposed to her twice. Having been the lover of the real Lord Byron, she could not accept the ersatz one.

Claire never forgave Byron and even felt resentful toward Mary for remaining friendly with him after Allegra's death. "Were the fairest Paradise offered to me upon the condition of his [Byron's] sharing it, I would refuse it," Claire wrote to Mary, for "there could be nothing but misery in the presence of the person who so wantonly willfully destroyed my Allegra." Mary had evidently tried to console Claire by mentioning that Willmouse, like Allegra, had also fallen victim to the unhealthy climate. Claire responded, "you were a mere girl at that time . . . with no one to warn you of the effects of climate, bestowing every care a mother's heart could devise, and most guiltless: He [Byron] was old and wicked and laid a plan to get rid of his child in a way that should be certain and yet not expose him to the blame of the world."

Claire liked to imagine that her daughter had not really died but had been kept hidden in a convent by Byron out of spite. Over time, she may have come to believe it. Trelawny reproved her in an 1869 letter:

> If I was in Italy I would cure you of your wild fancy regarding Allegra: I would go to the Convent — and select some plausible cranky old dried-up hanger-on of the convent about the age your child would now be, fifty-two, with a story and documents properly drawn up, and bring her to you — she should follow you about like a feminine Frankenstein — I cannot conceive a greater horror than an old man or woman that I had never seen for forty-three years claiming me as Father.

Mary herself did not escape Claire's criticism, for Claire never lost faith in Percy Shelley's ideals and believed that Mary had. She wrote,

> She [Mary] has compromised all the nobler parts of her nature and has sneaked in upon any terms she could get into society although she full well knew she could meet with nothing there but depravity. Others still cling round the image and memory of Shelley — his ardent youth, his exalted being, his simplicity and enthusiasm . . . but she has forsaken even the memory for the pitiful pleasure of trifling with trifles, and has exchanged the sole thought of his being

> for a share in the corruptions of society. Would to God she could perish without note or remembrance, so the brightness of his name might not be darkened by the corruptions she sheds upon it.

Mary was at times equally unforgiving. In an 1836 letter to Trelawny, she wrote: "Claire always harps upon my desertion of her — as if I could desert one I never clung to — we were never friends." Repeating what Claire had written her about Byron not long before, she added,

> Now, I would not go to Paradise, with her for a companion — she poisoned my life when young — that is over now — but as we never loved each other, why these eternal complaints to me of me. I respect her now much —& pity her deeply — but years ago my idea of Heaven was a world without a Claire — of course these feelings are altered — but she has still the faculty of making me more uncomfortable than any human being — a faculty she, unconsciously perhaps, never fails to exert whenever I see her.

While Mary was living at Field Place with Percy Florence and Jane, Claire came to visit; it would be the last time she would see Mary. Mary's bitterness, long suppressed, suddenly broke to the surface. Before the visit, Lady Shelley had offered to leave them alone, for she had met Claire earlier and disliked her. However, as she recalled, Mary cried out, "Don't go, dear; don't leave me alone with her. She has been the bane of my life ever since I was two!"

Late in her life, Claire lived in her niece's house in Florence, giving occasional interviews to English and American journalists who learned of her association with the great poets. In 1873, William Rossetti, a nephew of John Polidori, at Trelawny's request called to see some letters that Claire had supposedly been offering for sale. Rumors varied as to the nature of the correspondence, but since Claire had known both Shelley and Byron well, it was thought they might contain interesting material. Rossetti had difficulty in gaining admission to the house, but when he did he found "a slender and pallid old lady . . . with dark and expressive eyes." She was now an invalid due to a recent fall. He did not get the letters.

Edward Silsbee, a Boston art critic who worshipped Shelley, learned about the documents. He was so desperate to get his hands on them that he rented a room in the house where Claire and her niece lived. His hope was that when Claire, now quite old and in poor health, would die, he could persuade the niece to give or sell him the papers. Claire did indeed die, but the niece told Silsbee that he could only get the papers if he married her. He wasn't willing to go quite that far. A young American writer, traveling in Italy, heard the story of Silsbee's obsession and turned it into a novel. The writer could not have been more different from the Romantics Shelley and Bryon; he was Henry James, and the novel was *The Aspern Papers.*

"I would willingly think that my memory may not be lost in oblivion as my life has been," Claire wrote as the end neared. She died at eighty-one in 1879, and was buried in a churchyard near Florence. An inscription on her grave read, "She passed her life in sufferings, expiating not only her faults but also her virtues." She had suffered much for love, but it was her passion that makes her memorable. Though no story written by Claire ever appeared in print, her memory not only survives, but thrives: her journal and her letters have been edited and published in recent years. She was the one who brought the monsters of Diodati together. If she had never sent those persistent seductive letters to Byron, then *Frankenstein* would never have been written.

In her final years, Claire had converted to Roman Catholicism, her mother's religion. An English philosopher and essayist, William Graham, went to see her when she was eighty. He described her as a "lovely old lady: the eyes were still bright and sparkled at times with irony and fun; the complexion clear as at eighteen, and the lovely white hair as beautiful in its way as the glossy black tresses of youth must have been; the slender willowy figure had remained unaltered, as though time itself had held that sacred and passed by." He asked her about the Roman Catholicism and she said that it brought her comfort. When he asked Claire what she thought Shelley would think of her conversion, she replied, "I think Shelley would have forgiven me anything; and I am not sure that the thought of him did not lead to the thought of Christ." After Graham asked whether she had loved Shelley, Claire answered, "With all my heart and soul."

A year after Mary's death, her son went through her desk and found the journal that she had kept with Shelley in their 1814 elopement year. With it was a folded copy of one of Shelley's last poems, *Adonais.* Unwrapping the paper, Percy Florence found that it contained the charred remains of Shelley's heart, which Mary had kept with her all those years. It was something that she might have felt she would need if she were ever to put her lover back together again — as she had.

The monsters of Diodati have never been more alive than they are today. Both the vampire and Victor Frankenstein's creature are familiar figures in popular culture, found as animated cartoons, toys, puppets, and breakfast cereals; appearing in video games, television programs, comic books, movies, plays, Broadway musicals, and even a German ballet. Their fame has spread worldwide. To a great extent, this familiarity sprang from their depiction in two American motion pictures, both made in 1931: director James Whale's *Frankenstein,* in which the monster was played by then-unknown English actor Henry Pratt, who adopted the screen name Boris Karloff; and Tod Browning's *Dracula,* in which Bela Lugosi played the vampire aristocrat who had been the title character in Bram Stoker's 1897 novel. (Lugosi had created the role in a Broadway play four years earlier.) Karloff and Lugosi's portrayals — aided by makeup artists and costume designers — gave the monster and the vampire the outward forms by which they are now universally recognized. Whale was clearly influenced by the 1920 movie *The Golem,* directed by Paul Wegener (who also played the title role), which retold the medieval legend of Rabbi Judah Löw ben Bezulel creating a huge humanlike creature to protect the Jews of Prague from persecution. Though it has been asserted that Mary Shelley was inspired by the golem story, there is no evidence that she knew of it — though she certainly would have approved of the rabbi's method of bringing the creature to life: by placing a strip of paper bearing God's name into a pendant on its chest. Mary was very fond of the power of words.

It is appropriate that Frankenstein's creature and the vampire have seemed to thrive in tandem (more than once appearing in the same motion picture), for they represent opposite sides of the same image / reality dichotomy. Mary Shelley's monster is a being who longs for love and a connection to the human community, from which he is cut off because of his monstrous appearance. The vampire, whether Lord Ruthven, Count Dracula, or Anne Rice's Lestat, is physically attractive, sophisticated, even sexy — traits that conceal the decay and evil within. In short, he is the reverse of Frankenstein's creation. If anything, the stage and screen adaptations of Mary Shelley's novel have further heightened the monster's plight, for usually they have made him mute as well as ugly — they deny him the ability to explain himself, as he does in the novel. Feeling unloved, misunderstood, unjustly rejected are universal human experiences. Who has not felt the desire to be loved for ourselves alone? Who has not also thought that if we could show our true selves to the world, if we could only make people *understand* us, the result would be acceptance and affection?

Children in particular seem to love the monster; why else would a cereal manufacturer produce "Frankenberry"? Mary's creature — clumsy, unable to express himself, constantly getting into trouble — was made to feel unloved first of all by the person who created him. To children, he is a kindred spirit. To young Mary Godwin, a motherless child, a heartbroken girl whose persona was molded and stitched together by men of cold and selfish genius, such an unloved being was found not just on the pages of her book, but in the mirror.

The vampire, on the other hand, is the man we love to hate. Polidori felt all the emotions that Mary's monster feels, and he blamed his troubles on the person he most hoped to impress: Byron. Byron responded to Polidori's admiration with cruelty and ridicule. Supremely talented and handsome, Byron had within him something deeply ugly that made it difficult for him to reciprocate others' love. The idea that a beautiful person can be evil was not a new one: Polidori carried it a step farther, showing us that the appeal of beauty was stronger than the revulsion caused by evil. Byron's own heroes were tortured men who had a dark secret; Polidori showed that dark secret to be that they — and Byron himself — drew love and life from others, while giving nothing in return. The fascination we feel for the vampire comes from the fact that even though we know he is horrifying, we cannot resist admiring him.

Seldom, if ever, has a literary contest been as successful as the one prompted by Byron's challenge. It is rare for anyone to create a character, a novel, a work of art that has universal appeal. Mary Shelley and Dr. Polidori both did, striking a nerve in audiences that reverberates even today. In the final analysis, Mary's achievement was greater than Polidori's, for she had an even larger theme: the danger of science. The word "Frankenstein" today is virtually synonymous with the caricature of the mad scientist whose experiments get out of control. The story of Victor's quest to create a living being embodies issues that remain controversial today. What is life? What is a human being? How far can — or should — science go in prolonging, changing, or even creating life? Modern science has brought those possibilities out of the realm of imagination and into reality. Artificial intelligence, genetic engineering, cloning, stem-cell medical procedures, sentient robots, and even abortion all evoke the same questions Mary Shelley raised. The power of her story rests on the crucial premise that a human has dared to create life in a laboratory, and that the creature he brought to life has human characteristics: it not only thinks, but it also has emotions. At the heart of the book is the mystery of creativity and its consequences, something that concerned — even, at times, tormented — all five of the people at Villa Diodati. In their outsized passions, their remarkable talents, their distorted personal lives, their never-satisfied yearning for love — they were all monsters.

ACKNOWLEDGMENTS

We are indebted to the many scholars who have paved the way for us by assembling the letters and journals of the subjects of our book. To Betty T. Bennett, Paula R. Feldman, W. Clark Durant, Frederick L. Jones, Ernest J. Lovell, Jr., Leslie A. Marchand, Diana Scott-Kilvert, Marion Kingston Stocking, and Ralph M. Wardle — thank you for the work that will forever benefit all who study Mary Shelley and those who influenced her.

Thanks also to those who personally helped us with advice and information, including Stephen Wagner, curator of the Carl H. Pforzheimer Collection of Shelley and His Circle at the New York Public Library; Dr. Murray C. T. Simpson of the National Library of Scotland; Haidee Jackson, curator at Newstead Abbey; Virginia Murray of the John Murray Archive; and Martin Mintz and Sandra Powlette of the British Library. We appreciate the help we received from the staff of the New York Public Library's Map Division, who found us a detailed map of London at the time the Godwin family was living on Skinner Street. As always, we are grateful for the help of the staff of the Deborah, Jonathan F. P., Samuel Priest, and Adam Raphael Rose Reading Room of the New York Public Library; the staff of the Elmer Bobst Library of New York University; and to the staff of the Cohen Stacks of the City University of New York for pointing the way to a scarce and important volume.

Special thanks to Dr. Stephen Lomazow, world's greatest magazine collector, for lending us his copy of the September 1818 issue of *The Port Folio,* which contained the first American notice of Mary Shelley's *Frankenstein.*

We would be remiss if we did not acknowledge gratefully the heroic and skillful efforts of Little, Brown editor Geoff Shandler and copyeditor

Jen Noon to improve our manuscript, and we thank Al Zuckerman, our agent, for his support and hard work on our behalf. Our daughter Ellen, who was not yet born when we published our first book, is now a doctoral candidate at Columbia University who critiqued this manuscript for scholarship and style. Any mistakes, of course, are all ours.

NOTES

Abbreviations used in the notes:

BLJ: Marchand, Leslie A., ed., *Byron's Letters and Journals* (London: John Murray, 1973–1979).

CC: Stocking, Marion Kingston, ed., *The Clairmont Correspondence* (Baltimore: Johns Hopkins Press, 1995).

F1818: Shelley, Mary, *Frankenstein,* 1818 edition, ed. Marilyn Butler (New York: Oxford University Press, 1998).

F1831: Shelley, Mary, *Frankenstein,* 1831 edition, ed. Johanna M. Smith (Boston: Bedford Books, 1992).

JCC: Stocking, Marion Kingston, ed., *The Journals of Claire Clairmont* (Cambridge, MA: Harvard University Press, 1968).

JMWS: Feldman, Paula R., and Diana Scott-Kilvert, eds. *The Journals of Mary Shelley, 1814–1844* (Baltimore: Johns Hopkins University Press, 1995).

LMW: Wardle, Ralph M., ed., *Collected Letters of Mary Wollstonecraft* (Ithaca, NY: Cornell University Press, 1979).

LMWS: Bennett, Betty T., ed., *The Letters of Mary Wollstonecraft Shelley* (Baltimore: Johns Hopkins Press, 1980–1988).

LPBS: Jones, Frederick L., ed., *The Letters of Percy Bysshe Shelley* (Oxford: Clarendon Press, 1964).

PWPBS: *The Complete Poetical Works of Percy Bysshe Shelley,* edited by Thomas Hutchinson (London: Oxford University Press, 1961).

PLB: *The Poetical Works of Lord Byron* (London: Oxford University Press, 1961).

TLM: Shelley, Mary, *The Last Man,* ed. Anne Ruth McWhir (Peterborough, ON: Broadview Press, 1996).

Conception

3 weather conditions and reaction: Stommel.

3 "mad, bad, and dangerous to know": Eisler, 340.

3 ten thousand copies: ibid., 413.

4 "the Creator": CC, I, 25.

Chapter 1: Love Between Equals

7 "Mary": Sunstein, *A Different Face,* xv.

8 "My own sex": Wollstonecraft, *Vindication,* 81–82.

8 "A mistaken education": ibid., 114.

8 "An unhappy marriage": ibid., 115.

8 "It is vain": ibid., 257–58.

8 "hyena in petticoats": Tomalin, *Wollstonecraft,* 110.

9 "monarchy was": Constant, Benjamin, *De la Justice Politique* (Tubingen: Max Niemeyer Verlag, 1998), I, 371.

9 "There is certainly": LMW, 394.

10 "the first and most submissive": Godwin, William, *Memoirs of Mary Wollstonecraft* (London: Constable & Co., 1927), 9.

10 "parental affection": Todd, *Mary Wollstonecraft,* 4.

10 "the daughter": Wollstonecraft, *The Wrongs of Woman,* 1.

10 "Her father": ibid., 5.

11 "I am a little singular": LMW, 60.

11 "I cannot bear": ibid., 62.

11 "in her heart": Godwin, *Memoirs,* 119.

11 "better than all": LMW, 67.

11 "has a masculine": ibid.

11 "I must be independent": ibid., 107.

11 "toad-eating": Tomalin, *Wollstonecraft,* 16.

12 "a little patience": Godwin, *Memoirs,* 23.

12 "My child": Wollstonecraft, *The Wrongs of Woman,* 15.

13 "without someone to love": Tomalin, *Wollstonecraft,* 36.

13 "the grave has closed": Godwin, *Memoirs,* 35.

13 "I am now reading": LMW, 145.

13 "I am determined!": ibid., 159.

14 "the father of the book trade": Tomalin, *Wollstonecraft,* 67.

14 "I am . . . going to be": LMW, 164–65.

15 "Whenever I am tired": Tomalin, *Wollstonecraft,* 75.

15 "I grow too excited": ibid., 87.

17 "Bliss was it": Brody, Miriam, introduction to Wollstonecraft, *Vindication,* 20.

17 "I see the ardour": Tomalin, *Wollstonecraft,* 93.

17 "Out of the tomb": Mulvey-Roberts, Marie, "Mary Wollstonecraft Shelley" in Thomson, 390.

18 "And lo!": Tomalin, *Wollstonecraft,* 97.

18 "all women": Poovey, *Proper Lady,* x.

19 "This [virginity] lost": ibid., 23.

19 "rouse my sex": Wollstonecraft, *Vindication,* 231.

19 "I do not wish them": ibid., 156.

20 "I have been much pestered": Cracium, 112.

21 "I am a strange compound": LMW, 221.

21 "The public walks": Tannahill, 68.

23 "I have felt some gentle twitches": LMW, 237.

23 "I do not want to be loved": Tomalin, *Wollstonecraft,* 169.

24 "I do not chuse": LMW, 275.

24 "my soul is weary": ibid., 277.

25 "Love is a want": ibid., 302.

25 "I shall plunge . . .": ibid., 316–17.

25 "I do not shudder": Goethe, 126.

25 "I part with you": LMW, 330.

26 "bold and adventurous": Gilmour, 297.

27 "I remember": Brown, 1.

27 "perfectly willing": ibid., 2.

28 "It had never occurred": ibid., 7.

28 "the most self-conceited": Gilmour, 295.

29 "In the latter part": Brown, 23.

29 *Imogen:* Godwin, William, *Imogen: A Pastoral Romance from the Ancient British* (New York: New York Public Library, 1963 reprint of the 1784 edition).

30 "one of the most stupid": Sunstein, *A Different Face,* 172.

30 "tell all that I apprehended": Woodcock, *William Godwin.*

31 "With what delight": Woodcock, *Selections from* Political Justice, 12. Godwin's seminal work is today out of print. His opinions are not likely to reach a mass audience in the current political climate, no matter how relevant they might seem. *Selections,* printed during World War II in a city under attack from German bombers, includes Godwin's pronouncement: "The love of our country, if we would speak accurately, is another of those specious illusions which have been invented by imposters in order to render the multitude the blind instruments of their crooked designs."

31 "Damn the king": Marshall, 91.

31 groups of people raised the money: Smith and Smith, *William Godwin,* 22.

32 "he blazed as a sun": Tomalin, *Wollstonecraft,* 197.

33 "If ever there was a book": Godwin, *Memoirs,* 306.

33 "When we met again": ibid., 100.

33 "when the heart": LMW, 350.

34 "Mrs. Perfection": ibid., 340.

34 "My imagination": ibid., 337.

34 "Do not cast me off": Wardle, *Godwin and Mary,* 17.

34 "Can you solve this": LMW, 358.

34 "You tell me": ibid., 365.

35 "Mary Wollstonecraft, spinster": Tomalin, *Mary Wollstonecraft,* 213.

35 "I begin to love": ibid., 395.

35 "to threaten the earth": Sunstein, *Mary Shelley,* 18.

35 "I have no doubt": LMW, 409.

36 "Mrs. Blenkinsop": ibid., 411.

36 "Oh, Godwin, I am in heaven" and his reply, Tomalin, *Mary Wollstonecraft,* 226.

36 "20 minutes before 8": ibid., 228.

37 "I firmly believe": ibid., 229.

37 "destiny of woman": Thompson, 72.

Chapter 2: "Nobody's little girl but papa's"

38 "Reaching the cascade": Wollstonecraft, *Letters,* 152–53.

38 "One of my wife's": Paul, I, 285.

39 Nicholson's report: Mellor, *Mary Shelley,* 244.

39 "Damn you": Tomalin, *Mary Wollstonecraft,* 232.

40 "with disgust by every female": Williams, *Mary Shelley,* 17.

40 "For Mary verily": *Anti-Jacobin Review and Magazine,* 1801, IX, 518.

40 "I cannot but think": Polwhele, *The Unsex'd Females: a Poem* (London: 1798), 30.

40 "Hard was thy fate": Tomalin, *Mary Wollstonecraft,* 233.

41 "While I retain": St. Clair, 216.

41 "This day": ibid., 217.

42 "I am tormented": ibid., 208.

42 "Their talking about me": Paul, I, 364–65.

43 "Is it possible": Paul, II, 58.

44 "widow with green spectacles": Mellor, 6–7.

44 "That damn'd infernal": JCC, 15.

44 "a pustule of vanity": Rieger, xiii.

44 "Uncommonly mild": Tomalin, *Mary Wollstonecraft,* 230.

44 "les goddesses": Gittings and Manton, 9.

44 Burr's other impressions: *The Private Journals of Aaron Burr* (New York: Harper & Brothers, 1858), v. 2, 307.

45 "cadaverous silence": Tomalin, *Mary Wollstonecraft,* 230.

45 "learning and studying": Gittings and Manton, 8.

45 "Nothing could be more": Sunstein, 45.

45 "was too minute": Seymour, 62.

45 "Until I knew Shelley": LMWS, I, 296.

46 "spontaneous overflow": Wordsworth, William, and Samuel Taylor Coleridge, *Lyrical Ballads,* ed. W. J. B Owen (London: Oxford University Press, 1967), 157.

47 "Alone, alone": Coleridge, 154. This is from the 1798 version of the work. A slightly revised edition appeared in 1834.

48 "As long as I remained": Gittings and Manton, 5.

48 Godwin's history of Rome: Brown, 227.

49 "Her mother died": Williams, John, 12.

49 "I did not make myself": ibid., 24.

49 "My dreams": Shelley, Mary, introduction to *Frankenstein,* 20.

49 "nursed and fed": Poovey, *Proper Lady,* 115.

50 "In our family": ibid., 116.

50 "always thought": Walling, 24.

50 "more reflective": Mellor, 15.

50 "tell Mary": Williams, John, 34.

51 "I am quite confounded": Marshall, Florence A., *Life and Letters,* I, 28.

51 "beneath the trees": F1831, 20.

Chapter 3: In Love with Loving

53 "While yet a boy": PWPBS, 531.

54 "ancient books of Chemistry": Hogg, I, 305.

54 "should rise": Medwin, 28.

54 "a sort of": ibid., 27–28.

55 "It's not my wish": Blunden, 371.

55 "Never read a book": White, *Shelley,* I, 12.

55 "The habits": Hogg, I, 305.

55 "temper was violent": Gilmour, 45.

56 "Verses on a Cat": PWPBS, 838–39.

57 "like a girl": White, *Portrait,* 7.

57 "spirits" "almost on the borders": ibid., 9.

57 "The Revolt of Islam": PWPBS, 37–38.

58 Dr. Keate, the "Flogger," was said to have once flogged eighty boys in a single morning. Hogg, 43.

58 Classmate's recollections: Blunden, 34.

58 "Every night": Gilmour, 105.

58 "a thin, slight lad": Gronow, 123.

60 "His features": Hogg, I, 47–48.

60 "I myself": Tomalin, *Shelley,* 17.

60 "Books, boots, papers": Hogg, I, 55–56.
61 "his eyes close": Gilmour, 131.
61 "The moment he entered": Hogg, 14.
62 "Soft, my dearest angel": PWPBS, 864.
62 "He is such a Pupil": Hodgart, 33–34.
63 "Her complexion": Peacock, *Memoirs*, 338.
64 "quite like a poet's dream": Gilmour, 193.
64 "I was in love with loving": from Latin epigraph to *Alastor*, PWPBS, 15.
64 "*Your* noble and exalted": Gilmour, 207.
64 "radiant with youth": ibid., 193.
64 "Jealousy has no place": Tomalin, *Shelley*, 23.
65 "loathsome worm": Hodgart, 13.
65 "intended to fall": Cameron, *Young Shelley*, 177.
65 "He now became": Peacock, *Nightmare Abbey*, 47.
66 "Poets are the": Holmes, 585.
67 "A husband and wife": PWPBS, 806.
67 "Love is free": ibid., 807.
67 "It is now": Hogg, 306.
68 "There is no": *Complete Works of Shelley*, VI, 12.
68 "a wet-nurse": Peacock, *Memoirs*, 323.
68 "The contemplation": LPBS, I, 264–65.
69 "a dead & living": ibid., 265.
69 "I go on": Trelawney, 195.
70 "The originality": LPBS, I, 402.
70 "suffering, like a little": Grylls, *Mary Shelley*, 29.
70 "doth equal laws": PWPBS, 76. Canto 4, stanza 21.
70 "They say that thou": ibid., 39–40. Dedication, stanza 12.
72 "I followed him": Hogg, II, 147–48.
73 "They always sent me": Gittings and Manton, 11.
73 "The sublime and rapturous": LPBS, 403.
73 "Upon my heart": PWPBS, 522.
73 Account of Shelley at Godwin's: Holmes, 233.
74 "She was in my arms": JMWS, 6.

Chapter 4: Crackling Sparks and Free Love

75 "We are as clouds": PWPBS, 523.
76 "I had time": White, *Portrait*, 162.

76 "I said to Mary": JMWS, 7.
76 "As I left Dover": Tomalin, *Shelley,* 45.
77 "Mary was there": JMWS, 7.
77 "Shelley was also": ibid.
77 "We saw with extasy": JCC, 442.
78 Godwin's description: Cameron, *Golden Years,* 7–8.
78 "Jane has been guilty": Mellor, 22.
79 "a cold & stupid": JMWS, 9.
79 "Mary especially": ibid., 11.
79 "beds were infinitely": ibid.
80 "four-footed enemies": ibid., 13.
80 "so dreadfully dirty": Cameron, *Shelley and His Circle,* III, 347.
80 "We rest at Vendeuvre": JMWS, 14.
80 "he thought he was": Cameron, *Shelley and His Circle,* III, 350.
81 "the moment": JCC, 27.
81 "because we have no king": ibid., 28.
81 "like the white": JMWS, 17.
81 "Jane's horrors": ibid., 20.
82 "our only wish": ibid., 20–21.
82 Dippel story: Florescu.
82 "We read these verses": Shelley, Mary, *History of a Six Weeks' Tour,* 68.
83 "Delightful row": JCC, 42.
84 "Consider how far": LPBS, II, 396.
84 "But he is so beautiful": White, *Shelley,* I, 405.
84 "Here are we": JMWS, 81.
85 "Let it suffice": LPBS, I, 403.
86 "an Association": JCC, 48.
86 "the conversation": ibid.
86 "How horribly you look": JMWS, 32.
86 "I stood thinking": JCC, 48–49.
86 "Her countenance": JMWS, 33.
86 "engaging in awful conversation": ibid.
87 "How hateful it is": JCC, 50–51.
87 "Converse with Jane": JMWS, 36.
87 "Shelley and Jane": ibid., 37.
87 "in the morning": LMWS, 1.
87 "My beloved Mary": LPBS, 411.

87 "I cannot raise money": ibid., 410.

88 "She plagues my father": LMWS, 3.

88 "Press me to you": ibid., 3.

88 "Mary is unwell": JMWS, 45.

88 Information on Andrew Crosse: Haining.

89 "He was pleased": JMWS, 45.

89 ". . . get into an argument" and other quotes about Hogg: ibid., 46, 48.

90 "an overflowing": Murray, *Prose Works of PBS*, I, 282.

90 "Next month": Blunden, 134.

90 "As to his tenderness": ibid.

90 "Very unwell": JMWS, 49–50.

91 "You love me you say": LMWS, 6.

91 "I hope it will cheer": ibid., 9.

91 "Very ill all day": JMWS, 45.

92 "the Man whom": Mellor, 229.

93 "find my baby dead": JMWS, 68.

93 "My dearest Hogg": LMWS, 10–11.

93 "my little baby": JMWS, 70.

94 "I see plainly": ibid., 69.

94 "form her mind": Gittings and Manton, 26.

94 "I am no doubt": LMWS, I, 13.

94–95 Mary's May 12 and May 13 entries: JMWS, 78.

95 "I begin a new": ibid., 79.

95 "I am perfectly happy": CC, I, 9–10.

96 "We ought not": LMWS, I, 15–16.

97 "the very rooms": CC, I, 14.

97 "We have all felt": ibid., I, 15.

97 "William, *nepos,* born:" Grylls, *Godwin,* 207.

Chapter 5: The Most Dangerous Man in Europe

99 "She walks in beauty": PLB, 77.

99 "so beautiful": Lovell, *His Very Self,* 169.

99 "I was struck": Page, 82.

100 "His . . . lips and chin": Medwin, *Journal of the Conversations,* 233.

100 "That beautiful pale face": MacCarthy, x.

100 "Sleeping Beauty!" Gronow, 122.

100 "bloated and . . . fat": Eisler, 603.

101 "Nothing but hard biscuits": Page, 18.

101 "I especially dread": ibid., 143.

101 "a *cloven* foot": Medwin, *Journal,* 234.

101 "My dear Byron": Gronow, 123.

102 "Deformity is daring": PLB, 609.

102 "My passions were": MacCarthy, 23.

102 "I recollect all": Garrett, 11–12.

102 "used to come to bed": Eisler, 40.

102 "Now my *beau ideal*": Lovell, *Lady Blessington's,* 110.

104 "a very handsome man": Grosskurth, 8.

105 "I believe I have had": Marchand, I, 30.

105 "lame brat," Quennell, *Byron,* 130.

106 "a home, a world": Gilmour, 118.

106 "I will cut myself": BLJ, I, 49.

106 "My School friendships": BLJ, IX, 44.

107 "put 'the Ladies'": Quennell, *Byron,* 18.

107 "I will be obliged": BLJ, I, 78.

107 "Yesterday my appearance": ibid.

108 "That boy will be": ibid., 111.

108 "I wear *seven*": ibid., 114.

108 "I am buried": ibid., 158.

109 "Adieu, adieu!": PLB, 182.

110 "became the idol": Gronow, 325.

110 "On foams the bull": PLB, 192.

110 "If you make a proposal": BLJ, I, 220.

111 "The scene was savage": PLB, 201.

111 "that marble paradise": Minta, 41.

111 "dying for love": BLJ, I, 240.

111 "act of courtship": Eisler, 246.

112 "female apparel": ibid.

112 "I plume myself": BLJ, I, 253.

112 "I see not much": ibid., 238.

112 "Oh, thou Parnassus!": PLB, 189.

113 "At twenty three": BLJ, II, 47.

113 "I had but one friend": Gilmour, 266.

113 "Some curse": BLJ, II, 68.
113 "whom I once loved": ibid., II, 110.
113 "Ours too the glance": PLB, 63.
114 "I awoke one morning": Franklin, 50.
114 "the child of imagination": Mellor, 242.
115 "mad, bad": Minta, 175.
116 "She absolutely besieged": Page, 19.
117 "In 1815": Graham, 759.
117 "Follow without hesitation": Vaughan et al., 103.
119 "No man is safe": Eisler, 350.
119 "I should like": BLJ, II, 175.
119 "all the women": MacCarthy, 167.
120 "Of what consequence": Quennell, *Byron,* 61.
121 "Thy cheek, thine eyes": PLB, 268.
121 "a very pretty age": Minta, 178.
121 "I am much afraid": ibid.
121 "The great object": Garrett, 7.
122 "I felt as if": Minta, 181.
122 "We were married": BLJ, IV, 249.
122 "[H]ad Lady B": Longford, 71.
122 "the treaclemoon": BLJ, III, 175.
122 "She — or rather": BLJ, V, 91.
123 "You had better": MacCarthy, 275.
123 "An utter stranger": CC, I, 24–25.
124 "I have called twice": ibid., 27.
124 "I am now wavering": ibid., 30.
124 "Lasciate ogni": ibid., 31.
124 "If you think ill": ibid., 29.
125 "I will bring her": ibid., 36.
125 "Will you be so good": ibid., 39.
125 "Mary is delighted": ibid., 40.
125 "Have you then": ibid., 36.
125 "I was young": Graham, 760.
126 "if a girl of eighteen": BLJ, V, 162.
126 "God bless you": CC, I, n37.
126 "I am unhappily": MacCarthy, 273.
126 "I assure you": CC, I, 40.

Chapter 6: The Summer of Darkness

127 "I busied myself": F1831, 21–22.

128 "echo of the Infinite": Mellor, 70.

128 "We have had lately": BLJ, V, 86.

128–29 Mount Tambora statistics: *Encyclopedia Britannica,* 1969 ed., XXIII, 104.

129 "when first I stepped": Shelley, *Rambles in Germany and Italy,* I, 139.

129 "you will I suppose": CC, I, 43.

129 "desolate . . . sublime": Shelley, *History of a Six Weeks' Tour,* 93.

130 "the majestic": ibid.

130 "I feel as happy": LMWS, I, 18.

130 "saluted by": ibid., 18.

130 "I leave this": CC, I, 46.

130 "the curiosity to see": Minta, 183.

132 "a madman": MacDonald, 23.

132 "You wound my heart": ibid., 24.

133 "The sea dashed over": ibid., 60.

133 "As soon as he reached": ibid., 62.

133 "I am very pleased": Page, 148.

134 "First . . . I can hit": Eisler, 511.

134 "not much after . . . I detest the cause": BLJ, V, 76.

134 "I brought away": BLJ, V, 78.

134 "a curst selfish": Minta, 185.

134 "clouds were mountains": MacCarthy, 289.

134 "Lake Leman woos me": Longford, 98.

134 "I am sorry": CC, I, 46.

135 "You will hardly believe": Grosskurth, 278.

135 "It seems to me": BLJ, V, 131.

136 "the author of": Polidori, *Diary,* 101.

136 "I have been": CC, I, 47.

136 "Now — don't scold": BLJ, V, 92.

137 "We watch them": LMWS, I, 20.

137 "often whilst the storms": Polidori, *Vampyre,* xiv.

137 Oarsman's account: Lovell, *His Very Self,* 183.

137 "The sky is changed!": PLB, 222.

138 "the prettiest place": BLJ, V, 187–88.

138 "most intimate friends": Lewalski, 9.

139 "There is no story": MacCarthy, 295.

139 "it proved a wet": Walling, 28.

139 "at about a mile": CC, I, n53.

139 "With false Ambition": PLB, 91.

140 "Now you who wish": Polidori, *Diary,* 123.

140 "After a moment": Lovell, *His Very Self,* 182–83.

141 "I despair of": Tomalin, *Shelley,* 55.

141 "Beauty sat on": JMWS, 478.

141 "We often sat up": Walling, 28.

142 "the nature of": F1831, 22.

142 "What a pity": Grylls, *Godwin,* 151.

143 "phantasmagoria": JMWS, 56.

144 "excited in us": F1831, 25.

144 "You and I": Sunstein, 121.

144 "There were four": F1831, 21.

144 "I busied myself": ibid., 21.

144 "The ghost-stories begun": Page, 49.

145 "founded on the experiences": F1831, 21.

145 "more apt to": ibid., 21.

145 "Poor Polidori had": ibid., 21.

146 "In short, the man": Blunden, 134.

146 "Then drawing in": Grebanier et al., *English Literature,* IV, 201.

147 ". . . his lordship having": Polidori, *Diary,* 128.

147 "Have you thought of": F1831, 22.

148 "various philosophical . . . listener": ibid.

148 all, ibid., 22–23

149 all, ibid., 23.

Chapter 7: "A hideous phantom"

151 "Did I request thee": Milton, *Paradise Lost,* Book X, ll. 743–45, 232.

151 *"thought of a story":* F1831, 23.

151 "It was on a dreary night": ibid., 57.

151 "With an anxiety," ibid., 57–58.

152 "the wretch": ibid., 58.

153 "is an exceedingly": LPBS, I, 489.

154 "precisely in the spot": ibid., 486.

154 "himself quietly upon": Moore, Thomas, II, 23.

154 "I knew that my companion": LPBS, 483.
154 "a multitude of names": LPBS, 485.
154 "I vowed that I": PWPBS, 531.
156 "I eagerly inquired": F1818, 24.
156 "Whence, I often asked": ibid., 33–34.
157 "As the minuteness": ibid., 35–36.
157 "A new species": ibid., 36.
157 "Pursuing these reflections": ibid.
158 "Who shall conceive": ibid., 36–37.
158 "any person she": Tomalin, *Shelley*, 58.
158 "dreary night . . . dull yellow eye": F1818, 38.
158 "I thought I saw": ibid., 39.
159 one of Mary Wollstonecraft's children's books: *Original Stories from Real Life*, 20–27.
159 "[H]is conversation": F1818, 51.
160 "with sweet laughing": ibid., 47.
160 "While I watched": ibid., 56.
161 "I considered the being": ibid., 57.
161 "Thou art a symbol": PLB, 98.
162 "Whether with particles": Ovid, 4–5.
163 "The day was cloudless": JMWS, 113.
163 "[T]his appeared the most": ibid., 115.
163 "[A]s we went along": ibid.
163 "horrid avowal": CC, I, n53.
163 "Nothing can be more desolate": JMWS, 117.
164 "I . . . write my story": ibid., 118.
164 "This is the most desolate": ibid., 119.
164 "kiss our babe": ibid., 121.
165 "afterwards we all": JMWS, 125.
166 "a good man": BLJ, IX, 18.
166 "that none could believe": JMWS, 126.
167 "was, from the first": F1831, 20.
167 "No father had watched": F1818, 97.
168 "a true history": ibid., 104–05.
169 "the minutest description": ibid., 105.
170 "Remember, I shall be": ibid., 140.
170 "She was there": ibid., 165.

170 "While I still hung": ibid., 166.
171 "All men hate": ibid., 77.
171 "My dreadful fear": CC, I, 70.

Chapter 8: "I shall be no more . . ."

172 "He sprung from": F1818, 191.
172 "Do not think": ibid., 190.
174 "it is of the utmost": CC, I, 81.
174 "stupid letter from F": JMWS, 138.
174 "I depart immediately": CC, I, 85.
174 "In the evening": JMWS, 139.
174 "I have long determined": Paul, II, 242.
174 "when I shall be": F1818, 190.
175 "Mr. G. told me": Jones, *Gisborne,* 39.
175 "Go not to Swansea": JMWS, n140.
175 "From the fatal day": ibid.
176 "Her voice did quiver": PWPBS, 546.
176 "modify and change": Engar, Ann, "Mary Shelley and the Romance of Science" in Dabundo, 138.
177 "By painful experience": Einstein, Albert, *Out of My Later Years* (New York: New York Philosophical Library, 1950), 144.
178 "Is it wrong": Blunden, 161.
178 "I have not written": Tomalin, *Shelley,* 61.
178 "Too wretched": Hodgart, 15.
178 "far advanced": LPBS, I, n521.
179 "It seems that": ibid., 521.
179 "I don't think": JMWS, n151.
179 "Poor Harriet": ibid., 560.
180 "[Y]our nominal union": LPBS, I, 521.
180 "Of course you are": St. Clair, 415.
180 "was a change": LPBS, I, 539–40.
180 "The piece of news": Paul, II, 246.
181 "a marriage": JMWS, 152.
181 "Another incident": LMWS, I, 26.
181 "sends her affectionate": ibid., 26.
181 "You know": BLJ, V, 162.
182 "a house with a lawn": LMWS, I, 22.

182 "A fire in his eye": Blunden, 176–77.

182 "Claire has reassumed": LPBS, I, 395.

182 "Her eyes are": ibid.

183 "My affections are": CC, I, 110.

183 "Shelley's fullness": JMWS, n158–59.

184 "She loved Scythrop": Peacock, *Nightmare Abbey,* 95–96.

184 "I had a dream": LMWS, I, 32.

184 "My life might have": F1818, 7.

184–85 "I shall commit": ibid., 8–9.

185 "[My] ambition leads me": Beaglehole, J. C., 365.

185 "There, Margaret": F1818, 5–6.

185 "Learn from me": ibid., 35.

186 A modern feminist critic: Mellor, 274–86.

186 "Frankenstein discovered": F1818, 179.

187 "eloquence is forcible": ibid.

187 "Listen to my tale": ibid., 78.

187 "even power over": ibid., 178.

187 "The ice": ibid., 183.

187 "I am a blasted tree": ibid., 133.

188 "Seek happiness": ibid., 186.

188 "Yet why do I say": ibid.

188 "demon . . . voice of": ibid., 187.

188 "fallen angel": ibid., 189.

188 "I shall ascend": ibid., 191.

188 "He sprung from": ibid.

189 "How very vividly": JMWS, 172.

190 "igmatic . . . enigmatic . . ." et al.: Anne K. Mellor discusses in detail the changes Percy made to Mary's manuscript on pages 58–69 of her insightful book, *Mary Shelley: Her Life, Her Fiction, Her Monsters.*

191 "My health has been": LPBS, I, 428.

192 "I am just now": LMWS, I, 46.

192 "I am tired": ibid., 42–43.

192 "Poor little angel!": CC, I, 110.

192 "I know not": LMWS, I, 57.

193 "Devilman": Peacock, *Nightmare Abbey,* 211–12.

193 "Mrs. Shelley, tho'": LPBS, I, 583.

193 "The event on which . . ." et al.: F1818, 3–4.

194 "[*Frankenstein*] is piously dedicated": Brewer, *Mental Anatomies,* 17.

195 "perhaps the foulest toadstool": Mulvey-Roberts, Marie, "Mary Wollstonecraft Shelley." In Thomson et al., 393.

195 "Nothing attracts us": Rieger, "Dr. Polidori," 462.

195 "It is no slight merit": Walling, 34.

195 "the most wonderful": ibid., 23.

195 "a wonderful work": BLJ, VI, 125.

195 "Mary has just": CC, I, 111.

196 "Treat a person": Bloom, *Mary Shelley's Frankenstein*, 27.

196 "a thin patrician-looking": Sunstein, 147–48.

Chapter 9: The Ghosts' Revenge

198 "Who telleth": PWPBS, 524.

198 "We are all": LPBS, II, 1.

198 "The country is": JMWS, 197.

198 "we can see": ibid., 199.

199 "The snows": ibid., 201.

199 ". . . to inform you": LPBS, II, 5.

199 "for fear that": Gittings and Manton, 41–42.

199 "You write as if": LPBS, II, 10–11.

200 "Shelley has got to Milan": BLJ, VI, 37.

200 "Remember that I am": CC, I, 115.

200 "They dress her": Blunden, 212.

200 "I could never": JMWS, 67.

201 "Mrs. Gisborne is": LPBS, II, 114.

201 "we have a small": LMWS, I, 72.

202 "as beautiful as ever . . . extreme horror": LPBS, II, 36.

202 "face had become pale": Minta, 192.

202 "He associates with": LPBS, II, 58.

202 "So we'll go no more": PLB, 101.

203 "He is a person": PWPBS, 189.

203 "passionately attached": ibid., 290.

204 "I have done for": LPBS, II, 37.

204 "not well": JMWS, 224.

204 ". . . we have arrived": LMWS, I, 78–79.

205 "This is the Journal": JMWS, 226.

205 "All this is": LPBS, II, 40–41.

205 "I have not been without": ibid., 42.
206 "I sincerely sympathize": St. Clair, 460–61.
206 "Wilt thou forget": PWPBS, 553.
207 "not well": JMWS, 246.
208 "A most tremendous fuss": ibid., 249.
208 "with sweet laughing": F1818, 47.
209 "William is very ill": JMWS, 265.
209 "William is in the greatest": LMWS, I, 99.
209 "William is dead!": F1818, 52.
209 "I am going to write": LMWS, I, 100.
210 "I never know one": ibid., 101–02.
210 "Yesterday after an illness": LPBS, II, 97.
210 "My lost William": PWPBS, 581.
211 "Mourning in thy robe": ibid., 559.
211 "Ha! Thy frozen pulses": ibid., 560.
211 "My dearest Mary": ibid., 582.
212 "We cannot yet come": LPBS, II, 109.
212 "selfishness and ill humour": Seymour, 234.
212 "I had thought you": Mellor, 194.
212 "Your letters": LPBS, II, 227.
213 "I went to the Egham races": Walling, 34.
213 "What has been the fate": LPBS, II, 103.
213 "I begin my journal": JMWS, 293.
213 "That time is gone for ever": ibid.
214 "I am sorely afraid": CC, I, 127.
214 "a few days after my birth": Shelley, Mary, *Mathilda,* 155.
214 "He was a sincere": ibid., 153.
215 "One idea rushed on": ibid., 173.
215 ". . . rise from under my blighting": ibid., 180.
215 "His genius was transcendant": ibid., 191.
215 "He soon took great interest": ibid., 195.
215 "Woodville for ever": ibid.
216 "I am alone": ibid., 151.
216 "I go from this world": ibid., 210.
216 "disgusting and detestable": Jones, *Gisborne,* 44.
217 "small but healthy": LPBS, II, 151.

217 "he is my only one": LMWS, I, 114.

217 "after the frightful events": LPBS, II, 227.

218 "O Wild West Wind . . . Spring be far behind?": PWPBS, 577–79.

Chapter 10: A Dose for Poor Polidori

219 "Lord Ruthven had disappeared": Bleiler, 283.

219 "If there is in this world": Bunson, xi.

220 "But first, on earth": PLB, 262–63.

221 "a man of considerable": Bleiler, 287.

221 "his countenance": ibid., 291.

222 "A considerable change": MacDonald, *Polidori,* 100.

222 "sign of reconciliation": ibid., 102.

222 "I had no use for": BLJ, V, 122.

222 "We have parted": MacDonald, *Polidori,* 102.

223 "your letter produced": ibid., 108.

223 "pimp": Longford, 112.

223 "There were fifteen": MacDonald, *Polidori,* 122.

224 "The Doctor Polidori": BLJ, XI, 164.

224 "It is, however": MacDonald, *Polidori,* 144.

224–25 "Instead of making out": Lovell, *Medwin's Conversations,* 107.

225 "*delicate* declension": MacDonald, *Polidori,* 147.

225 "Dear Doctor — I have read your play": BLJ, V, 258.

227 "[Here is] a copy of a thing": Bleiler, xxxvi.

227 "As the person referred to": MacDonald, *Polidori,* 181.

228 "If the book is clever": BLJ, VI, 119.

229 "deadly hue . . . dead grey eye": Bleiler, 265.

229 "one whose strength": ibid., 273.

229 "conceal all you know": ibid., 276.

229 "Remember your oath!": ibid., 279.

230 "Lord Ruthven had disappeared": ibid., 283.

231 "death, he remembered": ibid., 280.

231 "The tale here presented": ibid., xxxvii.

233 "In every town": ibid., *Vampyre,* 268.

234 "departed this Life": MacDonald, *Polidori,* 237.

234 "I have been left": ibid., 238.

234 "I was convinced": Lovell, *Medwin's Conversations,* 104.

235 "I then said": MacDonald, *Polidori,* 241.

Chapter 11: The Littlest Victim

236 "I am ashes": PLB, 112.

237 "Which 'piece'": BLJ, VI, 92.

237 "She was not": MacCarthy, 360.

237 "My first wish": CC, I, 127.

238 "I wish to see": BLJ, VI, 213.

238 "very droll": BLJ, VI, 223.

238 "I was rather disappointed": Gronow, 212.

239 "celestial apparition": Marchand, II, 775.

239 "already the subject": ibid., 775.

239 "I was strong enough": ibid., 777.

239 "I am in love": BLJ, VI, 108.

240 "I am drilling very hard": BLJ, VII, 28.

241 "which shines among": ibid., VII, 80.

241 "I so totally disapprove": ibid.

241 "A letter from Mad[ame]": JCC, 145.

242 "she shall be taught": CC, I, 144–45.

242 "The woman is": BLJ, VII, 151.

242 "I must decline": ibid., VII, 162.

242 "Clare [*sic*] writes me": ibid, VII, 174–75.

243 "Each time she came": CC, I, n130.

244 "to become a good": Gittings and Manton, 58.

244 "the state of ignorance": CC, I, 163.

244 "The moral part": CC, I, 165.

245 "I am no enemy": BLJ, IX, 119.

245 "I am afraid that": ibid, IX, 123.

245 "Whether the convent": CC, I, n166.

245 "I send you": LPBS, II, 308.

245 reviews of *Don Juan*: Trueblood, 30–32.

246 "Saturday August 4th": JCC, 245.

246 "which you only can": LPBS, II, 319.

246 "ever been undisturbed": LMWS, I, 207.

246 "I write nothing": LPBS, II, 331.

247 "not much like": ibid., II, 334–35.

247 "Her light & airy": ibid.

247 "Before I went away": ibid.

247 "knows certain orazioni": ibid.

248 "a very pretty": ibid., II, 363.
248 "It was said that": Tomalin, *Shelley*, 103.
248 "My Dear Papa": BLJ, VIII, 226.
249 "sincere enough but": ibid.
249 "Just before Empoli": JCC, 253.
249 reviews of *Don Juan*: Trueblood, 37, 42.
249 "My dear Friend": CC, I, 170.
250 "L. B. would use": LPBS, II, 398.
250 "a shrug of impatience": Marchand, III, 975.
250 "I am truly uneasy": CC, I, 171.
250 "If there is any": Marchand, III, 992.
250 "extraordinary qualities": ibid.
251 "A mortal paleness": ibid., 993.
251 "felt the loss": MacCarthy, 419.
251 "The blow was stunning": BLJ, IX, 147–48.
252 "I tried the whole": CC, I, 199.
252 "I will not describe": LPBS, II, 415.
252 "I wish I had never": Grosskurth, 402.
253 memorial tablet: ibid., 404.
253 "the present doormat": Marchand, III, n1001.
253 "the epitome or miniature": MacCarthy, 420.
253 "While she lived": Marchand, III, 994.

Chapter 12: The Hateful House

254 "That time is dead": PWPBS, 546.
255 "It seems as if": LPBS, II, 211.
255 "A bad wife": JCC, 123.
255 "Heigh-ho, the Clare": JCC, 153.
255 "A better day": JMWS, 320.
255 "Claire is yet": LPBS, II, 218.
256 "disturb her quiet": ibid., 228.
256 "I should be very glad": ibid., 267.
256 "It was nearly seven": JMWS, n337–38.
257 "He is a great loss": LPBS, II, 297.
257 "The poor people": White, II, 243.
257 "where she sees": LMWS, I, 165.
257 "It is grievous to see": ibid., 172.

258 "He was inconstant": Hodgart, 91.

258 "Here are we then": LPBS, II, 448.

258 "an idealized history": ibid., 434.

258 "I never thought": PWPBS, 413.

258 "O Comet beautiful": ibid., 419.

258 "And all my being": ibid., 418.

259 "I make its author": LPBS, II, 263.

259 "died at Florence": ibid., n263.

259 "There are other verses": Norman, 144.

259 "an extremely pretty": LPBS, II, 256–57.

259 "Jane is certainly": LMWS, I, 180.

260 "Our ducking last night": LPBS, II, 286.

260 "was so full of *Ghosts*": BLJ, VIII, 74.

260 "they lock them up": Lovell, *Medwin's Conversations,* 73.

261 "six feet high": LMWS, I, 218.

261 "the personification of my": Trueblood, 114.

261 "He tells strange stories": JMWS, 391.

261–62 "She brought us back": Trelawny, 172–73.

262 "We talked and laughed": ibid., 197.

262 "Poor Mary!": ibid., 196.

262 "Thus on that night": JMWS, n390.

262 "Let me in my": ibid., 399–400.

263 "I commit them": LPBS, II, 437.

263 "The sea came up": PWPBS, 676.

263 "The gales and squalls": ibid., 677.

264 "Our near neighbors": ibid.

264 "I have lived too long": Minta, 203.

264 "I despair of rivalling": LPBS, II, 323–24.

264 "I always find the bottom": Trelawny, 190.

264 "Shelley was looking careworn": Gronow, 124.

265 "Less oft is peace": Norman, 94.

265 "languor and hysterical affections": LPBS, II, 427.

265 "No words can tell": LMWS, I, 244.

265 "I had no fear": JMWS, 562.

265 "I only feel the want": LPBS, II, 435.

266 "There it is again . . . lively imagination": Jones, *Gisborne and Williams,* 147.

266 "How long do you mean": LMWS, 245.

266 "Shelley had often": ibid.

266 "walk into a little wood": Moore, II, 388.

267 "They could hardly walk": LMWS, I, 245.

267 "be a comfort to me": LPBS, II, 433.

267 "Whether [my] life had been": PWPBS, 515.

267 "Then, what is life": ibid., 520.

268 "I have not a moments": LPBS, II, 444.

268 "I fear you are solitary": ibid., 445.

268–69 "for they say . . . going into convulsions": LMWS, I, 247.

269 "I had risen": ibid.

269 "I never can forget": Lovell, *Lady Blessington's*, 53.

270 "I went up the stairs": Trelawny, 218.

270 "Are we to resemble that": MacCarthy, 429.

270 "a dark and ghastly . . . soaring over us": Trelawny, 223.

271 "more wine": ibid., 223–224.

271 "We sang, we laughed": Hunt, II, 102.

271 "We have been burning": BLJ, IX, 197.

271 "I called him back": LMWS, I, 246.

272 "There is thus another": BLJ, IX, 190.

272 "Those who know": Norman, 15.

272 Other publications: White, *Hearth*, 330–31.

272 "Mr. Byshe [*sic*] Shelley": ibid., 325.

272 "Mr. Shelley is unfortunately": ibid., 329.

272 "Shelley the great Atheist": Norman, 22.

272 "To lose an eldest son": ibid., 19.

272 "That you should be so overcome": ibid., 20.

273 "All that I expressed": ibid., 20–21.

273 "He was the most gentle": Lovell, *Lady Blessington's*, 52–53.

274 "And so here I am": LMWS, I, 252.

274 "Drive my dead thoughts": PWPBS, 579.

Chapter 13: Glory and Death

275 "Now fierce remorse": JMWS, 491.

276 "What a scene": ibid., 435.

277 "But [except] for my Child": ibid., 428.

277 "romantic beyond romance": Williams, John, 94.

277 "Oh my beloved Shelley": JMWS, 429–30.

277 "No one seems to understand": ibid., 440–41.
277 "No one ever writes": LMWS, I, 290.
277 "I would, like a dormouse": ibid., 288.
277 "I am a lonely unloved thing": JMWS, 448.
278 "I cannot write": ibid., 462.
279 "Frankenstein is universally": ibid., n457.
280 "To examine the causes": Florry, 139.
280 "I was much amused": LMWS, I, 378.
280 "attack [on] the Christian faith," etc.: Florry, 5.
281 "lost divinity": JMWS, 443.
281 "But were it not": LMWS, I, 254.
281 "God has still one blessing": ibid., I, 297.
281 "queer, unamiable and strange": Norman, 55.
281 "The wisest & best": JMWS, 483.
282 "I was worth something then": JMWS, 471, 474.
282 "His life was spent": PWPBS, xiii.
282 "I am convinced": ibid., xiv.
283 "Sir T. writhes": LMWS, I, 444.
283 "All contemplative existence": Minta, 180.
283 "Shelley has more poetry": Lovell, *Medwin's Conversations,* 235.
284 "I do not think": JMWS, 439–40.
285 "The isles of Greece": PLB, 695.
285 *Blackwood's* and *Literary Gazette* reviews: Trueblood, 49–50.
285 "Yes! A grassy bed": Franklin, 179.
286 "that he considered": Gamba, 12.
286 "I was a fool": Marchand, III, 1123.
287 "Is the Girl imaginative": BLJ, XI, 47.
287 "Both [Byron's] character": Minta, 210.
287 "Be assured, My Lord": Marchand, III, 1140.
288 "I especially dread": Minta, 232.
289 "enduring the tedious details": Longford, 200.
290 "'Tis time this heart": PLB, 112.
291 "It [the seizure] was very painful": BLJ, XI, 113.
291 "Lyon, thou art an honest": Longford, 206.
291 "became pensive . . . fortune-teller in Scotland": Marchand, III, 1212.
292 "Come, you are": ibid., 1219.
292 "I fancy myself a Jew": ibid., 1217.

292 "I want to sleep now": ibid., 1228.

292 "the congenital malconformation": ibid., 1231.

293 "All Greece . . . grave of a great man": Minta, 275.

293 "With great grief": Franklin, 177.

293 "This [Byron's death] then was the": JMWS, 477–78.

294 "not a vestige": Eisler, 471.

294 "it went to my heart": LMWS, I, 436–37.

294 "honor and fame": MacCarthy, 539.

295 "Missolonghi groaned": Marchand, III, 1235–36.

295 "People take for gospel": Lovell, *Blessington's Conversations*, 220.

296 "I take a row on the lake": Lovell, *His Very Self*, 183–84.

296 Lady Caroline's sister: Matthews, XXXII, 258.

297 "At the age of twenty six": JMWS, 478–79.

Chapter 14: Mary Alone

298 "Alone — alone — all": JMWS, 573.

298 "The last man": ibid., 476–77.

298 "On this very day": LMWS, I, 438.

299 "Tears fill my eyes": JMWS, 485.

299 "I am under a cloud": LMWS, I, 438.

300 "Such writers as Byron": Norman, 97.

300 "vow I made": ibid., 72.

300 "his Satanic Majesty": Lovell, *Medwin's*, 12.

300 "a source of great pain": LMWS, I, 455.

301 "very gentle and feminine": Feldman, 612.

301 "very agreeable": JMWS, 501–02.

301 "seems to have known": Feldman, 613.

301 "The great charm of the work": LMWS, II, 101–02.

302 "the hope and consolation": ibid, I, 495.

302 "Loveliest Janey": ibid., I, 556.

302 "My friend has proved false": JMWS, 502–03.

302 "I need companionship": ibid., 498.

303 "Though I was conscious": LMWS, II, 25–26.

303 "emphatically a man": TLM, 35.

303 "his sensibility and courtesy": ibid., 20.

303 "You know me": LMWS, II, 72.

304 "Shelley's life so far": ibid, II, 194.

304 "What a folly is it": JMWS, 489.

304 "I stick to *Frankenstein*": CC, II, 341.

305 "If you would but know": ibid., 342.

306 "in this world": LMWS, I, 379.

306 "And now, once again": F1831, 23.

306 "While I followed": ibid., 45.

307 "Even now, as I commence": ibid., 38.

307 "Destiny was too potent": ibid., 46.

307 "The power of Destiny": LMWS, I, 572.

307 "a deformed and abortive creation": F1831, 46.

308 "He came to the university": ibid., 67.

308 "I lived principally in the country": ibid., 20.

308 "Teach him to think for himself?": Mellor, 211.

309 "In person he is": LMWS, II, 209.

309 "One day I said to him": ibid.

309 "When I mentioned Tennyson's": Norman, 220.

310 "Everything under the sun": Grylls, *William Godwin,* 240.

310 "In weighing well": Norman, 30.

310 "most people felt of Mr. Godwin": De Quincey, III, 25.

310 "O my God": JMWS, 548–49.

311 "The great work of life": JMWS, 559.

311 "It was a frightful": Walling, 135.

311 "I almost think": JMWS, 559.

312 "In the first place": JMWS, 553–54.

312 "His reading was not": PWPBS, 836–37.

313 "the beautiful and ineffectual angel": Bann, 37.

313 "The far Alps were hid": Shelley, *Rambles,* 148.

314 "Preserve always a habit": JMWS, 573.

315 "I had been resting": Rolleston, 27–28.

317 "Goodnight — I will go look": LMWS, I, 261.

317 "It is not": Sunstein, 384.

317 "Were the fairest Paradise": CC, II, 327.

318 "you were a mere girl": ibid.

318 "If I was in Italy": Moore, Doris, 446.

318 "She [Mary] has compromised": Grylls, *Claire Clairmont,* 254–55.

319 "Claire always harps": LMWS, II, 271.

319 "Don't go, dear": Rolleston, 41.

319 "a slender and pallid": Norman, 239.

320 "I would willingly think": Gittings and Manton, vii.

320 "She passed her life": ibid., 245.

320 "lovely old lady": Graham, 754.

320 "I think Shelley would have": ibid., 755.

320 "With all my heart and soul": ibid., 767.

BIBLIOGRAPHY

Contemporary Sources

Bennett, Betty T., ed., *The Letters of Mary Wollstonecraft Shelley* (Baltimore: Johns Hopkins Press, 1980–88).

Bleiler, E. F., ed., *Three Gothic Novels* (New York: Dover, 1966).

Coleridge, Samuel Taylor, *The Complete Poems,* ed. William Keach (London: Penguin, 1997).

De Quincey, Thomas, *Collected Writings of Thomas De Quincey,* ed. David Masson (Edinburgh: Adam and Charles Black, 1890).

Feldman, Paula R., and Diana Scott-Kilvert, eds., *The Journals of Mary Shelley, 1814–1844* (Oxford: Clarendon Press, 1987).

Gamba, Peter, *Lord Byron's Last Journey to Greece* (London: John Murray, 1825).

Godwin, William, *Memoirs of Mary Wollstonecraft,* ed. W. Clark Durant (New York: Gordon Press, 1972).

Goethe, Johann Wolfgang von, *The Sorrows of Young Werther* (New York: Holt, Rinehart and Winston, 1949).

Graham, William, "Chats with Jane Clermont [Claire Clairmont]," *The Nineteenth Century,* vol. 34, no. 201, 1893.

Gronow, Rees Howell, *The Reminiscences and Recollections of Captain Gronow,* abridged and introduced by John L. Raymond (New York: Viking, 1964).

Hale, Terry, ed., *Tales of the Dead: The Ghost Stories of the Villa Diodati* (Chislehurst, UK: Gothic Society, 1992).

Hogg, Thomas Jefferson, *The Life of Shelley* (New York: E. P. Dutton, 1933).

Hunt, Leigh, *The Autobiography of Leigh Hunt,* ed. Roger Ingpen (Westminster, UK: Archibald Constable, 1903).

Ingpen, Roger, and Walter E. Peck, eds. *Complete Works of Shelley* (New York: Gordian Press, 1965).

Jones, Frederick L., ed., *The Letters of Percy Bysshe Shelley* (Oxford: Clarendon Press, 1964).

———, ed., *Maria Gisborne and Edward E. Williams: Their Journals and Letters* (Norman: University of Oklahoma Press, 1951).

Lamb, Lady Caroline, *Glenarvon,* afterword by Anne Fremantle (New York: Curtis, 1973).

Lovell, Ernest J., Jr., ed., *His Very Self and Voice: Collected Conversations of Lord Byron* (New York: Macmillan, 1954).

———, ed., *Lady Blessington's Conversations of Lord Byron* (Princeton: Princeton University Press, 1969).

———, ed., *Medwin's Conversations of Lord Byron* (Princeton: Princeton University Press, 1966).

Marchand, Leslie A., ed., *Byron's Letters and Journals* (London: John Murray, 1973–79).

Marshall, Florence A., *Life and Letters of Mary Wollstonecraft Shelley* (London: Richard Bentley & Son, 1889).

Medwin, Thomas, *Life of Shelley* (revised) (St. Clair Shores, MI: Scholarly Press, 1971).

Milton, John, *The Poetical Works of John Milton* (London: Oxford University Press, 1961).

Moore, Thomas, *Letters and Journals of Lord Byron with Notices of His Life* (New York: George Dearborn, 1837).

Murray, E. B., ed., *The Prose Works of Percy Bysshe Shelley* (Oxford: Clarendon Press, 1993).

Ovid, *Metamorphoses,* trans. John Dryden (New York: Heritage Press, 1961).

Page, Norman, ed., *Byron: Interviews and Recollections* (Atlantic Highlands, NJ: Humanities Press, 1985).

Paul, C. Kegan, *William Godwin: His Friends and Contemporaries* (Boston: Roberts Brothers, 1876).

Peacock, Thomas Love, *Memoirs of Shelley* (New York: E. P. Dutton, 1933).

———, *Nightmare Abbey* (Harmondsworth, UK: Penguin, 1969).

Polidori, John William, *The Diary of Dr. John William Polidori,* ed. William Rossetti (London: E. Matthews, 1911).

———, *The Vampyre* (New York: Woodstock Books, 1990 reprint of 1819 ed.).

Rolleston, Maud, *Talks with Lady Shelley* (London: G. G. Harrap, 1925).

Shelley, Mary, *Frankenstein,* ed. Johanna Smith (Boston: Bedford Books, 1992).

———, *History of a Six Weeks' Tour* (Otley, UK: Woodstock Books, 2002 reprint of 1817 ed.).

———, *Mathilda,* ed. Janet Todd (New York: New York University Press, 1992).

———, *Rambles in Germany and Italy,* ed. Jeanne Moskal (London: William Pickering, 1996).

Stocking, Marion Kingston, ed., *The Clairmont Correspondence* (Baltimore: Johns Hopkins Press, 1995).

———, ed., *The Journals of Claire Clairmont* (Cambridge, MA: Harvard University Press, 1968).

Tannahill, Reay, ed., *Paris in the Revolution* (London: The Folio Society, 1966).

Trelawny, Edward John, *The Recollections of Shelley and Byron* (New York: E. P. Dutton, 1933).

Wardle, Ralph M., ed., *Collected Letters of Mary Wollstonecraft* (Ithaca, NY: Cornell University Press, 1979).

———, ed., *Godwin and Mary* (Lawrence, KS: University of Kansas Press, 1996).

Wollstonecraft, Mary, *Letters Written During a Short Residence in Sweden, Norway and Denmark* (London: Penguin, 1987).

———, *Original Stories from Real Life* (Washington, DC: Woodstock Books, 2001 reissue of 1791 ed.).

———, *A Vindication of the Rights of Woman,* ed. and introduction by Miriam Brody (London: Penguin, 1992).

———, *The Wrongs of Woman* (Oxford: Oxford University Press, 1998).

Woodcock, George, ed., *Selections from* Political Justice (London: Freedom Press, 1943).

Secondary Sources

Armstrong, Margaret, *Trelawny: A Man's Life* (New York: Macmillan, 1940).

Baldick, Chris, *In Frankenstein's Shadow: Myth, Monstrosity, and Nineteenth-Century Writing* (Oxford: Clarendon Press, 1987).

Bann, Stephen, ed., *Frankenstein: Creation and Monstrosity* (London: Reaction Books, 1994).

Barber, Paul, *Vampires, Burial, and Death* (New Haven: Yale University Press, 1988).

Beaglehole, J. C., *The Life of Captain James Cook* (London: The Hakluyt Society, 1974).

Bennett, Betty T., "Shelley, Mary Wollstonecraft," in *Oxford Dictionary of National Biography,* vol. 50, pp. 193–99.

Bennett, Betty T., and Stuart Curran, eds., *Mary Shelley in Her Times* (Baltimore: Johns Hopkins Press, 2000).

Bloom, Harold, *Mary Shelley's Frankenstein* (Broomall, PA: Chelsea House, 1996).

———, *The Ringers in the Tower* (Chicago: University of Chicago Press, 1971).

Blumberg, Jane, *Mary Shelley's Early Novels* (Iowa City: University of Iowa Press, 1993).

Blunden, Edmund, *Shelley: A Life Story* (New York: Viking, 1947).

Bowla, C. M., *The Romantic Imagination* (London: Oxford University Press, 1961).

Braudy, Leo, *The Frenzy of Renown: Fame and Its History* (New York: Oxford University Press, 1986).

Brennan, Matthew, "The Landscape of Grief in Mary Shelley's *Frankenstein,*" *Studies in the Humanities* 15 (1988), pp. 33–44.

Brewer, William D., *The Mental Anatomies of William Godwin and Mary Shelley* (Teaneck, NJ: Fairleigh Dickinson University Press, 2001).

———, *The Shelley-Byron Conversation* (Gainesville: University Press of Florida, 1994).

Brown, Ford K., *The Life of William Godwin* (New York: E. P. Dutton, 1926).

Bryant, Arthur, *The Age of Elegance, 1812–1822* (London: The Reprint Society, 1954).

Bunson, Matthew, *The Vampire Encyclopedia* (New York: Gramercy Books, 1993).

Burton, Anthony, and John Murdoch, *Byron: Catalogue for an exhibition . . .* (London: Victoria and Albert Museum, 1974).

Byrne, Richard B., ed., *Films of Tyranny: Short Analyses of* The Cabinet of Dr. Caligari, The Golem [and] Nosferatu (Madison, WI: College Printing & Typing Co., 1966).

Cameron, Kenneth Neill, *Shelley: The Golden Years* (Cambridge, MA: Harvard University Press, 1974).

———, *The Young Shelley* (New York: Octagon Books, 1973).

Cameron, Kenneth Neill, Donald H. Reiman, Stephen Wagner, Doucet Devin Fischer, eds., *Shelley and His Circle* (Cambridge, MA: Harvard University Press, 1961–96).

Carson, James P., "Bringing the Author Forward: *Frankenstein* Through Mary Shelley's Letters," *Criticism* 30:4 (Fall 1988), pp. 431–53.

Clubbe, John, "The Tempest-toss'd Summer of 1816: Mary Shelley's *Frankenstein*," *Byron Journal* 19 (1991), pp. 26–40.

Cochran, Peter, "Trelawny, Edward John," in *Dictionary of National Biography*, vol. 55, pp. 272–75 (London: Oxford University Press, 2004).

Copper, Basil, *The Vampire in Legend, Fact, and Art* (London: Robert Hale, 1973).

Cracium, Adriana and Kari E. Lokke, eds., *Rebellious Hearts: British Women Writers and the French Revolution* (Albany: State University of New York Press, 2001).

Crump, Thomas, *A Brief History of Science as Seen Through the Development of Scientific Instruments* (London: Constable, 2001).

Dabundo, Laura, ed., *Jane Austen and Mary Shelley and Their Sisters* (Lanham, NY: University Press of America, 2000).

Daiches, David, and John Flower, *Literary Landscapes of the British Isles: A Narrative Atlas* (New York: Paddington Press, 1979).

Eisler, Benita, *Byron: Child of Passion, Fool of Fame* (New York: Knopf, 1999).

Erickson, Carolly, *Our Tempestuous Day: A History of Regency England* (New York: William Morrow, 1986).

Feldman, Paula R., "Mary Shelley and the Genesis of Moore's *Life* of Byron," *Studies in English Literature* 20 (Autumn 1980), pp. 611–20.

Florescu, Radu, *In Search of Frankenstein* (Boston: New York Graphic Society, 1975).

Florry, Steven Earl, *Hideous Progenies* (Philadelphia: University of Pennsylvania Press, 1990).

Foreman, Amanda, *Georgiana: Duchess of Devonshire* (New York: Modern Library, 2001).

Franklin, Caroline, *Byron: A Literary Life* (New York: St. Martin's Press, 2000).

Frayling, Christopher, *Nightmare: The Birth of Horror* (London: BBC Books, 1996).

Frost, Brian J., *The Monster with a Thousand Faces* (Bowling Green, OH: Bowling Green University Popular Press, 1989).

Frost, R. J., "'It's Alive!' *Frankenstein:* The Film, the Feminist Novel and Science Fiction," *Foundation* 7 (1996), pp. 75–93.

Garrett, Martin, *George Gordon, Lord Byron* (New York: Oxford University Press, 2000).

Gelpi, Barbara Charlesworth, *Shelley's Goddess: Maternity, Language, Subjectivity* (New York: Oxford University Press, 1992).

Gilbert, Sandra, and Susan Gubar, *The Madwoman in the Attic: The Woman Writer and the Nineteenth-Century Literary Imagination*, 2nd ed. (New Haven: Yale University Press, 2000).

Gillespie, Charles, ed., *Dictionary of Scientific Biography* (New York: Scribner's, 1970).

Gilmour, Ian, *Byron and Shelley in Their Time: The Making of the Poets* (New York: Carroll & Graf, 2003).

Gittings, Robert, and J. Manton, *Claire Clairmont and the Shelleys* (New York: Oxford University Press, 1992).

Goetsch, Paul, *Monsters in English Literature: From the Romantic Age to the First World War* (Frankfurt-am-Main: Peter Lane, 2002).

Goldberg, M. A., "Moral and Myth in Mrs. Shelley's *Frankenstein*," *Keats-Shelley Journal* 8 (1959), pp. 27–38.

Gordon, Lyndall, *Mary Wollstonecraft: A New Genus* (New York: Little, Brown, 2005).

Grebanier, Bernard D. N., et al., *English Literature and Its Backgrounds* (Holt, Rinehart, and Winston, 1967).

———, *The Uninhibited Byron: An Account of His Sexual Confusion* (New York: Crown, 1970).

Grosskurth, Phyllis, *Byron: The Flawed Angel* (London: Hodder & Stoughton, 1997).

Grylls, Rosalie Glynn, *Claire Clairmont* (London: John Murray, 1939).

———, *Mary Shelley* (New York: Haskell House, 1969).

———, *William Godwin and His World* (London: Odhams Press, 1953).

Haining, Peter, *The Man Who Was Frankenstein* (London: Frederick Muller, 1979).

Harris, Janet, *The Woman Who Created Frankenstein: A Portrait of Mary Shelley* (New York: Harper & Row, 1979).

Hibbert, Christopher, *The Court at Windsor: A Domestic History* (New York: Harper & Row, 1964).

Hodgart, Patricia, *A Preface to Shelley* (London: Longman, 1985).

Hoeveler, Diane Long, *Romantic Androgyny* (University Park: Pennsylvania State University Press, 1990).

Holland, Tom, "Undead Byron," in *Byromania*, ed. Frances Wilson (New York: St. Martin's Press, 1999).

Holmes, Richard, *Shelley: The Pursuit* (London: Weidenfeld & Nicolson, 1974).

Honour, Hugh, *Neo-Classicism* (Harmondsworth, UK: Penguin, 1984).

Jacobs, Diane, *Her Own Woman: The Life of Mary Wollstonecraft* (New York: Simon & Schuster, 2001).

Jordan, Frank, ed., *The English Romantic Poets: A Review of Research and Criticism* (New York: Modern Language Association of America, 1985).

Kaplan, Morton, "Fantasy of Paternity and the Doppelganger: Mary Shelley's *Frankenstein*," in *The Unspoken Motive: A Guide to Psychoanalytic Literary Criticism*, ed. Morton Kaplan and Robert Kloss (New York: Free Press, 1973).

Kelly, G. D., "Godwin, Wollstonecraft, and Rousseau," *Women and Literature* 3:2 (Fall 1975), pp. 21–26.

Kelly, Linda, *Women of the French Revolution* (London: Hamish Hamilton, 1987).

Levine, George, and U. C. Knoepflmacher, eds., *The Endurance of Frankenstein: Essays on Mary Shelley's Novel* (Berkeley: University of California Press, 1979).

Lewalski, Barbara, *The Life of John Milton: A Critical Biography* (Oxford: Blackwell, 2000).

Longford, Elizabeth, *The Life of Byron* (Boston: Little, Brown, 1976).

Lovell, Ernest J., Jr., "Byron and Mary Shelley," *Keats-Shelley Journal*, January 1953, pp. 35–44.

MacCarthy, Fiona, *Byron: Life and Legend* (New York: Farrar, Straus and Giroux, 2002).

MacDonald, D. L., *Poor Polidori* (Toronto: University of Toronto Press, 1991).

McGann, Jerome, "Byron, George Gordon Noel," in *Oxford Dictionary of National Biography*, vol. 9, pp. 345–61 (London: Oxford University Press, 2004).

Marchand, Leslie A., *Byron: A Biography* (New York: Knopf, 1957).

Marshall, Peter H., *William Godwin* (New Haven: Yale University Press, 1984).

Matthew, H. C. G., and Brian Harrison, *Oxford Dictionary of National Biography* (London: Oxford University Press, 2004).

Masters, Anthony, *The Natural History of the Vampire* (London: Rupert Hart-Davis, 1972).

Maurois, André, *Ariel: The Life of Shelley*, trans. Ella D'Arcy (New York: D. Appleton & Century: 1942).

Mellor, Anne K., *Mary Shelley: Her Life, Her Fiction, Her Monsters* (New York: Methuen, 1988).

———, "Possessing Nature: The Finale in Frankenstein," in *Frankenstein*, ed. J. Paul Hunter (New York: Norton, 1996).

Minta, Stephen, *On a Voiceless Shore: Byron in Greece* (New York: Henry Holt, 1998).

Moers, Ellen, *Literary Women* (Garden City, NY: Doubleday, 1976).

Moore, Doris Langley, *The Late Lord Byron* (Philadelphia: J. B. Lippincott, 1961).

Murray, E. B., "Shelley's Contribution to Mary's *Frankenstein*," *Keats-Shelley Memorial Bulletin* 29 (1978), pp. 50–68.

Murray, Venetia, *An Elegant Madness: High Society in Regency England* (New York: Penguin, 1998).

Nardo, Don, ed., *Readings on Frankenstein* (San Diego: Greenhaven Press, 2000).

Nitchie, Elizabeth, *Mary Shelley* (Westport, CT: Greenwood Press, 1970).

Norman, Sylva, *Flight of the Skylark: The Development of Shelley's Reputation* (Norman: University of Oklahoma Press, 1954).

O'Neill, Michael, "Shelley, Percy Bysshe," in *Oxford Dictionary of National Biography*, vol. 50, pp. 200–12 (London: Oxford University Press, 2004).

———, "'Trying to Make It as Good as I Can': Mary Shelley's Editing of Shelley's Poetry and Prose," *Romanticism*, vol. 3, no. 2, 1997, Edinburgh University Press.

Origo, Iris, *The Last Attachment: The Story of Byron and Teresa Guiccioli* (New York: Scribner's, 1949).

Paglia, Camille, *Sexual Personae: Art and Decadence from Nefertiti to Emily Dickinson* (New York: Vintage, 1991).

Parissien, Steven, *George IV: Inspiration of the Regency* (New York: St. Martin's Press, 2001).

Perkins, Pam, "Godwin, Mary Jane," in *Oxford Dictionary of National Biography*, vol. 22, p. 616 (London: Oxford University Press, 2004).

Petre, Jean, *A Most Extraordinary Pair: Mary Wollstonecraft and William Godwin* (New York: Doubleday, 1975).

Poovey, Mary, "'My Hideous Progeny': Mary Shelley and the Feminization of Romanticism," *PMLA*, vol. 95, no. 3 (May 1980).

———, *The Proper Lady and the Woman Writer* (Chicago: University of Chicago Press, 1984).

Quennell, Peter, *Byron* (New York: Haskell House, 1974).

———, *Byron in Italy* (New York: Viking, 1957).

———, *Byron: The Years of Fame* (Hamden, CT: Archon Books, 1972).

———, *Samuel Johnson: His Friends and Enemies* (New York: American Heritage Press, 1973).

Richardson, Alan, *British Romanticism and the Science of the Mind* (Cambridge: Cambridge University Press, 2001).

Rieger, James, "Dr. Polidori and the Genesis of *Frankenstein*," *Studies in English Literature 1500–1900*, vol. 3, no. 4 (Augumn 1963), pp. 461–72.

———, *The Mutiny Within: The Heresies of Percy Bysshe Shelley* (New York: George Braziller, 1967).

Schoene-Harwood, Berthold, ed., *Mary Shelley: Frankenstein* (New York: Columbia University Press, 2000).

Schor, Esther, ed., *The Cambridge Companion to Mary Shelley* (Cambridge: Cambridge University Press, 2003).

Seymour, Miranda, *Mary Shelley* (London: Murray, 2000).

Small, Christopher, *Mary Shelley's Frankenstein: Tracing the Myth* (Pittsburgh: University of Pittsburgh Press, 1973).

Smith, Elton Edward, and Esther Greenwell Smith, *William Godwin* (New York: Twayne, 1965).

Smith, Susan Harris, "*Frankenstein:* Mary Shelley's Psychic Divisiveness," *Women and Literature* 5:2 (Fall 1977), pp. 42–53.

Spark, Muriel, *Mary Shelley* (New York: Dutton, 1987).

Stableford, Brian, "Frankenstein and the Origins of Science Fiction," in *Anticipations: Essays on Early Science Fiction and Its Precursors* (Syracuse, NY: Syracuse University Press, 1995), pp. 46–57.

Steffan, Guy, "Trelawny Trepanned," *Keats-Shelley Journal*, Winter 1954, pp. 67–73.

Stephen, Leslie, and Nkanjana Banerji, "Godwin, William," in *Oxford Dictionary of National Biography*, vol. 22, pp. 619–26 (London: Oxford University Press, 2004).

Stocking, Marion Kingston, "Clairmont, Clara Mary Jane," in *Oxford Dictionary of National Biography*, vol. 11, pp. 725–26 (London: Oxford University Press, 2004).

Stommel, Henry, and Elizabeth Stommel, "The Year Without a Summer," *Scientific American*, June 1979, pp. 176–86.

Summers, Montague, *The Vampire: His Kith and Kin* (New Hyde Park, NY: University Books, 1960).

Sunstein, Emily, *A Different Face: The Life of Mary Wollstonecraft* (New York: Harper & Row, 1975).

———, *Mary Shelley: Romance and Reality* (Boston: Little, Brown, 1980).

St. Clair, William, *The Godwins and the Shelleys* (New York: Norton, 1989).

Taylor, Barbara, "Wollstonecraft, Mary," in *Oxford Dictionary of National Biography*, vol. 59, pp. 996–1003 (London: Oxford University Press, 2004).

Thoma, Carole M., "Hogg, Thomas Jefferson," in *Oxford Dictionary of National Biography*, vol. 27, pp. 571–73 (London: Oxford University Press, 2004).

Thomson, Douglass H., Jack G. Voller, and Frederick S. Frank, eds., *Gothic Writers: A Critical and Bibliographical Guide* (Westport, CT: Greenwood Press, 2002).

Thompson, E. P., *The Romantics: England in a Revolutionary Age* (New York: The New Press, 1997).

Todd, Janet, "Frankenstein's Daughters: Mary Shelley and Mary Wollstonecraft," *Women and Literature* 4:2 (Fall 1976), pp. 18–27.

———, *Mary Wollstonecraft: A Revolutionary Life* (New York: Columbia University Press, 2000).

Tomalin, Claire, *The Life and Death of Mary Wollstonecraft* (New York: Harcourt Brace Jovanovich, 1974).

———, *Shelley and His World* (New York: Scribner's, 1980).

Toole, Betty Alexander, "Byron, (Augusta) Ada," in *Oxford Dictionary of National Biography*, vol. 9, pp. 343–45 (London: Oxford University Press, 2004).

Treasure, Geoffrey, *Late Hanoverian Britain, 1789–1837* (Mechanicsburg, PA: Stackpole Books, 2002).

Trueblood, Paul Graham, *The Flowering of Byron's Genius* (New York: Russell & Russell, 1962).

———, *Lord Byron* (New York: Twayne, 1969).

Uglow, Jenny, *The Lunar Men: Five Friends Whose Curiosity Changed the World* (New York: Farrar, Straus and Giroux, 2002).

Vaughn, William, Helmut Borsch-Supan, and Hans Joachim Neidhardt, *Caspar David Friedrich, 1774–1840* (London: Tate Gallery, 1972).

Veeder, William, *Mary Shelley and Frankenstein: The Fate of Androgyny* (Chicago: University of Chicago Press, 1986).

Walling, William, *Mary Shelley* (Boston: Twayne, 1972).

Weinberg, Alan M., *Shelley's Italian Experience* (London: Macmillan, 1994).

Weissman, Judith, *Half Savage and Hardy and Free: Women and Rural Radicalism in the Nineteenth-Century Novel* (Middletown, CT: Wesleyan University Press, 1987).

White, Newman Ivey, *Portrait of Shelley* (New York: Knopf, 1945).

———, *The Unextinguished Hearth* (Durham, NC: Duke University Press, 1938).

Williams, Anne, *Art of Darkness: A Politics of Gothic* (Chicago: University of Chicago Press, 1995).

Williams, John, *Mary Shelley: A Literary Life* (New York: St. Martin's Press, 2000).

Woodcock, George, *William Godwin: A Biographical Study* (London: Porcupine Press, 1946).

Ziolkowski, Theodore, "Science, Frankenstein, and Myth," *Sewanee Review* 89:1 (Winter 1981), pp. 34–56.

INDEX

ABOUT THE AUTHORS

Dorothy and Thomas Hoobler have written more than eighty books for adults, young adults, and children, and they have received numerous awards from library, educational, and cultural organizations. Their most recent novel, *In Darkness, Death,* won a 2005 Edgar Award. They live in New York City.